Paths of Wisdom

A Guide to the Magical Cabala

John Michael Greer

Paths of Wisdom

A Guide to the Magical Cabala

John Michael Greer

THOTH PUBLICATIONS
Loughborough, Leicestershire

A CIP catalogue record for this book is available from the British
Library.

Cover design by Bob Eames

Printed and bound in Great Britain

Published by Thoth Publications
64, Leopold Street Loughborough, LE11 5DN

ISBN 978-1-870450-25-6
Web address www.thoth.co.uk
email: enquires@thoth.co.uk

Dedication

For S. and R.
Companions on the journey

Contents

Part Three: Practice Of The Magical Cabala

Introduction

Cabala in the Golden Dawn Tradition

There was a time, not all that long ago, when the current renaissance of magic in the Western world seemed unthinkable to most people. The esoteric traditions of the West had been banished from sight by the dominant power of a materialist science and technology, and were preserved only in a shadowy underworld of magical lodges about which outsiders knew nothing and usually cared less. In the arenas where ideas were shaped and marketed - the universities, the churches, the media, and the broader realm of public opinion - magic was seen as something done only by primitive tribes, illiterate yokels, and lunatics: a folly civilized people had outgrown.

Times change. Three hundred years of technological advances have shown the other side of the promise of science far too clearly; a culture of supposedly rational scientific planning and action now threatens to produce a world better suited to machines than to human beings, a world in which statistics are the sole reality and efficiency is the only value. In response, a growing number of people have begun to look for less unbalanced, more human approaches to life, new or old ways of meeting the world in a deeper and more fulfilling manner. Some have turned to Eastern traditions, or to the teachings of surviving tribal peoples; some have ventured in wholly new directions; and others, increasingly, have begun to rediscover the ancient wisdom traditions of the Western world itself.

This book is about one form those Western wisdom traditions have taken - one system of theory, experience and practice which is directed toward a deeper understanding of ourselves and our world. That form or system is called the magical Cabala: more precisely, the Golden Dawn tradition of the magical Cabala.

These are hardly household words to most people nowadays, and it's worth taking a moment to talk about their meaning. What, then, is the Cabala, magical or otherwise? What is, or was, the Golden Dawn? And - perhaps the most important of all - what exactly is meant, in this age, by that troublesome word tradition, and why does it matter?

The Cabala

The word "Cabala" - also spelled "Kabbalah," "Qabalah," or any of a good half dozen other ways in English - comes from the Hebrew word קבלה , QBLH, "oral tradition." In its beginnings, the Cabala was a mystical offshoot of Judaism, a way of interpreting the traditions of Jewish worship and life which went beyond the outward observance of law and ritual to seek for direct personal experience of the spiritual side of things. The traditional Jewish Cabala focused, and still focuses, on interpreting the body of Jewish scripture according to special, mystical senses, and its practices are deeply interwoven with those of ordinary Jewish religious life.

The origins of the Cabala are still uncertain. The first definitely Cabalistic writings date from about 1150, but it's notoriously hard to pin down an oral tradition by way of written sources! Whether the sources of the Cabala are to be found primarily in older Jewish mystical teachings, or whether they include material from outside Judaism, is another point still very much subject to dispute. Cabalistic writings offer little guidance here; according to many of these accounts, the Cabala dates back all the way to the Garden of Eden, where it was revealed to Adam by the angels.

During the course of its history, though, the Cabala came to the attention of people with interests reaching far outside the realm of orthodox Judaism. The Renaissance, a time of renewal for so many things, saw a major revival of magic - the traditional art of shaping the hidden aspects of human awareness and experience. The surviving magical traditions of the Middle Ages were studied by some of the most brilliant minds of the age, and compared to a wide range of rediscovered wisdom teachings from the ancient world. To many of this new breed of Renaissance magicians, these methods of magical practice had potentials which went far beyond the ordinary understanding of magic: they saw magic as a way of personal and collective transformation which could open up the deeps of spiritual experience to the consciousness of the individual.

The Renaissance magicians' quest for ancient knowledge came across the Cabala early on, and it was found that many of the ideas central to Cabalistic thought could be combined with magical practice to form a new and powerful synthesis. Into the resulting fusion went compatible material from other sources: ancient Greek Hermetic and Neoplatonic philosophy, the mystical mathematics of Pythagoras, the traditions of alchemy, and a whole series of suppressed aspects of Christianity from ancient Gnosticism to the radical theologies of the late Renaissance itself. The result, evolved over several centuries, was a system of philosophy and practice which can be called the magical Cabala, a system which became the foundation for most of the teachings of Western magic from the Renaissance up to the present day.

The Golden Dawn

Many of these teachings, along with an astonishing array of odds and ends of lost knowledge, were gathered up in the late nineteenth century by an organization of English magicians known as the Hermetic Order of the Golden Dawn. Like the Cabala itself, the Golden Dawn has murky origins, and its own account of its beginnings is a Gothic tale featuring mysterious manuscripts in cipher and an untraceable German adept, borrowing many of the cliches of the occult novels of the time. Its real genesis seems to have been the work of two men, William Wynn Westcott and Samuel Mathers, both of them Freemasons and practicing magicians with a knack for research and synthesis, who assembled the basic framework of the Order's teachings and drew together a group of talented men and women around it.

Whatever its background, though, the system of magic and mysticism devised by the Golden Dawn's leading lights ranks, in scope, complexity and power, as one of the world's major esoteric teachings. One measure of this lies in its sheer scale. An adept of the Golden Dawn, at the completion of the full course of studies laid out in the Order's papers, was expected to have studied and practiced nearly every branch of occult knowledge known to the Western world, starting with the foundations of Cabalistic and alchemical theory and going from there into ritual magic, clairvoyance, astrology, geomancy, Tarot divination, practical alchemy, the design and consecration of talismans, and more. All these studies were linked together into a coherent structure of theory and practice, founded on the teachings of the magical Cabala, and this was taught step by step to members as they advanced through the different Grades or levels of the Order.

The original Hermetic Order of the Golden Dawn blew apart in the first of a series of ruinous schisms in 1900, as its organizational structure proved too brittle to handle the pressures of ordinary human misbehavior. From the ashes rose a series of successor Orders, some following the same course of studies developed by the original Order, others striking out in new directions. In time, much of the once-secret teaching material was published, most notably by Israel Regardie in his massive collection of the Order's papers, *The Golden Dawn*. These publications, along with those of major successor Orders such as Dion Fortune's Fraternity of the Inner Light and Paul Foster Case's Builders of the Adytum, have made the system of magic devised by the Golden Dawn probably the best-known of all magical traditions in the Western world.

To speak of a tradition in occult terms nowadays, though, is to court a good deal of confusion. The word routinely gets used as a synonyn for "system" or even "style," sometimes as a deliberate marketing ploy; the Such-and-Such Tradition sounds much more important and dignified than "some ideas I came up with this Thursday," especially when the latter is a more accurate description! The Golden Dawn tradition is certainly a system, and in a certain sense it defines a style as well - but it goes beyond this, in some important ways.

The word "tradition" comes ultimately from the Latin words trans, across, and *dare*, to give; *traditio* meant something given across or, as we would say, handed down. Central to the meaning of both words, Latin and English, is that a tradition is something that is passed on or passed down among people. It is not an individual creation, but a collective one, and usually one developed over time.

Habits of thinking common in our culture tend to be harsh on things of this sort; we tend to value what's original and novel, sometimes to the exclusion of any other factors at all. In the realm of magic, as elsewhere, these attitudes have resulted in a good deal of time spent reinventing the wheel, and a fair number of systems which treat current cultural prejudices as though they were universal truths. More subtly, any system of thought created by a single person is all but certain to share that person's strengths and weaknesses, imbalances and blind spots. In a system of magical philosophy and practice which aims at personal growth, this can be a serious defect, as it risks reinforcing problems instead of resolving them.

One way to sidestep many of these difficulties is the way of tradition. A traditional system, in the sense of this word we've explored, is the work of many minds and hands over many years, and its imbalances are most unlikely to match those of any given student - or any given age. Followed intelligently (as opposed to rigidly or unthinkingly!) a traditional system can provide a more balanced and more healthy framework for the sometimes difficult, sometimes risky, always unexpected path of inward transformation.

How To Use This Book

The heart of the Golden Dawn tradition, the core around which all the intricacies of the Order's work gathered, is a particular approach to the system of theory and practice I've called the magical Cabala. The purpose of this book is to offer a way into the Cabala of the Golden Dawn tradition for the novice who wonders what it's all about, the practicing magician who seeks a grasp of some of the deeper issues of his or her art, or the adept of a different system who wishes to sample the richness of this one. The material given in this book can be studied and practiced by itself, or combined with material from other books on magic; certainly any of the wide range of Golden Dawn-derived methods can be combined with it usefully.

For the beginner, the task of learning the ways of the magical Cabala can offer a significant challenge; there is a great deal of material to be learned, and some unfamiliar ways of looking at the world which need to be absorbed. There are at least two ways of handling the learning process, one traditional, one less so.

The Traditional Approach

In the days when the material we'll be covering was a secret tradition passed down within the lodges of the Golden Dawn and its successor orders, students received the theoretical material contained in this book a bit at a time, and in most cases these same students were practicing basic ritual and meditative work from the very beginning of their studies. Readers who would like to follow a version of this procedure might wish to use these guidelines:

The basic theory of the Tree of Life, the central diagram of the magical Cabala, is given in Chapters 1 and 2. These should be read first, and the material they cover should be learned as thoroughly as possible; it forms the foundation on which the whole structure of the Golden Dawn's Cabala is built.

The basic principles of practice are covered in Chapter 10, which should be read next. In many ways, this is the most important chapter in the book.

The first set of practices in this system are the Lesser Ritual of the Pentagram, given in Chapter 11, and the first stage of meditation, given in Chapter 13. It's best to read each of these chapters at least as far as the practice in question before beginning, because many of the basic concepts of ritual and meditation are covered in them.

These five readings cover the essentials of the system, and give the novice an opportunity to begin the practical work of magical training at once. The rest of Part One of the book (Chapters 3-6) should be studied next, and after that the symbolism of the Cabala, which is covered in Part Two (Chapters 7-9.) The rest of the material on magical practice, which makes up Part Three (Chapters 10-15), can be read at any time.

The Direct Approach

On the other hand, it's entirely possible to begin work on the material in this book by starting at the beginning and reading straight through to the end. This approach has the advantage that theory and symbolism are covered before the practices based on them are introduced; it has the disadvantage of placing several hundred pages of reading before the first steps in magical practice – and the practice, in a very real sense, is of more importance than any amount of theory.

A Note on Sources and Spellings

There is no one version of the magical Cabala accepted by everyone who works within the Golden Dawn tradition. One sign of a living system is that it grows and changes, and growth and change will inevitably lead different people in different directions. As a result, even the most basic details of theory, symbolism and practice vary from one teacher, book, or school to another.

The approach to the magical Cabala given in *Paths of Wisdom* is based closely on materials developed by the Hermetic Order of the Golden Dawn. The Golden Dawn's teachings, though, were in some places a hodgepodge, in others self-contradictory, and in still others simply incorrect. I have accordingly made changes where this was necessary, and discussed those changes where that is appropriate. The students who worked with this material in draft form as a correspondence course helped shape it through their questions, comments, and responses, and a handful of others – above all the two to whom this book is dedicated – played a central role in giving it what virtues it possesses.

A few other sources used in Paths of Wisdom should be noted here. Spellings and meanings of Hebrew words have been drawn from *Godwin's Cabalistic Encyclopedia* by David Godwin, and the meanings of angelic names are from Gustav Davidson's *A Dictionary Of Angels* - two books which belong on any Cabalist's bookshelf. On the thornier question of the interpretation of the "Path Texts" from the traditional "32 Paths of Wisdom," the translation by William Wynn Westcott (traditional in the Golden Dawn) has been used for the most part, but I have also referred to the translation by the late Rabbi Aryeh Kaplan.

Finally, I would like to mention the issue (if it is an issue) of spelling. It's been suggested that in in the magical community nowadays, a tradition consists of any three people who all spell the words "Cabala" and "magic" the same way. A great deal of importance has been attached to one or another variation; different spellings have been used as something not far from battle-flags in squabbles between groups. Be that as it may, *Paths of Wisdom* uses the standard dictionary spellings of both these words. Both are (or were) common English terms, and it seems reasonable to treat them as such.

Note to the Second Edition

Readers of some of my more recent books, particularly *A World Full of Gods* (ADF, 2005), may notice that my views on some important philosophical and theological topics have changed quite a bit since *Paths of Wisdom* was originally published in 1996. I have nonetheless decided to leave this book as it was, other than correcting a few errors of fact and style. The viewpoint it presents is fairly close to that of the mainstream Golden Dawn tradition, and my departure from those views was part of my movement from the Golden Dawn, where I had my original training, to the path I now follow. A number of people who have continued in the Golden Dawn tradition have told me they find *Paths of Wisdom* useful in their work. Let this be the excuse for its reprinting, if any is needed.

Part One

Principles
Of
The Magical Cabala

ChapterOne

The Tree of Life

One of the great difficulties in beginning work with the magical Cabala - and one of the reasons that this system of magic and mysticism has developed such a reputation for complexity and obscurity - is the sheer mass of material that has been built up over the years. As a living tradition more than four hundred years old, with its roots in other traditions many centuries older, it has been enriched by the efforts of generations of magicians, mystics and scholars. An immense store of tradition, lore, and experience has been amassed over this time. Like an ancient forest, it has grown thick with underbrush, and in all this underbrush it's easy to become so thoroughly lost that not only the forest but the trees themselves are hidden from sight.

Underlying all this, however, is a basic structure of great simplicity. It arose, as all mystical philosophies arise, out of the experiences of human beings facing the inner side of existence, and their attempts to describe those experiences. Such attempts are problematic, to say the least, because in a very real sense human language - any human language - can only express certain kinds of perceptions clearly.

The thinking mind, the part of us which creates and uses language, deals principally with the world of our everyday experience; language takes its meaning from that world, from the things most people perceive in common. And yet the attempt to talk about mystical experiences, which most people do not perceive, has to be made, if only to explain to others just what all the strange activities and experiences of the mystical path are about. In the process, mystics the world over have resorted to symbolism to hint at truths that cannot otherwise be expressed.

The founders of the Cabalistic tradition turned to the same resource to express their insights. In the course of time, however, they (like the founders of several other traditions) realized that the link between the symbol and the experience could be made to work in more than one way: not only could spiritual experiences be communicated in symbolic terms, but the symbols thus created could then be used by other people to experience these things for themselves. Working with this realization, Cabalistic adepts explored the subtle links between one symbol and another, and between the symbol and the thing it represents. Once these were mastered, the hidden doors to the higher levels of human experience lay open.

Symbol and Reality

Take a moment, now, to look at some nearby object: a cup, for instance. If you're like most people, you've probably always assumed that what you see is what's actually there. This assumption is so deeply ingrained in our ways of thinking that most of us never even realize it's an assumption.

As you look at that cup, though, think about how the image you see is actually formed. First of all, light waves strike the cup; depending on the atomic structure of the cup's surface, some of these waves are absorbed while others are reflected and scatter in all directions. Some of these reach your eyes, where they cause a set of chemical changes in your retina. These changes trigger cells in the optic nerve, which sends a pattern of electrical charges back through several different parts of the brain to the area at the upper back of your head, and there, by a process no one yet understands, the nerve messages are processed into the image of the cup that you actually see. We can only guess at the effects many of these stages have on the final image, but the one thing we can be sure of is that the cup and the image are not the same. The image is a representation of the cup in the mind's terms, a kind of mental model. It is, in a word, a symbol.

If at this point you go from looking at the cup to talking or writing about it, you will find yourself even deeper into the world of symbols. Instead of the cup or your image of it, you will be dealing with sounds made by a voice or marks made with a pen. These sounds and marks have only the most arbitrary relationship to the thing they represent, so that if you travel to another part of the world you may have to use a completely different set of them to make yourself understood. By contrast, anyone with normal eyesight who looks at your cup will see an image very similar to the one you see.

The central insight of the Cabalistic approach to symbolism is that this same distinction is true not only of the things we perceive with the five ordinary senses but of those perceived by the spiritual senses as well. The names, words, and concepts people use to describe the realms of experience beyond the ordinary physical world are arbitrary, and change from place to place and from time to time in much the same way that languages do. The basic images and experiences people have when they venture into the spiritual realms, on the other hand, are largely consistent between cultures and historical periods. This idea has gained some recent notice through the writings of the psychologist C. G. Jung, who made the same discovery independently. Where Jung's work dealt only with the psychological implications of the insight, however, the adepts of the magical Cabala have taken it much further.

Let's return to the cup for a few more moments. As we have seen, the word "cup" (or its equivalent in another language) is a symbol, which can be used to represent the image of the cup you see. The word takes its meaning from its link with the image, and apart from that link and its connections to other word- symbols it has no meaning at all. But the image itself is a symbol, representing the reality of the cup as such. We can know almost nothing about that reality. We can reason, if we happen to be philosophically minded, that it exists and causes the images and other sensations we experience; we assume, as well, that our mental representation of it is close enough, accurate enough, that we can make use of that representation as if it were the thing in itself - that, for example, if we pour coffee into the cup we perceive, it will stay there and not flow straight through the porcelain into our laps.

To the Cabalist, these same considerations are true of the universe in its totality. The words we use to describe the universe are symbols of our experience of the universe, which is itself a symbol of something else. About that "something else" we can know almost nothing.

Whether we use our ordinary senses to perceive the everyday world of matter, or develop those special senses which allow us to perceive other, hidden realms of being, all we can ever really experience are the symbolic images the "something else" creates in our minds. Still, after a fashion, we can reason about it. We can postulate that, in some sense, it exists. We know that it lies beyond the universe we experience, that it gives rise to that universe in some manner we don't understand. We know that its true nature is totally inaccessible to us. And as we consider these attributes, we may begin to realize that this "something else" sounds very much like what mystics of so many different places and times have called God.

The Veils of the Unmanifest

But this term, borrowed by mystical thought from the vocabulary of the established religions of the West, is as much a barrier as a help. We have already seen that the ultimate reality we are seeking cannot be clearly expressed in language. How, then, does one express the inexpressible? The question may seem absurd, but it's a necessary one. If the existence of an ultimate Reality is to be taken into account at all, we need to have some way to think about it, however inadequate. Just as language must be stretched to its limits to deal with experiences beyond the physical, the language of symbols must be stretched to its own, much broader, limits if it is to deal with the Reality which is beyond all experience whatever.

In seeking a way to tackle this problem, the creators of the Cabala - like mystics everywhere - turned to paradox as the only useable tool. At the outermost edge of its symbolism, then, the Cabala provides three paradoxical images for the Existence beyond all existence. They are called the Three Veils of the Unmanifest, to remind us that as symbols they necessarily conceal what they seek to express.

The first of the Veils is named AIN, which in Hebrew means Not or Nothing. If ultimate Reality is something utterly distinct from anything we can experience, then in human terms it can't be called "something" at all, but rather Nothing. If we try to speak about it, all that we can honestly say of it is what it is not. Here the symbol is, simply, Absence;

the Veil, the trap hidden inside the symbol, lies in taking the symbol literally and deciding that ultimate Reality simply doesn't exist.

The second of the Veils is named AIN SOPH, which means No Limit, Infinity. Everything we can know, however large or small, is finite. The sands on the beach or the falling raindrops may be beyond our ability to count, but a little logic shows that however large their numbers might turn out to be, the count will eventually reach an end. No matter how large a finite number we may choose, it falls short of infinity by an infinite amount, and the Cabalists of old saw in this absolute distinction a metaphor for the difference between the universe we experience and the ultimate Reality. Here the symbol is a Vastness like that of interstellar space, and the Veil lies in thinking this implies that the Ultimate is like the things we know, only bigger.

The third of the Veils is named AIN SOPH AUR, which means Infinite Light. One of the oldest and most universal of all symbolisms describes the world of ordinary experience as darkness and the spiritual realms which underlie it as light. Like the mental image of the cup, the image of spiritual light is based on experience: the energies of certain states of mystical awareness are very commonly perceived by human beings in the form of physical light. It's for this reason that terms like "illumination" and "enlightenment" are used to talk about spiritual experiences. In Cabalistic thought, the experience of inner light is a signpost pointing toward the attainment of the higher realms, and - as these realms offer a less constricted way of approaching the hidden Reality - light has been used to symbolize that Reality as well. Here the symbol is, of course, Radiance, and the Veil lies in mistaking that Radiance for the unknowable Existence it signifies.

In the practical work of the Cabalist the three Veils play only a minor role. Their place is as reminders and, to a certain extent, warnings, of the distinction between the symbolic and the real.

This distinction does need to be kept in mind. At the same time, awareness of the difference does not mean that the symbolic should be despised or rejected, as some philosophies claim. This attitude seems rather like that of the man who complained because he had nothing to eat but food, and nothing to wear but clothes! We are creatures of symbolic reality by our very nature, and our task is to comprehend and master that reality, not waste our time in a futile attempt to flee from it.

In the same way, the Cabalist doesn't seek to abandon the material level of experience, as some teachings urge. The whole of our universe, again, is a symbol which expresses ultimate Reality; every aspect and experience it contains has its value to us, its lessons to be learned. The everyday world is as holy as any other. The Cabalistic magician's goal is to be at home in all the levels of human experience, to travel from one to another at will, and in this way to embody the full potential of what it means to be human.

Symbols of Ultimate Reality

But what are these "levels of experience"? There are a number of ways to approach this idea, and a number of mistakes which are often made concerning it. Perhaps the most common of these latter is the notion that these "levels," "planes" or "worlds" - all three terms are used in different sources - are actually separate realms of existence, like the "other dimensions" of fantasy fiction. This is true only in the most metaphoric of senses; it's more useful, instead, to think of them as different modes of consciousness, different ways of seeing and symbolizing the same hidden Reality.

In the Cabala, each of these ways of looking at the world is defined by one of ten fundamental categories of being. We can begin to explore these categories by thinking about the idea of Reality itself, starting from the most basic concepts possible. Since these concepts are symbols, of course, they cannot reach the Existence beyond all symbolism; since they are symbols, on the other hand, they provide the foundation of the entire symbolic structure of the Cabala.

The first of these concepts is the idea of existence itself, and the first thing we can say about Reality is, simply, that it is.

The second concept is the idea of action. Reality seems to include the possibility of change and motion, and so we can apply another idea to Reality: it acts. The third concept is closely related to this; Reality also seems to include the possibility of an absence of motion, and so we can also say, it rests. The concepts of action and rest, however, cannot both apply at once; to include them both in our concept of Reality implies alternation, which is the root of the idea of Time.

So far, each of these concepts has dealt with Reality as a unity; we have had no need to postulate anything else. To go on, though, we'll have to move in this direction. In the context created by the first three ideas, action takes the form of distinct actions in time, and each new action extends the total range of action within Reality. This idea of increase or extension gives us another thing we can say of Reality: it extends. In the same way, we can speak of rests rather than of rest in the abstract, and each of these rests can be seen as the end or limit of an action; we can thus say, it limits. To speak of distinct actions and rests, though, is to suggest that the first of our concepts can be applied to them as well; once we have granted them existence, in turn, the other concepts follow, and we end up with many things rather than one, each existing, acting, resting, extending, limiting. We can put this in two ways: from the point of view of the one, it divides; from the point of view of the many, these are.

Once there is more than one thing in Reality, though, the possible range of concepts we can use goes up sharply. Any of the things which exist may contact others, and so we can say, these unite; once entered into contact, they may leave this state, and so we can say, these separate; these various unions and separations create a context which shapes and is shaped by the effects of all the other concepts, a context in which each thing which exists takes part; we can therefore say, these participate.

Finally, all these considerations apply to every action and rest, every union and division, and every participation of each existing thing. All these also exist, and take part in the full range of categories; their actions, rests, and so forth do the same; and this process continues out to infinity, creating an image of Reality made up of uncountably many things, all interacting in different ways - an image which seems very like the universe we experience in our everyday state of consciousness. This image represents the complete manifestation of the potentials contained in the original idea of being; we can thus say, last of all, it manifests.

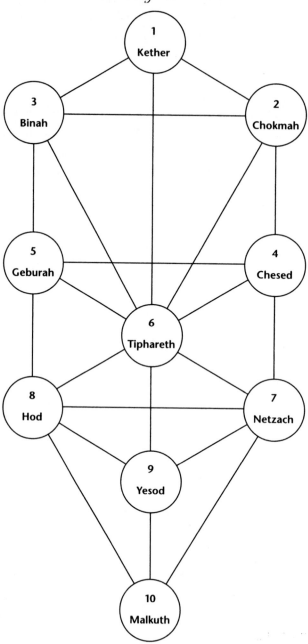

Diagram 1 - The Tree of Life

These ten categories - existence, action, rest, extension, limitation, multiplicity, union, separation, participation, and manifestation - form, from the perspective of the Cabala, the basic structures of human thought, and thus of the universe we are capable of perceiving. More, these are the grains of sand at the center of the pearls of the tradition; around each of them, layer by layer, has arisen one of the ten great symbolic patterns which make up the heart of the Cabalistic system: the Tree of Life.

The Tree of Life

The traditional diagram of the Tree of Life appears on page (page). You'll need to spend some time familiarizing yourself with it, because everything you'll be doing with this book will refer directly back to it. The ordering of the circles and lines - Spheres and Paths, respectively, are the terms we'll be using for the sake of simplicity, in place of the Hebrew terms Sephiroth and Netibhoth - is anything but random; each detail of the Tree's structure teaches specific lessons, which will become evident as your work with the Cabala progresses.

The first of the ten Spheres is KETHER, which means Crown. Its nature is absolute unity. On the diagram of the Tree, the three Veils are placed directly above Kether, referring to the idea that this Sphere is the simplest and least defined of all the realms of symbolic existence, the closest approach that symbols can make to the unknowable Reality beyond. Kether is said to be above all opposites and dualities. It has no attributes or qualities beyond pure existence; it and any quality it might have would make two, and it is always One. As a state of consciousness, it is awareness of unity with all things - not the intellectual notion that this is the case, which is easy enough to obtain, but the direct personal experience. This consciousness is the highest which human beings can achieve, and it represents the highest goal of all mystical practice.

The second of the Spheres is CHOKMAH, which means Wisdom. This is the source of creative energy and of expansion, similar to the Yang of Chinese philosophy. It is symbolically "masculine", in the sense that it creates by going outside of itself; for this reason, it also has the title of ABBA, the Supernal Father. In Chokmah the primal Unity descends from its original self-sufficiency into action, into creation. By doing so it changes from a unity to a duality: creator and creation, actor and that which is acted upon.

The third Sphere is BINAH, which means Understanding. This is the source of receptive energy and of contraction, and is much like the Yin of Chinese philosophy. Symbolically, it is held to be "feminine", in the sense that it creates by bringing what is outside into itself; for this reason, it is also named AIMA, the Supernal Mother. Binah receives the creative energy that is emanated by Chokmah, embodies it in form and, when its time is finished, absorbs it. As rivers flow downward to the sea, so all created things are said to return to Binah. Because of this, Binah is given the additional title of MARAH, the Great Sea.

These three Spheres are called the Supernal Triad. They represent the three highest powers of the universe that we can know, and the three highest states of consciousness we are able to reach. Between these states and the rest of human experience lies a barrier, which is called the Abyss.

All three Spheres of the Supernal Triad express Unity in its various aspects: unity of receptive form, unity of creative force, supreme unity transcending both of these. In order to enter these levels of experience, it's necessary to be able to perceive the entire universe - including the consciousness of the perceiver - as an unbroken whole. We don't naturally perceive things this way, of course. One of the first lessons each newborn learns from life is to divide experiences into "inside" (its own thoughts, feelings, and sensations) and "outside" (the world of objects in motion that it perceives around it). This is one of the most deeply ingrained of all habits of thought, but it is only true at certain levels of awareness. Above these, it must be set aside so that the experience of unity - an experience which Eastern mystics have called "Enlightenment," and Western mystics "union with God," can be attained.

In the midst of the Abyss is the quasi-Sphere DAATH, which means Knowledge. Daath does not arise from one of the basic categories explored above, and it is not a level of being in its own right; rather, it is the point of intersection between the forces of the Supernal Triad and those of the seven Spheres below the Abyss, at once a gate and a barrier between the realms of unity and those of individual existence.

The fourth Sphere, the first level of existence below the Abyss, is CHESED, which means Mercy. Like Chokmah, this Sphere symbolizes the outpouring of creative energy, and is considered "masculine". Chesed also has the quality of order, organization, law; long before the development of modern chaos theory, Cabalists understood that expanding energy leaves pattern in is wake. As a level of consciousness, Chesed is the deep awareness of inner structure, the ability to recognize the underlying patterns and possibilities of the world we experience. In human terms, it represents the memory.

The fifth Sphere is GEBURAH, which means Severity. As Chesed relates in some ways to Chokmah, so Geburah has certain similarities to Binah; it symbolizes a contracting and restricting force, and is considered "feminine". As the Sphere that balances Chesed's ordered creativity, though, Geburah represents destruction, dissolution, chaos. It is the power that clears away everything that has outlived its usefulness; that tears down excessive structure into simpler and more flexible elements. As a level of consciousness, it is the awareness of inner freedom, the power to break through self-imposed limitations and consciously choose one's own path in life. In human terms, it represents the will.

The sixth Sphere is TIPHARETH, which means Harmony. In the same way that Chesed reflects Chokmah and Geburah reflects Binah, Tiphareth is in a way a reflection of Kether below the Abyss. It represents the truth that every individual thing or being in the universe is a small unity, mirroring the great Unity of the universe itself. At the center of the Tree of Life, Tiphareth functions as a balancing force, harmonizing the powers of Chesed and Geburah, the "masculine" and "feminine" energies and the higher and lower levels of the Tree. As a level of consciousness, it is the awareness of self, that state of absolute inner honesty free of pride or guilt, in which we are able to see ourselves clearly for the first time. In human terms, it is the imagination.

Between these three Spheres and the four remaining ones lies a second barrier, reflecting the Abyss as the Spheres just discussed reflect the Supernal Triad. It is called the Veil of the Sanctuary. Like a veil, it partly conceals the things which lie beyond it, allowing only dim shapes and shadows to be seen. Thus the powers symbolized by Chesed, Geburah, and Tiphareth, and the levels of consciousness they represent, come only dimly into the world of our ordinary experience - unless they are deliberately brought through by a "rending of the Veil", an act of transformation in which the effects of this barrier are overcome. This act is in many ways the primary goal of Cabalistic training and practice; it takes many symbolic forms in the traditional writings.

Below the Veil of the Sanctuary is the seventh Sphere, NETZACH, which means Victory. This Sphere, like Chesed and Chokmah above it, is a source of outpouring energy, but Netzach is "feminine" rather than "masculine" in nature and its power has an attractive, indrawing function. All those forces which draw things together and bring them into interaction have their roots in Netzach, from gravity in the realm of physics to love among human beings. In human terms, Netzach represents the emotional nature.

Next is the eighth Sphere, HOD, which means Glory. Like Geburah and Binah directly above it, Hod is a center of limitation and form, but it is "masculine" in nature rather than "feminine", and the forms and divisions that rise from it pour forth as freely as the energies of Chokmah. Hod is the root of all those forces which divide and distinguish between things, and especially of every form of thought and perception. In human terms, Hod represents the intellectual nature and in particular the thinking mind.

The ninth Sphere is YESOD, which means Foundation. This is the great center of solidification on the Tree of Life, the Sphere in which the intangible energies of higher levels take shape as forces capable of affecting the material level of experience. As Tiphareth balances the opposed forces of Chesed and Geburah, so Yesod harmonizes those of Netzach and Hod, and unites within itself unbreakable stability and constant change. As the level of existence immediately beyond the physical, it is the world of visions, of dreams, and of psychic phenomena. In human terms, Yesod represents the instincts and the subconscious mind.

The tenth and last Sphere is MALKUTH, which means Kingdom. This is the world of matter we experience every day. To the Cabalist, as we mentioned earlier, Malkuth is as important as any of the other

Spheres, with lessons to be learned and powers to be contacted that are as valuable as any on the Tree of Life. It is the natural level of human beings, at least at this stage of their evolution, and any wisdom or power attained in any other Sphere must be in some way brought into action in Malkuth if it is to have any enduring human value. In human terms, Malkuth represents the physical body and the five ordinary senses.

These ten realms of being, then, make up the field of action in which the magical Cabalist operates. Although they have been presented here in cut-and-dried fashion, for the sake of clarity, it's a better representation of experience to think of them as colors or qualities in a spectrum linking spirit and matter, perfect unity and the diverse multiplicity of everyday experience. There is a certain amount of blending, in effect, at the edges, and each Sphere itself can be seen as embodying a complete Tree of Life - thus, for example, Malkuth contains aspects or reflections of each of the other Spheres within itself, and the Kether of Malkuth, the essential unity at the heart of the world of matter, has more than a little in common with the Malkuth of Yesod, the ultimate manifestation of the realm of subtle energies.

These blurrings of the sharp lines of theory have given rise, on the one hand, to an enormous amount of hairsplitting, and on the other to alternative ways of describing the spectrum of being within the Cabalistic tradition - systems which divide the continuum of existence into seven levels, or five, or three.

The system of ten Spheres nonetheless has remained central to the magical Cabala, for the simple reason that it provides a more complete framework for practical magic than any of the others. Time spent studying it will not be wasted.

Chapter Two

The Paths upon the Tree

So far, we've considered the Spheres on their own, as phases of the spectrum of being. This is only half of the complete picture. Each Sphere also stands at the center of a web of interactions linking it with other Spheres in certain specific ways, and these links can be used as bridges to move from one Sphere to another. There are twenty-two such links in all, and they are symbolized by the twenty-two Paths of the Tree of Life.

You'll find the Paths diagramed on the picture of the Tree of Life on page (page). Each Sphere, as you'll notice, is connected by Paths to at least three other Spheres, but no Sphere contacts all of the others. The arrangement of these Paths is used to teach a number of important lessons about the Spheres and their relationships, lessons which will be covered in detail later on in this book.

In one sense, the Paths represent the interactions between the Spheres, the play of energies between one aspect of the universe and another. These interactions have another significance, though. Each Path also represents a shift in awareness, a movement between different states of consciousness. In this sense, the Paths stand for the routes a traveler on the Tree must take to journey from Sphere to Sphere. This second sense is the foundation of all practical work with the Cabala, and you'll be using it more than the other. Both need to be kept in mind, and both will have their place at different times in the course of your work with this book.

Each of the 22 Paths has a number, a letter of the Hebrew alphabet, and a set of symbols and ideas associated with it. The numbers of the

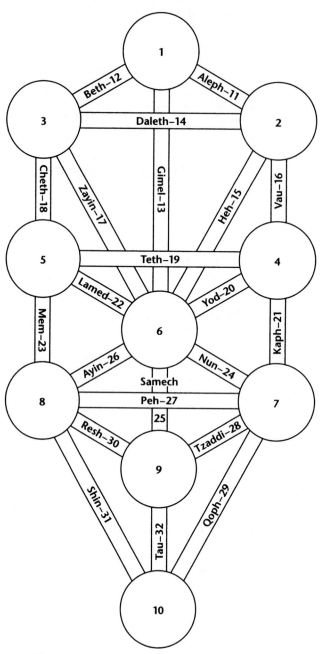

Diagram 2 - The Tree of Life (with Paths)

Paths run from 11 to 32, and not from 1 to 22 as one might expect; this is because traditionally the numbers from 1 to 10 were used exclusively for the Spheres. This system of numbering derives from the Sepher Yetzirah, or Book of Formation, an ancient mystical text that was one of the earliest sources of Cabalistic thought.

The attribution of the Hebrew letters to the Paths are also taken in large part from the Sepher Yetzirah. Speculations concerning the mystical meaning of the Hebrew language have always had a large place in Jewish mysticism, and played an important role in the origins of the Cabala itself. The belief in the special, "chosen" status of the Jewish people led writers of an earlier time into some rather extravagant claims: that Hebrew is the language the angels speak, for example, or that God only listens to prayers that are said in Hebrew.

Though they are still repeated by some of the more solidly doctrinaire writers on the Cabala, ideas such as these have no place in the magical Cabalistic tradition. Still, the Hebrew letters do have a place in our work, and not just as convenient labels. Centuries of use by mystics and scholars have given the Hebrew alphabet associations that may seem strange to modern minds. Each letter has a descriptive title, which dates back to the ancient picture writing out of which the Hebrew alphabet, like ours, originally developed, and each letter also stands for a number which is different from its Path number. The Sepher Yetzirah provides other associations, including the signs and planets of astrology, and divides the alphabet into "single" letters (assigned to the signs of the Zodiac), "double" letters (assigned to the seven traditional planets), and "mother" letters (assigned to three of the four elements). Still more correspondences, such as the cards of the Tarot deck, have been added in the last several centuries. As a result of all this, the Hebrew letters make up one of the most complete symbolic systems in existence, and would be valuable in Cabalistic work even if they were nothing more than abstract squiggles.

A few words need to be said about the last set of associations just mentioned. The act of divination - of foretelling the future or making sense of the present by means of some symbolic system - has been around a great deal longer than the Cabala. From the oracle bones

Table 1

Letter	Path	Title	Number	Astrological Correspondence	Tarot Trump
א, A	11	Aleph, Ox	1	Air	0, Fool
ב, B	12	Beth, House	2	Mercury	I, Magician
ג, G	13	Gimel, Camel	3	Moon	II, Priestess
ד, D	14	Daleth, Door	4	Venus	III, Empress
ה, H	15	Heh, Window	5	Aries	IV, Emperor
ו, U, V	16	Vau, Nail	6	Taurus	V, Hierophant
ז, Z	17	Zayin, Sword	7	Gemini	VI, Lovers
ח, Ch	18	Cheth, Fence	8	Cancer	VII, Chariot
ט, T	19	Teth, Serpent	9	Leo	VIII, Strength
י, I, Y	20	Yod, Fist	10	Virgo	IX, Hermit
כ, K	21	Kaph, Hand	20	Jupiter	X, Fortune
ל, L	22	Lamed, Goad	30	Libra	XI, Justice
מ, M	23	Mem, Water	40	Water	XII, Hanged Man
נ, N	24	Nun, Fish	50	Scorpio	XIII, Death
ס, S	25	Samech, Prop	60	Sagittarius	XIV, Temperance
ע, Aa	26	Ayin, Eye	70	Capricorn	XV, Devil
פ, P	27	Peh, Mouth	80	Mars	XVI, Tower
צ, Tz	28	Tzaddi, Hook	90	Aquarius	XVII, Star
ק, Q	29	Qoph, Back of Head	100	Pisces	XVIII, Moon
ר, R	30	Resh, Head	200	Sun	XIX, Sun
ש, Sh	31	Shin, Tooth	300	Fire	XX, Judgement
ת, Th	32	Tau, Cross	400	Saturn	XXI, World

The following letters have different shapes and number values when written at the end of a word:

Letter	Final Form	Number
Kaph	ך	500
Mem	ם	600
Nun	ן	700
Peh	ף	800
Tzaddi	ץ	900

Note that Hebrew is written right to left, not left to right as English is.

Table 1

of prehistoric China to the astrology columns of today's newspapers, people have turned to such things, and in the process have created sets of symbols which can be very useful in methods of mystical practice such as the ones we are studying. Several of these systems have in this way become attached to the Cabalistic tradition.

By assigning each of these Hebrew letters to a particular relationship between Spheres, and by expressing each of these by means of a cluster of associated symbols, Cabalists arrived at an alphabet which stood both for sounds and for basic ideas and experiences. These ideas aren't limited to the notions of mysticism or of philosophy. Just as the powers that are represented by the Spheres are found in every being and thing in the universe, the experiences represented by the Paths manifest themselves in the events of everyday life. Each of the important facets of human existence has its echo and its symbol in one of the Paths of the Tree of Life. The alphabet of Cabala, then, is an alphabet of human experience here on the material level.

At the same time, of course, the Paths offer a means of traveling beyond that level, of coming into contact with the deeper powers and realities hidden away within us and within the universe. This may seem like a paradox; in fact, it expresses one of the most important truths the Cabala has to offer. The keys to wisdom, to spiritual development, are not to be found in some dream world far off. They are to be found here and now, in the events of everyday life. Properly understood and properly used, the most ordinary of experiences can become a door into the higher levels of being.

The Names of God

Once the idea of an alphabet of symbols as well as sounds had been established by the early Cabalists, a whole range of uses for the idea were quickly developed. One approach, very popular in the devout Jewish circles in which the Cabala had its origins, involved using the idea of the symbolic alphabet as a way to interpret the holy books of Judaism. If each letter has an inner meaning, every word represents a sequence of such meanings, a kind of symbolic sentence that may have little or nothing in common with the word's ordinary meaning.

As each letter also stood for a number, these could be added together to produce a number for any given word; a belief arose that any two words which had the same number were connected in some mystical way, and an entire system of occult mathematics, called gematria, was created to analyze the words of Scripture according to their numbers. Other methods abounded. Over the years the belief grew that the whole of the Old Testament was a gigantic cipher, a secret message from God to humankind containing all of the wisdom of the universe in encoded form.

This belief can still be found today in Cabalistic circles within orthodox Judaism, but the main current of the magical Cabalistic tradition passed long ago beyond dogmatic reliance on any one traditional set of scriptures. Despite all the ingenuity of the Cabalists of old, it's a matter of question whether or not much of enduring value came out of the attempt to "decode" the books of the Old Testament. A number of the methods developed in that attempt, however, are of significant value. Though all this attention paid to words and their meanings may not have succeeded in finding hidden messages in Scripture, it will allow us to make sense of an important aspect of the Cabala: the strange words which tradition calls the Names of God.

What are these Names? Most of them come from the Old Testament, where they appear as the various titles and names of the tribal god of archaic Judaism. English translations of the Bible usually turn to various euphemisms to represent these - the Lord, the Almighty, the Lord of Hosts - or simply replace all of them with the single word "God". In the original text, however, a wide range of names and titles of God appear. Biblical scholars tell us that these come from different historical traditions, and from different writings that were combined in the fifth century B.C. to make the Old Testament we now know. In the traditional lore of Jewish mysticism, however, it is taught that the different Divine Names are intended to represent different aspects of God. Each Name, the traditional holds, is a symbolic form which expresses to human minds some part of the nature of an otherwise unknowable Reality.

The adepts of the Cabala took these ideas much further. They taught that every combination of letters symbolized some aspect of the Divine, some approach to the questions of existence that could be used in practical working. Of these, the traditional Divine Names found in Scripture were held to be at once the most useful and the highest, but every Name has its value, and methods were devised to create new Names to express specific truths or particular aspects of existence.

From the traditional Names, ten were selected and assigned to the ten Spheres of the Tree of Life, to represent the highest conception of Reality possible at each level of being. These ten Names of God will be an important part of our work in the course, and you'll be studying each of them in detail when we begin working with the individual Spheres later on. There is one Name, however, which holds an even higher rank in Cabalistic thought. Perhaps the most ancient of all the Names, it is considered so holy in Jewish tradition that it is referred to simply as ha- Shem, "the Name", and may never be spoken aloud. In the Cabala, its symbolism plays a role comparable to that of the Tree of Life itself.

The Tetragrammaton

This Name is called the Tetragrammaton, which means "Name of four letters". It is written יהוה , or in English letters YHVH. Biblical scholars tell us that this is to be pronounced "Yahweh", while esoteric tradition suggests several different pronunciations. Some modern linguists have suggested that it may be a very ancient form of the Hebrew verb "to be". If we turn to Cabalistic methods of analysis, we find that, in a very real sense, the Tetragrammaton does indeed express this concept. The four letters of this holiest of Divine Names make up a complete symbolism of processes of creation and the nature of existence itself.

Yod, the first letter, stands for the first spark of energy, the original initiating force that sets the creative process in motion.

In the Cabala, the letter Yod is associated with ideas of solitude, isolation, and innocence; it is the seed before it has begun to germinate, the child before the awakening of sexuality. The word Yod itself means "fist", the hand closed in upon itself, suggesting the same idea. Among the attributions of Yod are the astrological sign Virgo, the Virgin, and the Tarot Trump IX, the Hermit. Both of these carry forward the same symbolism. This first stage of creation, then, represents the initial force before it has come into contact with anything else. Traditionally, the Yod of Tetragrammaton is called the Father.

Heh, the second letter, stands for the environment in which the energy of Yod manifests itself. It is the matrix of the creative process, the existing pattern of things, stable and balanced and for that very reason unable to create on its own. Given a force from outside to set it in motion, however, it has immense power. The letter Heh, therefore, is associated with ideas both of receptiveness, passivity, and stability, and of strength in motion, calm but overwhelming as the current of a great river. The word Heh means "window", which suggests the receptive side of the symbolism, while Heh's attributions - the astrological sign Aries, the Ram, and the Tarot Trump IV, the Emperor - emphasize the more active side. In traditional writings, the first Heh of Tetragrammaton is called the Mother.

Vau, the third letter, stands for the product of Yod and Heh, the interaction between the pure creative force and the stable but receptive situation it encounters. It is the act of creation, the process of change as the old order of things gives way to the new. In the course of this phase, the energy of Yod is completely absorbed by Heh, and the environment of Heh is completely transformed by Yod. The first two letters, in a sense, destroy each other, leaving the third to carry on the process of creation. The letter Vau is thus associated with ideas of progress and continuation, of stability united with movement, of labor and endurance. The word Vau means "nail", again suggesting labor, the work of building. Vau's attributions include the astrological sign Taurus, the Bull, and the Tarot Trump V, the Hierophant, while in traditional writings the Vau of Tetragrammaton is called the Son.

Heh repeated, the fourth letter, stands for the conclusion of the creative process, the establishment of a new pattern of balanced forces. It represents crystallization, solidification, the return to stability. The associations and attributions of the letter remain the same, indicating that the new environment has many of the characteristics of the old, though the two are never identical. Traditionally, the second Heh of Tetragrammaton is called the Daughter. This new pattern, once established, is able to serve as the receptacle for a new outpouring of creative force, thus beginning the cycle anew; in some Cabalistic writings this is referred to poetically as "the Daughter being set upon the throne of the Mother". This changes the Tetragrammaton from a static linear sequence to a cyclical, never-ending process of creation and renewal.

Obviously, the idea of God that Cabalistic thought derives from the Tetragrammaton is very different from the one generally used by dogmatic theological traditions in Judaism, Islam, or Christianity. God as symbolized by the Tetragrammaton is more a process than a person: a verb, if you will, rather than a noun. The whole point of having and using the different Names of God, though, is that a range of different conceptions of the Divine, instead of just one, can be dealt with. An infinite Reality, after all, is not likely to fit too well into any single finite human concept! Other Names express other understandings of God, and among these are the familiar images of Deity such as First Cause, Omnipotence, and so forth.

One value of the Tetragrammaton comes from the fact that it allows us to see every act of creation as one expression of a single, universal process. Through it, any creative act of whatever kind can be analyzed in symbolic form. (For example, my intention to teach about the Cabala is Yod, my knowledge of Cabalistic tradition and the English language is Heh, the act of writing down these words on paper is Vau, and the book you are holding in your hands is the final Heh.) In the same way, the Tetragrammaton can be applied to the process whereby the universe that we experience comes into being, and it is here that this Name gains its greatest power.

The Cabalists of old expressed this by the saying that the Tetragrammaton contains the secrets of the creation of the universe. This claim is a lot less pretentious than it sounds. Unlike the ordinary Judeo-Christian idea of Creation, which holds that the creative process happened once, a long time ago, the Cabalistic teaching is that creation takes place constantly. The universe we know is created anew each moment by the interactions between our awarenesses and an unknowable Reality. Nothing remains the same for the smallest of moments. If we explore this process of creation through the symbols of the Tetragrammaton, we find the four letters representing four different kinds of existence, four steps between the universe we know and the supreme Power which lies behind it.

The Four Worlds

These are the four Worlds of Cabalistic tradition. The first World is called ATZILUTH, the Archetypal World, and stands for reality as it exists in itself, outside of our awareness of it. The second World is BRIAH, the Creative World, and it stands for reality as it exists in the factors which condition human (and other) awareness, and thus shape the way that Reality is experienced. The third World, YETZIRAH, the World of Formation, stands for the interaction between the first two Worlds, the long process of transformations that everything we perceive goes through before it reaches our awareness. The fourth World, finally, is called ASSIAH, the Material World, and stands for the result of all of these transformations, reality as we actually experience it, the symbolic realm of existence that human beings by their nature inhabit.

All this may seem very abstract, but it can be traced in every act of perception. Take a moment, as you did a little earlier, to look at some nearby object: the same cup, supposing you still happen to have it out. That cup exists, according to Cabalistic teachings, in four different ways; in fact, it would not be going too far to say that there are four different cups in front of you. There is the cup as you ordinarily perceive it and think of it, the cup in Assiah. There is the cup as a pattern of light particles reaching your eyes, electrical charges in your nervous system, and perceptions put together by your mind, the cup in Yetzirah. Then there is the cup as it already exists in your mind and memory, from the basic idea of "cup" to the memory that you filled this one with coffee and set it down next to your chair before you began reading this book, as well as the structures of sensation and perception that make the experience of that cup possible for you; all of this makes up the cup in

Briah. Finally there is the cup as it exists in itself, about which you can know literally nothing at all, the cup in Atziluth.

These same four kinds of existence, in Cabalistic thought, can be traced in the totality of the universe just as they can in the cup we have been examining. Here, too, it can be said without too much inaccuracy that there are four different universes about us at every moment: the universe of Atziluth, the real universe in its absolute unapproachability; the universe of Briah, the potential for perceiving a universe in the awareness of all conscious entities within that universe; the universe of Yetzirah, the sum total of the processes of awareness in all these entities; and the universe of Assiah, the myriad images of reality reflected in consciousness throughout the cosmos on all its levels.

Each of the ten Spheres of the Tree of Life thus exists in all four Worlds, just as the cup does, and many of the symbols that are assigned to each Sphere are divided up among the Worlds; thus, for example, the Names of God attributed to the Spheres represent the Spheres in the world of Atziluth. Traditionally, though, each Sphere is held to be particularly associated with one of the four Worlds. This is intended to point out that different levels of consciousness focus attention on different things, and that one or another of the four Worlds will seem most important as awareness rises from Sphere to Sphere. Thus Malkuth is linked with Assiah, since in the ordinary state of consciousness the universe of everyday experience is the only thing that seems real.

The Spheres from Yesod to Chesed are linked with Yetzirah, because at these levels reality appears as a constant process of interaction and change, a kind of dance of transformation in which the dancers are imaginary and only the dance is real. The Spheres Chokmah and Binah are linked with Briah, because at these levels reality seems to be primarily a matter of essential underlying pattern, from which the dance of Yetzirah takes its rhythm and form. The Sphere Kether is linked, finally, with Atziluth, since at this highest of levels all the phenomena of the experienced universe are seen to come directly out of the unknowable Reality symbolized, in a different sense, by the three Veils above Kether.

The Geometry of Being

This correlation between Spheres and Worlds can be understood in another way as well. The Tree of Life, as mentioned above, embodies a set of specific levels, states of being, and processes of transformation. Less obviously, it also embodies a specific geometry, which plays a central role in the structure of the whole and the organization of meaning within the diagram.

Few people even within Western esoteric traditions nowadays remember that the study of geometry was once an important part of those traditions, central to many aspects of study and practice. Still, any magician who has ever traced a pentagram in the air, or made a talisman of a shape determined by its planetary number, has experienced something of the power of geometric form. In an earlier age, before the great persecutions, enormous effort went into analyzing and understanding the inner effects of shape and proportion, and relating these to equivalent factors in philosophy, music and magic.

Important as they are, the fragments of this work which still survive cannot detain us here. Such considerations, however, underlie the essential structure of the Tree of Life, and can be explored to some extent through a simple exercise.

For this, you'll need a sheet of paper, a pencil, a ruler, and a geometer's compass - the kind you probably used in school, with a small pencil clipped to one side, is fine.

Start by drawing a line down the middle of the paper. Set the compass to any convenient width - two inches or so, perhaps - and, with the compass point near the top end of the line, draw a curve as shown.

Now move the point of the compass to the place where the curve you've drawn cuts across the line. Without changing the width of the compass, draw a circle around this point. The upper edge of this circle will touch the center of the original curve, as shown here.

Next, repeat the step above by moving the point of the compass to the place where the circle you just drew intersects the line, and tracing another circle of the same width. Then do the same thing one more time. You now have three and a half overlapping circles aligned along a straight line.

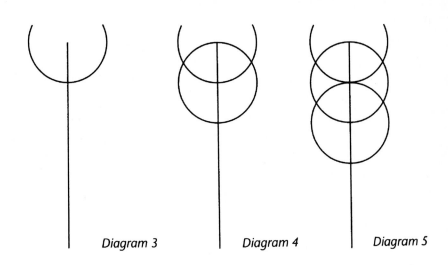

Diagram 3   Diagram 4   Diagram 5

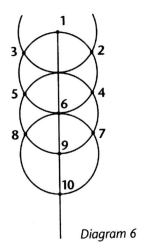

Diagram 6

Finally, mark the points numbered 1 through 10 on the diagram above. These points, of course, are the ten Spheres, and their positions match those on the traditional diagram of the Tree of Life. The three and a half circles represent the Four Worlds, with the undefinable reality of Atziluth symbolized, appropriately enough, by the open, incomplete curve at the top. In this diagram, as in experienced reality, the Spheres and Worlds define and are defined by each other.

From this approach to the Tree, the assignments of Worlds to Spheres given above may seem a little arbitrary, but in fact they express an important point. Those assignments give more than half the Spheres - the whole set of Spheres included in the Yetzirah circle - to the third World, Yetzirah, while the remaining Spheres are divided up among the other three. This imbalance is deliberate, and rises from practical considerations. The World of Formation, the realm of processes by which all conscious beings perceive the universe around them, is the major focus of work in the magical Cabala, because it is the realm most accessible to conscious understanding and change. Where the first two Worlds cannot be changed by human action, and the fourth (as the stable product of their union) resists change by its nature, the third World moves readily in response to will once its laws are understood and followed. Once set in motion, too, changes in the World of Yetzirah become manifest in the world of Assiah as part of the natural process of creation. Fluid and mutable, Yetzirah is above all others the World of magic, and it will be the primary field of the work ahead of you.

Chapter Three
The Polarities Of Being

The Spheres and Paths of the Tree of Life stand at the heart of Cabalistic symbolism and philosophy in the Golden Dawn tradition. In a real sense, though, a grasp of these levels and their interactions is only the first step in making sense of the Cabala. Woven among the branches of the Tree are a whole series of structures and interactions which we will call energy relationships. The use of "energy" as a metaphor here is not part of the traditional symbolism of the Cabala, but it conveys the dynamic, transformative quality of this aspect of the Tree to modern minds more clearly than older terminologies.

While it is a metaphor - the "energy" we're discussing won't show up on a meter or run your toaster oven - it can be useful to think of the Tree of Life as a structure along which a whole array of energies flow and surge. These energies are the driving forces of creation, the powers which form and sustain the universe at all its levels; they are also the forces which are used by the Cabalist in magic and other kinds of practical work. Like any form of energy, they can be dangerous when used clumsily or inappropriately, and a basic grasp of the principles by which they operate will spare the student some burned fingers.

The Principle Of Polarity

The most important of these principles, and the key to understanding the energy relationships of the Tree, is the concept of polarity. In some current magical circles this term is used to refer to the forces behind human sexuality, and this is appropriate in a sense: the principle of polarity certainly underlies sex, as it does any interaction between opposites. Sex alone, though, is only one rather small aspect of the whole field of polarity processes.

The essential idea behind the principle of polarity is that anything in the universe can be understood, in magical terms, as an energy relationship between two opposed forces, resulting in a third, balanced force. In this relationship, one of the forces is typically a centripetal force - that is, it tends to bring the things affected by it together, to a common center - while the other is typically a centrifugal force, and tends to drive the things affected by it away from one another. The balance and relationship between these forces determines the shape and direction of the resulting force of balance.

For instance, your physical body is formed through an interaction between the force of biological growth and that of death and decay; the interplay between these two produces a third force, which we call "life." Similarly, a group of people who come together to practice magic create an interaction between their mutual interest, on the one hand, and the divisive forces of their personal needs and goals, on the other; the fusion of these two may produce an egregor or group personality which harmonizes the group, or it may generate quarrels and divisive forces which split the group apart - and both of these outcomes involve, each in its own way, the establishment of balance.

It's important to understand what the definition given above does not say. Anything in the universe can be seen as a polarity relationship, but that does not mean that everything must be seen in this way, or that no other way is useful to the Cabalist. Quite the contrary! The Cabala is full of different, overlapping models and metaphors for the universe precisely because different conceptual tools work best to understand different parts of the universe, and make sense of different kinds of practical work. Like the small boy who was given a hammer for his birthday and decided that everthing in the world needed hammering, or like the proponents of modern science who try to fit all human experience to a model developed to make sense of physics, it's all too easy to mistake a metaphor's usefulness in one area for evidence that the metaphor should be applied everywhere - or, worse yet, for proof that the metaphor is somehow "true." Just as with the boy - or the scientists - the result of this sort of approach is usually a mess.

At the same time, the metaphor of energy and the model of polarity together form one of the most useful tools in the Cabalist's mental kit. Most of the complexities of Cabalistic thought, and many of the details of practical magic, become clear once these ideas are used to make sense of them.

The Pillars Of Wisdom

The presence of polarity relationships on the Tree of Life shapes the Tree's structure and symbolism in a number of ways, some obvious, some subtle. Probably the most visible of these is the positioning of the ten Spheres along three vertical columns or Pillars, which correspond to the three phases of the polarity process.

Diagram 7 shows the position of the Pillars on the Tree of Life. The pillars to the left and right can be seen as the negative and positive forces of the universe - the Yin and Yang of Chinese philosophy, to borrow a useful terminology once again. The pillar in the center is the balancing force that unifies and completes them. In one sense, these are downward extensions of the three Spheres that crown them, but this sense is not the limit of their importance; they are broader concepts with a greater range of applications.

The pillar on the right side of the Tree is called the Pillar of Force in some branches of Qabalistic tradition, and the Pillar of Mercy in others. It includes Chokmah, the Sphere of primary creative force; Chesed, the Sphere of order, structure, and law; and Netzach, the Sphere of love and attraction. It represents the outpouring, visible, active aspects of the universe, and is symbolically "male"; that is, it brings about creation outside itself, through the outward flow of its energy.

The pillar to the left is called the Pillar of Form, or in other sources the Pillar of Severity. It includes Binah, the Sphere of primary receptive form; Geburah, the Sphere of destruction, disintegration, and chaos; and Hod, the Sphere of intellectual thought and analysis. It represents the ingathering, hidden, receptive aspects of the universe, and is symbolically "female"; that is, it brings about creation within itself by drawing in that which is outside it.

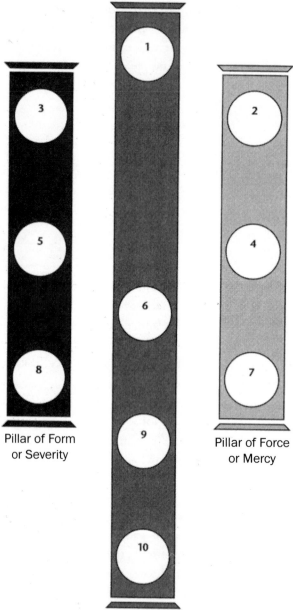

Pillar of Form
or Severity

Pillar of Force
or Mercy

Pillar of Consciousness
or Balance

Diagram 7 - The Pillars on the Tree of Life

The pillar in the center is called the Middle Pillar; its other names include the Pillar of Consciousness, of Mildness, and of Balance. It includes Kether, the Sphere of original and final Unity; Tiphareth, the Sphere of harmony and equilibrium; Yesod, the Sphere of fundamental force; and, of course, Malkuth, the Sphere of material reality. It represents the union and balancing of the conflicting forces of the two side pillars, the harmonizing force guiding them upwards into unity and downwards into material manifestation. Symbolically, it stands for the union of "male" and "female" natures in the act of creation, an exact reflection of the union of male and female in the act of love.

It's worth noting that, while the usual symbolism has each of the Pillars beginning and ending in one of its own Spheres, an alternative image has all beginning in Kether and ending in Malkuth. The beginning in Kether points out that all polarities resolve into perfect unity at the highest of levels; the end in Malkuth indicates that all polarities have their manifestation somewhere in the numberless oppositions of the realm of ordinary experience. These points have their applications both in deeper levels of Cabalistic theory and in magical practice.

The three Pillars are the most basic energetic elements of the Tree of Life, the framework upon which the entire system of the Tree's symbolism is organized, as well as the principal model of polarity relationships used in Cabalistic theory. Their importance is such that, in some senses, the Spheres placed upon them can best be understood as transformations of the essential energies of the Pillars themselves.

At the same time, the Pillars should not be seen as merely static forms. Their major role is as a context for a series of more extensive energy relationships, a dance of forces moving vertically and horizontally across the whole structure of the Tree. Like the frame of an infinite loom, they provide the structure on which the fabric of the universe is woven.

The Sword And The Serpent

Of these energy relationships, the vertical - running from Kether to Malkuth and back - are more important in practical terms, and should be considered first. They can be understood in two ways, the first from the top of the Tree down, the second from the bottom up. The first, traditionally, is held to convey the secrets of creation, while the second deals with the work of redemption, the transformation and healing of the human spirit; the first is of the macrocosm, the universe around us, while the second is of the microcosm, the universe within us; on the Tree itself, the first relates principally to the Spheres, the second to the Paths. Between them, these two patterns of energy flow make up the underlying structure of all practical work - meditative, visionary, ritual, mystical - in the magical Cabala.

The first or descending pattern follows the numerical order of the Spheres, from Kether down to Malkuth. Because of its zigzag course down the Tree, shown in Diagram 8, its most common name is the Lightning Flash.

This pattern is the primary course of creative energy through the Spheres, mapped onto the structure of the Pillars. If you trace the Flash on the Paths of the Tree, some of its meanings should be clear at once. Notice that the part of the Flash between the third Sphere, Binah, and the fourth, Chesed, does not follow any of the Paths; this gap is another representation of the Abyss, the most important of the barriers on the Tree. Note also the rhythm of the Flash from expansion to contraction, Mercy to Severity, and back to balance in the center; this rhythmic pattern, a moving response to the ebb and flow of polarity forces, appears again and again in the Tree's energetics.

The Lightning Flash has another significance in Cabalistic theory, as well, and an additional name: the Flaming Sword. Traditional lore holds that each of the Spheres, in the first phase of the creative act, takes shape as an unbalanced and unharmonized center of energy. This imbalance is personified as a demonic entity - the term we will be using is "Negative Power," in place of the technical term Shell or Shard (Hebrew Qlippah) - and the balancing and harmonizing of each Sphere by the descending energy of creation takes on the imagery of a war against the powers of chaos. As the Sword, the descent of energy from Sphere to Sphere becomes a weapon defeating and casting out destructive forces; in practical magic, the formula of the Sword is thus one of the principal tools of the magician against inner sources of imbalance, the reflections of these demonic forces within the microcosm.

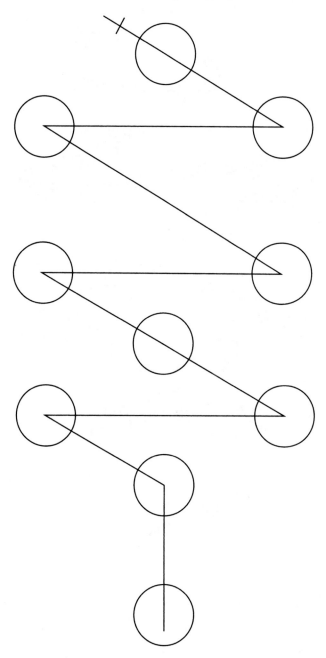

Diagram 8 - The Lightening Flash

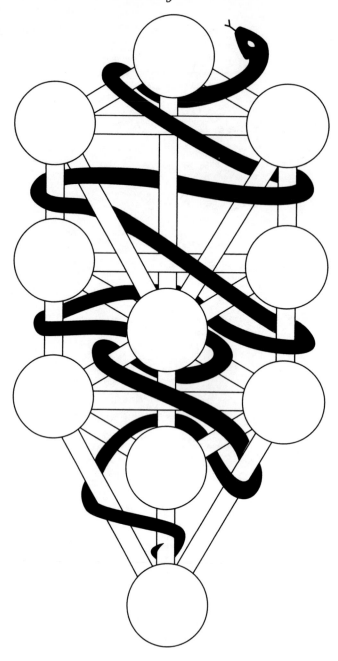

Diagram 9 - The Path of the Serpent

The descent of the Lightning Flash, then, brings the energies of the Tree down from the Sphere of absolute unity to the realm of everyday experience. That descent is balanced - is brought, in fact, into a polarity relationship - by an ascending current of energy rising from Malkuth back up the Tree to Kether. This rising current follows a complex, looping path, and in the traditional imagery of the Cabala it is therefore symbolized by the image of the Path of the Serpent, as shown in Diagram 9.

The course of the Serpent from Path to Path may seem strange, but it is anything but random. Nor does the Serpent's trail have as little to do with the ten Spheres as it may seem at first glance.

The Path of the Serpent, in fact, represents the opening of the Paths between Sphere and Sphere in the consciousness of the magical Cabalist. More precisely, it represents the opening of these Paths in a particular, carefully balanced order, rising up from the base of the Tree to its Crown and opening up the higher levels of human awareness and potential in perfect harmony. As a later chapter will discuss, this process of opening is the heart of the Cabala's approach to personal transformation; it is also, in the traditional lore, the fulfilment and completion of the entire process of creation.

The Path of the Serpent relates to the principle of polarity in two ways. First, the movement of the Serpent from side to side of the Tree, from Pillar to Pillar and back, echoes the zigzag route of the Lightning Flash at a higher level of complexity. Second and more critically, though, each Path between Spheres is itself a polarity relationship first and foremost, a force of balance created by the conflict between two Spheres in interaction. Each curve of the Serpent thus represents a polarity brought into balance; in terms of the human microcosm, it stands for the joining of two aspects of consciousness into a greater whole.

The Polarities Of The Tree

The role of the Paths as polarity interactions between the Spheres brings up another issue. In all polarity relationships, as mentioned above, one of the two primary forces has a centripetal or unifying effect, the other

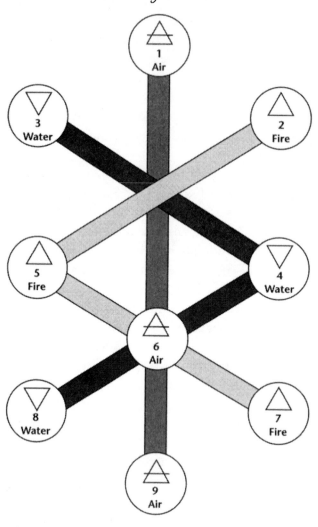

Diagram 10 - The Polarities of the Tree

a centrifugal or dispersing effect. In the relationships between Sphere and Sphere on the Tree, these roles are an important factor both in symbolism and in practical working, and the pattern that shapes them should be understood.

This pattern is not, as one might expect, simply that of the Pillars, although it derives from this. Rather, it follows the kind of back-and-forth motion on the Tree that also appears in the diagrams of the Sword and the Serpent. For the sake of convenience, traditional teachings use the four elements of ancient science to mark the polarity roles of the different Spheres, and this symbolism works as well as any.

Diagram 10, then, shows the way these roles map onto the Spheres of the Tree. In traditional terms, the element of Fire represents the centrifugal role, because material fire breaks up and disperses what it burns, while the element of Water represents the centripetal role, because when water is poured into water the two volumes mix together completely. Air and Earth, in turn, can be used to symbolize the resulting force of balance. The whole symbolism has its roots in the Tetragrammaton, YHVH, and can be developed further along the same lines

In tracing polarity roles on the Tree, the Spheres assigned to Fire and Water retain their role in every interaction; thus Geburah, for example, is always centrifugal in relationship with other Spheres. Spheres assigned to Air or Earth take the roles that balance the other Spheres with which they interact; thus Tiphareth, for example, is centripetal in relation to Geburah, but centrifugal in relation to Chesed. Finally, on the three Paths along the Middle Pillar, where Spheres in balance interact with each other, the higher Sphere functions as a centripetal force, the lower as a centrifugal one; thus Tiphareth is the unifying force on the 25th Path, but the dispersing and disuniting force on the 13th.

The Major And Minor Triads

Alongside this system of elemental patterns, there is another way of looking at polarity relationships on the Tree, one which has important practical applications. In this second system, the Paths are seen simply as mediators of the polarity process, and all three elements of the polarity relationship - both initial forces, and the resulting balanced force - are Spheres. The dance of forces on the Tree thus generates a series of triads of Spheres, each of which is linked together by a triad of Paths.

These triads introduce a greater level of subtlety to the Tree's energetics. In this context, the roles of Spheres in polarity relationships are much more fluid. In addition, the relationships themselves can take on some unexpected functions. Some of the triads involve two Spheres on one level and the third on a lower level; these represent interactions with a creative function - that is, processes aligned with the Lightning Flash, which participate in bringing the world into being - that separate into opposing forces during the ascent of the Path of the Serpent. Others involve two Spheres on a lower level resulting in a third on a higher; these are principally redemptive processes - aligned with the Serpent, and thus important to the work of transformation - which generate opposing forces during the descent of creative energies in the Lightning Flash. Still others unite Spheres on three different levels, and have a mixed function. These interactions will make a great deal more sense when seen in the context of the Path and Sphere symbolism, and will be covered in more detail later, but it's important that you have some sense of the possibilities involved.

Of these triads, three are of primary importance: the Kether-Chokmah-Binah triangle, the Chesed-Geburah-Tiphareth triangle, and the Netzach-Hod-Yesod triangle. Each of these triads link Spheres on each of the three Pillars, and each is based on one of the three horizontal Paths of the Tree - Paths which, as later chapters will show, carry enormous intensities of energy. These three triads also serve in their own right as the major horizontal energy structure of the Tree, comparable in its importance to the three Pillars. Here, they will be referred to as the Major Triads.

There has been a certain amount of confusion over these three triads and their relationship to the other symbolism of the Tree of Life. Some writers have assigned them to the first three of the Four Worlds, with Malkuth alone corresponding to the fourth; this is a useable symbolism, although it limits the meaning of the triads more than might be appropriate. Others, less usefully, refer to them as (in descending order) the Intellectual, Moral and Material Worlds; these are poor translations of Hebrew originals, and make gibberish of the triads' significance. The highest of the three - in traditional terms, the Supernal Triad - is not "intellectual" in any current sense of the word, nor are Netzach, Hod and Yesod "material" in any meaningful way.

One useful way to understand these triads is as modes of relationship between the three Pillars, the prime polarity of the Tree. As the Pillars extend across the barriers on the Tree, there are three such modes: one beyond the Abyss, one between the Abyss and the Veil, and one below the Veil. (Equally, it could be said that these three are one mode percieved from these three standpoints. In practical terms, these two ways of stating the matter are identical.) These three modes, plus a fourth which is their resolution in Malkuth, make up another expression of the Tetragrammaton; thus, the Supernal Triad is a mode of perfect unity, the second Major Triad one of receptivity but active power, the third one of dramatic transformation, and their manifestation in Malkuth of polarities as we ordinarily experience them.

Besides the major triads, there are also thirteen minor triads, triangular relationships of Paths linking Spheres, which have a lesser role in the energetics of the Tree. Three of these - the triangles marked out by Chokmah-Binah-Tiphareth, Tiphareth-Netzach-Hod, and Netzach-Hod-Malkuth - also connect the three Pillars together, but since they cross the Veil or the Abyss they do so with less intensity. The remainder connect two Spheres of one Pillar with one of another. Each of these minor triads establishes a polarity relationship of its own, and sets up energy stresses on the Tree which are balanced by other triads and held together by the overall polarity of the Pillars.

A word or two should be said at this point about the so- called "hidden Paths" of the Tree. Several modern Cabalistic schools have made much of the idea that any two Spheres not connected by one of the twenty-two traditional Paths are linked instead by a "hidden Path." While this concept can have certain uses in the realm of Cabalistic theory, it seems to have little relevance to the energetics of the Tree and, to the extent that one can generalize from personal experience, little value in actual magical working.

Similarly, there are several alternative arrangements of Paths on the Tree, connecting the Spheres in different ways. A number of these are at least as old as the one used by the Golden Dawn, while others are more recent productions. Certain proponents of one or another of these systems have made sweeping claims for the "truth" of their particular diagrams and the falsity of all others, but such claims miss the point; a system of symbols, a metaphor for an incomprehensible and indescribable reality, cannot be true - only useful. Whether these alternative systems are useful or not is a matter for personal experience, and beyond the scope of this book.

Practical Uses Of Polarity

All this material may seem, at this stage, far removed from issues of Cabalistic practice. In point of fact, though, the concepts of polarity and energy are critical to any understanding of the way the Cabala can be applied to the work of inner transformation and the arts of practical magic.

It is by way of a grasp of polarity relationships that the Tree of Life becomes a roadmap to the higher possibilities of human consciousness. Any state, by the principle of polarity, is the product of two opposed forces in balance, and the state of awareness you find yourself in, at this moment or any other, is no exception from the rule. To change that state, all that's necessary is that you identify the two forces that are holding that state in balance, and act on one of them. To identify such forces is one of the functions of Cabalistic theory; to act on them, one of the functions of Cabalistic practice.

For example, a Cabalistic magician who wishes to clear away a destructive emotional pattern might locate that pattern in Netzach, and trace the roots of the problem to issues of imagination and self-identity in Tiphareth, memory and concepts of spirituality in Chesed, and the interactions between these through the minor triad formed by the Paths of Yod, Kaph, and Nun. A ritual, a set of transformative Pathworkings, or some other form of magical response to the problem can then be put together, using an appropriate symbolism to restore a healthier balance - for instance, the consecration of a talisman to bring the positive aspects of Chesed more fully into operation, or a working of the Path of Gimel to clear away an unrealistically poor self-image. Once the principles are understood, the practice follows naturally.

The same is true of every level of Cabalistic practice, from the most basic forms of awareness training to the highest and most difficult realms of contemplation and ceremonial magic. A solid grasp of theory will spare the student many dead ends and much wasted effort in the practical realm.

Chapter Four

Macrocosm and Microcosm

In a way, the idea of practical application of many of the things we've mentioned begs a question. To apply polarity, or any aspect of the Tree of Life, to the workings of the human mind is to imply that this map of the universe is also a map of the human individual. This kind of multiple use of metaphor-maps is in many ways alien to our present culture's way of thinking; we don't commonly use chemistry as a key to psychology, for example.

And yet precisely this habit of thought is central to the philosophy of traditional Western magic. There is even a formal name for the concept: the Principle of Macrocosm and Microcosm. The macrocosm (literally, "big universe") is the cosmos around us, the microcosm ("little universe") is the individual human being; the principle uniting them is that any pattern which exists in one of these also exists in the other. The Tree of Life, for example, is a symbolic map of the universe; it is also a diagram of the human soul. In the same way, the human body is not merely the form of one rather unusual kind of animal on an out-of-the-way planet (though it is this, certainly); it is also an image of the universe as a whole.

This principle needs to be considered with some care, as it's easy enough to take it too far or in the wrong way. The mirroring of patterns between the universe and the human individual isn't absolute, especially on a material level. (Does the universe have feet?) On the other hand, the parallel between macrocosm and microcosm isn't simply a poetic simile. In certain contexts and in certain ways, the equivalence is exact.

One way to understand this is to return to some of the ideas covered back in Chapter One, and to look at how it is that human beings perceive anything at all. The chain of events which connect a cup of coffee with the image of that cup in your mind is, as we saw, long enough and complicated enough that the reality of the cup itself becomes a matter for philosophers to bicker over. Most of that chain of events, though, is defined either by the human senses and nervous system, or by the parts of the universe which those senses and that nervous system evolved to handle. Your image of the cup, therefore, is largely determined by the fact that it's being seen by a human being in a human environment. You perceive the cup - and everything else in the universe - in a human way, and the universe you perceive is thus a human universe, shaped in every detail by the reflected image of your own humanness.

Some philosophers have reacted to thoughts of this sort by rejecting everything we can perceive as "illusion." This kind of thinking misses the point. Once again, the universe of symbols in which we live is the only one is which we can live; it is our natural environment, our home. The transformations of the magical path reshape the magician's relationship to this realm of symbols, but they do not and cannot leave the symbolic behind. Even the highest levels of mystical experience are perceived by the mystic in a symbolic way.

Adam Cadmon

One of the ways in which the principle of macrocosm and microcosm is reflected in Cabalistic thought and symbolism may seem particularly strange from a modern viewpoint. This is the concept of Adam Cadmon. The word "Adam" (in Hebrew, ADM) means simply "human being," a point which might have saved a good many Western religious thinkers from the problems of too much literalism; "Cadmon", Hebrew QDMVN, means "primordial" or "archetypal." Adam Cadmon, the archetypal human being, is the universe envisioned in the form of humanity, the image of the individual human being projected onto the cosmos.

This symbolism has led to some strange speculations and some even stranger imagery. For our purposes, it's enough to note three things:

First, the diagram of the Tree of Life has often been seen as an abstract image of Adam Cadmon, and therefore of each individual human being as well. The implication of this idea is that every level of awareness and experience which exists in the universe exists in the individual as well - and vice versa.

Second, the diagram of the Tree of Life has also been seen as an image of each of the different levels or, to use the more common term, bodies, of Adam Cadmon, and therefore of each individual human being. Each of the ten Spheres is reflected in each level of human experience. From this, as the later parts of this chapter will show, come a series of practical formulae of magical working.

Third, Adam Cadmon is assigned to the World of Atziluth among the four Worlds. This needs to be understood with some care; the Primordial Human, like anything we can experience or talk about, is not of Atziluth itself. Rather, it serves as one of the most important symbols of the first World, the World of ultimate Reality. The lesson it has to teach is both humbling and of great practical importance: the closest we can come to that Reality, the best symbol we can use for it, is an image which is, ultimately, our own reflection.

Fifty Gates Of Understanding

The image of Adam Cadmon, though, is not the only way the magical Cabala speaks about the macrocosm. Another way, once very important in Cabalistic work, is a system known as the Fifty Gates of Understanding. This name was chosen to make a deliberate contrast with the Thirty-two Paths of Wisdom - in other words, the Tree of Life - and in this way to make a specific point: the Tree of Life, which corresponds to Wisdom or Chokmah, symbolizes the universe in terms of Force; the Fifty Gates, on the other hand, corresponding to Understanding or Binah, symbolize the universe in terms of Form.

These Gates are one development of a way of thinking about the universe which was once almost universal in the Western world, but which was discarded several centuries ago during the rise of materialist science. This way of thinking saw the universe as a ladder or chain - in modern terms, a spectrum might be the closest image - in which matter was at one end and God, however defined, at the other. In place of the rigid barrier between matter and spirit, natural and supernatural, which has been a feature of many modern philosophies and theologies, this approach envisioned the universe of our experience as a continuum uniting these two poles.

This concept obviously has much in common with the ideas central to the Cabala. The "Great Chain of Being," as it's been called, is an important part of the worldview which underlies all of the Western esoteric traditions, the magical Cabala among them. In Cabalistic circles, this idea was studied in detail, and the spectrum between pure matter and pure spirit came to be described symbolically as a series of fifty steps or stages called Gates.

The Golden Dawn made little use of the Fifty Gates, although W. Wynn Westcott, one of the Order's founders, included them in his translation of the Sepher Yetzirah. Still, the Gates and their symbolism can be a valuable tool to the Cabalistic magician. The Gates can be listed as follows:

1. Primordial matter, chaos.
2. Matter in manifestation: formless, empty and inanimate.
3. Natural forces of attraction and repulsion: the Abyss.
4. Separation and first rudiments of the four Elements.
5. Elemental Earth, from which all seed is as yet absent.
6. Elemental Water, acting upon the world.
7. Elemental Air, issuing from the abyss of waters.
8. Elemental Fire, warming and giving life.
9. Elements interacting through their Qualities (heat, cold, dryness, wetness).
10. Their attraction toward a mixture of all.
11. Emergence of metals through the division of Earth.
12. "Flowers" and "Saps" ordered for the generation of metals.
13. Seas, lakes, secret flowers among the cavities of the Earth.
14. Evolution of grasses, trees, and all plant life.
15. Processes of growth and reproduction in the plant kingdom.
16. Evolution of animal life in its simplest forms.

17. Evolution of insects, worms, and other invertebrates.
18. Evolution of fish.
19. Evolution of birds.
20. Evolution of mammals.
21. Emergence of humanity.
22. Human anatomy and physiology.
23. Human subtle anatomy, etheric structure, soul.
24. Human sexuality and reproduction.
25. The human being as a microcosm of the universe.
26. Five external powers: hearing, touch, sight, taste, smell.
27. Five internal powers: memory, will, imagination, emotion, intellect.
28. The human being as spirit.
29. The human being as angel.
30. The human being as image and likeness of God.
31. Sphere and spirits of the Moon.
32. Sphere and spirits of Mercury.
33. Sphere and spirits of Venus.
34. Sphere and spirits of the Sun.
35. Sphere and spirits of Mars.
36. Sphere and spirits of Jupiter.
37. Sphere and spirits of Saturn.
38. Sphere and spirits of the Zodiac and the fixed stars.
39. Sphere and spirits of the Primum Mobile.
40. Ishim, humanity as an angelic order.
41. Kerubim, angels of Yesod.
42. Beni Elohim, angels of Hod.
43. Tarshishim, angels of Netzach.
44. Malakim, angels of Tiphareth.
45. Seraphim, angels of Geburah.
46. Chashmalim, angels of Chesed.
47. Aralim, angels of Binah.
48. Auphanim, angels of Chokmah.
49. Chaioth ha-Qodesh, angels of Kether.
50. Ain Soph, the Limitless Divine.

The Cabalistic Cosmos

This long and somewhat arcane list may seem a little baffling at first glance. There is a structure underlying the Gates, though, and that structure is one we've already examined. The Fifty Gates divide up into five sets of ten Gates each, and each set represents the pattern of the ten Spheres, in reverse order, in one of five realms of existence. Gates 1-10 mirror the Spheres in the realm of elemental matter; Gates 11-20, in the mineral, vegetable, and animal kingdoms of Nature; Gates 21-30, in the realm of humanity; Gates 31-40, in the magical realm of spirits and planetary powers; Gates 41-50, in the realms of the angelic and the divine.

Each of these realms is discussed, to one degree or another, in the traditional lore of the magical Cabala, and each of them is the focus of certain kinds of practical magic. Although the central realm, that of humanity, is central as well to the work of the magical Cabalist, all five have powers and mysteries which are well worth exploring.

The realm of elemental matter and that of the angels share certain qualities in magical work. The four elements, in traditional cosmology, are basic states of matter, rather than "elements" in the modern sense of the word; they can be thought of as solid, liquid, gaseous and radiant matter, and as the patterns or reflections of these states on other levels of experience. The angels, on the other hand, are basic powers of spirit, manifestations of unity which hold the universe in existence and balance, and also as the patterns or reflections of these powers on other levels. Both represent the underlying structure of the universe, one from a material standpoint, the other from a spiritual; one, or more often both, are generally invoked at the beginning and end of a magical ritual to ground the ceremony in that structure.

The realms of Nature and of the spiritual powers offer a wider range of possibilities to the magician. The largely urban setting of the magical Cabala over the last several centuries has caused too much of the old magic of Nature to be lost to the tradition, but important lore still survives. The various classes of animal, plant, and mineral, according to tradition, each reflect some pattern of relationships between spiritual powers, and each can therefore be represented by letters of the Hebrew alphabet - letters which can be used to form a magical name or Word of Power. Each kind of animal bears an elemental, a planetary and a Zodiacal letter; each kind of plant bears a planetary and a Zodiacal letter; each kind of mineral bears a single letter - Zodiacal for ordinary minerals, planetary for metals, elemental for gemstones.

Certain plants also correspond to the energies of certain of the fixed stars, and all things in Nature have subtle relationships with the elements, whether or not these influence the magical name. Through magical and meditative work with these patterns of symbolism, it's possible to enter into communication with anything in this realm; to the Cabalistic magician, animals, plants and minerals alike possess life and consciousness, and have gifts to offer and lessons to teach.

The same is true of those entities we may as well call by the traditional name of "spirits." It's an oddity of modern culture that many people who are perfectly comfortable with the idea of a spiritual or "supernatural" realm of being become quite the opposite when it's suggested that such a realm might be inhabited. Be that as it may, most Western magical traditions accept and use the concept of spirits, intelligent beings who do not possess physical bodies. Often, as in the Fifty Gates, these beings are classified by way of the traditional system of planetary spheres, but this is more a shorthand than anything else; the range of spirits described in magical writings staggers the imagination.

There are two common and complementary mistakes which have been made over and over again concerning spirits by people in the Western world. The first of these is the orthodox Christian habit of assuming that all spirits are malevolent, dishonest and evil; the second is the corresponding habit, common in many New Age circles nowadays, of assuming that all spirits are loving, wise and good. Both of these attitudes are as foolish when applied to spirits as they would be if applied to human beings. There are helpful spirits and harmful ones, just as there are helpful and harmful people. It needs to be remembered, though, that spirits of every kind are alien to us; they think in different ways and act for different reasons than human beings do, and their actions cannot always be predicted. For this reason, those magicians who deal with spirits - and not all do, or should - typically (and wisely) use traditional methods of banishing and protection for the sake of safety.

Of the five realms of being traced out by the Fifty Gates, though, the third realm - that of humanity - is by far the most important. Partly this is because it is the realm closest to the human magician, and thus the strongest influence on his or her life; partly it is because this realm is home ground for human consciousness, and thus the easiest to enter and master. Partly, though, it rises from the special role of the human realm at the center of the system of Gates. The realms and beings of the spiritual and angelic levels do not reach down all the way into matter; those of elemental matter and the natural world do not reach all the way up into spirit. The human realm, and each individual human being, on the other hand, reach both ways to the ends of the chain of being. From the elemental matter of the physical body to the highest aspect of the spiritual self, the totality of the human being is a complete reflection of the Fifty Gates and of the universe as a whole.

Structures Of The Self

The magical Cabala has a special classification and a special set of Hebrew terms for the levels of being as they are reflected in the human individual. We'll be using these terms here, as English lacks good equivalents.

Diagram 11 shows the levels of the human organism as reflected in the Tree of Life. Since our culture's materialistic biases have made all but the lowest level of this structure foreign territory for many people, we'll explore the diagram from the bottom up.

At the bottom, corresponding to Malkuth, is the guph, the material body. This is the shape of physical matter of which most people think when the word "body" is mentioned. In the magical Cabala, however, the guph is held to be the least important of the various human bodies - little more than a shell of matter which allows the higher-level bodies to exist and to operate on the level of Malkuth.

Just above the guph, in the place corresponding to Yesod, is the nephesh, or as it's sometimes called, the etheric body. The ether, a term borrowed from nineteenth-century physics, is the substance of the

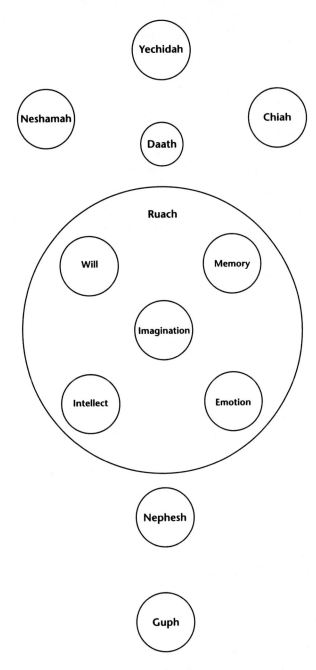

Diagram 11 - Levels of the Human Organism

Yesod level of experience; it structures and organizes the dense matter of the Malkuth level. The nephesh can be divided into two parts, one an egg-shaped shell of energies that extends up to several feet out from the guph, the other a denser sheath which mirrors the guph exactly; the first of these is called the aura or, in another context, the Sphere of Sensation, while the other is the etheric double. In its role as organizer of the physical body, the nephesh sets up currents of etheric substance - the meridians of Oriental medicine - which follow particular patterns of flow across the physical body's surface. The nephesh has a limited but real awareness and intelligence; it governs the realm of instinct, and the aspects of humanity which it has inherited from its animal ancestors. To some extent, it can be identified with the "subconscious mind" of current psychological theory.

Above this, corresponding to the Spheres from Hod up to Chesed, is the ruach, the conscious self. Just as this part of the Tree is made up of five Spheres, this aspect of the self consists of five faculties: intellect, emotion, imagination, will, and memory. The first two of these, corresponding to Hod and Netzach, are the ordinary thinking and feeling processes of the human mind. The other three, corresponding respectively to Tiphareth, Geburah and Chesed, are a little more complex.

This complexity enters the picture because the ruach reflects not only the Spheres but the Veil, the lower of the two great barriers of the Tree. In human terms, the Veil takes the form of a clouding of the ruach which blocks the full function of its three higher faculties. Thus, while mind and heart, the thinking and feeling processes, are more or less functional in most people, true imagination, will, and memory are not. We experience these things only in reflected form, often distorted, often weakened, rarely at even a fraction of their true potential.

At the same time, most of us have had experiences in which one or another of these faculties have shown an unexpected power. Many people have come across some memento of a previous time - a childhood toy, a letter from an old relationship - and found themselves recalling not merely the scattered images and facts of ordinary memory but a whole realm of remembrances, full of the indefinable flavor of one part of the past. Many people have made some willed decision, some choice, and found themselves swept along by a tide of unexpectedly favorable circumstances and of energy which has not seemed to come from within. Many people, too, have had moments of creative insight in which a mass of unconnected facts have suddenly clicked together into a pattern full of meaning.

All these common experiences are glimpses of the potential power of the higher faculties of the ruach. It would be easy to point, as well, to the role of these same faculties in the lives of men and women of genius, except that our society's cult of the exceptional has made most people unwilling to believe that they might be capable of the same levels of function. Nonetheless, this capability exists in everyone, and the disciplines of the magical Cabala are intended, in part, to begin the process of awakening it.

Above the ruach comes the human equivalent of the second of the Tree's great barriers. The nature of the Abyss, as it's expressed in human terms, follows closely on its nature on a broader scale; this is the point at which the personal gives way to the transpersonal, at which the self merges into unity. It is also the dividing line between the parts of the self which die with the physical body and those parts which do not. On this line, corresponding to Daath, is awareness itself, which may be turned downwards into the ruach or upwards into the eternal aspect of the self.

Like the Supernal Triad, which it mirrors, this highest aspect is made up of three parts. The lowest of the three is called the neshamah, and it corresponds to Binah on the Tree of Life. The neshamah is the root of the powers of perception and awareness in the human microcosm; receptive in its function, the neshamah is sometimes called the spiritual understanding. As the most accessible sphere of the Supernal Triad of the self, the neshamah represents all of these higher aspects of the self as they affect the lower, and the term neshamah is sometimes used to refer to the three highest levels when they are being treated as a unit.

Above the neshamah, although in another sense parallel to it, is the chiah or spiritual will, the highest active element, and the root of all the powers of action in the human microcosm. Finally, at the highest point of both the diagram and the human organism, is the yechidah, the spiritual essence of the self. In the theological language of the old texts, this part of the self is said to dwell constantly in the presence of God, and this is a fair image of its nature; it is the part of the self which most closely approaches the Reality beyond all appearances.

It is not, itself, that Reality. This needs to be stressed, because there's a point of view very common among today's alternative spiritualities which holds - to slip for a moment back into theological language - that this core of the self is in fact identical with, or a fragment of, God. This point of view can be highly appealing; in some ways, as a cultural phenomenon, it provides a useful counterbalance to the contempt for humanity that Western orthodoxies have so often displayed. Still, arrogance is as bad a habit as self-loathing, and as often as not the two come from similar sources.

The yechidah, then, is the Kether of the self; it is not the Ain Soph Aur, the Ain Soph, or the Ain; nor, above all, is it That which lies beyond all of these. It is the highest and most perfect level of the self, and the opening of contact between it and the conscious self is the highest of transformative experiences, but it still exists and operates at a symbolic level of being.

A Magical Anatomy

The classification given above is the most important application of the Tree of Life to the human microcosm, but it is far from the only one. As mentioned in the discussion of Adam Cadmon above, each aspect of the self from guph to yechidah also contains a complete Tree of Life, and several of these are important in the work of practical magic.

The Tree in the physical body, in particular, needs to be understood clearly, because it is the basis of a magical practice known as the Middle Pillar exercise, among the most effective basic practices in the toolkit of Cabalistic magic. This image of the Tree, fortunately, is a simple one; the Tree is simply mapped onto the standing human body, with Kether just above the head and Malkuth at the soles of the feet. The Pillar of Mercy is on the left side, that of Severity on the right; the effect is as though one were to turn around and back into a diagram of the Tree. The whole pattern is as illustrated in Diagram 12.

The physical body, obviously, does not contain Sphere-like organs at the points marked out by the Spheres. This does not mean, though, that the Spheres have no physical existence in the guph. The physical body, even on its own terms, is more than a lump of meat; it is also, in ways certain branches of medicine are beginning to rediscover, a structure of rhythms, of vibrational movements. Blood, lymph, cerebrospinal fluid, and other parts of the body pulse constantly in a complex rhythmic pattern, vibrating through the body as through the string of a guitar. The same mathematics which define where notes can be played on a stringed instrument also define harmonic points along any other vibrating object, and the human body is no exception to this rule.

The simplest and, at the same time, the most important of these mathematics of vibration is called the octave relationship. Pluck a guitar string, then press it down at its midpoint - dividing it in half - and pluck it again; the second note will sound like a higher equivalent of the first. In technical language, the second is called the octave of the first; two notes in an octave relationship have the same letter-name (for example, C) and harmonize perfectly with each other. If another point halfway between the middle and one end is pressed, and the short section of string plucked again, the result will be the same note again at a still higher octave. This process can be continued, dividing the string length in half over and over again and producing higher and higher octaves, until the intervals become too close together to measure.

The same process can be done, in a different way, with the vibratory system we call the human body. Imagine the body from head to foot as a string. The first octave point, the first division in half, falls at the level of the genitals; the second, dividing the distance between the genitals and the crown in half, falls at the center of the chest; the third, taking half of this last difference, falls at the throat. These octave points are the centers of the Middle Pillar in the guph, and by means of techniques covered in a later chapter they can be used to balance the energies of the body on all levels. Of less importance in practical terms, but still involved in the vibrational structure of the body, are the

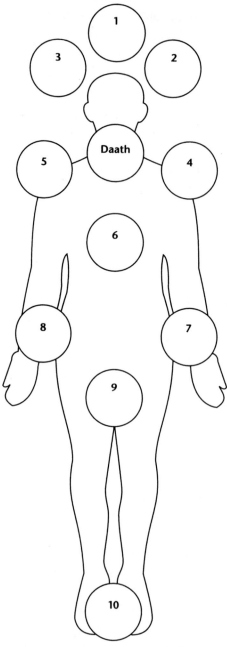

Diagram 12 - The Tree in the Physical Body

points where vibrations enter the "resonating chambers" of the legs, the arms, and the fluid-filled spaces in the brain; these form the Spheres of the two side Pillars in the guph.

The centers of the Middle Pillar are sometimes confused with the seven spinal centers or chakras of Hindu tradition, but these two sets of centers are not the same. The Middle Pillar centers are along the midline of the body, not along the spine, and they have little relationship with specific physical organs; the chakras, by contrast, are on the spine, and linked to endocrine glands and nerve plexi. The chakras have a role in some systems of magical Cabalism, but should not be confused with the centers discussed here. They are a different part of human subtle anatomy, and are developed in different ways.

The Sphere Of Sensation

The Tree of Life is also applied to the nephesh or etheric body in a particular way; here again, there are issues of magical practice which derive from this symbolism, although these are usually taken up at a more advanced level of training than the Middle Pillar exercise. The role of the Tree in the nephesh involves what has already been referred to as the Sphere of Sensation, and this Sphere needs to be understood if this part of the symbolism is to be followed.

What is the Sphere of Sensation? In simplest terms, as mentioned earlier, it is the aura, the egg-shaped outer layer of the nephesh which extends out several feet from the physical body. It is not, however, a simple featureless shape. Some texts refer to it as the Magical Mirror of the Universe, and this term is meant to be taken quite literally; the entire universe, in all its complexity, is reflected on its surface.

The Buddhist Garland Sutra makes use of an old Indian legend to express a similar insight. The god Indra, it was said, had a net infinitely large, in which each crossing of threads bore a brightly polished pearl. Each pearl reflected all the others, so that the whole net could be seen by looking at any one part. In this metaphor, the pearls are individual beings, the net the dance of becoming in which all beings are snared.

The Sphere of Sensation, then, can be imagined as one pearl of this Net, or - to turn to a more modern metaphor - as one piece of a hologram, in which the whole of the original image is contained. In practical terms, the Sphere of Sensation serves as the interface between consciousness and a certain class of images and perceptions, which are sometimes collectively labeled the "astral plane."

This term has caused a great deal of confusion, and has been used to cover a wild assortment of levels and phases of being. In the magical Cabala, the word "astral" usually refers to the range of perceptions which come through what is usually called the imagination: mental imagery, pictures in the mind's eye. While modern attitudes normally dismiss such things as wholly subjective, a product of wasted thoughts, Cabalistic teaching denies this outright. Some mental imagery does indeed come from within the mind, but some does not - and all of it, without exception, is reflected onto the Sphere of Sensation and, from there, out into the universe as a whole.

Mental imagery is thus both a way of perception and a means of action. As a way of perception, it allows the magician to perceive patterns moving through other minds, as well as the shapes of events not yet come to manifestation on the Malkuth level; as a means of action, it enables the magician to shape consciousness - his or her own, and others' - through images chosen and energized by the will. It is the principal tool of all visionary work, all divination, and most magic.

The Sphere of Sensation, as the instrument through which mental imagery works, has been studied with a great deal of thoroughness in Western magical circles. The symbolic structures of magic can be mapped onto it, and these maps used as ways of energizing specific patterns of imagery; thus, for example, there are charts in which the constellations are mapped onto the Sphere of Sensation as a basis for astrological magic.

These are advanced levels of work, however. More important for the present is another mapping, which traces out the Tree of Life in the Sphere of Sensation. In this system, the two side Pillars of the Tree are doubled, and curve around the outside of the Sphere; thus each person has two Binah centers in the Sphere, two Netzach centers, and so on. The Middle Pillar, though, is not doubled; it runs down the centerline of the body, and its centers in the etheric body are located at the same place as the corresponding centers in the physical body. This gives additional importance to the Middle Pillar exercise, which works with these centers on these and other levels.

The Microcosm And The Transformative Work

The Tree can also be traced out in each of the faculties of the ruach, in the neshamah, in the chiah and in the yechidah. So far, though, little has been done with these applications in the magical Cabala, and what exists is very nearly all theory, without connections in the realm of practice. There is, however, one more way to associate the Tree with the human microcosm - a way which focuses on the transformative process of spiritual development which the alchemists of old called the Great Work.

This attribution is shown in Diagram 13. Some elements of it, notably the lowest, derive from parts of Cabalistic theory that will be covered in the next chapter, and its full application will have to wait until the work of transformation itself is covered a little further on; still, the outline should be clear enough.

At the bottom is the Negative Persona. This can be seen as the sum total of the distortions and imbalances of the self. The word "persona" means "mask" in Latin; the Negative Persona functions very like a mask, hiding the actual shape of the self from all eyes - one's own included. For reasons which will be covered later, it is assigned to Malkuth.

Above this, but thoroughly entangled with it, is the Lower Self. This is the level of the self which is perceived by ordinary consciousness, made up of the lower part of the ruach, the nephesh, and the image of the guph held by the ruach - although not usually the guph itself. The word "personality" in its modern use matches the magical concept of the Lower Self quite closely. On the Tree of Life, it is assigned to the Spheres between Malkuth and the Veil.

Next on the diagram is the Higher Self. This is the level of the self which could be perceived by ordinary consciousness, but normally is not; it consists of all those potentials which lie beyond the Veil, unavailable until the Veil is parted. The glimpses of these potentials which do come through to the Lower Self often play a guiding and directing

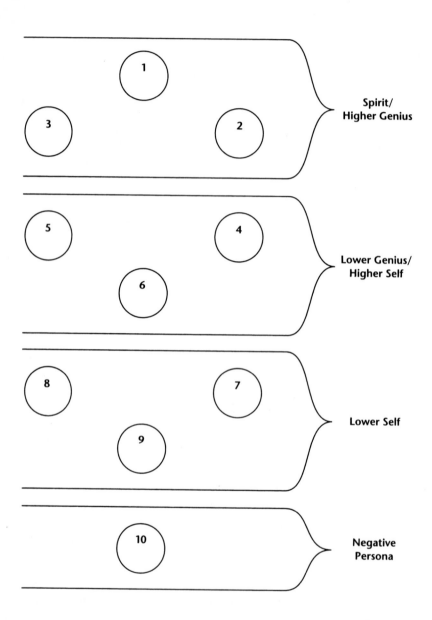

Diagram 13 - Levels of the Self Associated with the Tree

role. Because of this, the term genius, which meant a guardian spirit before it was watered down to mean an unusual talent, has been applied to this and the next level up. In this terminology, then - or the version of the terminology we'll be using; there are other uses for the same terms, a fact which does much to confuse an already difficult subject - this part of the self is also called the Lower Genius.

At the highest level of the self, finally, is the Spirit or Higher Genius, the part of the self beyond the Abyss, outside the range of ordinary consciousness altogether. This portion of the human microcosm, in an important sense, cannot be called part of the "self" at all; it exists in the realms of unity, beyond the levels where self and other are separate; it creates what we normally think of as the self, and the patterns of that self return into it at the end of physical life.

Some magical traditions, seeking to stress the difference between this overshadowing power and the ordinary personality, have risked one kind of confusion by referring to the Spirit as the "Holy Guardian Angel"; other traditions, with a higher degree of sophistication in the Cabala, have risked another kind of confusion by giving it the Name ADNI, Adonai, a Hebrew Name of God which means "Lord." Both these terms remain in present use despite their disadvantages, because both put a useful focus on the essential "otherness" of the Higher Genius. Both stress that this aspect of the human microcosm is not simply another way of talking about the Lower Self, or for that matter the Lower Self plus the Negative Persona.

This last point may seem elementary. It is not. The attitude which psychologists call inflation and the traditional lore of Cabalistic magic, borrowing a term from religion, calls spiritual pride is one of the most serious dangers of this work. Those who enter the path of magic with too great an appetite for flattery or too strong a need for ego reinforcement will very likely find these things, but they are also rather too likely to find fanaticism, megalomania and mental breakdown along the same route. The thing has happened far too often in the history of magic in the West.

ChapterFive

The Way of Creation

The material we've covered so far - on the nature of symbolism, the structure of the Tree of Life, the metaphors of energy and polarity which allow the Tree to be used in practice, the reflections of the Tree in macrocosm and microcosm - have all been by way of a first look at the philosophy of the magical Cabala, the governing system of ideas which underlies the system and gives it its shape and potentials.

In traditional Jewish Cabalistic texts, though, such things take up only a small amount of space. Detailed analysis of Scriptural verses, part of the quest to "decode" the Bible, takes up much more. A large part, though, goes to what can only be called the creation of a Cabalistic mythology: a vast account of the birth, history, and end of the entire universe, reaching over huge cycles of time and immensities of space, in which the myths of the Bible are used as springboards for astonishing speculations and the lives and history of human beings are part of a much greater drama of love, war, loss, and redemption among spiritual powers. While much of this drama was left behind by the magicians who adapted the Cabala to their own uses in the Renaissance and later, a significant part of the mythology of the Cabala was preserved, and plays a large role in the teachings of the Golden Dawn tradition.

This baroque scheme may seem pointless or worse to modern eyes, but four centuries of obsessive concentration on material experience has made our culture all but blind to what was once a common way of passing on information. The mythic structure of Cabalistic tradition, like any mythology, is a language of symbols which passes on knowledge in dramatic, easily remembered form. The myths of a culture express that culture's values and its image of the universe; those of a religion, the core concepts and elements of that religion's particular path to inner transformation.

So, too, the myths of the Cabala have a message to pass on. That message, and the myths which embody it, can be divided into two parts: one which deals with the present nature of the world and of humanity by tracing out the joined history of both; another which expresses the potential in humanity and the world by prophesying the joined future of both. In theological terms, we can call these the way of Creation and the way of Redemption.

At the same time, this structure is a myth, and its account of the past should not be taken for history in the naive sense - that is, as an account of events that "really happened." (For that matter, much of what passes for history in all ages, our own included, is made up of slightly disguised myth.) The traditional Cabalistic account of the origin of things provides a powerful set of metaphors for understanding the universe and the place and nature of human beings within it, but those metaphors will not necessarily jibe with the equally metaphoric theories of current scientific thought. Similarly, the structure of prophecy which dominates the magical Cabala's idea of the redemptive process should not be thought of as a blueprint for "the future." There is, after all, a different future for every person who lives into it, just as there is a different past for every person who remembers.

The Dawn Of Creation

Some idea of the divergence between Cabalistic tradition and the orthodox mythology of the Biblical faiths can be gathered from the Cabala's account of the beginning of the universe. This account emerged from the version given in Genesis through a series of stages, some of which can still be traced in the old texts; the methods of scriptural decoding mentioned in Chapter Two were used by many generations of scholars and mystics to fill out the bare bones of the Genesis account in a variety of directions, some of them bizarre to modern eyes. A portion of this material was later put to use in Western magical circles, and developed into a more or less coherent account; it is one version of this which we'll be discussing here.

In the magical Cabala's view, then, the origin of the universe came about in a process of three stages. The first of them can be called the phase of Withdrawal. Symbolically - and here we're standing at the uttermost limits of metaphor - the presence of God was said to fill all possible realms of Being so completely that there was no room for anything else to exist. Before the universe could be created, then, a space had to be cleared for it by the withdrawal of the divine presence. This act of withdrawal can be seen as the creation of nothingness, and thus relates to Ain, the first of the three Veils.

The second phase of Creation can be called the phase of the Primal Worlds. The old texts speak of this part of the process in veiled and often wildly contradictory terms, but the common thread running through these accounts is the idea that the dawning stages of creation saw the birth of a system of worlds or Spheres that came before the universe that now exists. Hurled forth, as the Golden Dawn's Philosophus Ritual phrases it, like sparks from a blacksmith's hammer, these original realms of being were each pure expressions of one part of the potential of the universe to be - unrelated, unpolarized, and therefore unbalanced, the world "without form and void" of Genesis. Another metaphor likens them to a swirling chaos rushing outward to the limits of the space formed by Withdrawal. Because of their imbalance, they could not endure, and with the coming of the next phase they disintegrated. The phase of the Primal Worlds established the range of possibilities open to the universe, and so corresponds to Ain Soph, the second Veil.

The third phase of the work of Creation can be called the phase of Descending Light. In this phase the presence of God which was withdrawn in the first phase was restored, but in a different manner: the manner of the Lightning Flash. In place of the undifferentiated sea of Being that, in this metaphor, predated Withdrawal, the Divine Reality entered into the universe in the form of ten creative powers, the ten Spheres of the Tree of Life. Around these ten powers, born from their energies, the whole spectrum of the universe from spirit to matter surged into being. The Seven Days of Creation described in Genesis can be interpreted here as the descent of the light through the seven lower Spheres of the Tree, the realms of manifestation below the Abyss. Because of the role of light in this phase, it relates to Ain Soph Aur, the last of the Three Veils.

The Negative Powers

In the phase of the Descending Light, the Primal Worlds are said to have been destroyed. They were not, however, without significance. In one of their aspects, they represented the potential for the Spheres of the Tree of Life to exist: containers, in a metaphorical sense, waiting to be filled by the descent of the Lightning Flash. In another aspect, they were the Spheres themselves in their original unbalanced form, waiting to be brought into harmony by the influx of energies from above.

A different aspect, though, has a more important role in many branches of Cabalistic thought and practice. As realms of imbalance, the Primal Worlds have a demonic role as forces in opposition to the creative light of Unity. Here the descent of the light takes the symbolic form of the Sword, shattering the realms of "Chaos and old Night"- shattering but not eliminating.

For the fragments of the Primal Worlds continue to exist in our present universe. Still wildly unbalanced, still in opposition to Unity, they are the Negative Powers, the demons of the Cabala and the sources of evil in the universe. As microcosm reflects macrocosm, they are mirrored in the human soul as the powers of ignorance and cruelty, selfishness and violence, and every other form of human evil.

The symbolism of the Negative Powers comes from the same sources as the elaborate demonologies of the orthodox faiths of the West. It would be a mistake to see them as identical to the devils of orthodoxy, though. They are not fallen angels, damned for eternity for rebelling against God. Rather, they are a necessary part of the process of creation; their role and their work is a part of what, in religious terms, could be called the will of God; nor are they flung into some sort of eternal Inquisitor's chamber for doing what amounts to their job. They are as much a part of the way of Redemption as they are of the way of Creation, and play a critical role throughout the mythic structure of the Cabala.

The Garden Of Eden

At the close of the three primal phases of Creation, the universe existed on all ten levels of awareness in a state of perfect harmony. This state corresponds to Adam Cadmon in his completeness; it is also described in the Cabala as Eden, continuing the use of scriptural metaphors. This Eden, however, has little in common with the one imagined by orthodox Christain and Jewish thought.

The principle of macrocosm and microcosm, discussed in the last chapter, is critical to understanding the meaning of Eden from a Cabalistic standpoint; what is true of Adam Cadmon is true, in another sense, of each human being. The myths that follow, then, can be read on at least two levels: first as a metaphor for the birth, transformation, and destiny of the universe; second as a metaphor for the origin, fall, and redemption of every one of us.

Diagram 14 shows the altar diagram of the Garden of Eden as shown in the Practicus Ritual of the Golden Dawn. This image is a specialized version of the Tree of Life, with a series of additional symbols added to it - some from Genesis, others from the Book of Revelations (another favorite source of metaphors on the part of magicians and mystics in the West).

The figure at the top of the diagram, crowned with stars, clothed with the Sun, and standing upon the Moon, is called AIMA ALHIM, Aima Elohim, the Supernal Mother. She is a synthesis of the three Spheres of the Supernal Triad, reflected through the symbolically feminine Sphere Binah, and thus stands for the highest spiritual powers present in the universe. At the same time, each part of this diagram also has its meaning in terms of the human microcosm; in this sense, the "woman clothed with the Sun" is the reflection of the Supernal Triad in the human soul, the immortal, transcendent part of the self, the neshamah.

From Aima Elohim, a current of creative energy descends to the center of the diagram, where it divides, forming a cross. Symbolically,

Diagram 14 - The Diagram of the Garden of Eden

this current was described as the river which, in Genesis, was said to flow out of Eden and divide into four streams, symbolizing the power of the Tetragrammaton. These streams are also shown in the diagram: the first, which is named Pison and attributed to Yod and Fire, flows from the point of division out to Geburah; the second, named Gihon, is assigned to Heh and Water and flows out to Chesed; the third, named Hiddekel, is linked to Vau and Air and flows down to Tiphareth; the fourth, which is named Phrath or Euphrates, is associated with final Heh and Earth and completes the descent from Tiphareth to the base of the diagram in Malkuth.

The point of division of these currents of energy is at Daath, the quasi-Sphere in the Abyss. Here as in the diagram of the Tree, Daath serves as both bridge and barrier; the part of the diagram above it is traditionally named the Higher or Supernal Eden, that below it the Lower Eden, and Daath stands as the gate between them.

Below Daath on the diagram, with his head at Tiphareth and his feet at Yesod, stands a second human image, crowned but otherwise naked. This represents Adam. Literal interpretations of Adam as the first man miss the point; as mentioned earlier, the word "Adam" in Hebrew simply means "human being." Adam is humanity in the abstract: in one sense, Everyman; in another sense, the sum total of human beings and of human potential, past, present and to come, as well as the image of humanity reflected in the universe as a whole. He wears a crown to symbolize contact with the descending energies of Kether, and reaches out to Chesed and Geburah to symbolize his balance between the great polarities of the Tree. In microcosmic terms, this figure represents the ruach, the conscious self or personality, made up of the faculties of memory, will, imagination, emotion and intellect.

Below Adam, standing on Malkuth, is another crowned figure, the figure of Eve. Here again literal interpretations miss the point; the name "Eve" (in Hebrew, ChVH, Chavvah) comes from a word meaning "Life." Eve in the macrocosm can be seen as, precisely, the power and potential of biological life - in a sense, Mother Nature. In the microcosm she is the nephesh, the instinctive and animal side of the human soul, the part we share with other physically incarnate beings. Thus every living human being, male or female, is both Adam and Eve, spirit and animal combined, with the immortal presence of the neshamah or Spirit the third element of the polarity. It's important to note that in this diagram, the figure of Eve is also crowned, and her hands support the Pillars of Force and Form. She is thus linked with the Supernals, as Adam is, and her special role is that of maintaining the balance of the entire system.

At the bottom of the diagram, in the place corresponding to Malkuth, is another symbol drawn from the Book of Revelations. The dragon with seven heads and ten horns has been given many meanings down through the years, depending on various symbolic, religious, and political circumstances. Here, however, it also stands for the Serpent of the Eden myth, and represents the presence of the Negative Powers. The ten horns stand for the ten Spheres, the seven heads to the seven hells of their realm: Gehenna, the Kingdom of Shells.

In ancient Jerusalem the valley of Gehenna was the place where garbage from the city was taken to be burnt. Borrowed as a image for the Hell of orthodoxy, it nonetheless makes a useable metaphor for the mode of existence of the remnants of the Primal Worlds in the current universe. Shattered and cast out by the descent of the Sword, the unbalanced energies that made up the Primal Worlds are said to have been driven to the outermost parts of Malkuth, at once the densest levels of matter and the furthest reaches of the process of Creation. There, as the diagram shows, they sleep: less metaphorically, they are present but inactive, potentials not yet made manifest.

From the tenth Sphere, above them, sprout the branches of the Tree of Knowledge of Good and Evil, continuing the Eden symbolism. This tree represents the possibilities of true self- awareness, for good or ill; it reaches up toward the higher Spheres of the Tree, but also down into Gehenna. It rises from Malkuth because the material realm, with all its contending forces, is the one level of existence in which human beings can truly come to know themselves and their powers.

Above, like a promise, the Spheres below Daath are shown bearing branches of their own, linking them symbolically with Eden's Tree of Life. This Tree, too, has a Serpent, though it is not shown in the diagram: the Serpent whose windings trace the Paths which lead from Malkuth to the Tree's summit in Kether.

The image as a whole can be read in a number of ways, in a microcosmic as well as a macrocosmic sense. Common to all of these interpretations is a sense of innocence, but also one of unfulfilled potential. Adam remains separate from the realm of matter, and the possibilities of self-awareness, knowledge and mastery represented by the Tree of Knowledge are still untouched. This stage is the time of infancy before objects have separated out from the "buzzing, blooming confusion" of experience; it is also the first stage of spiritual or magical practice, before the stirrings of that fear of change and growth magicians have symbolized as the Watcher of the Threshold. In a broader sense, it refers to the stages of our species' evolution before the birth of true self-awareness, when the instincts and natural drives represented by Eve held the pillars of the emerging self in balance: the long animal prehistory of Homo sapiens' precursors, at once the infancy of our species and the first stage of its own spiritual development.

In any of its readings, this figure is an image of beginnings, and in the broader sense those beginnings are already past. It is with the next diagram that the world we experience begins to take shape.

The Fall

The state symbolized by Eden is in perfect balance, but that balance is static; it cannot survive the coming of change. The nature of the change that overtakes it, and the results of that change, are shown in Diagram 15, the altar diagram of the Fall from the Philosophus Ritual.

Orthodox ideas of "original sin" and the like have made the notion of a Fall, a major turn for the worse in human history and human nature, highly suspect in many modern eyes. Still, this idea is not unique to the monotheistic religions of the West. The appalling behavior of human beings toward each other and toward the world in which they live has led people of many cultures and times to suspect that some central flaw lies behind the many manifestations of human destructiveness. Many Eastern traditions - Buddhism is a good example - have tended to see this flaw as beginningless, although curable; by contrast, the Westernworld has tended to see human evil as a temporary affliction with a definite beginning as well as an end. In the last analysis, the difference may simply be one of cultural style.

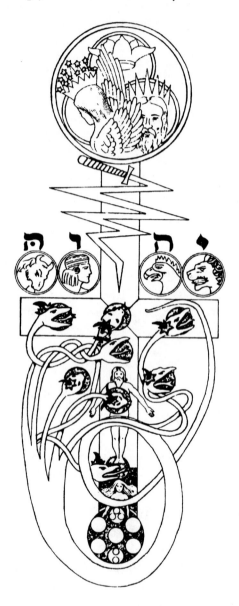

Diagram 15 - The Diagram of the Fall

The Cabalistic myth of the Fall derives, ultimately, from the same Biblical narrative that gave rise to the bleak stories of the orthodox faiths. Here again, though, the Cabala has its own approach and its own ways of interpretation. These can best be followed by going over the Diagram of the Fall, in this case from bottom to top.

At the foot of the diagram is the realm of Gehenna, refuse heap of the cosmos. In the diagram of Eden the red dragon representing the Negative Powers slept here, inert. Now, though, the Powers are awake, and sweep up in a great double arc to surround the Sphere Malkuth and attack the other Spheres below the Abyss. In their place, fallen into the Kingdom of Shells, is the Eve of the previous diagram.

The story in Genesis recounts how Eve tasted the fruit of the Tree of Knowledge of Good and Evil. This part of the tale was absorbed into the Cabalistic myth, but in a very different sense. The Tree of Knowledge here is precisely that, the knowledge of self-awareness that makes true choice possible. Eve, life, has here attained this self-awareness - but in the process the two Pillars she held in balance have been left unsupported. In the diagram, the Pillars are gone, the balance of the system shattered, and Eve herself has descended into the realm of pure imbalance.

With the descent of Eve, the figure of Adam has also fallen from his previous place; his feet now rest on Malkuth, and his head reaches only to the space between Netzach and Hod. Neither he nor Eve have kept their crowns, for the direct descent of energies from the Supernals has been cut off. The dragon, once seven-headed, has grown an eighth head to correspond to Daath, the point of division of the four rivers of Eden, and wears the crowns that mark its contact with the Higher; its venom desecrates the descending waters and transforms them from the rivers of Eden into those of Hell.

But the dragon of the Negative Powers, of radical imbalance and evil, cannot pass the Abyss into the levels of Unity. The gate of the Higher Eden is closed to it. In Genesis, the gate of Eden after the Fall is said to be guarded by "cherubim, and a flaming sword." The same is true here, but the Cabala gives these words a good deal more meaning. Cherubim - in modern magical parlance, the spelling "Kerubim" is more common - are not the fluffy infant angels of European art, but the angelic powers governing the four elements and representing the four letters of the Tetragrammaton; often, as in the diagram, they are symbolized by the images of a lion, an eagle, a human being, and an ox. The flaming Sword, in turn, images the Lightning Flash of creation and the original shattering of the Primal Worlds.

Above, at the top of the diagram, the unity of Aima Elohim has been broken as well. Her figure remains, but turned away, as though mourning. Beside her is the face of the Supernal Father, representing Chokmah, and over all hovers the Crown of Kether. Destruction below is mirrored by division above.

As with the last diagram, this set of mythic images can be read in a number of ways, macrocosmic and microcosmic. On a planetary scale, it represents the coming of age of our species, the awakening of self-awareness and of individual responsibility within one portion of the animal life of Earth. The forces of nature, manifested in instinct and in environmental pressure, no longer hold humanity in balance in the world; instead, the same biological drives which once maintained that balance goad humanity toward excess in every direction, and the forces released by these drives - forces which go far beyond the human, or the natural - contaminate every aspect of humanity's thought and action. One might even see in the fate of Eve, cast down into Gehenna, the fate of so much of the natural world at human hands, made into a realm of garbage and fires. For his part, Adam, humanity, with his feet now firmly on the ground of Malkuth but the crown of inner guidance vanished from his head, is left to find his way as best he can.

Equally, the diagram could be read in microcosmic terms, as a map of the human soul in its present condition. In this reading, the nephesh and its primal instincts, once the great source of balance in the self, now lead to imbalance; desires become addictions, fears become obsessions; responses evolved to protect against beasts of prey warp into habits of lethal violence, so that men and women have become beasts of prey themselves. These imbalances contaminate the whole of the ruach, the conscious self, and to make matters worse the ruach has fallen below Tiphareth and no longer has direct access to its own higher faculties; the Veil has drawn shut. Above, in place of the gentle inner guidance of the neshamah, looms a barrier, and beyond it the neshamah itself has turned away; what comes through the barrier, if anything does, is more often a command than an insight, a driving force from behind than an understanding of the goal ahead.

There are other readings. In any of them, the same sense of disaster and of loss dominates. Still, it would be a mistake to read in too much of the orthodox attitude to the Fall, to start passing blame or bemoaning the event. The Fall was not a crime or an accident. Rather, it was – is – a necessary stage in any process of awakening. Most children go through the equivalent several times in the course of their growth: the "terrible twos" with the awakening of self-awareness, adolescence with the onset of sexual energies. In the same way, most students of any spiritual tradition pass at least once through the state which mystics have called "dryness" and magicians the encounter with the Watcher on the Threshold, a state in which boredom, disgust and fear rise up to oppose the awakening of the inner life.

So, too, our species. For self-awareness to be gained, the balancing role of instinct had to be relinquished; for evolution to proceed, the static peace of Eden had to be left behind. Nor is the Diagram of the Fall without its own kind of promise. The Kerubim and the Flaming Sword upon the Abyss are more than simple barriers; they offer a way onward, for the Fall marks the end of the way of Creation and the beginning of the way of Redemption.

ChapterSix
The Way of Redemption

The mythic structure of the Cabala, as the last chapter mentioned, deals with the present and the future as well as the past. In dealing with these, in particular, it's important to stay clear of certain easy mistakes. One of these is the habit, already discussed, of taking the metaphors of myth as literal descriptions of what we usually call "fact" - to do as orthodox religions in the West have done, for example, and identify Adam, Eve and the serpent as historical figures in the same sense as George and Martha Washington. Another, equally common, is the habit of dismissing myth as meaningless because it is not a description of ordinary fact.

A subtler mistake, though, affects many attempts to make sense of mythic metaphors like those we're examining here. This is the failure to recognize that myth, symbolic though it is, has practical implications.

A Native American tale from the Puget Sound country describes how Moon, a mythic hero, was pursued by a forest fire. As he ran from the flames, he asked each thing he passed if it could shelter him. The various trees and plants of the forest could not, but finally he came to a trail. The trail answered, "Lie down in me, and I will shelter you." And so it happened; the fire and smoke passed over Moon and left him singed but alive.

It would be possible to interpret this tale in any number of symbolic senses, or to spend one's time debating whether Moon actually existed, when and where the forest fire took place, and so on. The Coast Salish people who told this story to their children, on the other hand, had at least one other point in mind. If one is caught in the woods by a fire, lying down in a deeply rutted trail does in fact offer a better chance of survival than most other possible responses - and the practical value of this fact remains whether the story used to communicate it has any historical "truth" or not.

The same point is true of the mythology of the magical Cabala. (Admittedly, these symbolic narratives of fall and restoration will not give you much help if you happen to be caught by a forest fire; different myths have different purposes.) The Cabala's tale of Primal Worlds and descending Light, of Eden and the Fall may or may not have any relationship to the kind of facts scientists and historians seek; their principal importance lies elsewhere. They are designed to help the Cabalist interpret and respond to the various stages, experiences and transformations that are encountered in the process of magical training.

This is above all true of the second stage of the magical Cabala's mythology, the stage we have called the way of Redemption. This part of the narrative weaves legend, prophecy, and practical advice into the same fabric, and it isn't always possible to untangle these different threads. An eye to the meaning of the myths in terms of the experience of practice is probably the best way to take hold of this sometimes confusing subject.

Emergence Of A New Myth

One further difficulty in talking about the way of Redemption in the magical Cabala is that this part of the tradition's mythic structure is currently passing through a phase of major transformations. Until this century, most accounts of the redemptive process in magical literature used the language and symbolism of Christianity to a degree few modern magicians would tolerate. To some extent, as well, this was not simply a matter of language; most of the magicians of the Western tradition, the adepts of the Golden Dawn among them, considered themselves Christians, although their "Christianity" admittedly would rarely have passed theological muster. In the source materials of the Judaic Cabala, similarly, the way of Redemption was interpreted in the light of Jewish belief in the Messiah, and in the special, chosen status of the Jewish people.

At the same time, a set of very different images has been evolving within the Western magical tradition itself. These images drew, like the tradition itself, on ancient Hermetic and Neoplatonic teachings, European folklore and folk magic, and more recently on ideas brought in from Oriental sources. From the early seventeenth century, when the first Rosicrucian writings began to catalyze the process, to the emergence of the first explicitly non-Christian magical orders in the first part of this century, these two mythic structures existed in a kind of uneasy symbiosis, borrowing from each other and blurring at the edges but destined, in the end, to split apart.

This split is by no means complete. Still, the two myths have drawn far enough apart that it is possible to separate them out, and to present a version of the magical Cabala's own mythic structure on its own terms, separate from the Christian backdrop of older accounts.

The chief difference between the older, half-Christian mythology and the newer structure can be defined fairly clearly. The older myth accepts the Christian idea that the life of Jesus of Nazareth was, in some sense, a turning point in the redemptive process, and gives Christianity a privileged place among the world's religions; the newer myth does neither. Instead of placing the burden of redemption on the shoulders of a messiah, the magical myth returns it to the individual, and places the individual not in the glaring light of an arbitrary divine judgement but in the broader context of a Path.

The Journey Of Seth

To begin exploring the way of Redemption in terms of this developing mythology, paradoxically enough, it may be useful to turn to an ancient Jewish legend. Adam and Eve, in the Genesis account, had three sons whose names are recorded; the first two, Cain and Abel, gained an unpleasant fame as the first murderer and his first victim. The third, however, was named Seth, and had a different destiny. The Bible says little about him, but legend tells that he journeyed back to the gate of Eden and spoke to the angels who guarded the gate. From them, according to one story, he received the secret teaching which was to become the Cabala.

This is one of a number of different legends of the Cabala's origin given in Jewish sources; others name Abraham, Moses, or Adam himself as the first Cabalist. For our purposes, though, the story of Seth is perhaps more useful, because it links up with the symbolism of the two diagrams discussed in the last chapter. Although it has apparently not been done - the nearest equivalent, the diagram on the lid of the Pastos in the Golden Dawn's Adeptus Minor Ritual, uses Christian imagery - it would be entirely possible to design a third diagram around the legend of Seth's journey to Eden; such a diagram would have a significant place in this discussion, because that journey symbolizes the whole process of the way of Redemption.

Turn back for a moment to the diagram of the Fall. Above the desecrated Lower Eden, guarding the way to the Higher, are the four Kerubim and the Sword. These are symbols of creative power, as we've seen, as well as images of the original breaking of the Primal Worlds. They are also, and critically, the central elements of Cabalistic teaching. In the ten Spheres marked by the fiery Sword and the four letters of the Tetragrammaton, the whole of the Cabala is symbolized, and the gate of Eden becomes a revelation as well as a barrier.

At the same time, the journey to that revelation involves a shift in level as dramatic as the one brought about by the Fall. From Malkuth, in the midst of the red dragon's coils, the route leads up the poisoned rivers of Earth and Air to Daath, at the furthest reach of the dragon's coils. Only here, where the descending river of energy from the Supernals still runs clear, is it possible to perceive the guardians of Eden's gate - but once this is done, and the power of the Flaming Sword and the Great Name experienced, that power can then be turned upon the dragon and the Negative Powers driven out from the Lower Eden.

Our imagined diagram, then, might show Seth risen to Daath, his hands extended to Chesed and Geburah to restore the balance of the Pillars, while the heads of the dragon fall back from the Spheres they have attacked. In fact, imagery very like this appears on the Pastos, although the Christian element in the symbolism makes Jesus the central figure and maps the whole pattern onto the crucifixion. Either way, the meaning is much the same.

There are, then, three stages to this journey of return. The first involves getting free of the entangling coils of the dragon; the second, rising up to Daath, and receiving the gifts of the guardians there; the third, using those gifts to cast down the dragon and cleanse the defiled Garden. These three stages summarize the entire work of the way of Redemption.

Two points need to be noted, though. The first is that the dragon is to be vanquished, not slain. The Negative Powers have a place in the scheme of things from beginning to end. In the macrocosm, they can be seen as the primary energies of existence, unmixed and therefore unbalanced, which must be harmonized rather than destroyed. In the microcosm, their reflections are powerful if chaotic forces moving through the self, destructive if uncontrolled but potential sources of enormous strength once brought into balance and discipline. In either interpretation, they are returned to their own realm, but there remain awake. Thus the previous state of Eden is not restored, nor is the Fall prolonged; instead, a third state having elements of both brings the entire system into a renewed harmony.

The second point, though, is more ominous. In the legend, it is not Adam, humanity, which accomplished the journey, but Seth the son of Adam - or, in an older but still evocative translation, the "Son of Man." Humanity, in its ordinary state, remains barred from Eden's gate. This can be interpreted in a macrocosmic sense: that humanity must pass through further ages of evolution before it can accomplish the work of redemption. It can also be interpreted in a microcosmic sense: that the individual must go beyond the human in order to complete that work. Either way, the journey back to Eden takes on the image of a pilgrimage of terrifying length.

The Two Paths

At the same time, the journey of Seth introduced a new factor into the process. According to the tale, he passed on what he had learned to others, and they to others still. From that legendary origin, a secret tradition of wisdom came into being. That tradition was never widespread, for there were few in any generation who had untangled themselves enough from the coils of the dragon to listen and understand. Nonetheless, it never died out, and as others completed the journey to Eden and returned with their own experiences the tradition took on breadth, complexity, and subtlety.

The keynote of that tradition rises from the divergence between the two senses - macrocosmic and microcosmic - of the diagrams we've been studying. Put simply, the way of Redemption can be trodden by all of humanity together, following the slow route of evolution. It can also be walked, much more quickly, by any individual human being. These two paths, collective and individual, reach the same goal by approximately the same stages; the difference between them is purely a matter of time.

It is to the collective path - the Open Path, as it's called - that the traditions and practices of ordinary religion belong. At its best, religion fosters habits of decent behavior and reverence for the transcendent, and these are important factors in furthering the march of human evolution. More significantly from a Cabalistic perspective, religious disciplines can also lay the foundations for individual progress, by giving opportunities to learn self-discipline and self- knowledge, and by fostering an attitude toward the world which goes beyond the simple satisfaction of biological drives.

It is to the individual path, on the other hand - the Secret Path, to give it its proper name - that the world's systems of mysticism and magic relate. In their healthy forms, at least, these also foster attitudes and ways of growth which further the collective movement of humanity. Their major function, though, is to show individuals the route to Eden's gate, to help them to do themselves, quickly, what the rest of humanity is doing over evolutionary time. They also provide, or try to provide, protections against the real risks of the journey.

From these two paths, in turn, arise two different histories of humanity. The first, outer history is the record of our species' collective evolution, the long chronicle of blood, misery and occasional brilliance which is the business of the ordinary historian to study. The second, inner history is less tangible, a matter of secret traditions and hidden organizations, books and unwritten lore handed down across generations, sudden appearances and long silences. This latter history is the history of the Secret Path.

Some aspects of this second, secret history have become a subject of much interest in academic circles in recent years, as scholars have begun to notice the role that magical traditions and secret societies have played in the cultural and political life of the West. Other aspects remain largely untouched, at least in part because the magical traditions of the Western world have become mixed up over the years with a great many strange ideas about the history of the world and of humanity.

Thus, for example, a great deal of talk about Atlantis and other "lost civilizations" has circulated in the magical community for several centuries now. There has been more nonsense written about Atlantis, quite probably, than about any other single subject; furthermore, most of it has been wasted breath, because the existence or nonexistence of an ancient Atlantic continent really makes very little difference to the work of the practicing magician. The myth of Atlantis is a powerful one, and it has a great deal to teach the magician, particularly about the arrogance of power; it's also true that a certain amount of evidence, none of it unarguable, suggests that there may have been cultures during the Ice Age more advanced than current archeological theory is willing to admit. None of this makes Atlantis the burning issue it has sometimes been in magical circles.

Similar issues, or non-issues, clutter any attempt to talk about the inner history of the world. Still, this much seems certain: there is a tradition, or a group of traditions, passed on from very early times, which teaches a set of philosophies and techniques aiming at the total regeneration of the individual human being on all levels. The magical Cabala is one offshoot of that tradition, and its teachings one subset of those philosophies and techniques. Beyond this, the fine points of the secret history can be left to scholars.

The Ladder Of Initiation

The way of Redemption, as mentioned above, may be divided into stages; the magical Cabala has used a number of different systems of these, to make sense of the processes of the redemptive work. One system, perhaps the most common in the tradition's history, divides the sequence into three stages or "degrees;" this system was the framework used earlier for the three stages of Seth's journey. These three degrees were sometimes merely numbered, sometimes given the quasi-Masonic titles of Apprentice, Companion or Practical Brother, and Master.

More recently, though, the detailed Golden Dawn system based on the Tree of Life has become more or less standard in magical parlance. This system has the additional advantage that it extends beyond the core work of the Secret Path to include the highest stages of attainment, stages which come into play after the damage of the Fall is healed. Each stage, or "grade," of the sequence has a title and two numbers; the first number gives the order in which these grades are reached, while the second indicates the grade's position on the Tree. The whole system is given in Table 2.

Table 2

Number	Grade	Meaning	Sphere
0=0	Neophyte	"New Plant," Novice	(none)
1=10	Zelator	Zealous One	Malkuth
2=9	Theoricus	Theoretical Student	Yesod
3=8	Practicus	Practical Student	Hod
4=7	Philosophus	Philosophical Student	Netzach
5=6	Adeptus Minor	Lesser Adept	Tiphareth
6=5	Adeptus Major	Greater Adept	Geburah
7=4	Adeptus Exemptus	Exempt Adept	Chesed
8=3	Magister Templi	Master of the Temple	Binah
9=2	Magus	Magician	Chokmah
10=1	Ipsissimus	"Most Oneself"	Kether

The first stage is the 0=0 or Neophyte grade. As the numbers suggest, this is not so much a stage of its own as the beginning of the inner quest, the awakening to a part of life beyond biological drives and social roles.

The next four grades, from 1=10 to 4=7, represent the stages of the work between this awakening and the opening of the Veil. In the Zelator grade - the word is garbled medieval Latin, and means "zealous one" - the student learns to work zealously at the practical work of the tradition. In the Theoricus grade, he or she begins to perceive nonphysical forces and presences on the Yesod level, and studies basic theory. In the Practicus grade, he or she masters the practical work and learns to shape the forces of the nonphysical realm. In the Philosophus grade, he or she comes to understand the deeper issues behind the theory, and learns to combine theory and practice, idea and application, into a way of self-transmutation.

Between these four grades and the next three comes a transitional phase, called the Portal. Where the first five grades of this system can be assigned to the first stage of the journey of Seth, this one is assigned to the second; at this point, the tools which have been developed are put to use in the ascent of consciousness through the Veil.

The achievement of this work is the keynote of the next three grades, from 5=6 to 7=4. The grade of Adeptus Minor is devoted to stabilizing consciousness on its new level, completing the work begun with the first passing of the Veil. That of Adeptus Major is dedicated to using the powers of this new level to break the hold of the Negative Powers on the self and clean up the shambles caused by their presence. That of Adeptus Exemptus is directed to attaining self-knowledge and, through this, a mastery of the process of rebirth.

With the crossing of the Abyss, the achievement of the consciousness of Unity discussed earlier, comes the grade of Magister Templi. The chief work of this grade is the work of teaching. The grade above this, Magus, has the task of participation in the work of Creation in the macrocosm itself; while the work of the highest grade, that of Ipsissimus, cannot be understood from any lower grade at all. (The word "ipsissimus", by the way, is a clever if untranslatable Latinism meaning roughly "most completely oneself.")

These three highest grades have another role in the mythic structure of the Cabala, one which has a certain amount of practical importance beyond its theoretical role. It has been taught in many branches of the magical tradition of the Cabala that those who achieve these levels pass beyond ordinary life into another kind of life or activity, a hidden mode of existence or of embodiment which represents, for the individual, what the completion of the whole evolutionary process represents for humanity in general. The awkward but useful term "Inner Plane adepts" has been used for such beings.

Some groups have tended to exalt the status and powers of these beings to an embarrassing degree, and certain pathologies of magical training have their root in this sort of folly. At the same time, the phenomenon is a real one; certain kinds of magical working bring about contact with these entities, a contact which is marked by the communication of important knowledge and the transmission of very high levels of magical power. Such contact is generally held to be the difference between a true magical order and a mere study group.

The process of climbing the ladder of grades is referred to, in a number of contexts, as the Way of Initiation, and the attainment of any given grade can be called the initiation of that grade. This language risks a certain amount of confusion, however, because "initiation" can also refer to the class of magical ceremony which is used to accelerate the inner development of a member of an order or working group. To add to the confusion, the Golden Dawn used the grade structure given here as a framework for a set of initiation ceremonies. As a result, the "initiation of the grade of Adeptus Minor" might be the transforming experience of passage through the Veil, or it might be a useful but by no means equally powerful ceremony - or, for the right person at the right time, it could be both at once. In this book, therefore, when initiations and grades are mentioned, they will refer to actual stages in the transformative process charted above.

It may be worth mentioning, finally, that the same sequence of grades can be used to map out the course of the Open Path as well as its hidden counterpart, and this offers some unexpected insights into human history. At present, it may be safe to suggest, much of humanity stands at the Practicus grade, with the strengths as well as the weaknesses of Hod and the intellect dominant in our cultures and our ways of thought. The awakening of Hod's potentials of reason and communication out of the often murky image-based consciousness of Yesod has occupied our species for more than two and a half millennia now, and the process is far from finished. Evolution is not a fast process - a fact that points up the value of the Secret Path of mysticism and magic.

The End Of History

What can be said, finally, of the future? Like the orthodox religions of the West, with their Second Comings and messianic prophecies, the magical Cabala has produced an enormous body of prophecy and prediction down through the years, extending the mythic structure we've explored into distant ages. Very little of this material has practical application in Cabalistic work, though, and a great deal more shows signs of the same sort of wish-fulfillment and fantasy one finds in so many Christian and Jewish prophetic works. Like the prophecies of the orthodox, too, the visions of future transformation which have emerged from the Cabalistic tradition have one thing overwhelmingly in common: those which have been put to the test in a literal sense have, almost without exception, been wrong.

There would be little point in mentioning this here, except that the old habit of apocalyptic prophecy remains very much alive in the magical community at present - and that habit can be a lethally dangerous one. The Solar Temple's self-immolation in Switzerland and Canada in 1994 is a recent echo of the same spirit which led hundreds of people in the year 1000 to brick themselves up in high towers, where they starved to death waiting for Jesus to appear: useful reminders, both of these, of the need to keep watch on the difference between myth and history.

Visions of the New Age, like those of the New Jerusalem, are valuable as myths; they show us images of human possibility, and of the deep structure of things on which those images are based. The future itself will go its own way, and - even in the eyes of the Cabalistic myths we've been exploring - that way is likely to show a fair resemblance to the past. In terms of the outer history, cultures and civilizations will rise and fall, and new ones rise from the rubble; quite possibly scholars of some future age will dismiss legends of our moon landings as so much fairy- tale, as our scholars dismiss stories of ancient civilizations. In terms of the inner history, the tradition of the Secret Path will continue, persecuted or ignored or celebrated, and those who are ready to take its path will encounter it.

That path will still be needed for a very long time to come. As a species, we are still not far from the bottom of the Tree of Life, and it's said that every human soul must follow either the Open Path or the Secret Path to the Tree's summit before Adam becomes Seth and our present humanity awakens into the radiant Son of Man.

Part Two

Symbolism
Of The
Magical Cabala

Chapter Seven

The Tree Below The Veil

From the traditions and myths covered in the first part of this book to the detailed correspondences of the Spheres and Paths of the Tree - the subject of this second part - may seem like a substantial jump. The same principles of symbolism and symbolic thinking govern both, however, and the principles of the magical Cabala provide the foundation on which the correspondences rest.

Traditionally, works covering the Tree of Life have presented the Spheres in their descending order, following the Lightning Flash of the way of Creation. By contrast, the three chapters of this section will follow the opposite order, rising from Sphere to Sphere and Path to Path along the route of the Serpent. This sequence, rather than the other, determines the order of practical work on the Tree - and it is in practical work that the magical Cabala has its chief value.

Malkuth, the Tenth Sphere

Title:	MLKVTh, Malkuth (Kingdom).
Name of God:	ADNI, Adonai (Lord).
Archangels:	MThThRVN, Metatron, Prince of Countenances; SNDLPVN, Sandalphon (Twin Brother).
Angelic Host:	AIShIM, Ishim (Humanity).

Astrological Correspondence:
> AaVLM YSWDWTh, Olam Yesodoth (Sphere of the Elements).

Tarot Correspondence:
> the four Tens and four Pages or Princesses of the pack.

Elemental Correspondence:
> Earth.

Path Text:	*"The Tenth Path is the Resplendent Intelligence, because it is exalted above every head, and sits on the throne of Binah. It illuminates the splendor of all the Lights, and causes an influence to descend from the Prince of Countenances."*
Magical Image:	A young woman in a robe of mixed earth colours, her feet bare and her hair unbound, sitting on a throne of roughly shaped black stone.
Additional Symbols:	The altar, the equal-armed cross, the temple, the Tree of Knowledge of Good and Evil.
Colours:	in Atziluth - clear yellow.
	in Briah - citrine, olive, russet, and black.
	in Yetzirah - as Briah, but flecked with gold.
	in Assiah - black rayed with yellow.

Correspondence in the Microcosm:
> GVP, Guph, the physical body.

Correspondence in the Body:
> The feet.

Grade of Initiation: 1° =10□ , Zelator.
Negative Power: LILITh, Lilith, the Woman of Night.

One of the chief traditional images of the work of the Cabalist likens it to the ascent of a ladder, which has its foot on the Earth and its upper end in the heavens. Like anyone who intends to climb a ladder, though, the student of the magical Cabala needs to make sure of the ladder's footing before taking the first upward step. The foot of the Cabalistic "ladder" is in Malkuth, the tenth and lowest of the Spheres, and so it's here that we begin the upward journey through the symbolism of the Tree of Life.

The Sphere Malkuth, in its most basic sense, is the everyday material world in which most human beings live out the whole of their conscious lives. It is the universe as we perceive it with our five ordinary senses. In the state of consciousness that corresponds to Malkuth, the world appears to be made up of various kinds of physical substance in motion. Before Einstein and the early quantum theorists, this was the only aspect of existence that most scientists accepted as real and worthy of attention, and even today remnants of this attitude get in the way of many branches of scientific research.

An opposite but complementary attitude, the idea that the material world is basically unreal or not worth notice, has played a similar role in hampering spiritual research, in our culture and in many others. In some spiritual traditions - Gnosticism is an example - this has been taken even further, to a belief that material existence is fundamentally evil, a delusion and a snare to be escaped at any cost.

Both of these typically unbalanced attitudes have influenced the magical Cabala at various points in its development, but overall a wiser attitude has prevailed. From a Cabalistic perspective, the realm of physical matter is as real as any other we can perceive. Because Malkuth stands at the foot of the Tree of Life, though, it has a special status as the completion of the work of Creation; any power or wisdom attained at a higher level must be brought into manifestation on the level of Malkuth if it is to have any lasting significance.

Those traditions which see ordinary reality as evil or unreal often talk a great deal about contact with the higher levels of existence as "liberation". In a sense, this is entirely valid, because the experience of less constricted states of consciousness can free us from attitudes and assumptions that limit us, the "mind-forg'd manacles" of which the poet William Blake wrote or - in the language of Cabalistic myth - the coils of the Serpent. The real liberation, however, is not to be found by using these experiences as an escape. It's found by coming back to the everyday world with the new perceptions gained at higher levels, and, because of these, being able to clearly see the mysteries and power of a realm of being we too often take for granted. To use mythical language once again: the magician ascends to heaven so that he or she may return with its gifts to Earth.

*　*　*

Like the material world itself, the symbolism of the tenth Sphere contains some startling possibilities under an apparently dull image. The title of this Sphere, for instance, is Malkuth, which means "kingdom." A kingdom is the sphere of action and power of a king; as we'll see further up the Tree, kingship in a Cabalistic context has to do with a great deal more than an outdated political system.

The Name of God assigned to Malkuth, the symbol of the highest reality comprehensible from the perspective of this Sphere, is ADNI, which is pronounced Adonai and means, simply, Lord. Like the English word that translates it, Adonai is a personal title of honor and reverence; it would be easy to see in this nothing more than the usual idea of the divine which has pervaded Western culture since the triumph of monotheism in the early Dark Ages.

In one sense, that interpretation has some validity, but it only scratches the surface of a much more complex issue. All over the world, for thousands of years, the great majority of people have thought of the power or powers that rule over the world as, in one way or another, essentially human. (This way of thinking about divinity emerged from an older pattern, which saw the divine in animal form; that older pattern still exists, of course, in surviving tribal cultures.) The sheer familiarity of this notion may hide just how strange it is. Why, one might reasonably ask, should the reality beyond all appearance be symbolized by a person?

The answer, as suggested in an earlier part of this book, is that human consciousness tends to work that way. A species which routinely talks to pets and swears at broken tools, which projects its own experience of personhood on everything it encounters, will have an easier time thinking about transcendent powers if it can think of those powers in some personal form. More specifically, human beings have an easier time thinking of divinity in personal terms when they are functioning at the Malkuth level of awareness.

Human perceptions of divinity in Malkuth, then, are to some extent a product of human perceptions of humanity. At the same time, these perceptions exist in a constant if subtle tension with the higher levels of human awareness. In one way or another, all these levels are operating in each of us at every moment, and the perceptions of divinity present at these other levels have little in common with that of the Malkuth level. This tension may have more than a little to do with the unnerving way in which certain kinds of mystics have tended to become the worst of Inquisitors.

✳   ✳   ✳

The Name Adonai has more to teach as well. Like all the Names of God, it can be read letter by letter in accordance with the symbolic alphabet of the Cabala.

א Aleph, the first letter, represents creative energy in its purest form, free and unlimited. It is associated with the beginnings of cycles, with springtime, youth, and morning, and also with folly and intoxication. The word Aleph itself means "ox", suggesting agriculture and the spring plowing. Among the various attributions of Aleph are the element of Air and the Tarot Trump 0, the Fool.

ד Daleth, the second letter, expresses ideas of fertility and generation, the joyful union of opposites. In it the creative energy of Aleph takes form and bears fruit. The symbolism of Daleth is largely biological, even sexual; Daleth represents Nature in all her forms, but particularly refers to the instincts and energies of reproduction. The word Daleth means "door", and is often interpreted as a symbol of the womb. Other attributions of the letter Daleth are the planet Venus, sacred in Classical tradition to the goddess of Love, and the Tarot Trump III, the Empress.

Nun, the third letter, is a symbol of radical change, of transmutation and decay. As Daleth can be said to refer to love, Nun refers to death; as Aleph stands for the beginning of the cycle, Nun stands for its ending. The word Nun means "fish", which is an image of life hidden beneath the waters, and also (since fish are cold and do not breathe) a traditional death- symbol as well. Some of the attributions of Nun are the astrological sign Scorpio, the Scorpion, and the Tarot Trump XIII, Death.

Yod, the fourth letter, should be familiar to you as the first letter of the Tetragrammaton. Its associations, as you may recall, include solitude and innocence, the seed bearing within itself the secret spark of life. The word Yod means "fist", the closed hand, again suggesting containment and concealment, while the attributions of Yod include the astrological sign Virgo, the Virgin, and the Tarot Trump IX, The Hermit.

Taken together, these four letters trace the outline of a familiar sequence. In Aleph, creative energy bursts forth; in Daleth, it gives rise to form and fruitfulness; in Nun, these reach their completion and perish, leaving a seed hidden in Yod by which the cycle can begin anew. These four phases are morning, day, evening, and night; spring, summer, fall, winter; birth, life, death, and the after-death state. The Name Adonai governs all these, and contains in itself the cycles of existence which shape our lives on the Malkuth level. It's worth noting in this context that those religions which most strongly focus on the personhood of divinity also tend to organize their worship around a seasonal calendar derived from this same cycle.

The Name Adonai often appears as part of two other Names of God that are assigned to the tenth Sphere. The first of these is ADNI MLK, Adonai Malak, which means "Lord and King". This Name stresses the link between Adonai and Malkuth, the Kingdom. The second is ADNI HARTz, Adonai ha-Aretz, which means "Lord of the Earth".

It stresses the place of this image of God as the primary aspect of the divine in the world of physical matter.

*   *   *

The next two entries on the table of symbols, the Archangels and the Angelic Host, are concepts that came to the Cabala out of the religious world of Judaism. The realm of nonphysical powers that affect human life is a complex one, not easily reduced to any kind of orderly system; most cultures of the ancient world reacted to this common experience by creating sprawling pantheons of gods and goddesses to represent the diversity of forces. Of ancient cultures in the West, only the Jews seem to have rejected this approach. The uncompromising monotheism of Jewish religion after the Babylonian exile made such a system impossible. Instead, ideas borrowed from Persian sources were reshaped to give rise to the idea of angels, nonphysical beings of various kinds and powers subservient to God.

This would be nothing more than a footnote to religious history except for two points. The first of these is that it was this system of angels, rather than any of the various pagan pantheons, which became the framework for ceremonial magic in the West from the early Middle Ages onward. The second is that (at least from a Cabalistic viewpoint) the various transcendent powers in the universe do seem to function as though they were governed by a higher unity, and so the old belief in angels makes a quite adequate symbolism for discussing and working with these powers.

In the magical Cabala two classes of angelic beings have a central role in this context. Just as the Names of God attributed to the ten Spheres of the Tree are assigned to Atziluth, the archangels are assigned to Briah, and the angels to Yetzirah. In the same way that the ultimate reality is most easily conceived by human beings in Malkuth in the form of a person, lesser expressions of transcendent power can be best expressed in the same way. This expression is not just a convenience for theorists; a large part of the apparatus of ceremonial magic makes use of it in intensely practical ways.

With these points in mind, we can turn to the archangels and angels of Malkuth. Unlike the other Spheres, which have one archangel each, Malkuth has two. The first of them is named Metatron, and is also the archangel of the first Sphere, Kether. Alone of the Archangels, his name has no meaning in Hebrew (in point of fact, it is a Hebrew form of Mithras, the name of a Roman savior-god of Persian origins). For reasons which will be discussed later on, Metatron is known as the Prince of Countenances; he represents a secret link connecting the highest and lowest of the Spheres.

Cabalistic traditions make a distinction, a useful one, between the aspect of Metatron assigned to Kether and that assigned to Malkuth, a distinction which involves a different spelling of the archangel's name. Metatron in Malkuth is held to be the transformed Enoch, taken bodily into heaven according to the Biblical myth, and to function as a celestial scribe recording all the acts of humanity; his name was spelled MThThRVN, as given in the table above. Metatron in Kether, by contrast, is seen as a transcendent power, the "Lesser Tetragrammaton" created before the birth of the universe, and his name was spelled with an additional Yod, MIThThRVN. Of this we'll have more to say in Chapter Nine. In either form, Metatron may be visualized as an angelic figure of pure light.

The second archangel of Malkuth is named Sandalphon. As Metatron expresses the spiritual energies coming into Malkuth from above, Sandalphon expresses the spiritual energies of Malkuth itself; these two archangels are usually paired in the traditional symbolism, and are associated with the two angelic figures atop the Ark of the Covenant, Metatron on the right hand, Sandalphon on the left. As Metatron is linked with Enoch, Sandalphon is often equated with Elijah, the other Old Testament figure who is said to have ascended directly into heaven. Despite this and the meaning of the name, Sandalphon is often represented as female; she is called the Reconciler for Earth, and the Celestial Soul of Earth. She represents the driving force of evolution, the constant upward striving toward the spiritual on the part of every created thing. As the counterpart to the bright radiance of Metatron, she is sometimes envisioned as a luminous figure clad in dark garments.

The Angelic Host or class of angels attributed to Malkuth is the Ishim; this word literally means "humanity," but its connotations may be better expressed by the phrase Souls of the Perfected. Angels, according to the old belief, carry out the purposes of the Divine in the created world, and the point of this correspondence is to point out that human beings are - at least potentially - capable of filling the same role as participants in the great work of Creation.

The archangels and angels assigned to the Tree of Life also have another function; they represent the Briah and Yetzirah aspects of each of the Spheres. Thus Metatron and Sandalphon symbolize the patterns within consciousness which play so large a part in shaping our experience of the material world, patterns which have roots in the descent of forces from higher levels, represented by Metatron, or in the evolutionary process which Sandalphon represents. The Ishim, in turn, symbolize the processes of human perception which bring us knowledge of the realm of matter.

The next three attributions are relatively straightforward, covering the equivalents of Malkuth in astrological, Tarot, and elemental symbolism. The only one of these that merits special comment is the astrological correspondence, which is Olam Yesodoth, the Sphere of the Elements. Just as the Divine, archangelic and angelic names correspond to the first three of the four Worlds, the astrological symbol for each Sphere represents that Sphere in the world of Assiah.

Next on the table comes the Path Text. This is a quotation from a Cabalistic teaching document borrowed from Jewish sources centuries ago. The Thirty-two Paths of Wisdom, written by an unknown Cabalist perhaps a thousand years ago, was translated into Latin by Johannes Rittangelius in 1642. Because these commentaries on the Spheres and Paths of the Tree have usually been printed along with the Sepher Yetzirah, they have often been called (inaccurately) the "Yetziratic Texts;" under any name, though, they are among the best summaries of Cabalistic teaching in existence.

In the Text, Malkuth is said to be "exalted above every head" because it is the completion and fulfillment of the whole Tree of Life, and thus in a sense the most important of all the Spheres. It "sits upon the throne of Binah" because Binah is the origin of form, and Malkuth its end result; Malkuth is also, in a special sense, the final Heh of Tetragrammaton, and Binah the first Heh. It "illuminates the splendors of all the Lights" because in it all the Spheres (which are also called "Lights") become visible to human beings. Finally, the influence that "descends from the Prince of Countenances" refers to the dual role of Metatron as archangel of both Kether and Malkuth, and to the hidden link involved in this dual attribution.

Most of the remaining symbolism requires little comment. The Magical Image, which will be used extensively in the practical work to come, is a traditional figure which expresses the basic ideas of Malkuth in pictorial form. The additional symbols are all used to represent Malkuth in various Cabalistic writings and traditions, and can be used as topics for meditation.

The Colors assigned to Malkuth have symbolic meanings, but they derive principally from practice rather than theory and their chief use is in practical workings. Visionaries who have explored the various levels of the Tree of Life using the higher senses have found that the various energies of Malkuth are commonly perceived in the form of these colors. As the table indicates, the first color represents the Divine energies in Malkuth, the second the archangelic, the third the angelic, and the fourth the planetary energies. (By the way, "citrine" is a brownish yellow, "olive" a deep brownish green, and "russet" a rich rust-brown color.)

The next three entries, the correspondence in the microcosm, the correspondence in the body and the grade of initiation, have been covered in earlier chapters, and are listed in these tables purely for reference purposes.

The Negative Power of the tenth Sphere is Lilith, a legendary figure around whom some very strange stories have gathered. She was said to be a night-demon who stole and devoured young children, who seduced men sleeping alone and bred monsters and evil spirits from their seed. She was identified with the desert and the ocean, with all the aspects of Nature that are hostile to human beings. She was traditionally pictured as a beautiful and seductive woman who changes into a hairy, twisted monkey-like demon. Jewish writers in the Middle Ages made her the villain of an ugly little fable in which she was Adam's first wife, cast aside by him and cursed by God because she insisted on being treated as an equal and not merely as Adam's property. Before this, however, she seems to have been an evil spirit feared by many different peoples in the Middle East, and even further back the dim figure of the original Lilith can be made out: a pagan goddess, ruling over the destructive powers of Nature and of human nature.

Her image and her symbolism combine death and sexuality, desire and fear. This duality is the key to understanding her place among the symbols of Malkuth. The Negative Powers, again, stand for the energies of the Spheres out of balance, and when the Malkuth aspect of our consciousness is out of balance we become obsessed with material things, with our desire for some things and our fear of others. Our desires and our fears can come to dominate every part of our lives, chasing us this way and that the way dogs chase a rabbit. For most people the strongest desires are those tied to sex, the strongest fears those linked with death; embodying both of these, Lilith becomes a primary symbol of the forces keeping us out of balance with the world of matter, and thus unbalanced on other levels of existence as well.

The power of Lilith, it should be understood, is not limited to those parts of life that can be called purely material; after all, from a magical perspective, neither sex nor death are primarily material events. The imbalance which Lilith represents is a matter of attitude, not of objects, and it is entirely possible to become driven by fears and desires that have even less to do with the realm of matter. Critically, this can be true of spirituality. It is all too easy for the spiritual realms to become just one more object of desire, the realm of everyday life one more object of fear, and all your efforts simply a matter of digging the trap deeper.

This is one of the reasons why meditation is so important as a foundation for any kind of esoteric work. Since we start the work from the Malkuth level, the imbalances represented by Lilith form one of the principal obstacles in the way. In the calmness of meditation, fear and desire can be set aside for a time, and the mind of the student can begin to get used to the experience - often a novel one - of considering something outside a context of cravings and obsessive wants. Over time, this same clarity percolates out into ordinary thinking as well, and makes it possible to operate freely on the Malkuth level without being dominated by it.

Path 32, the Path of Tau

Letter of the Path: ת , Tau (Cross).
Name of God: YHVH ALHIM, Tetragrammaton Elohim.
Astrological Correspondence:
    Saturn.
Tarot Correspondence:
    Trump XXI, the World.
Esoteric Title: Great One of the Night of Time.
Path Text: *The Thirty-second Path is the Administrative Intelligence, and it is so called because it directs and associates the seven planets in all their operations, all of them in their own due courses."*
Mythological Principle:
    Descent into the Underworld.
Experiences of the Path:
    Travel underground, descent, burial; underground rivers; crossing a narrow bridge; removal of garments or ornaments; relics of ancient times; the starlit night sky.
Entities of the Path: Monstrous beings; phantoms of the dead; the Watcher of the Threshold.
Magical Image: An arch of a deep indigo color, with the letter Tau in brilliant white upon the keystone. The door within the arch bears the image of Trump XXI.
Colours: in Atziluth - indigo.
    in Briah - black.
    in Yetzirah - blue-black.
    in Assiah - black, rayed with blue.

The Thirty-Second Path connects Malkuth, the Sphere of ordinary reality, to Yesod, the Sphere of dreams, visions, psychic phenomena, and the subtle forces which lie beyond the material world. The symbolism of this or any other Path is sparser and less detailed than that of a Sphere; it is not, however, less important. The names and images given above are signposts pointing toward the transformation of consciousness represented by the Path; through practice, they become keys by which that transformation can be experienced.   The first entry is the Letter of the Path, which is ת, Tau. This is the last letter of the Hebrew alphabet; it has the sounds T and Th, and its name means "cross". More exactly, it is the word for what is still often called the Tau cross, a cross shaped like our letter T. In ancient times this kind of cross was an instrument of slow and agonizing death; crucifixion was an established practice long before the Romans took it up. There are, according to those who study such things, few ghastlier ways to die. Victims routinely survived for days before exposure, shock, and simple exhaustion killed them. As a symbol of protracted suffering, the letter Tau fits well with a Path which tradition associates with Time and the realm of the dead.

The Path of Tau is said to be "the reflection of the Sphere of Saturn"; it represents, in a different mode, something of the sense of form, of limitation, and of sorrow that can be found in the Sphere allotted to Saturn, Binah. The second and third entries on the table derive from this connection.

The Divine Name governing the Path is YHVH ALHIM, Tetragrammaton Elohim, the Name of God assigned to Binah; its symbolism will be covered in detail when we reach the third Sphere itself. The Astrological Correspondence is, of course, Saturn, and here the connections with the Path symbolism are exact and extensive. Saturn, as the slowest and outermost of the seven planets known to the ancients, is associated with ideas of time, old age, and restriction. When portrayed in art as a human figure, Saturn is shown as an old man in dark clothing, carrying the scythe that is also wielded by the figures of Time and of Death.

The Tarot Attribution is Trump XXI, The World. The usual picture upon Trump XXI shows a female figure, naked except for a scarf covering the genitals, dancing in the center of an oval which in some versions is a wreath, in others an ellipse made of seventy-two circles. She holds a wand in each hand. Outside of the oval, in the corners of the card, are the heads of a man or woman, a lion, an eagle, and a bull: the symbolic animals of the four Elements. It is a strange image, and tradition makes it stranger still by stating that the scarf conceals male genitals, and the central figure is thus a hermaphrodite: male and female combined in one form, the union and reconciliation of opposites.

In working with imagery of this sort, it's valuable to try to tease out the meaning of the symbols: to note the four elements in the card and connect them to Olam Yesodoth, the Sphere of Elements in Malkuth's symbolism, for instance, or to connect the bisexuality of the dancer with the balancing of polarities on the Middle Pillar. This is a significant part of the work of studying the Cabala, and forms a foundation for the system of meditation that will be presented later. At the same time, it's equally important to approach the symbols in a more immediate way, to simply look at them, turn them over in the mind's eye, make them a part of one's mental furniture. Images of this sort communicate their meaning through unconscious as well as conscious channels, and often it's the things that slip in through the back door of unconscious perception that prove the most valuable in meditation and other forms of practical work.

The same is true of the Esoteric Title of the Path, "Great One of the Night of Time". The Esoteric Titles are poetic images originally applied to the Tarot Trumps. They do embody precise definitions of the Paths, and often draw on the traditional lore of Western mysticism and magic. Thus Time appears in this title as a reference to Saturn, and the Night of Time can be contrasted with the Day of Eternity; the whole looks back to an ancient image of the cosmos which sees time as a "moving reflection of Eternity" created as well as measured by the planets, under the rulership of Saturn, Lord of Time.

Still, much of the value of these titles is as spurs to the imagination and expressions of what, for want of a better term, might be called the "atmosphere" of the Paths. They should be thought about, meditated on, allowed to develop their own subtle meanings.

The Path Text, which comes next, will benefit from close analysis. The Path of Tau is called the Administrative Intelligence because it represents the influence of Yesod, the Sphere of the energies that shape physical reality, on Malkuth, the material world itself. It is said to direct the courses of the seven planets because these, in the ancient vision of time mentioned above, are governed by Saturn in their timekeeping function; there is also a reference here to certain points of Cabalistic philosophy, in which the planets are the material reflections of the seven Palaces, the Spheres in active manifestation, and the Path of Tau is the Path by which the balanced forces of the whole Tree descend into Malkuth.

With the next part of the symbolism we begin to stray into matters of practical importance. The mythological principle and the experiences and entities assigned to each of the Paths are primarily given as guides to Pathworking, although they can also be used to help gain a clearer sense of the Path on a more theoretical level. They should be taken as hints, not as hard and fast definitions; your own journeys along may or may not contain any of the experiences or entities mentioned, although it's a good bet that something similar will turn up much of the time.

It is in this sense that the 32nd Path is given the mythological principle of Descent into the Underworld. Most traditional mythologies contain legends of living people who journeyed to the land of the dead; from the legends of Orpheus and Ishtar to Dante's Divine Comedy, the image is a potent one, and rarely missed by the storytellers of any society. Such tales have a tendency to follow similar lines, down to points of fine detail. These tales are closely parallelled, as well, by the experiences of shamans in their trance voyages to the Underworld - and by Cabalists venturing along the Path of Tau. Often - again, not universally, but often - there are ghosts and monstrous creatures along the way, caverns and narrow passages, the rush of underground water, the unnerving journey across a bridge as narrow as a sword's blade; at times the traveler must give up something - anything from a small gift to the flesh on his or her bones - as the price of the descent. At the end of the journey comes the return to light and air, and very often the light is the light of stars.

One of the entities often met with on this Path has a somewhat broader role: the Watcher of the Threshold, symbol of the fear that bars the way to transformation. Although the Watcher can make its presence felt at any point, this Path is perhaps its most common lurking spot; Saturn's involvement with time and death make the Path of Tau congenial ground. It will sometimes happen that the Watcher will take concrete form in a working of this Path, appearing as a monster barring the way. While this can be unnerving, it usually marks a turning point in the work of the student. Once the Watcher is squarely faced on any level, its power dwindles.

Yesod, the Ninth Sphere

Title:	ISVD, Yesod (Foundation).
Name of God:	ShDI AL ChI, Shaddai El Chai (Almighty Living God).
Archangel:	GBRIAL, Gabriel (Strength of God).
Angelic Host:	KRVBIM, Kerubim, Powers of the Elements.

Astrological Correspondence:
LBNH, Levanah (the Moon).

Tarot Correspondence:
the four Nines of the pack.

Elemental Correspondence:
Air.

Path Text:
"The Ninth Path is the Pure Intelligence, so called because it purifies the Numerations; it proves and corrects the designing of their representation, and disposes the unity with which they are combined without diminution or division."

Magical Image:
A beautiful and very strong naked man standing upon a cube of stone, his arms raised in the position of Atlas holding up the sky.

Additional Title: The Treasure House of Images.

Colors:
in Atziluth - indigo.
in Briah - violet.
in Yetzirah - very dark purple.
in Assiah - citrine, flecked with azure.

Correspondence in the Microcosm:
the nephesh.

Correspondence in the Body:
the genitals.

Grade of Initiation: 2=9, Theoricus

Negative Power: GMLIAL, Gamaliel, the Obscene Ones.

Yesod, the ninth Sphere, is perhaps the most problematic of all the realms of the Cabala. Of all the Spheres above Malkuth, the world of physical matter, it is closest to our ordinary experience; its patterns and forces form the structure on which material existence is founded. In human terms, too, it touches on familiar ground, for Yesod governs dreams and visions, instinct and biological drives, the animal aspects of human consciousness and the subtle forces of life. All of these are part of the common ground of human life.

At the same time, all these things have been regarded with deep suspicion by a culture committed to the idea that every part of human experience must be explainable in purely material terms. Until the discoveries of the quantum physicists forced the concept back into currency, the idea that immaterial patterns might structure the material world was rejected outright by the scientific community. On the side of the microcosm, there are still important schools of psychology which deny flatly that human beings possess any instincts at all, while dreams and other experiences of the Yesod level receive attention for the most part only so long as they can be made to fit into materialist models of the human mind.

These confusions, and the intense discomfort behind them, have their root in cultural conflicts too intricate to explore here. Still, their legacy is a factor that must be dealt with by the Cabalistic magician. The habits of thought fostered by our culture's material bias make it easy to dismiss much of the Yesod level as unreal, because not solidly physical - and such a dismissal leaves the magician without some of the more important tools the tradition offers.

✳   ✳   ✳

One of the more useful examples of an idea rejected by our culture, but necessary to our work, is the idea of a life force: a pervasive vital energy present in all living beings, which causes the rather strange phenomenon we call "life". Very few ideas have been so thoroughly denounced by the scientific community as this one; distinguished scientists can still be reduced to spluttering indignation by a mention of it. (It has only been a few years since the editors of the British journal *Nature*, as stodgy a periodical as anything in print, lambasted a book which strayed too far in this direction as "a good candidate for burning.")

At the same time, very few ideas in all of human history have been as persistent and widespread as this one. Outside of modern Western civilization, practically every culture around the world and across time has named this energy and considered it of high importance. In the martial arts of the Orient, which name it ch'i or ki, this energy plays a crucial role and provides the force by which a bare human hand or foot can shatter boards, bricks, or blocks of stone. In many traditional systems of medicine, this same energy is identified with breath and seen in the critical factor in all healing.

What makes the entire issue so fascinating is that the field of vital energy around the human body can be perceived directly by the human senses. One simple way to experience this is to shake your hands thoroughly and then hold them out in front of you, facing each other, the fingers spread and the hands cupped as though you held a volleyball. Pay attention to the "empty" space between your hands. After a moment, move your hands gently in and out, as though squeezing the ball, and notice the sensations which result.

The tingling and faint pressure you are feeling comes from the interaction between energy centers in your hands. The substance of those centers, and of the unseen but almost tangible presence between them, is the life force, the basic "stuff" of life, concentrated by the action of your etheric body. In the terminology this book uses - there are several other ways of speaking of these matters within the Western magical tradition - this "stuff" is ether, the substance of the Yesod level of being. Although it concentrates most strongly in living things, the ether is present in all forms of physical matter; thus, in a sense, all things are alive, as mystics and tribal peoples around the world have always believed. Fluid and constantly shifting, it nonetheless serves as the foundation for material existence, holding the particles of matter in a latticework of forces like beads strung upon the meshes of a net.

* * *

Because Yesod is the closest of all the higher Spheres to the familiar realm of Malkuth, it plays a central part in those phenomena which our culture has come to label "supernatural." This troublesome word has been condemned by some recent writers, who point out that everything can be seen as natural on its own level, and that the strange and seemingly miraculous effects which can be achieved through esoteric practices are nothing but the working of natural laws that we don't yet understand. This is true in a certain sense, but all the same the idea of the supernatural has a certain value. The point it makes is that other levels of being function in different ways, follow different rules, and produce different results than the "natural" realm of Malkuth.

This is the sense in which we can call Yesod the Sphere of the supernatural. As the level of existence immediately above the material, Yesod is the source of most of the nonphysical phenomena that affect the physical world. Most of the time, when people have a supernatural experience - that is, an experience which violates the rules of ordinary reality - what has happened is that they have encountered some aspect of the realm of Yesod, either because the energies of that Sphere were present at a higher intensity than usual, or because their awareness had been shifted by some means to the Yesod level of consciousness.

There are a fair number of people who seem to think that the ability to bring about this shift, and to gain various "psychic powers" in the process, is proof of an advanced stage of spiritual development. On the Tree of Life, of course, the ninth Sphere is indeed closer to the spiritual end of the spectrum than the tenth - but the difference is rather smaller than many of the current crop of metaphysical hucksters tend to claim. From a broader perspective, psychic phenomena are only slightly better evidence of inner growth and wisdom than plain physical strength would be. They are, to a much greater degree than most people realize nowadays, normal functions of human consciousness, and their development - while it does require the exercise of ordinary patience and effort - has very little to do with the transformative work of the magical Cabalist.

*   *   *

All these issues should be kept in mind in dealing with the traditional symbolism of Yesod. Much of this symbolism ties directly into Yesod's role as the Sphere of the ether, and if this is kept in mind the images and ideas given should be fairly simple to interpret. Thus the title of this Sphere, Yesod, means "foundation", and thus refers to the role that the subtle energies of Yesod play in organizing and giving structure to the particles of physical matter. Just as the entire structure of a building rests on and rises from its foundation, so the material world of Malkuth depends wholly on the structure given to it by the etheric world of Yesod.

The Divine Name in each Sphere stands for the highest conception of absolute Reality possible in that Sphere. Because of this, it can offer a glimpse directly into the heart of its Sphere's inner meaning. The Name of God corresponding to Yesod is ShDI AL ChI, Shaddai El Chai; Shaddai means "Almighty," Chai means "living", while El is an ancient word whose only known translation is "God".

The first and third elements of this Name suggest the tremendous currents of energy and life that flow through the universe in its Yesod aspect, and the central element suggests that these currents can best be seen as manifestations of a single unity. It is from this conception of the ultimate reality that the idea of pantheism, of the Divine as a life present in all things, comes into being; here, too - in the words of the often-quoted magical saying - "God is pressure."

The letters of the Name, as with each of the traditional Names of God, can be read as a further expansion of the Name's meaning.

Shin, the first letter, represents overwhelming power descending from above into the world of matter. It is associated with ideas of destruction and renewal, with radical change, with choices that cannot be undone and decisions permitting no appeal. The word Shin means "tooth," suggesting the process of eating in which food is destroyed in order to be transformed into living flesh. The attributions of Shin include the element of Fire, which has the same symbolism of power and transformation, and the Tarot Trump XX, Judgment.

Daleth, the second letter, is an image of fertility in all its forms, the creation of new life through the union of opposites. Closely linked to Nature in all her aspects, Daleth expresses ideas of generation, sexuality, and love. Attributions of Daleth include the planet Venus and the Tarot Trump III, The Empress.

Yod, the third letter, has its usual meanings of innocence and isolation as the hidden spark of life. The word Yod means "fist," and its attributions include the astrological sign Virgo, the Virgin, and Tarot Trump IX, The Hermit. It concludes the first part of the Name.

Aleph, the fourth letter, symbolizes the perfect freedom of unbound energy, of inspiration, intoxication, or insanity. It is connected with ideas of springtime, morning, and childhood, and it symbolizes the original outpouring of force before the establishment of form. The word Aleph means "ox;" its attributions include the element of Air and the Tarot Trump 0, The Fool.

Lamed, the fifth letter, stands for the concept of balance on all levels. It includes ideas of equalization, adjustment, and atonement; in human terms, the force it represents corresponds closely to the Eastern concept of karma, the pattern of cause and effect by which every action we do, for good or ill, returns to us in time. As Aleph is the ox, the word Lamed means "Ox-goad" - the ancient tool for controlling and directing oxen - and the attributions of Lamed include the sign of Libra, the Scales, and the Tarot Trump XI, Justice. Lamed also concludes the second part of the Name.

Cheth, the sixth letter, expresses the idea of obedience to divine power, of receptiveness to energies from the higher levels of existence. It is associated with ideas of responsibility and self-discipline, of faith, and of the human soul as a vehicle for the indwelling force of the Divine. The word Cheth means "fence", suggesting the concepts of containment and enclosure. Among its attributions are the astrological sign Cancer, the Crab, the most receptive of the signs, and the Tarot Trump VII, The Chariot.

Yod, the last letter, repeats the meanings outlined above. This sequence can be interpreted in several ways. Perhaps the most useful involves dividing the Name into its three elements. In this context, Shaddai, Almighty, can be understood as the outpouring of infinite energy (Sh) descending into the world of Nature (D) and scattering sparks of the Divine throughout the universe.(I). Chai, Living, suggests that every living thing is a vehicle or container (Ch) for that Divine spark (I). El, the Divine in and of itself, expresses the paradox of perfect freedom (A) which manifests itself in perfect balance (L). The whole Name thus offers a pantheistic image of absolute Reality - an image true on its own level, however incomplete on others.

Similar patterns show in much of the other symbolism of this Sphere. The Archangel of Yesod, for instance, is an expression of the same image of the ninth Sphere as Power; the name Gabriel means "Power of God", and suggests that the Briah aspect of the ninth Sphere can be understood in terms similar to that of the Atziluth aspect. The Angelic Host of Yesod, the Kerubim, are slightly more complex - as an earlier chapter mentioned, they serve as images of the inner side of the four elements and as symbols of the letters of the Tetragrammaton - but power is still central to their meaning; they represent the power of the Tetragrammaton (in theological language, the creative power of God) as it manifests in the material world from above.

The astrological correspondence of Yesod is the Moon, for two reasons, one theoretical, one practical. The theoretical reason is simply that just as Yesod is the closest Sphere to Malkuth, the Moon is the closest of the traditional planets of astrology to the Earth. In the days when the Earth was seen as the motionless center of the universe, the Tree of Life was mapped directly onto the planets in a highly literal fashion; in the end, it made for poor astronomy, but very good symbolism.

The practical reason is a little more subtle. The experiences of magicians over several hundred years have shown that the flow of etheric substance in the physical world increases and decreases in regular patterns. There are, in effect, tides in the Unseen, and the Moon affects these as strongly as it does the tides of the ocean. This influence is powerful enough that certain kinds of ritual work can only be done effectively at certain lunar phases. The association of the Moon with Yesod followed naturally from this.

The Path Text, here as always, is worth a great deal of study and meditation. It points up a different aspect of Yesod than do the symbols that we've discussed so far. The ninth Sphere is said to "purify the Emanations" - Emanations being another name for the Spheres -

because it receives the energies of all the higher Spheres, focuses them, and transmits them in the clearest possible manner down the 32nd Path to Malkuth. This transmission consists of the "representations" (in another translation, "images") of the Spheres - in other words, their reflection in Yesod, which is called "the Treasure House of Images" - and it is these which form the "seven planets" of the Path of Tau's Path Text. That transmission, finally, is a unity "without diminution or division;" it is only in Malkuth itself, in the world of matter, that this unity is finally broken into the multiplicity of separate things we experience each day. The ether, the substance from which the images of the Yesod level are shaped, flows freely through all of them without division, just as ocean water can rise up in wave after wave without being divided by the movement.

Much of the remaining symbolism can pass without discussion here. The last two entries on the table, however, require some comment, if only to avoid misunderstanding.

The Correspondence in the Body assigned to each Sphere refers to the location of an energy center in the guph, the physical body, where the forces of the Sphere in question are concentrated. In the case of Yesod, that center is located in the genitals, and is deeply involved with many aspects of sexuality. Despite the common notion that sex is the most physical of activities, most of sex takes place on the etheric and higher levels. Deprived of these, sex becomes nothing more than friction, and - since the etheric aspects of sex link, through the nephesh, to the instinctive drives that energize the whole affair - not especially enjoyable friction at that.

Some of the most closely guarded teachings of traditional Cabalism deal primarily with sex. This secrecy may have been more a matter of social prudery than anything else, but it was taken with a great deal of seriousness; in the early part of this century one Cabalistic magician, Dion Fortune, got into a great deal of trouble with the leadership of one of the Golden Dawn's successor Orders for publishing a relatively mild book on the subject. The teachings involved have been published a number of times, and aren't really relevant to an introductory work of this sort. Still, the basic principles can be made clear.

Sex, as mentioned a moment ago, is much more a matter of the etheric body than the physical one. There are technical methods which make use of this fact - methods of synchronized breathing are among them - but the more important applications go in another direction. The etheric body itself is a vehicle for the ruach, and the union of etheric bodies (which is what happens in sex) can, and often does, become the basis for a corresponding union of one or more levels of the ruach. When this happens in ordinary life, sex becomes the basis of love; when it happens between two people who have made some progress toward the parting of the Veil, the energies of the union can rise to levels of the ruach not normally accessible, and open these up to consciousness; when it happens between two people who stand on the edge of the Abyss, the joining of two can flower into the experience of the union of all. The mating of lovers in this context becomes not merely a poetic simile for, but an experience of, what mystics have called - in equally sexual terms - the mating of God and the world.

In the realm of magic, though, what can be used for transcendent ends can also be used for selfish and destructive ones; in the language of alchemy, the raw material of the Universal Medicine can also be made into a deadly poison. The same is true, typically, of sexuality. This is symbolized in Cabalistic terms by the image of the Negative Power of the ninth Sphere, the Gamaliel or Obscene Ones. Their traditional image shows a crowd of naked, filthy giants with the heads of bulls, joined physically to one another the way Siamese twins are joined. They represent the energies of sex degraded, reduced to a reflexive grasping for sensation in which others exist only as objects to be used for the satisfaction of cravings. The possibilities of the ascending union of levels of the self are lost in the pursuit of some new experience novel enough to break through the numbness of mere friction on nerve endings. There are other forms of imbalance at the Yesod level, other ways of distorting the function of the nephesh, but few are so costly in terms of human potential or - unfortunately - so common in today's society.

Path 31, the Path of Shin

Letter of the Path: ש , Shin (Tooth).

Name of God: ALHIM, Elohim.

Astrological Correspondence:

     Fire.

Tarot Correspondence:

     Trump XX, Judgement.

Esoteric Title: Spirit of the Primal Fire.

Path Text: *"The Thirty-first Path is the Perpetual Intelligence, and why is it so called? Because it regulates the motions of the Sun and Moon in their proper order, each in an orbit convenient for it."*

Mythological Principle:

     Rebirth through Fire.

Experiences of the Path:

     Sensations of heat, thirst, and pain; travel across a desert, or through fire; burning away of the physical body; images of other incarnations.

Entities of the Path: The Grigori or Watchers; salamanders, elemental spirits of Fire.

Magical Image: An arch of a clear red colour, bearing on its keystone the letter Shin in brilliant white. The door within the arch bears the image of Trump XX.

Colours: in Atziluth - glowing scarlet orange.

     in Briah - vermilion.

     in Yetzirah - scarlet, flecked with gold.

     in Assiah - vermilion, flecked with crimson and emerald.

The Path of Shin is the second of three Paths leading up from Malkuth, the realm of ordinary material reality, to the Spheres beyond. Like the Path of Tau, it thus connects to the world we ordinarily experience. From this common point, however, these two Paths diverge sharply. The Path of Tau moves by patient steps in the direction of the forces which lie just behind the material world, and it ends in Yesod, the Sphere of subtle energies and dreams. The Path of Shin, by contrast, is a Path of test and trial and of sudden, dramatic change, and it ends in Hod, the Sphere of ideas and intellect.

There's another difference, a vital one, between these two Paths. The Path of Tau is part of the Middle Pillar, the great central axis of the Tree; it is perfectly balanced between the opposing poles of the other two Pillars. The Path of Shin, on the other hand, is not. It connects the Middle Pillar with one of the two great polarities, but it does not touch the other, and because of this it must be balanced by its equivalent on the Tree's other side - the Path of Qoph, from Malkuth to Netzach - in order to come into balance with the energies of the Tree of Life as a whole.

The Path of Tau, therefore, is a balanced way from material reality to the realms of experience beyond it, but the Path of Shin is not. This is a point of some practical importance, because each of the three Paths which start in Malkuth can represent an approach to the first stages of the Cabalist's upward journey, a means of coming to grips with higher aspects of reality. All three have been used at various times, by various mystical traditions; all three can be found in use at the present time. A grasp of these three Paths thus has a great deal to offer concerning the nature of the links between ordinary and magical states of consciousness.

*   *   *

The first of the symbols of the 31st Path is the Hebrew letter Shin. The word Shin means "tooth"; teeth are instruments of change, and carry out the first phase in the everyday miracle of nutrition, the transformation of dead matter into the energies and tissues of a living body. Shown in a smile, they suggest warmth and friendliness; bared in the jaws of a threatening animal, they warn of immediate danger. At the same time, teeth are among the hardest parts of the body, and after death they survive long after the rest of the body has fallen to dust. Symbolically, then, they cause change in food and express change in feelings, but resist change themselves.

The Path of Shin is governed, as the traditional phrase has it, by "the reflection of the Sphere of Fire." This attribution is a key to the nature of this Path. Fire symbolizes energy, will, force; it expresses the power that sets things in motion and brings about definite change. Like the symbol of the tooth, fire has an ambivalent nature: burning in the fireplace, it expresses warmth and hospitality; raging out of control, it threatens pain and death. It transforms almost everything that it encounters but remains always itself, bound by its own specific laws.

This attribution is the source of the next two symbols of the Path. ALHIM, Elohim, is the Divine Name tradition assigns to the element of Fire. Here it represents the highest spiritual influence that operates on this Path. The astrological correspondence of the Path is, simply, fire, and links the Path to the fiery Zodiacal signs of Aries, Leo and Sagittarius.

With the next entry, the symbolism begins to enter into deeper waters. The Tarot Correspondence of the Path of Shin is Trump XX, Judgement. The image which typically appears on this card looks, at first glance, like nothing more than an orthodox image of the resurrection of the dead from Christian mythology: the Last Trump, so to speak, pictured here in the next-to-last Trump. In the upper half of the card, an angel bends down, blowing a trumpet to call the dead from their graves. Below, human figures rise up from the ground.

As with the imagery of Eden discussed earlier, though, the image of Judgement Day shown here need not be interpreted in a strictly orthodox sense. Some of the oldest traditions of Western mysticism and magic made use of a pun linking the Greek words soma, "body," and sema, "tomb," to suggest that the descent of the human spirit into physical matter involves qualities of loss and limitation like those we normally associate with the idea of death. The physical body, in these teachings, was seen as the tomb of the soul, and the image of resurrection in the Western magical tradition has therefore tended to point not so much to a revival after death as to a radical transformation of what we call life. To ascend from Malkuth to a higher Sphere, then, is the true resurrection; to descend, as we will see, is the true entombment.

In the Golden Dawn, this aspect of the card's symbolism was supplemented with a set of associations and images relating to the

Fire symbolism of the Path. Similarly, the Esoteric Title of the Path refers to fire, in its basic elemental sense. The Path Text, by contrast, illuminates a different aspect of the Path's meaning. This text, unlike any of the others, is phrased as a question and its answer; this is meant to point up the role that this Path plays linking Malkuth to Hod, the Sphere of communication and thought. The whole Path Text can be seen as a discussion of the nature and effects of this link.

The 31st Path can be called the Perpetual Intelligence because in magical thought the interaction between what are usually called "mind" and "matter" is not a rare phenomenon in the universe, limited to certain odd-looking apes living in an out-of-the-way corner of one unremarkable galaxy. Rather, mind is always present in matter; the microstructure of crystals and the sweep of galaxies alike show the order and regularity of mind's presence. As a Path descending from the Pillar of Severity to Malkuth, the Path of Shin shows mind in its role as a restrictive and formative power, a role central to the Cabala's understanding of mind and its workings. Mind, finally, works through division in the context of Malkuth, separating one thing from another, classifying, dissecting; this is why the Path Text refers to Sun and Moon, the classic images of primary duality in the Western magical tradition.

✳   ✳   ✳

The mythological principle of this Path, Rebirth through Fire, brings us to the threshold of the practical applications of the Path of Shin. Of the myths of rebirth through fire, perhaps the best known are the legend of the Phoenix, born from its own ashes and therefore immortal, and that of Hercules, half-god and half-human, who - poisoned by the centaur's blood, but unable to die - burned away his human half on a pyre and ascended to Olympus to sit among the gods.

These myths express the deep resonances of the Path within the human psyche, and offer vital clues to its use in practical terms. The Path of Shin, leading from material reality into the realm of pure mind, requires that those who travel it be able to free their awareness from the limitations of the material level. There are several indirect ways to do this, involving other Paths and other Spheres, but there is also a direct way. That way is to be found in suffering.

This is the principle at the root of those spiritual traditions which rely on asceticism to gain access to the spiritual levels of being. Methods of deprivation such as fasting, celibacy, and enforced wakefulness, as well as the direct inflicting of pain and discomfort on the body, have been used for thousands of years by mystics, seers and shamans as a means to shake their minds free of the grip of Malkuth. This approach to self-imposed Rebirth through Fire represents an intentional, even artificial, method of ascending the 31st Path.

Unquestionably, such methods can and do work. At the same time, the Path of Shin is not balanced in terms of the whole pattern of the Tree of Life, and if it becomes the main Path of spiritual development that development is likely to be unbalanced as well. In the magical Cabala, the Path of Tau serves as the primary upward route, and access to Hod is made by way of the images and energies of Yesod and the gentler fires of the 30th Path.

At the same time, the Path of Shin has its own place in the work of the magician. Life in fallen Malkuth provides plenty of opportunities for suffering, even for those who have no interest at all in seeking it out; all by itself, this world of ours turns out enough pain, disappointment, frustration, grief, and heartbreak to satisfy anyone's need for suffering. Meditations and workings on the Path of Shin offer one way to help the magician handle the impact of ordinary human unhappiness, and to turn that unhappiness into a way toward attainment. Suffering on the material plane is a great teacher, and when it cannot be avoided it should be approached thoughtfully and used as a tool for transformation.

$$* \quad * \quad *$$

The remaining symbols are intended principally as background for your Pathworkings. As always, these specific events and beings may or may not show up in the course of your inner journeys on this Path; they are intended to give you an idea of the things which you may encounter, not to define your Pathworking in advance. Of the experiences of the

Path, most should be self-explanatory. The last of them, though, may need some comment.

Certain kinds of meditative work, and exercises using certain symbolisms, tend quite often to produce the experience of remembering other lives. These apparent memories range from dim sensations or single fleeting images to full-blown recollections of the details of a life lived at another time in history. Such experiences are common enough in the Western magical tradition that those branches of that tradition not too tightly bound to Christian orthodoxy have tended to treat reincarnation as an ordinary fact of life. Groups in the Golden Dawn tradition, in particular, have generally done so, and the tendency for memories of other lives to surface in some kinds of magical practice has much to do with this.

While it can be interesting to experience such things, it's important not to become obsessive about them. It's also important to remember that wishful thinking, fantasies, unresolved desires, and even books you've read can contaminate these apparent memories. The "glamor factor" can be a tipoff to this sort of thing; the vast majority of people, throughout history, have been peasants, herdsmen, housewives and other ordinary people, not kings and queens, and a series of "past lives" of unbroken glamor and excitement probably has more to do with daydreams and personal feelings of insecurity than with anything else.

The two types of entities of the Path given in the table are commonly met with on the Path of Shin, though of course there are many other kinds. The Grigori or Watchers, as the first type have been named, often appear as immense looming human figures looking down from above. They rarely if ever speak; their function is to keep watch over the sufferings of the Path, and to observe the way in which travellers on the Path face these. The Salamanders are elemental spirits of fire, the stirrings of consciousness within this aspect of the physical world. They may appear as living, dancing flames. Traditionally they are said to be less evolved and less intelligent than human beings, although more energetic; the experiences which they provide are generally more useful than any advice they may offer.

Path 30, the Path of Resh

Letter of the Path: ר , Resh (Head).
Name of God: YHVH ALVH VDAaTh,
Tetragrammaton Eloah va-Daath.

Astrological Correspondence:
the Sun.

Tarot Correspondence:
Trump XIX, the Sun.

Esoteric Title: Lord of the Fire of the World.

Path Text: *"The Thirtieth Path is the Collecting Intelligence, and is so called because astrologers deduce from it the judgement of the stars and the celestial signs, and the perfections of their science, according to the rules of their resolutions."*

Mythological Principle:
Awakening of the Mind.

Experiences of the Path:
Meadows, forests, and other areas of rich vegetation; temples, schools, and observatories; instruction by nonphysical beings; flight or ascent.

Entities of the Path: Lions and other solar animals; sages and teachers.

Magical Image: An arch colored clear orange, bearing the letter Resh in brilliant white on the keystone. The door in the arch bears the image of Trump XIX.

Colours: in Atziluth - orange.
in Briah - golden yellow.
in Yetzirah - rich amber.
in Assiah - amber, rayed with red.

The Thirtieth Path, like the Thirty-first, offers a way to Hod, and its symbolism is likewise dominated by images of fire. Its starting point, however, is not the recalcitrant plane of material reality but the responsive, subtle, ever-changing realm of Yesod. If the fire of the Path of Shin manifests itself principally as heat - burning away the impurities of the self, searing the attachments to the material world - the fire of this higher Path, the Path of Resh, reveals itself above all as light. In place of the shattering power of the Path of Shin, the Path of Resh places conscious awareness, understanding, and the workings of the mind. In human terms, it works not by will but by perception, and its primary symbol is that oldest of all symbols of the conscious mind, the Sun.

In working with this Path, then, you'll be dealing with the functions of consciousness in your own mind, exploring the very part of yourself which allows you to explore anything at all. To some extent, this is familiar territory for most people in Western civilization. The obsessive materialism of our society has resulted in a valuing of the conscious mind and its functions over all the many other aspects of human consciousness, because rational consciousness is a more obviously effective tool for manipulating matter than those other aspects. Locked into a purely material focus, however, the conscious mind cannot even begin to reach its full powers, and even in the most ordinary acts of awareness there are potentials which are hidden from a purely materialistic approach.

Take a moment, as you did back in Chapter 1, to be aware of some object in the space around you - the same cup once again, if you happen to have it out. As you look at it, and experience the symbolic image that it produces in your mind, watch the way that the image affects your awareness. As you concentrate on it, notice the way that the image occupies the forefront of your awareness, while other things fade off into the background, and still others aren't in your awareness at all.

At any moment, you can turn your attention to something else, and this new object will move to the forefront while the cup takes a place in the background. It's as if you stood in a darkened room, holding a flashlight witn a narrow beam; at any given moment, a few things in the room will be brightly lit, others will be dimly lit, while the rest will remain unseen in the darkness.

The flashlight's beam, in this metaphor, is the conscious mind, and the darkness that hides everything around it is the rest of the realm of human awareness, which (for the moment) we can class together as the "unconscious mind." In a more ancient version of the same metaphor, these two are associated with the Sun and the Moon. This older image points to an important truth about these two great divisions of the mind, because it's not really accurate to speak of the unconscious mind as darkness. The unconscious has its own kind of awareness, shadowy and diffuse but much more inclusive than the narrow, focused beam of consciousness. It's possible to learn to connect up to this unconscious, moonlit awareness, and to use it in harmony with the solar clarity of conscious awareness; doing so is a significant stage in the work of the magician.

In this lesson, though, we'll be exploring the narrow beam of the conscious mind. As mentioned above, this beam has possibilities that have not often been explored in modern times. The beam can be varied in a number of ways, some obvious, some less so. As you saw for yourself a few moments ago, it can shift focus from one object to another. This is only the simplest of its transformations, though. It can also shift its focus from one level of existence to another, moving from Sphere to Sphere upon its own reflection of the Tree of Life; in this way, it turns from material objects in Malkuth to, say, images in Yesod or patterns of logic in Hod - or, once the barriers on the Tree have been opened, to the deep structures of manifestation in Chesed or the supreme unities above the Abyss.

The "flashlight beam" of conscious awareness can vary in yet another way, however, and in this lies one of the keys to its special power. It can change not only its direction but also its intensity. There are many degrees of consciousness, just as there are many levels on which it can operate, and it's been an important teaching of mystics since the beginning of history that, compared to the degrees of clarity and perception which the human mind is capable of reaching, our ordinary state of "waking" consciousness is very little more than a kind of shallow sleep.

* * *

Two points concerning the use of symbols in the Cabala make the traditional imagery of the Path of Resh a little more obscure than some of the other material covered so far in this chapter. Because of limitations within Western magical symbolism, some of the symbols used by Cabalists have to do double or even triple duty on the Tree of Life. Each of the seven traditional planets, for example, is associated with both a Sphere and a Path, and more often than not the two are nowhere near one another on the Tree! At the moment we're considering the Path attributed to the Sun, but many of the points mentioned so far relate equally to Tiphareth, the Sphere attributed to the Sun and the level at which true conscious awareness has its center. The two, Path and Sphere, have certain things in common, and this is among the reasons one symbol serves for both. A crucial distinction divides them, however. The Sphere is a level of being in itself, and the source of the solar consciousness discussed above; the Path is a relation between levels, and represents one way of putting that consciousness to work.

This point is crucial to an understanding of a part of the Tree's structure which has caused a good deal of confusion down through the years. Some of the symbolic links between one Sphere and another seem out of place, or even outright misleading. From Yesod, the Sphere of the Moon, it's possible to travel directly to Tiphareth, the Sphere of the Sun, but if you try to take the Path of the Sun to get there you'll find that you've been detoured to Hod. Like a road sign pointing in the wrong direction, the attributions of the Path seem out of step with those of the Spheres around it, and the same thing happens again in several other places on the Tree of Life.

As so often happens in the Cabala, this puzzle conceals an important point. In traveling from one Sphere to another, the most obvious approach doesn't always work. In this particular case, trying to get from Yesod to Tiphareth simply by focusing awareness on the solar consciousness of the higher Sphere will take you to Hod, not to Tiphareth. Why? Because, until the Veil of the Sanctuary has been passed, human awareness can only grasp a dim reflection of the true consciousness of Tiphareth. This reflection has its own uses, and when it's focused on the images of Yesod it reveals the patterns and ideas of Hod behind them; thus, it appears on the Tree as the 30th Path. It requires a different approach, however, to break through the Veil and come into contact with the level of awareness of which the Path of Resh is little more than a shadow.

*   *   *

With these points in mind, we can begin to examine the symbolism of the 30th Path. The Letter of the Path is ר, Resh, which means "head". This refers to the brain, the physical basis of awareness, and also to the sense organs located near it. The head is often used as a symbol to represent the conscious and intellectual side of human nature, in contrast to the heart which symbolizes the emotional and subconscious side; this has more to do with the specific biases of Western culture than with the deep structure of the self, but it still serves as a useful shorthand. The head can also symbolize leadership, direction, and organization. Just as the brain organizes and directs the activities of the body, the person holding a leadership position in an organized group is often called its "head".

The Path of Resh, in the old phrase, is "the reflection of the Sphere of the Sun"; it expresses in its own way some of the energies of Tiphareth. This connection gives rise to the next two entries on the table. The Name of God, Tetragrammaton Eloah va-Daath, is the Name corresponding to Tiphareth, and thus the aspect of ultimate Reality most active at the very heart of the Tree of Life. The Astrological Correspondence, as already mentioned, is the Sun. As the center and prime mover of the solar system, the Sun symbolizes many of the same ideas of power and organizing force we mentioned in connection with the letter Resh, and as discussed earlier it is also an ancient symbol for the conscious aspects of the self.

The Tarot Correspondence, at first glance, is part of the same symbolism, but it has more complex overtories. Trump XIX is called the Sun, and its most common image shows a meadow flourishing beneath a rayed golden sun. Behind the meadows is a low stone wall, and before this stand two naked children, a girl and a boy, holding hands. The wall and the children, images of division and of sexual polarity, seem at first glance to contradict the ideas of unity and of centeredness we've already discussed, but there's more to it than that.

The lesson of Trump XIX is that conscious awareness is based on a kind of inner separateness from the world, a drawing back from the objects of perception. As you look at this page, you're aware of the page, and aware of yourself being aware of the page; the more solar, more conscious your awareness becomes, the more clearly you're aware of both. You see the mental image of the page as something entirely separate from yourself, and you can observe it, think about it, as something outside of yourself as observer and thinker. This is an illusion, but in its place it is a highly useful one, preventing the kind of blurred overlapping of self and surroundings that can make unconscious ways of thinking as murky and inexact as they too often are. In the Trump, this division between the observer and the observed is symbolized by the wall, separating the sun from the meadow on which it shines.

The two children also refer to division, but in a different sense. Symbolizing sexual polarity, and distinctions in general, they remind the viewer that the conscious mind thinks in terms of differences. In a very real sense, all the mind can perceive is difference; the idea of "hot" exists only because it can be contrasted with "cold", for instance, and the same is true of every other distinction. The conscious mind functions by recognizing these distinctions, and it functions creatively by recognizing distinctions it had not before perceived. For this reason, the figures in the Trump are children, representing some new realization of difference, and they hold hands to point out that all opposites are in fact the products of a unity - as "hot" and "cold" both are functions of one continuous spectrum of temperature.

The Esoteric Title, Lord of the Fire of the World, relates this Path to the elemental symbolism of Fire; one of its points is that the will is to be guided by the intellect. The Path Text, in turn, deals with another of the applications of solar consciousness. The Path of Resh is called the "Collecting Intelligence" because the conscious mind at its best does not merely flit from object to object like a flashlight beam moved randomly, but notices, compares, collects, and brings together random bits of information into a coherent whole. The references to astrologers in the next phrase come from the fact that astrology was the broadest of the sciences in Rittangelius' time, and the foundation of most attempts to think about the universe as a whole; the entire human process of science, of conscious exploration of the laws of nature, is implied here. The careful work of deduction and calculation that the text suggests is very much a matter of the 30th Path.

The next four entries are meant largely as background for Pathworkings on the Path of Resh. The Mythological Principle of the Path, the Awakening of the Mind, refers to those legends and legendary images which deal with the dawning of conscious human awareness. Many of these tell of teachers, "culture heroes" who taught traditional ways of life to the first ancestors. Some of the early students of folklore, with more insight than they realized, called legends of this sort "solar myths;" their attempts to reduce these images to simple astronomy were too simplistic to be workable, but the connection of many such myths to solar symbolism is hard to argue.

The Experiences and Entities of the Path, finally, should be self-explanatory for the most part. The "solar animals" mentioned among the entities represent one facet of the great medieval lists of correspondences, in which animals, plants, stones, and nearly everything else imaginable were assigned to the seven traditional planets, the four elements, or some other scheme of symbolism. The lion, hawk, rooster, and stag are all solar animals; any good dictionary of symbolism will give others. These correspondences, in their own way, are a good expression of the Path of Resh itself; at their worst, they represent nothing more than an urge to classify taken to berserk extremes, while at their best they serve as a valuable tool for making sense of an otherwise confusing world. In the use of the conscious mind, both these possibilities always have to be considered.

Hod, the Eighth Sphere

Title:	HVD, Hod (Splendor).
Name of God:	ALHIM TzBAVTh, Elohim Tzabaoth (Gods of Armies).
Archangel:	RPhAL, Raphael (Healing of God).
Angelic Host:	BNI ALHIM, Beni Elohim (Sons of Elohim).
Astrological Correspondence:	
	KVKB, Kokab (Mercury).
Tarot Correspondence:	
	the four Eights of the pack.
Elemental Correspondence:	
	Water.
Path Text:	*"The Eighth Path is called the Absolute or Perfect Intelligence, because it is the mean of the Primordial; it has no root by which it can cleave or rest except the hidden places of Gedulah, which emanate from its own proper essence."*
Magical Image:	A winged hermaphrodite, wearing an orange loincloth and sandals, holding a staff in its right hand and a lantern in its left.
Additional Symbol:	the Caduceus.
Colours:	in Atziluth - violet purple.
	in Briah - orange.
	in Yetzirah - reddish russet.
	in Assiah - yellowish brown, flecked with white.
Correspondence in the Microcosm:	
	the intellect in Ruach.
Correspondence in the Body:	
	the right hip.
Grade of Initiation:	3=8, Practicus.
Negative Power:	SMAL, Samael (the Liars).

With Hod, the ascent of the Tree of Life reaches the base of one of the two side Pillars. As part of the Pillar of Severity, Hod has a formative function in the Tree's balance of energies; it gives rise to limit through division and distinction, separating out different elements of the universal patterns reflected into it from Chesed. It thus corresponds to analysis in the literal sense of the word - "breaking down" unities into their component parts.

On a subjective level, Hod is the realm of intellect, of language, and of rational thought. Familiar ground for most people nowadays, these aspects of the world can be comfortable enough that it's easy to forget just how equivocal and evasive they actually are. The same words that can be used to speak the truth can also be used to lie; the same habits of logical thought which can make perfect sense out of one portion of experience can generate utter confusion and misunderstanding when applied to a different part. Remembering this ambivalence is crucial to understanding Hod, and will throw a great deal of light on the symbolism of this sometimes perplexing Sphere.

Computer programmers have a useful notion called the Law of GIGO. This "four-lettered name" of sorts stands for the phrase "Garbage In, Garbage Out," and the point it makes is that the best computer program in the world is only as good as the data it has to work with: if you feed nonsense in, you'll get nonsense back.

This same rule applies equally well to the human intellect in all its functioning. Start with false assumptions and you'll end up with false conclusions, no matter how perfectly logical the steps in between. If you assume that the Moon is made of green cheese, then with perfect logic you can end up proposing that the Apollo astronauts should have taken wine and crackers with them. This example is harmless enough; human history would be a good deal less bloody if the workings of the GIGO law were always so harmless.

At the same time, the flexibility that makes the intellect vulnerable to the GIGO trap can be used in other, more constructive ways, and helps make the human mind the instrument of astonishing power that it is. The ability to feed the machinery of the intellect a carefully chosen piece of nonsense - to imagine things that don't exist, and then to think about their consequences in detail - is at the heart of human creativity in science, in the arts, and in daily life.

In the ancient world, this aspect of reality was symbolized by the god Hermes or Mercury, the messenger of the gods. Mercury was the god of arts and sciences, of trade, of medicine, and of magic; he was also the god of tricksters, liars, and thieves. Here, too, the same duality between communication and deception presents itself. This duality at the heart of the eighth Sphere points out issues of awareness and ignorance that are vital to a clear understanding of the work of the Cabalist.

*　　*　　*

The symbolism of Hod arises out of these same themes of duality and of paradox. The name of the Sphere, HVD or Hod, can be translated "splendor" or "glory." Other words with essentially the same meaning have very different roles on the Tree; thus, for instance, the Path Text for Kether refers to that Sphere as the "Primal Glory," while that for Chokmah names the second Sphere the "Second Glory." On the one hand, then, the eighth Sphere functions as an image of these higher levels, particularly when seen from the context of the mists and moonlight of Yesod; the light-symbolism of the Path of Resh is important here. On the other hand, Hod can also be a counterfeit of the higher levels, when ideas and doctrines held in the intellect are treated as more important than the experiences they were invented to express.

The Name of God assigned to Hod, ALHIM TzBAVTH or Elohim Tzabaoth, expresses the same duality in several ways. The first element of this Name is itself a Name of God in its own right, one of the most important; all three of the Spheres which make up the Pillar of Severity bear Divine Names which include it. Where the Names encountered so far in the ascent of the Tree have been relatively straightforward, however, this one is anything but that.

The complexities of the Name Elohim start from the structure of the word itself. Like many languages, Hebrew has different grammatical forms for masculine and feminine words. The root of the word elohim is elohe, a feminine word meaning, essentially, "goddess;" onto this is placed the suffix -im, which is a masculine plural! The result is a strange hybrid which might be translated "goddesses/gods."

Obviously this implies a concept of Divinity that has had little place in the established religions of the Western world, a concept which includes multiple forms and both genders. Here, more than anywhere else, the Cabalistic concept approaches that of the sprawling pantheons of the ancient pagan faiths. This closeness has been used by more than one Cabalist as a way to interpret those older faiths - a way which sees the gods and goddesses of the ancient world as each revealing and expressing, in a form human beings can grasp, some essential aspect of a transcendent Unity.

A letter-by-letter analysis of the Name Elohim reveals the same pattern, taken to another and a deeper level.

Aleph, the first letter of the Name, is also the first letter of the Hebrew alphabet; its symbolism includes the element of Air and the Tarot trump 0, the Fool, and its meaning contains ideas such as freedom, innocence, and indefinability.

Lamed, the second letter of the Name, provides balance to the free energies of the first; the letter-name Aleph means "ox," while Lamed means "ox-goad." As a symbol, Lamed's meaning includes ideas of polarity, harmony, balance and judgement. Its correspondences include the zodiacal sign Libra, the Balances, and the Tarot trump XI, Justice.

Heh, the third letter of the Name, represents the product of the first two, the outpouring of creative force set in motion by the union of perfect freedom and perfect balance. At once receptive and energizing, Heh provides a matrix of energy for the emerging patterns of being: passive if left to itself, it is capable of immense force once set in motion by something beyond it. The word Heh means "window," symbolizing the passive aspects of this letter's meaning, while other parts of its symbolism - the zodiacal sign Aries, the Ram, and the Tarot trump IV, the Emperor - express the more active side.

Yod, the fourth letter of the Name, symbolizes isolation, containment, withdrawal. It represents the division of the outpouring energy into separate sparks of force, the transition from unity to multiplicity. The word means "fist," another image of containment, and the attributions of this letter include the zodiacal sign Virgo, the Virgin, and the Tarot trump IX, the Hermit.

Mem, the fifth letter of the Name, represents the end of the sequence, the reabsorption of creative energy back into the original matrix. Mem expresses ideas of receptivity, acceptance, and sacrifice, of the final phases of every pattern and the final stages of every life. The word Mem means "water," and as water is the most receptive of the four traditional elements this carries the same symbolism. Mem's correspondences include the element of water, and the Tarot trump XII, the Hanged Man.

Taken together, the letters of the Name Elohim spell out a way of understanding the Atziluth level of Reality that is sharply different from the one represented by the Tetragrammaton, but at the same time complementary to it. In the Name Elohim, existence is imaged as a cycle of transformation in which the One, as infinite energy in perfect balance - the Name AL, which is contained in Elohim - becomes many, and the many return to the One. In some ways, this vision of being takes the perspective of the individual consciousness, facing its source and goal, while the vision implied by the Tetragrammaton takes the perspective of universal consciousness considering the universe as a whole.

At the same time, the image of existence expressed in this Name should not be confused with the vague type of pantheism which makes the ultimate Reality nothing more than the sum total of things in the universe. That Reality remains beyond human understanding and perception, and all the Names of God are merely models of it, ways to grasp some part of its function in the realms of human experience. The attempt to reduce Reality to any set of definable factors or components - be these the contents of the universe or the clauses of some doctrinal statement - is common enough in the current gamut of alternative spiritualities, but from a Cabalistic perspective it remains a mistake, the one valid meaning of the word "idolatry." It is also, and critically, one of the central risks in work on the Hod level.

In the eighth Sphere, the Name Elohim is combined with a second word, TzBAVTh, Tzabaoth, which means "of armies." Originally, perhaps, the title of an ancient war-god, this element has come to be used in a much broader sense in Cabalistic thought. The "armies" referred to can be seen as the hosts of individual conscious beings in the universe, and in this way the name Elohim Tzabaoth, Goddesses/Gods of Armies, has to do with the relationship between the grand cycle of creative power symbolized by the Name Elohim and the infinite complexity of the universe it creates.

✳ ✳ ✳

The Briah correspondence of Hod, the Archangel Raphael, contains yet another perplexity. As you'll recall, each of the four great archangels of traditional magic is assigned to one of the four elements. Each of the Spheres of the Tree, similarly, has an elemental correspondence. If the Cabala followed straightforward patterns in its inner structure, these two elemental symbolisms would govern the way in which the archangels as Briah correspondences relate to the Spheres. Instead, the archangel Raphael, who corresponds to the element of Air, is assigned to Hod, which corresponds to Water - and Gabriel, archangel of Water, is assigned to Yesod, a Sphere of Air!

This may be confusing, but it is anything but accidental. The archangels as they operate in Malkuth, the Sphere of our ordinary experience, are not quite identical to the archangels in their function as symbols applied higher on the Tree of Life. In Malkuth, the archangels function as ideals or goals of the elements, particularly of the elements as aspects of the individual. Thus Raphael, "Healing of God," expresses the idea that the intellect (Air in the microcosm) achieves its highest form when it becomes an instrument of healing. In the same way, Gabriel, "Strength of God," teaches that the emotions reach their best expression by becoming a source of inner strength.

On the Tree of Life as a whole, however, the archangels represent the Briatic aspect of each of the Spheres, the aspect present in the perceiving consciousness of an individual being - or of the universe as a whole. Here Raphael functions as a symbol of healing in a different though related sense. Healing, above all, is a process of restoring balance to the system being healed, and it requires that the different factors making up that balance be recognized, distinguished, and separately understood. The capacity to do this is central to the experience of the eighth Sphere; it creates the capacity to perceive the universe in an intellectual way, and gives rise to ordered patterns of thought such as language and logic. Just as the surgeon's knife separates tissues in order to allow them to reunite cleanly, so the distinctions and divisions of Hod become the source of a renewed unity further down the Tree in Yesod.

As if the above weren't enough, there is yet another difficulty in Hod's Briah symbolism to be dealt with. In the traditional lore of Cabalistic magic, the Archangels assigned to Hod and Tiphareth have at times been interchanged, with Raphael attributed to the Sixth Sphere and Michael to the Eighth. The Golden Dawn's documents followed this alternate scheme. On the whole, though, the archangel of healing fits best in the Sphere assigned to Mercury, whose caduceus is still one of the standard symbols for medicine; as we'll see in Chapter Eight, too, Michael's name and imagery identifies him clearly with the symbolism of Tiphareth.

✳   ✳   ✳

The next four symbols attributed to Hod need little comment. The Yetzirah correspondence of Hod, reasonably enough, is the angelic order of Beni Elohim, Sons of Elohim. These are the manifestation of the Name Elohim in the formative realm of Yetzirah; they are also the "Sons of God" who, in legend, came to the daughters of men and taught them all the arts and sciences, including those of magic. The Assiah correspondence of Hod, similarly, is Kokab or Mercury, and connects the eighth Sphere to the astrological and mythological meanings of that planet. The Tarot and elemental correspondences of Hod, for their part, are covered elsewhere.

The Path Text, on the other hand, will require careful study and meditation. As with all the texts, it provides an exact description of the Sphere and its nature, but it comes at the topic from its own distinct angle.

The Text covers three primary points. First, Hod is called "the Absolute or Perfect Intelligence;" second, it is described as the "mean of the Primordial;" third, it depends for its existence on Gedulah, which is a second name for Chesed, the fourth Sphere of the Tree.

The first point is clear enough. Hod can be called "absolute" or "perfect" because at its level, the universe is expressed as pure idea fully expressed; above Hod, the patterns of existence are not yet fully manifest, while below it these patterns have descended into the complexities of etheric and physical substance. The second point, too, can be interpreted easily; Hod is the "mean of the Primordial" - the word "mean" here means "average" or "midpoint" - because its place at the bottom of the Pillar of Severity makes it the last restricting and balancing Sphere on the Tree, imposing a final shape on the forces descending from the primordial Sphere, Kether.

The third point, on the other hand, lands us once again in complexity. As the eighth Sphere, Hod receives its primary inflow of energy from the seventh, Netzach; as the lowest Sphere of the Pillar of Severity, it receives a secondary inflow from Geburah and, ultimately, from Binah. Its other relationships depend principally on Path connections - to Tiphareth, to Yesod, and to Malkuth. Why, then, is Chesed's role stressed here?

Despite the lack of visible connections, Hod and Chesed do share one correspondence in common - the elemental attribution of Water. They also share some interesting mythological links: Mercury is the messenger as well as the child of Jupiter in Classical myth. Similar linkages, elemental and mythological, form a mirror-image relationship between Geburah and Netzach.

Something subtle and important is involved here, a polarity relationship which is not resolved by the usual Path-based energy flows of the Tree. In both these cases, as in the corresponding case of Yesod and the shadow-Sphere Daath, the resolving factor is not a Path but a Sphere: the sixth Sphere, Tiphareth, which balances and harmonizes the entire Tree of Life. The ring of Spheres surrounding Tiphareth, like that (on a higher level) surrounding Daath, forms a hexagram of balanced but powerfully polarized forces, and these in turn provide much of the shattering power which the experience of Tiphareth so often contains. From these considerations come several formulas of practical magic, notably the Ritual of the Hexagram.

On an experiential level, Hod's dependence on Chesed can be expressed in simpler terms. The "hidden places of Gedulah," which emanate from Gedulah's essence, stand for the experience of Reality symbolized by the Divine Name in Chesed. This experience, according to the teachings of the Cabala, has as its keynote a sense of the overall order of things, of the universe as a revelation of transcendent law. This experience in turn provides Hod with its context - its "root," in the language of the Text - without which the constant mental activity of Hod can find no solid ground from which to begin or end. Without a foundation in a personal experience of the universal order, the mind can run (as so many minds, including many apparently "sane" ones, have run) off into illusion, obsession or unrecognized fantasy. Here again, "garbage in" equals "garbage out."

✳   ✳   ✳

The additional symbol given here for Hod derives, as much of the imagery of the magical Cabala does, from Classical myth. The Caduceus, a winged staff entwined by twin serpents, was one of the symbols of the god Mercury, and as mentioned before it is a common symbol of medicine. In the Golden Dawn, though, it was used as an important instructional image.

This image can be read in two ways. The first considers the Caduceus as an image of the Tree of Life itself. The foot of the staff, where the tails of the two serpents touch, represents Malkuth; the crossing of the serpents above this is Yesod, and the one above that Tiphareth; the head of the staff is Kether, while the Spheres of the two side pillars are symbolized by the wings, the serpents' heads, and the middle of their bodies.

The second way of reading the Caduceus relates its shape to the shapes of certain Hebrew letters, and to these letters' correspondences. The uppermost part, comprising the wings and the staff's head, resembles the form of the letter ש , Shin, symbolizing Fire. The middle part, from the serpents' heads to the widest coils of their bodies, is similar to the letter א , Aleph, symbolizing Air, while the lowest part has some resemblance to the letter מ , Mem, symbolizing Water. In this interpretation, the Caduceus becomes a symbol of the three Mother letters, and thus of the powers of the elements: Fire above, Water below, Air between them, and Earth formed by the union of all three.

Both these ways of reading the Caduceus have another importance beyond their symbolic one. Both can be applied, as any of the symbolism of the Tree or the elements can be applied, to the human microcosm, and in this way both give rise to formulas of practical magic. As a representation of the Tree, the Caduceus expresses the formula of the Middle Pillar, while the elemental form of the Caduceus provides a less well-known formula working with energies in the head, heart, and belly.

✳   ✳   ✳

The same words which can be used to speak the truth can also be used to lie. This point, mentioned above, bears repetition here, for it has a relevance to the last of the correspondences of Hod: the Negative Power of the eighth Sphere, which is named Samael and called, traditionally, the Liars.

The Samael are given the image of dogs with the heads of grinning demons. They represent deliberate dishonesty in all its forms, from the most obvious to the most subtle. Their presence, in terms of individual experience, can be traced whenever the intellect strays from its proper role and begins to mask perceived reality behind webs of its own spinning.

In some ways, questions of dishonesty are among the most vexed of ethical issues, for as we've seen every communication is in some sense a falsification, a distortion of a reality no finite consciousness can effectively express. Still, just as there is a difference between the two kinds of symbols discussed in Chapter One - the first kind drawn from direct experience, the second kind constructed as a response to that experience - there is a difference between the dishonesty present in every act of communication and the kind put in deliberately, out of self- interest or malice.

Hod is familiar ground for many people in our current culture, and in the same way the Liars are perhaps the most familiar of the Negative Powers. Because of that very familiarity, they can be the most difficult of all to see clearly. The work of comprehending and balancing these

Powers, through the honesty of self-knowledge, thus represents a major challenge to the Cabalistic magician.

Diagram 16 - The Caduceus

Path 29, the Path of Qoph

Letter of the Path: ק , Qoph (Back of Head).

Name of God: AL, El.

Astrological Correspondence:
Pisces, the Fishes.

Tarot Correspondence:
Trump XVIII, the Moon.

Esoteric Title: Ruler of Flux and Reflux, Child of the Sons of the Mighty.

Path Text: *"The Twenty-ninth Path is the Corporeal Intelligence, so called because it forms every body which is formed beneath all the worlds, and the increment of them."*

Mythological Principle:
Emergence from Water.

Experiences of the Path:
Journeying over or through water; darkness or dim light; intense odors and textures; visions of the prehuman past.

Entities of the Path: Sea and water creatures, prehistoric animals, animal oversouls.

Magical Image: An arch of reddish purple or magenta, bearing the letter Qoph in white on its keystone. The door within the arch bears the image of Trump XVIII.

Colours: in Atziluth - magenta.
in Briah - buff, flecked with silver-white.
in Yetzirah - pale translucent pinkish-brown.
in Assiah - brownish-gray stone.

The Twenty-ninth Path, the Path of Qoph, is the last of the three Paths linking Malkuth with the rest of the Tree, and thus the last of the three ways by which the Cabalist can rise above the purely material level of consciousness. Like the Paths of Tau and Shin, which share the same function, the Path of Qoph has much to teach about the limitations that exist at the material level of experience, and about how these limitations can be overcome. The Path of Tau deals with the limits that arise from the essential nature of existence and of time, and the Path of Shin with those which are imposed by the laws and patterns governing the world around us. The Path of Qoph, on the other hand, is concerned with the equally real limitations inside of us. Here is the place of many of the problems of perception and illusion, of symbols and the reality behind them, which were discussed at the beginning of this book. Traditionally, for this reason, the Twenty-ninth Path has come to express ideas of illusion and delusion, of dream, fantasy, and hallucination.

One useful way to begin to explore the nature of this elusive and disorienting Path is to compare it with the Path of Shin, its mirror-image on the other side of the Tree of Life. These two Paths are similar in ways, precise opposites in others. In their macrocosmic sense, as channels for energy descending from the higher levels of the Tree, these Paths bring the forces of the two Pillars directly into the realm of Malkuth. Just as the Path of Shin, transmitting the powers of the Pillar of Form into the world of matter, gives rise to order and to natural law, so the Path of Qoph establishes the energies of the Pillar of Force in Malkuth, setting them to work within all material things that move, change, and grow. In our world, therefore, the Path of Qoph is manifested above all in life and living things.

In their practical application, as two of the three routes by which human beings can turn the focus of their awareness to the realms of experience above the material, these two Paths have a similar function but involve very different techniques; in turn, although they both lead to higher levels of awareness, their destinations are not the same. As mentioned earlier, the methods of practice that are associated with the Thirty-first Path involve self-denial and suffering. This is the Path of the ascetic, and its work is a turning away from the senses and the body, emptying them until that which lies beyond them shines through. The approach of the Twenty-ninth Path, by contrast, involves the senses completely in the work. Through robes, incense, and all the paraphernalia of ritual; through poetry, music, dance, and art; through eroticism and every kind of physical experience - the means is not important, so long as it floods the senses and, through them, the emotions, with a sense of the presence of something greater than the merely material. Both of these approaches, the ascetic and the sensual, appear in most religious traditions, although their coexistence is often an uneasy one; much of the feuding between Catholic and Protestant branches of Christianity, for example, arises from precisely this opposition.

This polarity is typical of the way in which the forces of the two side Pillars interact. Typical, too, is the role of the Middle Pillar in this conflict. Where the Path of Qoph involves filling the ordinary senses, and the Path of Shin requires that the ordinary senses be emptied, the Path of Tau goes beyond the entire issue by opening up new senses, attuned to higher levels of reality, and because of this more readily able to perceive the descent of forces and forms from higher levels still.

✻　✻　✻

The traditional symbolism of the 29th Path is relatively straightforward if the points just covered are kept in mind. The letter of the Path is as good an example as any. The Hebrew word QVP, Qoph, literally means "the back of the head", which ties into the points we've mentioned above in two ways. First, in anatomical terms, the parts of the brain toward the front of the head are the areas linked with our distinctively human qualities, while those at the back - particularly the cerebellum, the medulla, and the brainstem - are linked to those qualities which human beings share with other animals. The back of the head, then, serves as a symbol for our inner relationship with the biological world, and so with the life imagery of the 29th Path. (The differences between different parts of the brain, it's worth noting, were understood to some extent long before the rise of modern medicine. Then as now, injuries to different parts of the head produced different long-term results in those who survived them, and the healers and sages of the past were quite as observant as their modern counterparts.)

The second link between the back of the head and the symbols of the 29th Path is subtler, but no less exact. Human eyes, shaped by evolution for depth perception, are paired and aimed forward; unlike rabbits and many birds, we cannot look behind ourselves without turning. The back of the head, then, is a physiological blind spot, and for this reason it can stand for human psychological blind spots as well, those places in everyone's life where thought and awareness are drowned in illusion, misperception, and fantasy. In turn, many of the blind spots in many lives have the forces of this Path at their root.

The Name of God which corresponds to the Path of Qoph is AL, which is pronounced El. This is the Name of God that rules the element of Water, and that Element is one of the most important symbolic influences on the Path of Qoph. The Name El is also attributed to the Sphere Chesed; for all its apparent simplicity, it is one of the most important of all of the Names of God, and its implications have a profound bearing on many points of Cabalistic philosophy and practice.

The influence of the element of Water appears again in the next entry, the Astrological Correspondence for the Path. This is Pisces, the Fishes, one of the three signs of the Zodiac which are assigned to Water. As slippery and elusive as this Path, the Fishes again draw attention to the connotations of life and living things that we've already mentioned. Additionally, the traditional image of the sign, two fishes linked but swimming in opposite directions, has a special significance that can be applied to the Path; in esoteric systems of astrology, it has often signified the opposing pulls of material and spiritual experience on the human soul.

Many of these same points are expressed again in the Tarot Correspondence for the Path of Qoph, which is Trump XVIII, The Moon. The usual image of this card shows a waxing moon rising between two dark towers. Below the towers, a wolf and a dog stand on a sandy beach, and at the very water's edge a crab or crayfish crawls up onto the land. It's a strange picture, and one which has gathered a large number of different and often contradictory explanations over the years. The core of its meaning, however, is simple enough. The water and the animals restate the ideas that we've already discussed, with a slight variation; the animals themselves were chosen from among those traditionally attributed to the Moon, in keeping with the title of the Trump.

Here, again, the misleading nature of the Paths' relationship to Sphere symbolism is an issue. Just as the Path of the Sun doesn't lead to the

Sphere of the Sun, neither the Path of the Moon nor the Path bearing the Moon as its Tarot attribution leads to Yesod, the Sphere of the Moon. This points up one of the pitfalls in a simplistic approach to esoteric work. Without the slow patient effort necessary to open and train the higher phases of the mind through meditation and ritual, such glimpses of Yesod's forces as can be seen from the Malkuth level are just another set of sensations; accepting these as "higher awareness" can lead the unwary into a murky realm of confusion and fantasy. Too many followers of the present rush of spiritual fads have fallen into exactly this kind of trap. While it is possible to achieve authentic inner growth in this way - the 29th Path does in fact lead up from Malkuth to a higher Sphere - the trip there is full of potential blind alleys, and demands an extraordinarily difficult process of balancing with Hod and its energies if the Veil is to be penetrated and the high experience of Tiphareth gained.

It is equally true that the same difficulties apply to the use of the Path of Shin as a primary route into the higher levels of Being. Very few people in today's society, however, are likely to willingly take up a spiritual path based on intentional suffering and absolute self-denial. The appeal, and the danger, of the Path of Qoph is that it seems to require little or no effort; all that's needed, or so it seems, is a receptive attitude toward life, and a willingness to do things most people enjoy anyway. If only it were so easy!

✳   ✳   ✳

The next entry, the Esoteric Title of the Path, connects with both the lunar symbolism of the Tarot attribution and the deeper meanings of the Path. "Flux and reflux" are old terms for the flow and ebb of the tides, which are indeed ruled by the Moon. The oddly genealogical phrase "Child of the Sons of the Mighty," on the other hand, ties into Cabalistic symbolism. The Mighty or Mighty Ones referred to in a number of these titles are Chokmah and Binah, seen in their symbolic roles as Abba, the Supernal Father, and Aima, the Supernal Mother. The Sons of the Mighty are the six Spheres assigned to the World of Yetzirah, from Chesed down to Yesod - "Sons" because Yetzirah is governed by the letter Vau of the Tetragrammaton, the Son. What, then, is the child of these Sons?

The answer, once a commonplace of magical philosophy, is given in the Path Text for the Path of Qoph. Every corporeal thing at the Malkuth level of existence - every "body," whether we perceive it as animated or not - receives and expresses the powers of the higher Spheres in the realm of matter. The "Child of the Sons of the Mighty" is Nature, the sum total of processes by which every body is formed, and by which their "increment" or reproduction is brought about. In modern terms, it can be thought of as evolution in the strict scientific sense, the process of natural selection which fits living things to their environments.

✳   ✳   ✳

The remaining elements of the Path symbolism are intended for practical use. The mythological principle of this Path, Emergence from Water, touches on a vast array of myths and legends from around the world. Nearly every mythology has an account of a hero, a teacher, or the world itself emerging out of the waters. The Biblical story of the infant Moses in the bulrushes is one example of the type. Many of these myths are rooted in the symbolism of birth, and closely allied is the rite of baptism, a practice by no means unique to the Judeo-Christian tradition. This focus on birth marks another example of the polarity between this Path and the 31st, which is often expressed in myths concerning death.

The Experiences and Entities of the Path, which follow, derive from the symbolism which we've already examined, and most of the entries here should be self-explanatory. The place of darkness in the experience of this Path is an important one; it represents the obscuring of human consciousness, its submergence in a more basic, more biological level of awareness. The same factor gives odors and textures an important place in the experiences of the 29th Path. To many animals, the sense of sight is of little importance compared to other senses, especially smell and touch. Contact with the prehuman aspect of ourselves will tend to waken both of these; Pathworkings on this Path can leave the magician's sense of smell heightened for several hours afterward.

Path 28, the Path of Tzaddi

Letter of the Path: צ Tzaddi (Fish-hook).

Name of God: YHVH, the Tetragrammaton.

Astrological Correspondence:
Aquarius, the Water Carrier.

Tarot Correspondence:
Trump XVII, the Star.

Esoteric Title: Daughter of the Firmament, Dweller between the Waters.

Path Text: *"The Twenty-eighth Path is called the Natural Intelligence, and by it the nature of all that exists beneath the Sun is completed and perfected."*

Mythological Principle:
Awakening of the Heart.

Experiences of the Path:
Forests, meadows, and other scenes of vegetation, seen by night; mist, starlight; boundaries between land and water, and between opposites generally.

Entities of the Path: Nature spirits, birds and animals of the night.

Magical Image: An arch of violet, bearing the letter Tzaddi in brilliant white upon the keystone. The door in the arch bears the image of Trump XVII.

Colours: in Atziluth - violet.
in Briah - sky blue.
in Yetzirah - bluish mauve.
in Assiah - white, tinged with purple.

The Path of Tzaddi comprises the relationship between the Spheres of the Pillar of Mercy and the subtle forces of Yesod. In important ways, it mirrors the patterns of the Path of Qoph on a different level, just as the Sun of the Path of Resh across the Tree mirrors the fire of Shin. The Path of Qoph governs the realm of biology, of the forces of life as expressed on the most material level of existence; similarly, the Path of Tzaddi relates to the same realm, but in a less concrete way.

The 28th Path has to do with the complex web of relationships which link together all living things, human beings among them. It includes much of what is currently called ecology, although its scope is wider that that of any single science. It also relates to the forces of instinct and emotion, the links between biology and consciousness.

Like the Path of Qoph, too, the Path of Tzaddi is involved with evolution and the slow transformation of living things through time. There's an important difference in the way these two Paths interact with this process, though. The Path of Qoph, connecting Netzach with the passive substance of Malkuth, governs those aspects of evolution which fit each living thing to the circumstances of its environment. The Path of Tzaddi goes beyond this; connecting the energies of Netzach with the living currents of Yesod, it governs a more active form of the evolutionary process, in which living things break from mere reaction to the conditions around them but change and progress in new and unexpected ways. Additionally, the evolution of the 28th Path is directed, not random, and moves toward goals that may exist only as possibilities. Where the Path of Qoph looks to the past, that of Tzaddi looks toward the future.

✳   ✳   ✳

All these factors come together in the traditional symbolism of the 28th Path. The letter of the Path, Tzaddi, is an adroit symbol of many of the issues just mentioned. A fish-hook is an instrument of control, but it can only work if the fish swallows it voluntarily. Some kind of bait is thus necessary. In the same way, the directing forces of nature often use "bait" - for example, sexual pleasure - to shape the behavior of living beings.

The fish-hook of Tzaddi also has a reference to a higher Path, the 24th, which carries the letter Nun, "fish;" this will be dealt with when that Path is discussed. Finally, there is also the simple link between the fish-hook and the element of Water. Although the 28th Path has the elemental attribution of Air, much of its symbolism is connected with Water. This allows for a closer link with the Path of Qoph, just as the fire of the Sun in the symbolism of the Path of Resh connects it more closely with the elemental fire of the Path of Shin. It also serves as another example of the symbolic interchange of Air and Water, which was covered in our discussion of Hod and which plays an important role on this Path.

✳   ✳   ✳

The Name of God assigned to this Path is the Tetragrammaton, appearing here in its role as the Divine Name governing the element of Air. This attribution is expanded in the next of the correspondences, the astrological sign linked with the Path of Tzaddi; this is Aquarius, the Water Carrier, a symbol which contains in itself most of the points discussed so far. As a constellation, Aquarius takes the shape of a man pouring water out of a jug, but this sign nonetheless is assigned to the element of Air. In astrology, Aquarius marks traits such as optimism, humanity, and hope for the future. The image of a figure pouring out water, too, fits well with this Path's position as a channel by which the energies of the Pillar of Mercy pour down into Yesod, and thence to Malkuth.

There is another level of symbolism to this attribution as well. Gareth Knight, a perceptive scholar of the Cabala, has pointed out that the traditional symbol of Aquarius - two identical zigzag lines, one above the other - contains a subtle Cabalistic reference. The upper line can be seen as an image of the Lightning Flash or Flaming Sword, the descending path of creative energy through the Spheres of the Tree. The lower line, in turn, represents the reflection of that path of energy within every individual thing in the universe. The symbol thus represents the mirroring of macrocosm and microcosm, but there is more to it than this. In Cabalistic theory, the Lightning Flash in the macrocosm creates and sustains its images in the many microcosms of creation; in the same way, all higher-level energies create and govern their equivalents on lower levels of being. On the 28th Path, this process is perhaps the dominant force, and any working which calls on the forces of this Path must take the role of higher-level forces into account.

The Tarot correspondence expresses many of the same points through a related symbol. The traditional image of Trump XVII, the

Star, shows a naked woman kneeling between land and water, one foot on the shore, the other in the sea. She holds a vessel in each hand, and from these water pours out on land and sea. Behind her is a tree, in which a bird perches, and above the scene a brilliant seven-pointed star shines down.

This image has some obvious parallels to the astrological figure of Aquarius, and these are important to the Trump's meaning. Important, too, is the star for which the Trump is named. In traditional lore, this is Venus, the Morning Star, which is also the astrological correspondence of Netzach. As the goal of this intensely goal-oriented Path, the seventh Sphere dominates the Path's Tarot image. The seven points of the star, and the seven smaller stars which cluster around it in many versions of the card, carry on the same attribution. The bird and tree can be seen as symbols of nature; at the same time, the bird is an ancient symbol of the soul, and in Cabalistic terms the image of a tree usually refers to the Tree of Life. The bird atop the tree, then, can also be seen as an image of the ascent of the human soul to the supreme experience of Kether, the final goal of all who travel on the Tree.

The Esoteric Title assigned to this Path derives, again, from the Tarot symbolism, but includes references that may not be immediately obvious. The "firmament" mentioned here is the sphere of the starry heavens which, in ancient astronomy, was believed to surround the earth. Above it and below it, in the same traditions, were endless abysses of water; it was from this source, in Biblical myth, that the waters of the Flood came. To be a "Dweller between the Waters," then, is to inhabit the natural world as we know it, as distinct from the incomprehensible realms beyond.

The firmament is also the astrological correspondence of Chokmah, and can be used as a symbol of the Pillar of Mercy which derives from Chokmah. In Gnostic myth, the stars and Zodiacal signs were assigned to the powers of Mercy, the Aeons, while the planets were governed by the restrictive forces of Severity, the Archons; like many of the teachings of the old Gnosis, this opposition was taken to some extreme conclusions, but the basic principle holds. As "Daughter of the Firmament," then, the 28th Path here shows its function as a product of the descending energies of the Pillar of Force.

*   *   *

The Path Text for this Path is, for a change, fairly straightforward, but it touches on issues which are of the highest importance in understanding both this Path and the Cabala as a whole.

The Path of Tzaddi, the Text states, is the Natural Intelligence, and its function is to complete and perfect the nature of everything under the Sun. The word "natural" is another of those which has been diluted nearly to meaninglessness by generations of politicians and ad copywriters, but it once had an exact meaning deriving from its root, a word meaning "to be born." Nature, then, is what is born rather than made. It refers both to the world of nature outside us, and to the world of human nature inside us: the wilderness around us, as well as that within.

The Path Text thus unites the ecological and instinctive aspects of this Path with its future-oriented and goal-seeking operations. On this Path, and in all the phases of life in which this Path's energies take part, instinct and biological factors become the driving forces of evolution. Yet there is a limitation to the working out of these forces, a limit expressed in the simple words "beneath the Sun."

The phrase "everything under the Sun" is a common cliche, and this was as true in ancient times as it is in ours'. It's worth remembering, though, that the Path Texts contain nothing meaningless, and this small phrase carries a great deal of meaning. The Sun which looms over the Path of Tzaddi is Tiphareth, the great central Sphere of the Tree of Life. "Everything beneath the Sun" in Cabalistic terms means the four Spheres below the Veil, and the Paths that connect them with one another. To ordinary human consciousness, indeed, these are "everything beneath the Sun," since the Veil prevents any awareness of the higher levels of Being from below. The point stresses here, though, is that the forces represented by the Path of Tzaddi have their effect on the portion of the Tree below Tiphareth, and there alone.

The implications of this are of high importance in Cabalistic work. If the forces of Nature, taking this term in its broadest sense, do not operate beyond the Veil, then the Rending of the Veil involves going outside of Nature, beyond the reach of instinct and of the ordinary driving forces of evolution. Normal ideas of "human nature" cannot be safely applied to those who have achieved the experience of Tiphareth. This is the alchemical "work against Nature," and its result is the power of transmutation: in this context, the ability to go beyond the human, to transform the self at every level of its manifestation.

With every power comes a corresponding risk; here, especially, this old adage holds true. Given the power to transform the self in accord with will, it is entirely possible to use this ability to descend to subhuman, even to demonic, levels rather than to ascend toward the heights. This is one of the reasons why the methods of the Secret Path were so carefully guarded in times past. The history of this century contains at least one example of the effects of the transmuting powers put to their worst possible use, though a clear understanding of the phenomenon of Nazi Germany and of its supreme mage, Hitler, has been quite effectively blocked through a combination of wilfull inattention and crackpot obscurantism.

*   *   *

The remaining symbolism of the path of Tzaddi is primarily of use in practical work, and needs little comment. You may wish to compare these symbols with their equivalents from the Path of Resh; the polarity between these two Paths can be seen more clearly here than anywhere else. Thus, the mythological principle of the Path of Tzaddi is the Awakening of the Heart, contrasting the great myths of love with the cultural myths of the Path of Resh, and the experiences and entities met with on the 28th Path form obvious polarities with those on the 30th.

Opposite yet equivalent, these two paths represent the two poles of many of those conflicts which beset those beneath the Veil: feeling versus thinking, heredity versus environment, nature versus culture. A thoughtful study of these opposites will help bring clarity to some of the more vexing controversies of the present, and over time will lead to the point of balance between these opposites - a point of balance which is the beginning of the way to Tiphareth.

Path 27, the Path of Peh

Letter of the Path: פ , Peh (Mouth).

Name of God: ALHIM GBUR, Elohim Gibor.

Astrological Correspondence:
Mars.

Tarot Correspondence:
Trump XVI, the Tower.

Esoteric Title: Lord of the Hosts of the Mighty.

Path Text: *"The Twenty-seventh Path is the Exciting Intelligence, and it is so called because through it every existent being receives its spirit and motion."*

Mythological Principle:
The War at the World's End.

Experiences of the Path:
Images of struggle and combat; scenes of mass destruction; conflict between fire and water; sudden changes in imagery and scene.

Entities of the Path: Warriors; the Wild Hunt, the Gatherers of the Slain; carrion birds, such as vultures and crows.

Magical Image: An arch of a brilliant blood red, bearing the letter Peh in intense white on its keystone. The door in the arch bears the image of Trump XVI.

Colours: in Atziluth - scarlet.
in Briah - red.
in Yetzirah - Venetian red.
in Assiah - bright red, rayed with azure and emerald.

In the course of the last several sections, the polarity interactions between the two Spheres at the base of the side Pillars have played an increasingly important part. The interplay between the two side Pillars is not limited to this type of indirect process, though. The Pillars also come into contact directly, through three Paths running horizontally across the Tree of Life. The lowest of these Paths, and the one which concerns us at present, is the 27th Path, the Path of Peh.

This Path shares many features with the two higher horizontal Paths - the 19th, connecting Geburah and Chesed, and the 14th, connecting Binah and Chokmah. Like them, it joins Spheres which have not only opposite natures but also, in terms of energetics, opposite genders. Because of the first of these oppositions, all three Paths carry enormous flows of energy; because of the second, these energies have a strongly sexual quality and a powerful role in the creative process.

There are some important differences among the horizontal Paths, though, and these play a major part in giving the Path of Peh its particular qualities. The 14th Path, located above the Abyss, exists at so transcendent a level that the idea of conflict itself has not yet emerged from the original unity of Kether, and so the opposing forces on this Path fuse harmoniously into a single creative energy. The 19th Path, though below the Abyss, mirrors the harmonies above it in certain ways, and the nature of the Spheres it connects is such that, although it carries stronger energy flows than any other Path of the Tree of Life, these flows are always under perfect control.

The 27th Path is below the Veil, however, and at this level no such protections exist. Hod and Netzach are each at the base of one of the side Pillars, each expressing the nature of the Tree's horizontal polarity in the most fully developed form. Some part of the opposition between these two has been explored while comparing the 31st and 29th Paths, and it is honed and strengthened in the interplay of the 30th and the 28th. Now, in the 27th, the forces involved meet head on in a single Path. The outcome can only be an explosion.

"Explosive", in fact, is probably the single best description of the Path of Peh in all its aspects. It is a Path of revolutionary change, of overwhelming force which blasts apart the existing order of things. The workings of its energies can seem like senseless destruction, but this is an illusion. As the highest of the Paths entirely below the Veil, the 27th Path has a purifying function; in its macrocosmic sense, as a channel for descending energies, it clears away old and outworn patterns of existence to make room for the new to be born; in its microcosmic sense, as a route of ascent for the Cabalist, it turns its powers against the inner obstacles to higher awareness in preparation for the journey through the Veil.

This Path's energy, therefore, is harsh but necessary, a cleansing force that sweeps away the clutter in our universe as well as in ourselves. Because of its important place on the Tree, dominating the Paths below the Veil, it also serves as a useful reminder that the quest of the magician is not without its rough spots!

There is a certain kind of rather prissy spirituality, all too common nowadays, which holds that once one gets beyond the material level, everything is well-behaved sweetness and light. It's true enough that this can be found on the magician's journey, but so can power, passion, suffering, stark terror, and astonishing joy. The purpose of work with the Cabala isn't the restriction of experiences to a narrow range of things labeled "good"; rather, the work is intended to open up the student to new experiences and new levels of existence. Only when every facet of the universe, positive or negative, can be perceived as a a unity can the highest levels of attainment be reached. The union of opposites in the 27th Path can also serve as a reminder of that fact.

✳   ✳   ✳

The first of the symbols assigned to this Path is the letter Peh. The Hebrew word "peh" means "mouth", which may seem odd as an image of radical transformation. Still, as an image, the open mouth full of bared teeth summons up feelings of danger and fear of a sort often associated with the radical changes of this Path. As an organ, the mouth begins the process of digestion, changing solid food into a form that the rest of the body can begin to use - and in the process, destroying the food's original form completely.

There is another connection between this Path and the mouth, an esoteric one linked to the details of practical magic. One of the most powerful transformative techniques in the magician's toolkit is a method of making vocal sounds, a method known as the Art of Vibration. Certain sounds, made in certain ways, can transform the state of awareness of one who makes or hears them, and this effect can be as sudden and dramatic as the shattering of a glass by a singer's voice.

Those who have mastered this technique achieve levels of control over consciousness, both in themselves and in others, that seem miraculous to the uninstructed; abilities of this sort are at the back of a great deal of the folklore about "magic words" and "words of power", and play an important role in many systems of mysticism, magic, and the martial arts.

The next several entries all have to do with the ideas of conflict and destruction which loom so large on this Path. First of these is the Name of God governing the Path, which is ALHIM GBUR, Elohim Gibor. This is the Name of God attributed to Geburah, the fifth Sphere, the great power of destruction and purification on the Tree of Life, and the most similar of all the Spheres to this Path.

Next comes the Astrological Correspondence, which is Mars, traditionally the planet of the god of war. In modern astrology, Mars is the prime source of energy in the horoscope; it governs will, courage, and inner strength, as well as its older meanings of violence and conflict. In an age when warfare means impersonal mass destruction, and when no one is a noncombatant, it's as well that we have the alternative! Nowadays the old virtues of the warrior may be out of place in many issues of conflict between people, but they retain a real value and a place in dealing with the conflicts within each of us. In the work of the Cabalist, certainly, courage, self-discipline, and the willingness to keep on going despite the odds are all qualities that need to be cultivated. Meditation on the symbols of this Path can be of use in developing them.

The next entry is the Tarot Correspondence, which is Trump XVI, the Tower. Here is an image of destructive force in its plainest aspect. From out of a dark sky, a bolt of lightning stabs down against the top of a tall stone tower. The blast lifts up the tower's top and sends flames throughout the structure. Two figures in crowns and rich clothing have been hurled from the battlements and plummet through the air toward the rocks below. In some versions of the card, three great holes have been blasted out of the stonework, while in others the entire tower collapses under the lightning's force.

The appearance of utter disaster expresses one part of the Trump's meaning, but there is another side to the image. As a symbol, the tower (or any other fortification) suggests defense against what's outside, but also the imprisonment of those within; it is at once protection and prison. The destruction of the tower in the Trump, then, is also a liberation, and the two figures thrown from the battlements are prisoners set free from bondage.

Most often, and particularly in its application to the human microcosm, both of these meanings will apply at once. Any set of beliefs or opinions, for example, is at once a defense against mental chaos and a barrier to accurate perception, and when it is overwhelmed by events and has to be discarded this occurence is both the loss of a way of understanding the world and an opportunity to find a new and better one. Each act of destruction is also a new birth - and, inevitably, every new birth is also an act of destruction, an ending for old things and conditions of being.

The following entry, the Esoteric Title of the Path, includes much of what we've discussed by way of a symbolism of sheer power: "Lord of the Hosts of the Mighty." As with other such titles, the "Mighty" are Abba and Aima, the Spheres Chokmah and Binah; their "Hosts" - the word is equivalent to Hebrew TzBAVTh, Tzabaoth, an element of the Names of God governing Hod and Netzach - the myriad individual things in a universe dominated by the polarity between the bases of the two Pillars.

In the next entry, the Path Text, many of the points already raised are developed yet further. The Path of Peh is called the Exciting Intelligence; "exciting" is another word watered down to the point of meaningless in recent times, but in its original sense it meant "calling forth," "rousing," "awakening" - all far from meaningless ideas in relation to the Path of Peh. From this Path, everything which exists receives spirit and motion: motion, as an effect of the energizing nature of the Path; spirit, as a reflection of the role of the polarities of the Pillars in the descent of light in the Lightning Flash. Both movement and manifestation are a function of polarity relationships of the sort the Path of Peh shows forth.

The mythological principle of this Path might simply be called War, but those wars of legend which come at the end of the world or of a world-age most closely fit the pattern of the 27th Path. Once again, the core principle at work is polarity; the two sides at war - be they the angels and devils of Revelation, the gods and giants of Ragnarok, or the heroes and villains of a hundred less obviously apocalyptic myths - form the two opposed powers of a polarity interaction which is resolved only through the shattering of the existing order and the dawn of a new epoch.

Of the remaining entries, the only one which may need commentary is one of the classes of entities often met on the Path of Peh. The Wild Hunt or Gatherers of the Slain - a band of spectral warriors riding through the sky - is a common image from European folklore, but appears in many other contexts as well; it has not often been noted, for example, that the American cowboy ballad "Ghost Riders In The Sky" preserves exactly the same legend in a slightly different form. Like many of the entities met with on this Path, the Gatherers will take on threatening, nightmare forms, and the fear they sometimes bring can be one of the more important obstacles of this part of the work.

Netzach, the Seventh Sphere

Title:	NTzCh, Netzach (Victory).
Name of God:	YHVH TzBAVTh, Tetragrammaton Tzabaoth (Lord of Armies).
Archangel:	HANIAL, Haniel (Grace of God).
Angelic Host:	ThRShIShIM, Tarshishim (Brilliant Ones).

Astrological Correspondence:

NVGH, Nogah (Venus).

Tarot Correspondence:

the four Sevens of the pack.

Elemental Correspondence:

Fire.

Path Text: *"The Seventh Path is called the Occult Intelligence because it is the refulgent splendor of all the intellectual virtues, which are perceived by the eyes of the intellect and the contemplations of faith."*

Magical Image: A beautiful naked woman. Her hair is long and unbound, and she wears a crown of deep red roses and green leaves; this is her only ornament.

Additional Symbol: the rose.

Additional Title: the Gate of the Mysteries.

Colours: in Atziluth - amber.

in Briah - emerald.

in Yetzirah - bright yellow-green.

in Assiah - olive, flecked with gold.

Correspondence in the Microcosm:

the emotions in Ruach.

Correspondence in the Body:

the left hip.

Grade of Initiation: 4=7, Philosophus.

Negative Power: AaRB TzRQ, A'arab Tzereq (the Ravens of Dispersion.)

In a certain sense, Netzach is the most important Sphere on the Tree to the practical Cabalist. Its additional title, "the Gate of the Mysteries", expresses something of this importance. As the highest Sphere below the Veil, it represents the highest level of experience that ordinary human consciousness can reach on its own, and the closest approach that fallen humanity makes to contact with reality under ordinary circumstances.

For people raised within Western cultures, these roles may seem oddly placed on the Tree, for Netzach's chief attribution in the human microcosm is the complex set of reactions we usually label "the emotions." For centuries, Western civilization has had an intensely ambivalent relationship with human emotional life. On the one hand, the major cultural traditions of the West are strongly biased in favor of the intellect and against the emotions; in Qabalistic terms, they veer from the Middle Pillar over to the Pillar of Form, with all of the loss of balance which that implies. Much of Western culture treats the emotions with distrust and contempt; standards of behavior and manners often require that feelings be hidden away whenever possible, piled up in a sort of inner attic like so much outworn rubbish. Choices are supposed to be made "rationally", without emotional "interference". Attitudes such as these have resulted in buildings, cities, institutions and social systems, designed logically and with the best intentions in the world, which have proven to be sterile and inhuman because their designers paid no attention to human emotional needs.

On the other side of the balance, a pervasive undercurrent within Western culture has gone to the other extreme, and glorified the emotional life while despising and condemning the intellect. The results have been equally disastrous because the approach is equally unbalanced. The whole debate - Classical versus Romantic, culture versus counterculture - is more than a little reminiscent of a quarrel between two surgeons, one of whom favors right-handedness and wants to cut off everyone's left hand, the other of whom favors left-handedness and proposes to remove everyone's right hand. The idea that it's useful to have two functioning hands at the same time seems to have entered the debate all too rarely!

As one person within a sprawling and overcrowded society, the Cabalist can have only a limited role in resolving these ancient confusions. The same resolution, though, must take place within the self if the conflictiing forces of the two side Pillars are to be resolved and the way up the Middle Pillar opened. There's little value to simply bludgeoning the emotional side of the self into silence, as a few of the most intellectual of the Western world's spiritual traditions would have it. Equally, there's little value to drowning the rational side of the self in a torrent of unthinking emotion and basing every decision on pure feeling. Balance, the balance of the Middle Pillar, is here as ever the key to spiritual progress, and some level of it has to be achieved before any great progress in the work of the magician can be made. For the modern Cabalistic magician, the achievement of such balance may require more attention to be paid to emotional issues, or it may require less; certainly, though, it demands that the emotional life be understood and its needs and perspectives brought into the larger context of the whole self.

The foregoing may suggest - and rightly so - that work with Netzach requires a willingness to deal with powerful energies. Netzach stands at the foot of the Pillar of Mercy, and represents the most developed expression of the Force side of the Tree of Life. As the highest Sphere below the Veil, too, it receives the descending power of the Lightning Flash at an earlier and thus less diffuse stage than do any of the other Spheres which are accessible to ordinary consciousness. It will come as no surprise, then, that much of the symbolism of the seventh Sphere ties in directly with images of power.

There is another side to Netzach's symbolism, though. On the Tree of Life, the seventh Sphere has the role of a unifying force, binding together the countless individual entities which are created at the level of Tiphareth. The power of Netzach is the power of joining, and in human terms this power is expressed as love. The imagery of love, for this reason, plays as important a part in Netzach's symbolism as does the imagery of power. In many of the symbols, too, the two appear together as the two sides of a single whole. The true nature of their union is one of the inner secrets of the seventh Sphere.

* * *

These considerations will help make sense of the traditional symbolism of Netzach. As you study the symbols, it's well to keep in mind the roles that power, love, and their interaction play in the imagery and ideas of the Sphere.

First is the title of the Sphere, Netzach, which means "victory". In its broadest sense, this is simply the outcome of power effectively used: the defeat of obstacles and the gaining of a desired goal. In terms of Cabalistic philosophy, though, it has a more specific reference, symbolizing a particular "victory" that is part of the manifestation of being down the levels of the Tree of Life. At the Tiphareth level of the creative process, individual beings first come into existence out of the interplay of macrocosmic energies of force and form. As the newly-formed microcosms descend further, there's a certain risk that they might turn wholly inward, each one a universe to itself closed off from any outside interaction. The major role of Netzach in the work of Creation, then, is to conquer this tendency and bind each created being to everything else in the universe. This victory is a victory of power, but also one of the power of union - in human terms, of the power of love.

The next entry, the Name of God assigned to Netzach, expresses the same power in an exact form. The Name, representing the highest understanding of reality possible from the standpoint of the seventh Sphere, is YHVH TzBAVTh, Tetragrammaton Tzabaoth, which can be translated "Lord of Armies". This Name shares its second element with the Divine Name in Hod, Elohim Tzabaoth. The similarity is not accidental, of course. The tension of opposites between Hod and Netzach extends all the way up to the manifestations of absolute Reality in these two Spheres. Above the Veil, this tension is resolved in the harmony of Tiphareth, while below the Veil it provides the driving polarity behind the power of Yesod, but at the level of these two Spheres themselves it appears in its most intense form.

The opposition between these two approaches to Reality may be traced directly in the Names themselves. The Name Elohim Tzabaoth refers to Reality as unity arising from multiplicity, the whole which is greater than the sum of its parts. This is the point of view of pantheism, the concept that all things which exist are part of God; in the language of theology, it sees divinity as immanent - that is, participating in the universe of human experience, within the world rather than beyond it.

The opposite viewpoint is expressed in the Name attributed to Netzach. In place of the complex, plural Name Elohim, the straightforward creative energy of the Tetragrammaton gives this Name its essential nature. Combined with the second element, Tzabaoth, which literally means "of armies" and symbolically points to the relationship between the Divine and the armies of individual things that make up the world we experience, the Name Tetragrammaton Tzabaoth represents what in theological language would be called the idea of God as transcendent - that is, completely distinct from the universe of human experience, creating from beyond rather than shaping from within.

The nature of these conflicting images of the Divine is not difficult to understand, given the nature of the two Spheres involved. The intellect in Hod perceives things by analysis, by taking them apart and seeing how the pieces interact, and so the image of ultimate Reality most appropriate to the intellect and to Hod is the complex web of intertwined powers expressed by the Divine Name Elohim. The emotions, by contrast, operate by synthesis, by bringing separate things together and making a unity of them. The image of the Infinite most appropriate to Netzach and the emotions, then, is the powerful creative unity expressed symbolically by the Tetragramrnaton. It's important to remember, though, that the opposition between these two Names is not defined by their roles in these two Spheres; each one appears a total of three times on the Tree of Life, and each appearance marks a different phase of the complex interaction of these two powerful symbols.

$$* \quad * \quad *$$

The Name Tetragrammaton Tzabaoth expresses the nature of Netzach in the world of Atziluth, the realm of absolute existence beyond all perception. The next two symbols, the Archangel and Angelic Host, symbolize the energies of Netzach in the worlds of Briah and Yetzirah - respectively, the reflection of Atziluth in consciousness, and the interaction between the reality and the reflection. About Haniel, the Archangel of Netzach, very little in the way of legends or traditions appear in the traditional lore; he may be understood as the potential in consciousness for love in all its aspects. The Tarshishim, or Brilliant Ones, are similarly neglected in magical lore. Their symbolism, one of radiant jewellike light, is general enough - in a sense, vague enough - to be applicable almost anywhere on the Tree. An additional complication is that some texts use the word Elohim as the name of an angelic host, and correlate it to Netzach in this context; this rather awkward symbolism has generated a fair amount of confusion in some circles, although it does have the advantage of relating the Yetzirah aspect of Netzach to the unity of creative forces which the word Elohim usually symbolizes. The neglect of these parts of the seventh Sphere's symbolism may well derive from the Western world's cultural difficulties with emotional life.

The astrological correspondence of Netzach, on the other hand, has gathered enough lore around it to nearly make up the difference. Nogah, Venus, the expression of Netzach in Assiah, governs love in all its manifestations and is thus a force far too potent for any culture to suppress entirely. On the other hand, both the symbol of Venus and the idea of love have been confused thoroughly with the much more restricted realm of human sexual activity.

It's as well to be clear about these matters. Sexuality at its deeper levels, as already mentioned, contains some of the supreme mysteries of the magical Cabala, for the joining together of two human beings in a sexual context involves forces and interactions on levels that reach far beyond the material realm. Still, it isn't the whole of life, or of magic, nor is it the only basis for an emotional bond between two people. Sexual activity in the usual sense is primarily a matter of Yesod, not of Netzach, and the love that is the human keynote of Netzach can manifest in many other ways. The common tendency to collapse every kind of human intimacy into a purely sexual context is yet another of the marks of our culture's blindness to the life of the emotions.

*　　*　　*

With the next part of the symbolism we pass from the material aspects of Netzach up into the higher reaches of its meaning. At first glance, the Path Text assigned to Netzach may seem confusing or worse. Its description of Netzach as the "splendor of the intellectual virtues" appears to contradict most of what we've said about Netzach so far. Beneath the seeming contradiction, though, the Text presents a subtle approach to some of the highest aspects of the seventh Sphere, one well worth following.

Begin with the first phrase of the Text. Netzach, it states, is called the Occult Intelligence. The word "occult" now carries a heavy burden of connotations, but its original meaning is, simply, "hidden." To call Netzach the Hidden Intelligence can be understood in more than one sense; Western culture at the time when the Text was written was nearly as blind to the value of the Netzach side of experience as ours is, and this part of the Text can certainly be read as a reference to that blindness. It also suggests, however, that the aspect of Netzach with which the Text is concerned is hidden, and cannot be perceived directly. The only approach left is the indirect one, exploring the Sphere through its effects elsewhere on the Tree, and this is exactly what the Text proceeds to do.

Netzach, the Text goes on to say, is "the refulgent splendor of the intellectual virtues." This difficult phrase expresses a complex but important point, which centers on the concept of virtue. This word isn't meant in the rather prim sense it's usually given nowadays, but rather in the older sense in which one refers to the "virtues" - that is, the powers or effects - of an herb or a stone. The implication here is that Netzach can be seen in some sense as an effect of the powers of Hod. By describing the seventh Sphere as "refulgent" (that is, radiant) "splendor", too, the Text not only identifies the two Spheres (since the word Hod literally means "splendor" or "glory") but also suggests the specific function of Netzach in this context: it serves to lead from Hod toward the symbolic Light of the higher levels of the Tree.

Implicit here is the realization that Netzach is not only the opposite of Hod, but also its superior, closer to Kether and the original source of the energies of the Lightning Flash. On the way of Redemption, the experience of Netzach emerges out of the mastery of the realm of Hod, just as each Sphere's stage on the upward journey emerges from that of the Sphere immediately below it.

The last part of the Text is intended to point toward the ways in which this stage of the work can be reached. Two are given: "the eyes of the intellect" and "the contemplations of faith". The first of these, clearly enough, refers to Hod, and suggests that by careful study of the rational side of the self, it becomes possible to see clearly that the power of rational thought is not the summit of human consciousness it sometimes claims to be - to recognize the limitations of the intellect, and thus become its master rather than its slave.

What of the second, though? Faith, in a magical context, should not be understood in Tom Sawyer's sense of "believin' what you know ain't so;" rather, faith is basic trust in the universe, and in the processes and driving forces at work in it. As a later chapter will discuss, the Cabala traces faith to a root in Binah, the highest Sphere of the Pillar of Form, the source of the fundamental patterns and structures of our experience. To seek Netzach through "the contemplation of faith," then, is to rely on the natural processes of harmony within the universe to balance the experiences of Hod with those of its counterpart.

It's interesting here to note that both these two routes to Netzach derive from Spheres on the Pillar of Form to reach a Sphere on the Pillar of Force. This in itself has a good deal to teach about the role of balance and polarity in the work of the magician.

✳　　✳　　✳

Of the remaining symbols of the Sphere, the rose is by far the most complex, but its intricacies rise out of a vast body of cultural connotations for which there is no place here. Students of the Cabala who lack the time to go chasing through the literature on the subject can think of the rose as a symbol of love, which summarizes its meanings fairly well.

The additional title given to Netzach, the Gate of the Mysteries, refers to the seventh Sphere's place both as the highest Sphere below the Veil and the Sphere least well integrated into the ordinary thought processes of Western culture. Both of these concerns make it imperative that this Sphere be encountered and its forces brought into balance before the Parting of the Veil can be attempted and the higher levels of the ruach brought through into consciousness.

The final element of Netzach's symbolism is the Negative Power assigned to the Sphere, and here the symbolism plunges at once into some very deep waters. The Negative Power of Netzach, the unbalanced, primal form of the Sphere, is called A'arab Tzereq, the Ravens of Dispersion. It is pictured in tradition as a vast flock of ravens with demon's heads, pouring like smoke out of the crater of an erupting volcano. Ravens are thieves, and eaters of the dead; they serve as a potent image of an energy which feeds on other energies and concentrates where the forces of life are weakened or dispersed.

In their reflection within the human microcosm, the Ravens are to the emotional side of the self what the Samael, the Liars, are to the intellectual side. They represent the principal source of suffering and destructive behavior in emotional life. That source has rarely been well understood in the West, for our culture's intense ambivalence toward the emotions has left it as ill equipped to deal with the weaknesses of Netzach as it is to grasp the seventh Sphere's strengths.

Still, the Negative Power of Netzach is not a complete mystery; it has a name, and that name is envy. Envy is the emotional attitude which treats the happiness of others as a loss to the self. Implicit in envy is the idea that there is only so much happiness and so much misery to go around; given that assumption, it's only sensible to hoard the happiness for oneself while pushing off the misery on everyone else. The assumption isn't even remotely true - the amount of happiness in the world is limited only by our willingness to help create it, and to refrain from actions which lessen it - but at one level or another it pervades the way most people think about their emotional life.

Envy drives much of the frantic folly of our competitive, overconsuming society, in which keeping up with the Joneses is more important than figuring out if the place the Joneses are headed is a place any sane person would want to be. Envy, more than any other factor, breeds the distrust of other people that makes human relationships of any kind so difficult in so many lives. And since envy is a corruption of the Pillar of Force and so tends to energize and cause action, it also has an enormous role in all the manifestations of human violence.

To master the Ravens and bring the energies of Netzach into balance in the self thus involves the renunciation of envy and the willingness to experience the happiness of other people as good in itself. In a culture pervaded by envy, this may not be an easy task, but it marks a necessary stage in the personal development of the Cabalistic magician.

Chapter Eight

The Tree Between
the Veil
and the Abyss

Above Netzach, the Paths of Wisdom which make up the Tree rise above the realms of experience normally accessible to human beings. The process of opening up these higher ranges of human possibility - and in particular, of opening up the five Paths which cross the Veil - is the central work and the principal challenge facing the magical Cabalist, and the focus of most kinds of magical workings which go beyond purely practical goals. The Paths and Spheres between the Veil and the Abyss, then, have important lessons to teach concerning magical practice. At the same time, they lay the foundation for the summit of the Cabalist's journey - the crossing of the Abyss to the realms of Unity beyond.

Path 25, the Path of Samech

Letter of the Path: ס, Samech (Prop).
Name of God: ALHIM, Elohim.
Astrological Correspondence:
  Sagittarius, the Archer.
Tarot Correspondence:
  Trump XIV, Temperance.
Esoteric Title: Daughter of the Reconcilers, Bringer Forth of Life.
Path Text: *"The Twenty-fifth Path is the Intelligence of Probation or Temptation, and it is so called because it is the primary temptation by which the Creator trieth all righteous persons."*
Mythological Principle:
  Ascent to Heaven.
Experiences of the Path:
  Upward flight; climbing a stair, ladder, or rope; encounter with images of the self; facing a series of barriers or tests.
Entities of the Path: Centaurs and other half-animal beings; angelic figures.
Magical Image: An arch of clear medium blue, bearing the letter Samech in brilliant white on its keystone. The door in the arch bears the image of Trump XIV.
Colours: in Atziluth - Blue.
  in Briah - Yellow.
  in Yetzirah - Green.
  in Assiah - Deep vivid blue.

Up to this point, the route we've been tracing up the Tree of Life has taken the Paths in the reverse of their numerical order. At each stage of the journey, that order has approached each Sphere starting from the lowest Sphere which connects to it; thus the journey to Netzach, for example, begins with the Path of Qoph (linking Netzach to Malkuth), goes on to the Path of Tzaddi (linking to Yesod), and then passes to the Path of Peh (linking to Hod). The ascent to each Sphere, then, in some sense goes back over ground already covered, and this repeating rhythm of ascent is an important source of balance in the upward journey.

With the Path of Samech, though, the Path numbers part company with the ascending sequence of the Paths. The sequence continues as before; of the three Paths leading up to Tiphareth, the first to be taken begins in Yesod, the second in Hod, the third in Netzach. The numbers, however, no longer follow suit. The route of ascent goes from the 27th Path to the 25th, then to the 26th, then to the 24th, before resuming numerical order.

This detail of symbolism can be used to stress an important point. Up to now, the journey up the Tree has involved a steady progress from level to level, uninterrupted by breaks or major obstacles. As the Path of Samech is reached, though, the route of ascent comes within range of the first of the two great barriers on the Tree: the Veil of the Sanctuary.

In the traditional lore of the magical Cabala, the three Paths leading up to Tiphareth are pictured as a narrow way leading between two fierce guardians. The guardians are the 26th Path - symbolized by Tarot Trump 15, the Devil - and the 24th Path - symbolized by Trump 13, Death. The narrow way is the 25th Path. Once this last Path has been opened up, the others become accessible, but to take on these others before the lessons of the 25th have been learned is to court significant trouble.

The reason for this, as for so many things in the magical Cabala, is balance. The Path of Samech rises up the Middle Pillar of the Tree, in perfect balance between the forces of the two side Pillars; the other two do not. As we'll see, the Paths of Ayin and Nun have an unusual relationship to the Pillars and their energetics, and this relationship makes those Paths a potent source of imbalance if they are handled incautiously.

✳   ✳   ✳

To understand what is involved in the opening of the Veil, the central work of the Path of Samech, it's necessary to touch on issues which go back to the first points covered in this book. To review these, the reality that each human being experiences is symbolic in nature; at every step in the process of perception, the flow of information goes through changes and distortions so thorough that the final result, the mental image "in here", has only the most theoretical connection to the original object of perception "out there". Each person, therefore, lives in a world that's made up of largely arbitrary mental images, arranged in largely arbitrary patterns created by consciousness.

This pattern-making faculty is one of the most important functions of the human mind, for it is the power by which each of us in effect creates the universe in which we live. In Cabalistic terms, it is the true imagination, the Tiphareth of the human microcosm. To make use of this magical power, though, it's necessary to bring its operations into conscious awareness and control - and this is much easier said than done.

Most people never do. Instead, the pattern-making faculty remains unconscious, and comes to be directed by unconscious needs and drives. The influence of the various Negative Powers also comes into play, twisting the patterns in unhelpful ways. As a result, most of the time, people remain passive to their own worldmaking powers, treating the misery and frustration of their lives as the result of fate or other people's malice when so much of both arises from their own uncontrolled minds. At the same time - critically - people's understanding of themselves suffers the effects of the same process; one's self-image is as much a product of the imagination as one's image of the world, and it can slip from conscious understanding and control in the same way and with similarly destructive results.

It is exactly this habit of inner passivity which is the Veil. Such a habit can be comforting - it is always nice to be able to blame all one's troubles on someone else - but it stands squarely in the way of the work of Redemption, and for that matter of any real progress in magic. Nor is it enough to do as some currently fashionable schools of thought suggest, and decide that you "create your own reality." You don't; that is precisely the problem. The task you face as a magician is that of learning to do so.

The difficulty here should not be understated. The passage through the Veil has been called "a controlled nervous breakdown," and while this isn't precisely accurate it gives a fair approximation of the character of the experience. Much of what you know about yourself and your world is a fantasy spun by unconscious and often destructive drives. The power available to these drives is such that this fantasy generally includes many of those "truths" you believe most strongly. To pass through the Veil is to risk the loss of these things - the loss of much of what you think of as your identity.

The typical reaction to this loss is stark terror. As with the Watcher at the Threshold, though, this terror can be overcome only by facing it and enduring it. The temptation not to do so, to flee from it and from the self-knowledge it hides, is the primary risk of this Path. It is not a minor risk; that way lies madness.

The passage through the Veil can't be faked, and it can't be forced. It can be fostered by meditation, ritual, and the other practices of magical training, but in the end it comes in its own time and in its own way. On another level, though, practical work with the symbols of this transformation can make the passage itself less harrowing by providing the mind with ways of making sense of its experience, and with imagery and ideas which keep the goal of the journey in mind. This is one of the great strengths of the traditional lore of the magical Cabala

*   *   *

The Path of Samech provides the primary route through the Veil. In a real sense, then, it forms the focus of all the principles and practice of the magical Cabala; everything done before it is faced serves as a preparation or a support for it; everything done after the Opening of the Veil follows from it, as a consequence of it. As a later chapter will show, even the crossing of the Abyss is in some sense a reflection of this work on a higher and broader level.

The symbolism of the Path of Samech is thus above all the symbolism of visionary and mystical experience, of ascent to higher realms of existence; its myths are the myths of ascent to heaven, from Jack and the Beanstalk to the Ascension of Christ. A secondary element, also important, is added by symbols of balance between polarities. These two aspects will appear again and again in the images and ideas assigned to the Path.

This is true, certainly, of the first symbol to be covered. The Hebrew word "samech," the name of the letter assigned to this Path, means "prop" or "support." Traditionally, it is linked to a visionary experience of the Patriarch Jacob. During his wanderings, he went to sleep beneath the open sky at a certain place, with a stone beneath his head for a pillow. As he slept, he saw a vision of a ladder reaching from Heaven to Earth, with angels going up and down on it. After he awoke, he named the place Bethel, Hebrew for "House of El." The Name El has a role in the 25th Path's symbolism; more important here, though, is the image of the ladder. This is among the most common and pervasive symbols of the Path of Samech, for it suggests an ascent through a series of levels or steps - a standard description of the experience of this Path.

The Name of God assigned to this Path is ALHIM, Elohim, the Divine Name corresponding to Fire. The element of Fire is appropriate here because physical fire always rises upward; in astrological tradition, too, Fire governs the Zodiacal sign Sagittarius, which is the astrological correspondence of this Path.

The image of Sagittarius, the Archer, is a centaur - a being half-man and half-horse - armed with a bow and arrows. The centaur unites human and animal, reason and instinct, in a powerful symbol of the balance which characterizes this Path. Additionally, there are few better illustrations of the power of opposites in balance than the bending of a bow; the outward pull of the bow's two ends and the forward and backward pull of the archer's arms all bring energy to bear on the arrow, and when this energy is released in the right way the result is to send the arrow flying toward its target.

The image of the arrow ties into Cabalistic teachings in another way, one which is also linked closely with this Path. The letters of the three Paths which begin in Malkuth - Qoph, Shin, and Tau - taken together spell QShTh, Qesheth, the Hebrew word for "bow". As mentioned earlier, these three Paths can be used to represent the three basic approaches to spiritual experience, the sensual, ascetic, and meditative ways. These three approaches, seemingly opposed, can be used together in magical work to provide motive power for the magician's ascent. In this symbolism the Path of Samech becomes the arrow, soaring upwards through the Veil, and the title "the Path of the Arrow" is commonly used for the 25th Path. The word Qesheth also means the rainbow, symbol of promise and also of the "Peacock's Tail" phase of alchemy, when rainbow colors shining in the vessel announce the approach of success in the Great Work.

Finally, Sagittarius is traditionally ruled by the planet Jupiter, the most beneficent planet in medieval systems of astrology, to which in turn is assigned the Divine Name El. The sign Sagittarius is thus precisely Bethel, the House of Jupiter.

✳   ✳   ✳

With the next symbol, the Tarot correspondence, we enter on a more complex set of issues. In the Tarot, the Path of Samech is assigned to Trump XIV, Temperance. In nearly all published decks, this card has a very simple form: a winged, angelic figure, standing with one foot on land and one in the water, pouring water from one cup or vase into another. This is simply a conventional image of the virtue of temperance or moderation. The two vessels, which have been given so many bizarre interpretations over the last century or so, refer to nothing more arcane than the once-common practice of adding water to strong wine in order to weaken its intoxicating effects. As a symbol of the balancing of opposites, of course, the Trump image has its application to the symbolism of the 25th Path, but at a fairly basic level.

The complexity in this attribution is the fact that, according to the Golden Dawn's traditions, the present image on Trump XIV is not the original one. At some point in the past, the Order's documents claim, an older and stranger image was withdrawn from general use for reasons of secrecy, and was replaced by the more innocuous one used today. Whether this is true or not - and there is admittedly no evidence whatsoever for it besides the bare claim itself - the alternative version does bring in deeper aspects of the Path's symbolism.

On the alternative Trump, a woman wearing a crown of five points stands over a cauldron. In her right hand, she holds a cup, and pours water from it into the cauldron; in her left hand is a torch, and flames fall from it to blend with the water. Around her waist is a chain, and two other chains extend from this to collars about the necks of two animals, a lion on the left, an eagle on the right.

This Trump has much to do with alchemy, as well as with Cabalistic magic, but the heart of its meaning will be clear enough. In the union of fire and water in the cauldron, the concept of the balance and fusion of opposites is expressed with great clarity. The lion and the eagle expand on this same point; the lion represents the astrological sign Leo, the strongest of the Fire signs, while the eagle is one of the symbols of the sign Scorpio, which is the strongest of the Water signs. The crown of five points symbolizes the five Paths that cross the Veil, and it also suggests the five Spheres above Tiphareth, the further goals of this transformative Path.

∗   ∗   ∗

The Esoteric Title and Path Text attributed to the 25th Path are, for a change, relatively straightforward. The Path of Samech is called the Daughter of the Reconcilers because, as a Path of the Middle Pillar, it carries energies descending from Kether and Tiphareth, the great reconciling centers of the Tree, and it is the Bringer Forth of Life because life on all levels is the product of balance between polarities; in the words of the Neophyte Ritual of the Golden Dawn, "Unbalanced Power is the ebbing away of Life."

The Path of Samech may also be called the Intelligence of Probation or Temptation, and the "primary temptation by which the Creator trieth all righteous persons," because the temptation to turn away from that balance - to leave the Middle Pillar in the direction of Force or Form - is the principal test which must be faced before the Veil opens and the higher potentials of the self awaken. More, the concept of balance is at the heart of the Cabalistic concept of "righteousness," or (to use a word which has had its meaning a little less corrupted by religious politics) of ethics. Centuries of intensely dualistic thinking in the West have left too many people thinking that any given kind of goodness is necessarily the opposite of some corresponding evil. Most often, though, virtue holds the middle ground between two conflicting vices. Thus courage is opposed to cowardice, but also to recklessness; fairness stands against selfishness, but also against self-abnegation; real generosity is no more spendthrift than it is penny-pinching. The Middle Pillar here as elsewhere is the Cabalist's guide.

The mythological principle of this Path, as mentioned earlier, is the Ascent to Heaven. Like the underworld journey of the 32nd Path, myths of this sort appear with great frequency in the world's mythologies, sometimes with details which copy Cabalistic imagery to a remarkable extent; one whole class of such tales involves the route to heaven being opened by an archer who shoots an arrow into the dome of the sky, a second that sticks into the nock-end of the first, and so on to form a ladder of arrows all the way to the ground.

Of the experiences and entities commonly met on this Path, the only one which may need comment is the centaur and his kin. Beings half animal and half human are a symbol of balance between apparent opposites, but they also suggest the relationship between the biological and spiritual sides of humanity - a relationship which has much to do with the other two Paths which rise up to Tiphareth.

Path 26, the Path of Ayin

Letter of the Path: ע, Ayin (Eye).

Name of God: ADNI, Adonai.

Astrological Correspondence:
         Capricorn, the Fish-Goat.

Tarot Correspondence:
         Trump XV, the Devil.

Esoteric Title: Lord of the Gates of Matter, Child of the Forces of Time.

Path Text: *"The Twenty-sixth Path is called the Renovating Intelligence, because the Holy God renews by it all the changing things which are renewed by the creation of the world."*

Mythological Principle:
         Meeting with the Powers of Life.

Experiences of the Path:
         Wild and desolate landscapes; storms and other expressions of the forces of nature; submergence of human consciousness in the animal self.

Entities of the Path: Wild animals; feral humans or half-human creatures; satyrs and other wilderness spirits. Magical Image: An arch of a deep indigo colour, bearing the letter Ayin in brilliant white on its keystone. The door in the arch bears the image of Trump XV.

Colours: in Atziluth - indigo.
         in Briah - black.
         in Yetzirah - blue-black.
         in Assiah - cold dark grey, nearing black.

The Path of Ayin, in the metaphor mentioned earlier, is one of two fierce guardians upon the narrow way to Tiphareth. Like the Path of Nun, its opposite and complement, this Path serves to some extent as a barrier to the Cabalist's ascent; in the traditional lore of the magical Cabala, its role is a forbidding one.

It's worth taking a moment to see why this should be so. On the Tree of Life, the way individual Paths relate to the major dynamics of the Tree has much to say to their energetics and their character. A transverse Path like the Path of Peh balances intensely polarized energies because of its horizontal route; a vertical Path like the Path of Samech bears the pure energy of one of the Pillars between external polarities, and its balance has a different (and less explosive) quality.

Of the diagonal Paths, eight run from higher Spheres on one of the side Pillars inward to lower Spheres on the Middle Pillar. As channels for the power of Creation, these Paths form descending triads which impart balance to the universe; as routes for the upward journey of Redemption, they allow levels of consciousness gained along the Middle Pillar to be extended and differentiated through the powers of Force and Form. In both functions, these Paths tend to establish and maintain balance of themselves, and they are thus more easily traveled than either horizontal or vertical Paths.

The four remaining diagonal Paths, on the other hand, move from higher Spheres on the Middle Pillar to lower Spheres out to the side. As descending Paths, they establish new dualities, which must then be resolved into balanced triads; as routes of ascent, they seek to rise from the conflict of opposites to a resolution on a higher level. In both functions, these Paths involve a disruption of stability and balance, and there is thus a certain built-in difficulty in traveling them.

The 11th and 12th Paths, at the top of the Tree, are less strongly affected by this factor because they exist above the Abyss, in the realm of unity. The 24th and 26th Paths do not have this advantage. They are made additionally difficult by the fact that they cross the Veil, one of the primary barriers on the Tree, and so their resolution in Tiphareth is far from an automatic matter!

For this reason, these two Paths are among the major challenges the Cabalist faces in the work of Redemption. Even if the relatively safe techniques of meditation and Pathworking are used as the principal methods of ascent, there are certain risks involved in traveling them, and certain traps to be watched for in their symbolism and theory.

*　　*　　*

These points should be kept in mind as we turn to the symbolism of the Path of Ayin. Many of the correspondences of the Path have two faces, one dark, one bright. The dark side refers to the dangers mentioned above, and to some related factors in human experience which we'll discuss shortly. The bright side refers to the macrocosmic role of the Path, its nature as a channel of energies linking the harmony of Tiphareth to the patterns of Hod. The two are respectively the threat and the promise of the Path: the danger that must be faced in order to travel this Path, and the goal to be won at its end.

This duality comes through with great clarity in the first of the Path's symbols. The Letter of the Path is Ayin, which means "eye". The image of an open eye conveys little to most people in today's developed societies, but in the Western world until quite recent times this symbol often represented the Evil Eye, a destructive power by which sorcerers could curse and kill with a single glance. This belief, though it took strange forms, was founded on a reality; magical methods to cause depression, sickness and death have been common in every culture, and the use of the gaze as a vehicle for such things is far from rare.

From its associations with destructive magic, the eye has often been used as a potent symbol of spiritual evil. At the same time, the eye has another set of meanings, which touch the opposite end of the ethical spectrum. As a symbol of perception and awareness, it has been used to represent the human soul; from its roundness and its connection with light, it has often been a symbol of the sun; and from this latter, in ages when people were more comfortable with material images of ultimate Reality, it came to be a common symbol of God. To this day, it appears in this role on the seal on the back of every US $1 bill.

How is this duality to be reconciled? When one symbol can be used to represent both the divine and the demonic, it's a safe bet that the teachings expressed through it are of a fair degree of complexity. Still, there is a common theme to both these uses of the symbol, and that theme is power.

The Path of Ayin brings the energies of Tiphareth to the Pillar of Severity, and it does so in the part of the Tree which is accessible to ordinary consciousness. It can be understood, in an important sense, as Tiphareth's formative power, its ability to bind and limit. From below the Veil, this power has its roots in mystery, in realms of consciousness which can only be grasped in the most indirect of ways; from above the Veil, it is a natural function of the transcendent balance of the Sphere of the Sun.

The magician who ascends to the Tiphareth level gains the ability to make use of this power, to one degree or another. Much depends, though, on how that ascent is handled, for the process (as we'll show later) is not an all-or-nothing matter; glimpses and brief periods of heightened consciousness precede the full opening of the Veil. Even a glimpse of Tiphareth is a source of power, however. Reached by way of the balanced path of Samech, that glimpse will tend to awaken powers in a more or less balanced way, a way which brings the human soul into increased harmony with the higher realms of being. Reached by way of the unbalanced and unbalancing Path of Ayin, by contrast, that glimpse will open up further possibilities for imbalance. In particular, to work toward Tiphareth from the Pillar of Severity will tend to awaken powers of control, binding and domination: the tools of sorcery.

This Path, then, is preeminently the Path of the sorcerer, the magician whose highest goal is his or her own personal power. To choose such a goal is to shut off the possibilities for further ascent on the Tree, for balance is the price and prerequisite of the work of Redemption; still, it's a choice which has been made (and is still made) by a significant number of magicians. From the perspective of the magical Cabala, their decision is at once tragic and rather silly - tragic in that it sets in motion balancing processes in the macrocosm which exact their own price from the sorcerer, a price most often paid in suffering; silly in that, by grasping at the petty powers of selfish and destructive magic, the sorcerer loses the far greater powers to be gained beyond the Veil. Still, it's part of the nature of things that human beings have the right to their own choices.

*　　*　　*

The next several symbols express a different aspect of the Path's meaning. They also share a common focus on the element of Earth, the most stable and the most restricting of the four - and the most appropriate to this Path, by which the energies of creation stream outwards from the Sphere of harmony and balance, toward the last, most developed expression of the Pillar of Form.

The Name of God attributed to the Path of Ayin, therefore, is Adonai, the Name assigned to Earth. The astrological correspondence, similarly, is Capricorn, one of the three signs of the Zodiac which are attributed to the element of Earth. In astrology, the Capricorn personality is conservative and practical; at best it is constructive and preserving, at worst miserly and obsessed with forms. Its traditional symbol is a bizarre composite creature, the fish-goat, which has the front half of a goat and the back half of a sea-serpent. This can be understood, and correctly, as a reference to the myriad forms taken by biological life in our world - a reference which we will consider shortly - but it contains another set of meanings as well. The sign Capricorn is ruled by the planet Saturn, and in ancient times the image of the fish-goat was used not for the sign but for the planet. Here, to a great extent, these older meanings are appropriate.

The symbolism of Saturn will be familiar, at least in part, since the Path of Tau is attributed to it. As you'll remember, the experience central to Saturn is the experience of time, and this is true on the Path of Ayin as well as on that of Tau. The two Paths are not identical, however. On the Path of Tau, free of other influences, time is sensed as duration pure and simple: the constant onward flow, intangible but always present, in which we live just as a fish lives in water. In practical terms, time in this sense manifests itself as process, and in particular as the sometimes achingly slow process of spiritual growth. On the Path of Ayin, on the other hand, the sense of time is influenced by the symbolism of Earth and the movement toward the side of form, and so it comes through not simply as time but as time past, time as history. In practical terms, this aspect of time manifests itself as the influence of history, the weight of the past pressing on every choice and on every new thing. Here time becomes the ally of form; here is the home of the truth - partial, like the truth of every unbalanced Path, but true nonetheless - that "there is nothing new under the sun"

✳   ✳   ✳

Some sense of the influence of history, certainly, will be needed in order to make sense of the next part of the symbolism. The Tarot correspondence of the Path of Ayin is Trump XV, the Devil. This Trump shows a conventional image of the Devil, horned, clawed, and hairy, standing on a cubical block of stone. Depending on the version, the Devil may hold various things in his hands - an inverted torch, a cornucopia - or may gesture in some symbolic manner. Two lesser demons, horned and tailed, stand to either side of him, and chains fasten them to the cubical stone.

This figure has often been seen as an image of the spiritual evil mentioned earlier, and it has that significance in certain senses. The Devil of Christian mythology, though, is only the latest in a very long line of similar figures, many of whom have little to do with evil in the usual sense of that word. If you've had any exposure to Greek mythology, for example, you will have little trouble recognizing the figure of Pan, the horned and hooved god of nature whose name literally means "all".

The worship of the Horned God, lord of animals and of the forces of the natural world, can be traced to prehistoric times, and has left some remarkable traces in the world's religions. His worship often occurs with that of the Great Mother; this is appropriate enough, as Binah is the Sphere corresponding to mother-goddesses, and Binah as Saturn plays such a large role in this Path.

The Horned God stands at the interface between the human and the animal, ruling the many aspects of human life which we have in common with other living things. From one viewpoint, this is his (and our) strength, but it is a strength which contains a critical weakness, the weakness of imbalance. Human beings share many characteristics with the animal realm, but we are animals only in part. To lose sight of the difference here is to falsify human nature and human potential - and it is symptomatic that modern scientific ideologies, which begin from Hod, routinely make just this error.

It may also be worth noting that the desire for power which motivates the sorcerer is itself biological in nature: the normal animal drive for dominance, bloated and distorted by humanity's loss of the balancing functions of instinct through the Fall. Here again, the dominance of one half of the human totality leads to the loss of humanity in the best sense of that word.

✳   ✳   ✳

Next in the Path's symbolism is the Esoteric Title, which sums up much of the material just covered while adding another element of its own. As a Path strongly linked to Saturn, the Path of Ayin is very much a "child of the forces of Time," and the Path's correspondence with the element of Earth makes it also a "lord of the gates of matter." At the same time, this second phrase also suggests this Path's functions in the process of death and rebirth, a process which will be examined a little later in this chapter.

The Path Text also has a great deal to do with the Path's connections with Saturn and Earth, but it focuses on the broader effects of these linkages, as well as on the role of the path as the formative power of Tiphareth. As the Renovating Intelligence, the 26th Path functions as a force of stability in the universe - not a stability opposed to change, but rather a stability which includes and moves through change. By renewing "all the changing things" through the continuous process of Creation, the energies of the Path of Ayin have a crucial role in the deeper patterns of balance on the Tree.

The mythological principle, the Meeting with the Powers of Life, refers to legends of human encounter with the archaic forces of nature and instinct, symbolized by magical animals and, especially, by wild men and women - those powerful images of feral humanity which serve as a valuable challenge to our more civilized aspects.

You may notice that the experiences and entities assigned to this Path show similarities with those of the 28th and 29th Paths further down the Tree. Although these are on the other side of the Middle Pillar, seemingly unconnected from the Path of Ayin, the links between its symbolism and theirs are not accidental. Such reflections of imagery from Path to Path and from side to side occur often on the Tree of Life, and rise from subtle balancing processes between the Pillars. It can be useful to keep track of those you notice, and to think about their implications.

Path 24, the Path of Nun

Letter of the Path: נ , Nun (Fish).

Name of God: AL, El.

Astrological Correspondence:
Scorpio, the Scorpion.

Tarot Correspondence:
Trump XIII, Death.

Esoteric Title: Child of the Great Transformers, Lord of the Gates of Death.

Path Text: *"The 24th Path is the Imaginative Intelligence, and it is so called because it gives a likeness to all the similitudes which are created in like manner similar to its own harmonious elegancies."*

Mythological Principle:
Meeting with the Powers of Death.

Experiences of the Path:
Images of death, burial, and decay; travel through deep water, or through blood; visions of the dead and of the future.

Entities of the Path: Skeletons and other death-figures; cold-blooded animals.

Magical Image: An arch of a deep greenish-blue bearing the letter Nun in brilliant white on its keystone. The door in the arch bears the image of Trump XIII.

Colours: in Atziluth - greenish blue.
in Briah - dull brown.
in Yetzirah - very dark brown.
in Assiah - livid indigo-brown, like a beetle's shell.

The 24th Path is the second of the two guardians which wait along the way to Tiphareth. Many of the points raised in the discussion of the first guardian, the 26th Path, apply equally well here; Paths which mirror each other's position on opposite sides of the Tree of Life tend to mirror meanings and symbolism as well. Like the 26th Path, the 24th is inherently unbalancing, because its energetics are oriented outward toward one of the side Pillars rather than inward toward the Middle Pillar. Like the 26th Path, the 24th has symbolic links with the Path of Tau, the underworld journey of time and death. Like the 26th Path, too, the 24th is one of the most difficult to travel of all the Paths, and its symbolism has many of the same elements of danger discussed in the context of the Path of Ayin.

Each of these similarities, in turn, becomes an opposition as the principle of polarity comes into play. Where the 26th Path tends toward imbalance in the direction of form, restriction, rigidity, the 24th tends toward imbalance in the opposing direction of force, extension, dispersal; the one brings imprisonment, the other disintegration. Where the connection between the 26th and 32nd Paths is expressed through the symbolism of time, that between the 24th and 32nd Paths functions primarily through the imagery of death. Death, too, is the heart of the experience of the 24th Path. Where the 26th Path calls up concepts of supernatural evil and sorcery from the far past, the 24th Path shows the Cabalist the one future event each of us must someday face.

This confrontation with death brings with it an awareness of the reality and the universal nature of change. To the traveler on this Path, nothing is constant or permanent except change itself, and even the most enduring of created things is seen as a transitory presence caught in the midst of its passing away. This sense of transience dominates the experience of the 24th Path, tying into the Path symbolism at every point. Like the sense of enduring pattern that shapes so much of the 26th Path, the perception of transience is a partial truth, accurate on its own terms but misleading if applied too broadly.

$$* \quad * \quad *$$

The symbolism of this Path builds on many of these issues in a number of ways, some obvious, some subtle. The Letter of the Path is Nun, which means "fish". To the people of ancient times, the fish was at once resource, symbol, and paradox; warmth and breath were the proofs of life known to the ancient world, and yet the fish had neither but was obviously alive. Because of this, and because it flourished in a world in which no human being could live, it became a symbol of the afterlife, of the mysteries of the after-death state. In the mythologies of many coastal peoples, the land of the dead is located across or beneath the sea, and the harvesting of fish for food has been seen as a gift from the dead to the living, repaid by the living when they themselves go to join the dead.

The letter Nun also possesses a more specific role in the context of Cabalistic theory. The Path of Nun is the Path of the Fish, while the 28th Path, the Path of Tzaddi, is the Path of the Fish-hook. Implied here is a close and specific relationship between these two Paths, a relationship of control.

The 24th Path, for several reasons, is a Path of high and turbulent energies. Its movement away from balance and toward the side of Force and its place along the route of the Lightning Flash both contribute to this. The balance of the Tree as a whole requires that these energies be brought back in toward the center, toward harmony. All three of the Paths leading up to Netzach from below play a part in this, but the brunt of the work is borne by the Path of Tzaddi. Like a hook and line in the mouth of a fish, the cyclical natural patterns of Tzaddi restrain the unstable energies of Nun, drawing them back in to the Middle Pillar at Yesod.

This detail of symbolism contains an important practical teaching. The 28th Path governs natural cycles and processes, and its symbolism focuses on the direction of these toward goals in the future. This focus is precisely what's needed to master this difficult Path, on any of its levels.

*   *   *

The next two symbols of this Path have largely to do with the elemental attributions of Nun. The first, the Name of God associated with the 24th Path, is AL, pronounced El. A Name that we've seen before, El is assigned to the element of Water, and its link with the 24th Path comes from this connection. Water, among the elements, symbolizes the emotions, and also ties in well with the fish symbolism of this Path. The imagery of water also suggests the similar imagery of the 29th and 28th Paths, which connect to the 24th by way of Netzach.

The second, the astrological correspondence, is of a more complicated nature. Scorpio, the Scorpion, also corresponds to Water, but is associated with power, passion, sexuality, and violence. It is the great transformative sign of the Zodiac, and in magical lore it is said - unlike any of the other signs - to have three images, representing three different phases of transformation.

The scorpion is the first and lowest of these. Ancient legend tells that a scorpion trapped by a brush fire and unable to escape will sting itself with its own tail, turning its poison on itself to escape the pain of death by fire. Fanciful as it is, this story symbolizes one human response to the transience and change that permeates the world: self-destruction.

The second of the images of Scorpio is the serpent. A serpent in motion winds from side to side in response to the shape of the ground, but its path goes straight toward its goal. It represents the attitude which works with change rather than being overwhelmed by it.

The third and highest of the images of Scorpio is the eagle. According to legend, the eagle is the only creature that can look directly at the sun. In flight, the eagle soars high above the earth, and nothing below is hidden from it. The eagle thus symbolizes the highest human response to the forces of the 24th Path. Its legendary link with the Sun signals a connection with Tiphareth, and in fact this mode of dealing with change - transcending fear of it through personal experience of what is eternal - is one of the gifts of the parting of the Veil.

✳   ✳   ✳

The remainder of the Path symbolism is above all a symbolism of death. As the most drastic change most of us can imagine, its place here is a clear one, and the imagery is anything but subtle about the role of death in the Path.

Thus the Tarot correspondence is Death. In many of the early Tarot decks this card has no name at all - simply a number and a picture. This habit came from nothing more mysterious than the fact that the French word for "death" was considered obscene in the Middle Ages; the starkness of a nameless card fits the quality of this Path well.

The usual image on this Trump corresponds closely to the traditional picture of Death, a grinning skeleton wielding a scythe. Older decks, and some modern ones, show this figure harvesting a grisly crop of cut-off heads and hands. This can be seen as a reference to the end of all human thought and action in death.

It can express another meaning, though, to the observer of alternative spirituality in the West. Just as the Path of Ayin contains a trap which must be faced by the magician in the ascent to Tiphareth - the trap of sorcery - so the Path of Nun has a trap of its own. That trap lacks a common name; for our purposes, we can borrow a term from the language of theology, and call it quietism.

What is quietism? In essence, it is the idea that the spiritual path demands the giving up of all desire and the surrender of the self into a passive relationship with the Higher. In its extreme form, as practiced by some religious movements, it requires the absolute acceptance of everything that happens and the abandonment of all willed action; at this extreme, the quietist does nothing except listen for the "inner voice" of God and obey it without question or thought. More broadly, though, all those teachings which place the individual in a passive role with regard to his or her own spiritual development can be seen as quietist to one degree or another.

In fairness, it must be said that quietist ideas rarely cause the same sort of human suffering that sorcery often generates. On the other hand, quietism is quite as much of an obstacle to the aspiring magician as is sorcery. The work of transformation is precisely that: work. It requires a series of dramatic changes in the relationships between the various parts of the self, and these changes do not happen by themselves. Furthermore, one of the major sources of energy driving this process is precisely the force of human desire, which the quietist seeks to extinguish.

In an important sense, sorcery and quietism thus mirror one another as two sides of one mistake, and that mistake is the failure to reconcile the biological and spiritual sides of the human totality. The sorcerer turns toward the goals of the animal self, and ignores the potentials of the spirit; the quietist turns toward the spirit and ignores the needs of the animal self. Both end in spiritual stagnation. It is as though both seek to chop themselves apart at the neck; the only difference lies in which of the resulting parts they propose to throw away.

This is the lesson hidden in the symbol of the centaur, which plays a role in the mythology and the experience of the Path of Samech. The centaur represents the fusion of spirit and body, transcendent awareness and animal nature, the lessons of the nonphysical levels and those of the physical world. Where the sorcerer seeks merely to fulfill desires, and the quietist to extinguish them, the way of the centaur - and a good part of the way up the Path of Samech to Tiphareth - is to balance them with the needs and perspectives of the spirit, so that the body receives what it needs without usurping the roles of the higher aspects of the self. Ultimately, and critically, the desires of the animal self are themselves reflections of forces which exist at higher levels of being, and they can be brought into harmony with these higher forces in the perfect balance of Tiphareth.

*   *   *

The next part of the symbolism, the Esoteric Title, reflects its equivalent on the 26th Path to a high degree. The one is the Lord of the Gates of Matter, the other the Lord of the Gates of Death; the one is the Child of the Forces of Time, the other the Child of the Great Transformers. The 26th Path can thus be seen as a power of the realm of Form, linked with matter and duration, while the 24th takes on the corresponding role of a power of the realm of Force, linked with the separation of spirit from matter and the process of change.

There is another, more specific meaning contained in these titles, though. As Lord of the Gates of Matter, the Path of Ayin represents that set of transformations which bring a soul into incarnation; as Lord of the Gates of Death, the Path of Nun represents that complementary set which bring the soul back out again. The entire cycle from death to rebirth can in fact be traced out on the Tree, and doing so provides a useful model for the process.

We can begin in Malkuth, with the death of the physical body. From there the cycle rises up the Path of Qoph. This Path corresponds to the first phase of the after-death process, in which the higher phases of the self detach from the etheric body. This separation, sometimes called the Second Death, can fail to occur, and such failures are among the causes of ghosts. During the three days or so that the separation is said to take, the soul remains in a realm of illusion, where imaginary beings and events ranging from the pleasant to the horrible appear and disappear.

The completion of the Second Death leaves the soul in Netzach, where the life just completed is evaluated in emotional terms, an experience which has helped to give rise to myths of heaven and hell. From there, by way of the Path of Nun, these emotional energies are themselves resolved back into clear awareness, and the freed soul itself returns to its center in Tiphareth.

At this point the process of death gives way to that of rebirth. Leaving Tiphareth by the Path of Ayin, the soul takes on the form-creating powers as well as the sharp limitations of that Path, and in Hod comprehends in intellectual terms the pattern of the life to come. From Hod, the soul then descends into a new body in Malkuth by way of the Path of Shin, coming under the power of the forces governing material experience.

In tradition, it's said that there is another way in which this process can be carried out, one based on certain deep transformations of the various bodies or layers of the self, and linked in Cabalistic lore to the state of the Inner Plane adepts mentioned in an earlier chapter. This alternative way can also be traced on the Tree. It has its beginning in Yesod instead of Malkuth, because the etheric body rather than the physical one is the focus of experience and the anchoring point of the self. It passes to Netzach by way of the Path of Tzaddi, and then to Tiphareth by the Path of Nun; it descends from Tiphareth by the Path of Ayin to Hod, and from Hod to Yesod by the Path of Resh. It thus avoids both the illusions of Qoph and the constraints of Shin, and allows the process of rebirth to take place under conscious direction.

*   *   *

It is with the Path Text that some of the deeper implications of this Path come out. The Path of Nun is here described in several terms - the Imaginative Intelligence, harmony - which seem to refer not to it but to the Sphere Tiphareth at its upper end. It is also imaged as giving a "likeness to all the similitudes" - that is, to all things similar - "...to its harmonious elegancies."

The archaic language of the Text makes the meaning contained here more obscure than it needs to be. What is being said is that the Path of Nun is a pattern for many other things; it gives its image to a range of "similitudes" or reflections. That image is the image of death. All change in the universe, in this sense, is a reflection of death, and as change is universal so is death; the blank gaze of the Reaper's skull looks out at us from everything we see - including our own reflections in the mirror.

Critically, though, the Text does not (as so many people do) portray this as an evil. The image of death is "harmonious," "elegant;" it comes from Tiphareth, not from the Kingdom of Shells. To the magician, certainly, death is a known quantity, and the awareness of death's nearness a useful tool. From the standpoint of the magical Cabala, too, the cycle of death and rebirth can be seen as a model for the opening of the Veil: a radical change, beyond which lies new life.

This is also the lesson of the mythological principle of this Path, the Meeting with the Powers of Death. Any number of legends and folk tales describe an encounter between a living human being and Death personified; one of the great works of Hindu philosophy, the Katha Upanishad, uses just such an encounter as its framing story. One very common feature in such legends is that the mortal who handles such an encounter in the right way receives a gift from Death. The nature of the gift varies in the legends, but in a broader sense the gift of death is always wisdom.

Tiphareth, the Sixth Sphere

Title:	ThPARTh, Tiphareth (Beauty).
Name of God:	YHVH ALVH VDAaTh, Tetragrammaton Eloah va-Daath (Lord God of Knowledge).
Archangel:	MKAL, Michael (He Who Is As God).
Angelic Host:	MLKIM, Malakim (Kings).

Astrological Correspondence:

ShMSh, Shemesh (the Sun).

Tarot Correspondence:

the four Sixes and four Knights or Princes of the pack.

Elemental Correspondence:

Air.

Path Text:

"The Sixth Path is called the Mediating Intelligence, because in it are multiplied the influxes of the Emanations, for it causes that influence to flow into all the reservoirs of the blessings, with which these themselves are united."

Magical Images: A naked child with golden hair, standing with its arms upraised; a king in robes and crown of gold, dark-haired, bearded, seated on a throne, holding a sword in his right hand and a wand topped with a lotus blossom in his left; a naked man crucified on a black leafless tree, tied to the tree at wrists and ankles with bloody ropes.

Additional Symbols: The cube, the cross of six squares, the truncated pyramid.

Additional Title: Microprosopus, the Lesser Countenance.

Colours: in Atziluth - clear rose pink.

in Briah - golden yellow.

in Yetzirah - rich salmon-pink.

in Assiah - golden amber.

Correspondence in the Microcosm:

the imagination in Ruach.

Correspondence in the Body:
                    The solar plexus.
Grade of Initiation: 5=6, Adeptus Minor.
Negative Power: ThGRIRVN, Tagiriron (the Disputers).

With Tiphareth, the route of the magician's ascent reaches the heart and nerve center of the Tree of Life. Set at the Tree's exact midpoint, Tiphareth functions as the primary balancing and harmonizing power within the structure of meshed realities which the Tree maps out. Each of the other Spheres, except Malkuth alone, links with Tiphareth directly, and polarities and symmetries passing through Tiphareth shape the whole fabric of the Tree in ways ranging from the dramatic to the subtle; energies pairing Chesed and Hod, Geburah and Netzach, and Yesod and the quasi-Sphere Daath harmonize in Tiphareth; every Sphere of the two side Pillars, every one of the horizontal Paths of the Tree, trace out polarizations of energy which resolve in the sixth Sphere.

Seen from another standpoint, of course, Tiphareth is also the level of awareness at which most of the techniques of the Cabalistic magician take aim. From still another, in turn, it is the faculty of imagination in the ruach, the principal tool of magic, the power with which consciousness assembles the world out of the million unrelated perceptions provided by the other parts of the self.

Perhaps the most useful of these various ways of looking at the sixth Sphere, though, is also one of the simplest. Tiphareth is the middle of the line connecting Kether and Malkuth, the halfway point between absolute unity and the infinite diversity of the world of ordinary experience. In theological language, it is the midpoint between the human and the divine; in a more philosophical mode of speaking, it is the point of contact between the experience of the self as an individual and the experience of the self as an aspect of the unity of all things.

Traditions of Cabalism influenced by Christian mythology have identified Tiphareth with Jesus as a way of suggesting the same point. In the magical Cabala, however, the implications of this idea go in directions that have little in common with Christian orthodoxy. To the Cabalistic magician, the point of contact between himself or herself and the infinite unity symbolized by Kether is not to be found in a person who lived two thousand years ago. Nor is it to be found in the power structure of a church - or, for that matter, of a magical Order. It exists, constantly and necessarily, within each of us. Once the Tiphareth level of awareness has been opened up to the conscious self, this contact becomes a gate between the personal and the infinite, and as higher levels are awakened in turn the magician learns to pass through the gate at will and to live and work magic on both sides.

This dance of interaction between individuality and unity is also, in a broader sense, the resolution of all those conflicts which shape the expressions of the Tree below the Veil: nature versus culture, animal versus spiritual, and so on. From the perspective of the sixth Sphere, all of these become different possibilities within the experience of individual existence, more appropriate in some circumstances, less so in others. All, in turn, can be understood as expressions of some aspect of Kether's unity, and therefore partial and incomplete by themselves. Like the human and animal halves of the Path of Samech's centaur-symbol, these apparent opposites join together into one whole.

*　*　*

The symbolism of the sixth Sphere reflects these issues closely. The title of the Sphere, Tiphareth, can be best translated as "beauty". The idea of beauty includes concepts such as harmony, balance, and grace - all closely linked to Tiphareth - but as an experience it cannot be classified in such cut-and-dried terms. Attempts to define the essence of beauty have driven philosophers to distraction for centuries. To the mystic and the magician, this is only to be expected, for in esoteric terms beauty can be best understood as a kind of transparency to the Higher; a thing of beauty expresses nonphysical experience in (or, rather, through) material form. In many ways, the experience of beauty is a close relative to the experience of contact with the Tiphareth level of being - an experience often called "enlightenment." In great works of artistic or natural beauty, this relation can approach identity.

The Name of God attributed to Tiphareth is YHVH ALVH VDAaTh, Tetragrammaton Eloah va-Daath, and may be very roughly translated as "Lord God of Knowledge". A better if somewhat looser interpretation might be "God made manifest in the sphere of Mind." This Name is the longest of any on the Tree of Life, and one of two made up of three separate elements. The meanings expressed in this Name are correspondingly complex.

We can begin untangling some of these meanings by studying this Name of God in terms of its elements. The first, YHVH, is of course the Tetragrammaton, the primary Cabalistic image of reality as a creative process. The third, VDAaTh, is the name of Daath, Knowledge, the transitional quasi-Sphere set in the Abyss, with the prefix "va-" (roughly, "of") added to it for grammatical reasons.

Between these two is the second element, ALVH, Eloah. This is a Name of God in its own right, derived from the same root as the Names El and Elohim. Of all the Divine Names used in the Cabala, Eloah is probably closest in meaning to the English proper noun God, with the same connotation of a single personified deity. It thus represents the conjunction of human and divine we've already discussed, the idea of the human individual as a symbol for the absolute reality beyond the Three Veils. This idea has already been introduced in another form, that of Adam Cadmon, but these two differ slightly in emphasis; Adam Cadmon is the divinized Human, Eloah the humanized God.

A further meaning of the Name Eloah can be grasped by considering the letters that make it up. The first two letters, Aleph and Lamed, express the same idea of perfect freedom in perfect balance that is shown in the first part of the Name Elohim. The last two letters, Vau and He, symbolize the same concept of progressive change leading to a new pattern of reality that appears in the second half of the Tetragrammaton. The Name Eloah, then, can be thought of as the product of the joining of these two Names - their child, to use the language of myth.

More broadly, Tiphareth can be seen as the product or child of the basic "masculine" and "feminine" energies of existence, whether these are symbolized by Chokmah and Binah, by the Names YHVH and ALHIM, or by the Yod and Heh of the Tetragrammaton itself. The Divine Name ALVH is an effective expression of this. In its role as

Name of God for Tiphareth, it unites with the Tetragrammaton to stress its connection with the primary creative Power, and with the title of Daath to stress its place as a product of the Supernals.

The next three symbols all express variations on a single theme, the idea of Tiphareth as the central ruling force on the Tree of Life. Though each of these symbols applies to a different one of the four Worlds, all express the same patterns in these different contexts.

Thus, the Archangel of Tiphareth is Michael, who is also Archangel of the element of Fire. The name Michael literally means "similar to God"; as the Briah correspondence of Tiphareth, the reflection of the sixth Sphere in the receptive structures of consciousness, it represents the closest approximation or image of reality itself which can exist in human awareness below the Abyss, an image in which - in Cabalistic theory as well as in Biblical mythology - we ourselves are made. In another sense, one developed by some of the major Cabalistic magicians of the Renaissance, this approximation of the Ultimate can be understood as the presence or reflection of God within the created universe, and so as a second, creative power shaping the world of human experience; this idea and its implications will be explored a little later.

The two following symbols are rather less complex. The Angels assigned to Tiphareth are the Malakim, the Kings; their symbolism is simple and exact, using human political structures of an earlier age to suggest ideas of rulership and centrality, and thus of the processes of centered consciousness vital to the functioning of the imagination. In magical practice, the Malakim are considered to have rulership over the four elements and the elemental spirits who inhabit them. The astrological correspondence of Tiphareth is the Sun; even in the days when the Earth was believed to be the center of the universe, the Sun was recognized as the source of light and life, and the most important of the traditional planets, and traditional astronomy put it exactly halfway between Earth and the sphere of the stars.

✳   ✳   ✳

Despite its convoluted language, the Path Text for Tiphareth deals with the sixth Sphere's function in a straightforward manner. Both "influxes" and "influence" here refer to what we've called the flows of energy on the Tree of Life, and primarily the descent of power down the Lightning Flash from its source in Kether. Both "Emanations" and "reservoirs of blessings" here refer to the ten Spheres of the Tree. The literal meaning of the Text, then, is that the Sphere Tiphareth rules the patterns of energy flow through the Tree of Life as a whole. Its role as the Mediating Intelligence and as the image of the Imageless gives it power to mediate between the ten Spheres and the forces which ultimately create and sustain them.

There is a further implication in this Text, one which brings up an aspect of the Tree of Life that has not yet been discussed. To say that in Tiphareth "are multiplied the influxes of the Emanations" implies that the sixth Sphere has a part to play in the transformation of the Tree's energy flows from the simplicity of the Lightning Flash to the complexity of the Serpent. In fact, Tiphareth's role here is primary. The Paths collectively, as a whole, derive from the sixth Sphere and are functions of its specific power.

To understand this fully, it's necessary to keep in mind that the Tree of Life diagram which we've been using is merely one rather abstract way of representing the dance of energies that makes up the totality of human experience. The Spheres are not separate from one another in any real sense, least of all the spatial one suggested by the Tree diagram; each one is present in all of the others, and all ten are present at once in every aspect of existence. It's because of this that a Path connecting Malkuth to Hod can at the same time be a function of the energies of Tiphareth, and that your experience of this same Path (in Pathworking, for example) can take place in Yesod's realm of images and subtle forces.

Older writings on the Cabala suggested something of this aspect of Tiphareth's role by way of images borrowed from Biblical sources. As you may recall from the discussion of the way of Creation, the two Trees of Eden have Cabalistic significance; the Tree of Knowledge of Good and Evil can be assigned to Malkuth, the Tree of Life to the Spheres above it and especially to Tiphareth. The serpent of the Genesis myth, the Dragon corresponding to the Negative Powers, in this symbolism is the Serpent of the Tree of Knowledge. The Tree of

Life, in turn, has its own serpent, that which forms the ascending route of the Paths, and this latter is also the brazen serpent Nehushtan which, in Biblical mythology, Moses placed on a pole to cure the Israelites from snakebite in the wilderness. The serpent on the pole is the pattern of Paths structured around the Middle Pillar, symbol of the whole way of Redemption, and the snake whose bite it cures is in one sense the Serpent of the Tree of Knowledge.

✷   ✷   ✷

The next three headings are meant to introduce some of the vast body of associated symbols which have gathered around Tiphareth in Cabalistic lore. Of all of the Spheres, the sixth has by far the most complex symbolism. Partly, this is because the Tiphareth level of awareness is the primary goal of most systems of mysticism and transformative magic, and as a result it has attracted more attention than some of the other levels. In addition, though, Tiphareth's role as a harmonizing force causes it to appear in many different aspects, each appropriate to the polarities involved.

One measure of this complexity is that, alone of the Spheres, Tiphareth has not one but three Magical Images assigned to it. These images have an enormous range of implications, both in Cabalistic theory and in magical practice; in their most basic sense they represent Tiphareth's roles in relation to the Supernals, to the Spheres from Chesed to Yesod, and to Malkuth respectively, but they go far beyond this. They are reflected in a great many of the myths and religious traditions of the past, as well as in the imagery of many sects of Christianity.

It's worth dwelling briefly on this point, because the apparently Christian nature of much of Tiphareth's imagery has made many people uncomfortable with this part of the Cabala. The success of Christianity in the ancient world was based on the fact that Christian imagery, theology and myth all borrowed a great deal from the older traditions of Classical paganism. Divine child, solar king and sacrificed god are images of vast age, and even the fine details of their Christian version often come from pagan sources.

One good example is crucifixion. As mentioned in Chapter 7, this terrible method of execution was not a Roman invention; it dates back ultimately to traditions of divine kingship, in which the king became a human sacrifice at the end of a certain period. Two different traditions might govern such a king's death; some were decapitated or dismembered and their fragments scattered over the fields; others were suspended in the air, and despatched by some means which did not let their blood touch the earth. The first type often appears in the myths together with a sword and a shield, stone or platter, the second with a spear and a cup. In Christian mythology, they are represented by John the Baptist and Jesus, respectively; their pagan equivalents are innumerable.

Crucifixion and hanging were the most common methods used to arrange the latter form of sacrifice, though there were others; the prize for the strangest certainly goes to the Welsh, whose Celtic zest for the bizarre had one mythic sacrificial king impaled by a spear while standing stark naked on a streambank with one foot balanced on the rim of a cauldron and the other resting on the back of a goat! With the passage of time, both of the former methods (although, fortunately, not the latter) became ordinary methods of execution, but enough of the old lore survived into Roman times to give the Christian icon of the Crucifixion a subtle but deep connotation in many minds. In turn, of course, the history of Christianity has loaded the cross with a great deal more in the way of meaning, much of it inappropriate to the work of the Cabalistic magician. There were, however, many different methods of crucifixion, and the magical image suggested here uses one which will be less likely to call up unintended connections.

The reason why the imagery of crucifixion has been used for Tiphareth's sacrificial element (rather than, say, replaced with the high strangeness of Llew Llaw Gyffes' death on goatback) will become plain when the additional symbols of Tiphareth are concerned. The cube and the cross of six squares are actually two forms of the same symbol, because a cube unfolded makes a six-square cross. The six sides of the cube and squares of the cross relate these symbols to Tiphareth in numerical terms, but their relationship to each other is by far the more important factor. The cube's stability and solidity can be seen as a reference to Malkuth, but unfolded it becomes the sacrificial symbol of

Tiphareth. Implied here is the whole tradition of the Fall, the human soul bound to the cross of purely material experience; in turn, the image also symbolizes the first stage of the journey of Seth and the work of Redemption it represents, while the King represents the second stage and the radiant Child the third.

After these complexities, the truncated pyramid provides a breathing space of simplicity. A truncated pyramid is, simply, a pyramid which has had its top cut off, leaving a flat square top. Here the point of the pyramid symbolizes Kether, the square base Malkuth; the removal of the point represents the hiddenness of the Supernals, and the flat top's location between point and base expresses Tiphareth's intermediate function.

$$* \quad * \quad *$$

The additional title given in the table is another matter. The word "Microprosopus" means "the small face" or, in the more ornate language of older Cabalistic writings, the Lesser Countenance, and it represents a subtle and important concept in the Cabalistic understanding of existence.

We've seen that the absolute Reality behind all experience is impossible to define, or even to perceive directly, and seen also that what we can know or guess about it identifies it with that transcendent, transforming power which mystics have called God. In the Cabala, the closest human approach to this Reality is symbolized by Kether, and in a more abstract sense the Reality itself in its ten aspects is represented by the various Names of God. But there is another representation as well, less direct but more accessible to human consciousness.

This third image of Reality is the reflection of the first below the Abyss. It's an old adage that a whole is greater than the sum of its parts. Similarly, below the Abyss, where the totality of the Infinite is refracted like light through a prism into a spectrum of individual beings and things, there remains a unity which relates all these things together. Its harmonizing role links it to Tiphareth, but it is present in all seven of the lower Spheres and can be perceived from any of them. When human beings do perceive it, they generally describe the experience as that of "seeing God," but this is only partly accurate, for the Lesser Countenance is a reflection of a reflection, and colored by the Sphere from which it is perceived. (This is the origin of many of the world's religious disagreements.)

Until the Abyss is faced, on the other hand, this is the closest approach the human mind can make to the Supernals, and an experience worth seeking. So long as its limitations are understood, and the dangers of a literal interpretation of the experience remembered, the vision of the Lesser Countenance is an important step on the path of initiation; the method of magical prayer, by which this may be sought, is the subject of a later chapter.

∗   ∗   ∗

The dangers and limitations just mentioned, on the other hand, take us from the highest to the lowest aspects of Tiphareth's symbolism, for these are the keys to understanding the Negative Power of the sixth Sphere.

The Tagiriron or Disputers are traditionally pictured as huge giants wrestling with one another. Their meaning is twofold, for - like any other aspect of the Spheres between the Veil and the Abyss - they appear in an indirect form below the Veil, but in a direct form above it. Below the Veil, their meaning is clear enough; they stand for arrogance, that attitude which sees the self as the sun around which the rest of the universe rotates. This is a common failing of magicians, as it is of all those whose creative work is central to their own lives; still, the habit of arrogance is a denial of unity, and thus a serious roadblock on the way to the higher reaches of human experience.

There's a tendency, as mentioned in the last chapter, for dualistic habits of thinking in our culture to make virtues and vices seem like the opposite ends of a spectrum, when it's more useful to think of virtue as a point of balance between unhealthy opposites. The issue of arrogance is a case in point. The toxic arrogance of classical Roman culture drove the early Christians to the opposite extreme of morbid humility and self-abasement, to the point that hatred of the self was considered the foundation of all virtue. In recent times this process has repeated itself in the other direction, as people disgusted by Christian self-hatred have headed back toward the other extreme. Self-respect, however, is neither arrogance nor abasement, but balanced self-knowledge joined to a recognition of the place of the self within unity.

Above the Veil, by contrast, the Tagiriron stand for something more insidious. The spiritual path, like anything human, has its destructive possibilities. We can think of these as the sicknesses or pathologies of the path, and they can be symbolized by the six Negative Powers which exist above the Veil. Three of those Powers, those assigned to Spheres between the Veil and the Abyss, stand for pathologies in the relationship between the magician and the world; the other three, those assigned to the Supernals, stand for the much deeper pathologies which affect the relationship between the magician and the Infinite.

The first of these to be faced is the Tagiriron, and this confrontation often arises from the gradual nature of the opening of the Veil. For this rarely takes place all at once; rather, in the course of regular practice, brief glimpses of the Tiphareth level of awareness begin to come through, often unexpectedly. These become more frequent and more sustained with further work, until finally it becomes possible to enter the Tiphareth level at will. In the interval, though, these glimpses provide higher-level insights to a mind which may then be left to deal with them on lower levels alone.

So long as these insights are treated as simple personal experiences, all is likely to be well. Too often, though, the power contained in such perceptions leads them to be treated as revelations from God, to be believed absolutely and where possible forced down other people's throats as well. The result is that particularly toxic form of fanaticism which seems to be the province of the failed mystic, in which disagreement with the "truth" is the worst of sins, to be stopped by any means available. Large religious movements have been born out of this process, and too often the intolerance at their core has been reflected in lakes of human blood.

Glimpses of the realm beyond the Veil have a part to play in certain kinds of insanity as well; magic and madness are not so far apart as many magicians like to think. They are also a constant occupational hazard of the religious mystic, who is often warned explicitly in traditional texts to regard any such glimpse as a delusion and a snare. This latter attitude is an extreme, though, and an unnecessary one. So long as these "tremblings of the Veil" are recognized for what they are - transitional experiences, not final revelations - the danger represented by the Tagiriron can be avoided and the potentials of the higher levels of the self achieved.

Path 23, the Path of Mem

Letter of the Path: מ , Mem (Water).
Name of God: AL, El.
Astrological Correspondence:
                         Water.
Tarot Correspondence:
                         Trump XII, the Hanged Man.
Esoteric Title: Spirit of the Mighty Waters.
Path Text: *"The Twenty-third Path is the Stable Intelligence,*
and   *it is so called because it has the virtue of consistency*
                         among all numerations."
Mythological Principle:
                         Self-sacrifice.
Experiences of the Path:
                         Images of water in its various forms, and
                         particularly of the ocean; travel through
                         underwater caves; images of drowned people,
                         sunken ships, and lost cities of the Atlantis
                         type.
Entities of the Path: Spirits of elemental Water; underwater
                         phantoms; the Drowned Giant.
Magical Image: An arch of pure deep blue, bearing the letter
                         Mem in brilliant white upon its keystone. The
                         door in the arch bears the image of Trump
                         XII.
Colours: in Atziluth - deep blue.
                         in Briah - sea green.
                         in Yetzirah - deep olive green.
                         in Assiah - white, flecked with purple.

The Path of Mem is the first of two Paths leading up to Geburah, the central Sphere of the Pillar of Severity, and it is also one of two paths which form that Pillar on the Tree. In its role as part of the process of Creation, it forms the channel by which the power of Geburah takes shape in the intricate patterns of Hod; in its role as one of the routes of Redemption, it opens the way by which the intellect can overcome its limitations and become a vehicle for the workings of the will.

Both these aspects of the Path are strongly influenced by its position on the Tree of Life. Since it runs vertically along one of the Pillars, it is in balance in terms of the Tree's horizontal polarities; at the same time, since its place is all the way over to one side, this balance is of a peculiar type. On the Pillar of Form itself, the opposing principle of Force is effectively absent. The balance that exists on this Path is thus a function of the total dominance of one power; it has perfect stability because no opposing force has the power to influence or disturb it.

This special relationship to the Tree's polarities shapes the Path of Mem in unexpected ways. It gives this Path, in particular, a certain similarity to another of the Paths through the Veil, the Path of Nun. These Paths share elemental symbolism, and relate to similar qualities of passivity and sacrifice. They can be seen as the Severity aspect of the parting of the Veil, since one moves in the direction of the Pillar of Form while the other forms part of it. (In turn, the Paths of Ayin and Kaph represent the Mercy or Force side of the same process.)

In a sense, these four Paths can be thought of as a pair of roads which both fork, one side turning toward Severity, one side toward Mercy. The forks in the roads are at Hod and Netzach, and while the roads themselves are in some sense far apart the branches which go in similar directions have something of the same nature. Still, there are critical differences, and the most important of these derive from the Paths' relationship to Tiphareth. Those Paths which end at the sixth Sphere interact with the overall balance of the Tree. Those which rise to other Spheres do not, and their role in the Tree's energy structure is thus a limited and a somewhat static one. On the other hand, the inherent balance of these latter makes them useful as Paths of ascent, and techniques deriving from their symbolism play a significant part in the toolkit of the Cabalistic magician.

✳   ✳   ✳

The static quality just mentioned is one of the most noticeable factors in the Path of Mem's symbolism. Generally, the symbols of this Path are among the simplest and most consistent of any Path of the Tree of Life. Four of the entries, in fact - the Letter of the Path, the Divine Name, the Astrological Correspondence, and the Esoteric Title - all refer principally to one symbol, the element of Water.

The name of the letter, Mem, means "water", and its form is traditionally said to symbolize waves on a troubled sea; like four other letters, it has a final form used at the end of a word, and this is said to represent the sea in calm weather. The Divine Name, AL, is the Name of God associated with Water; it is also the Name assigned to Chesed, which has Water as its elemental correspondence. The astrological correspondence is, simply enough, elemental Water; the esoteric title is "Spirit of the Mighty Waters". Nowhere else on the Tree do so many symbols speak with a single voice.

With the Tarot Correspondence, the first of the symbols not directly linked with Water, we enter a new phase of the Path's meanings. Trump XII, the Hanged Man, shows the decidedly odd image of a man hanging head downwards by one foot. Decks differ concerning his surroundings; some place him on a cross or a gibbet, while the Golden Dawn deck hangs him in a sea cave, a nice reference to the water symbolism of the Path. Many modern decks, influenced by Christian imagery, put a halo about the man's head and a serene expression on his face.

There has been, as one might expect, an enormous amount of effort put into explaining this odd picture, and as one might equally expect the original meaning of the image has generally been lost in the shuffle. People who were alive during the latter part of World War II, though, may recall it in another context. After the Italian dictator Mussolini was put to death by his people, his body was suspended by its feet in much the same way as the figure on the card. Italian tradition set out this fate for the bodies of those who betrayed their country. It's worth noting that some early Tarot decks named this Trump not the Hanged Man but the Traitor, and showed nothing more exotic than the corpse of an executed man hung up by one ankle and left to rot.

It's important to realize, though, that the Tarot in its original form seems to have had nothing at all to do with the Cabala; the connection between these two has evolved over several hundred years, and brought about certain changes in each. The image of a traitor's body moldering on a gibbet has little to say to the 23rd Path. On the other hand, the modern form of the card has a great deal to say here. It represents the control of Hod's patterns by Geburah's power, the suspension of thought, the intellect disciplined by will. Also, on a more practical level, it represents a route through the Veil which plays a critical role in esoteric work.

In the discussion of the Path of Ayin earlier in this chapter, some of the risks which are part of an intellectual attempt to pass through the Veil were suggested. To return to the metaphor of the forked roads mentioned earlier, the intellect can choose either the direction of Mercy or that of Severity; it can either seek to act or seek to abandon action. Before the Path of Samech is opened, both these choices lead nowhere. To choose action, to try to think one's way through the Veil, is likely to end in sorcery, as an intellectual understanding of the nonphysical becomes the tool of uncontrolled desires fired by reflections of the imagination in Tiphareth. On the other hand, to choose inaction in this context is to risk complete passivity and bring an end to any progress whatever.

The opening of the Veil by the Path of Samech changes this situation utterly. Once Tiphareth is achieved, to choose action is to take conscious hold of the natural creative power of the imagination. In turn, to choose inaction is to still the mind's activity so that what is beyond may manifest itself, and to bring the intellect under the control of the will reflected from Geburah.

On its own, this approach is incomplete and can create imbalance, but it can be readily balanced with the complementary approach of the Path of Kaph on the other side of the Tree, and both brought into relationship with the Path of Samech on the Middle Pillar. Reflected below the Veil, this is the essential formula of meditation. Above the Veil, in its pure form, it becomes the formula of the enlightened consciousness.

* * *

The Path Text is almost entirely free of such complexities. In it, the Path of Mem is called the Stable Intelligence, because "it has the virtue

of consistency among all numerations." These "numerations," as
elsewhere in the Path Texts, are the Spheres of the Tree, and as we've
seen the symbolism of this Path is indeed consistent to a degree no
other aspect of the Tree can equal.

Why should this be so? The answer is partly a function of the static
nature of the Path's energetics, but it has a deeper side as well. The
Path of Mem is essentially passive and receptive in nature, as its Water
symbolism suggests, but this very passivity makes it invulnerable to
change; lacking shape, it cannot be reshaped; it resists nothing and so
cannot be resisted. Whatever passes through it, it remains itself.

This is also one lesson of the mythological principle of this Path, which
is Self-sacrifice. In one sense, this principle is one half of a paradox
which is resolved in Tiphareth, where solar king and sacrificed victim
are one and the same. Still, the myths of self-sacrifice belong principally
to this Path, and can be best understood from its standpoint.

What is sacrifice? The word literally means "making holy." In the
terms we're using, to sacrifice a thing is to move it up the levels of
the Tree, away from manifestation and toward Unity. This involves, in
some sense, the destruction of that thing's presence on the lower level.
But destruction can be understood in many ways, and its more concrete
aspects are rarely useful in practical terms - to say nothing of the ethical
issues involved.

Ultimately, the one truly worthwhile sacrifice is the sacrifice of the
self. This sacrifice is identical with the way of Redemption as it's been
outlined elsewhere in this book. Its difficulty - and it is difficult, perhaps
more difficult than any other human act - is, however, a function of
misunderstanding. The true self is precisely what is not sacrificed. Like
the Path of Mem, what is real in each of us remains untouched by the
transformations which pass through it. The problem, of course, lies in
realizing this.

Traditional lore represented something of this paradox in an image
which is also one of the entities often encountered in work on the
Path of Mem. The Drowned Giant, like all undersea things, represents
something which has passed below the surface of consciousness,
hidden but still present. Where other images of this sort can refer to
forgotten memories or the relics of past phases of biological or spiritual

evolution, the Giant symbolizes the Higher Self microcosmically, and macrocosmically the ultimate Reality itself. In vision he often appears as a vast human shape at the bottom of the sea, drowned but sleeping, dimly seen amid seaweed and mud. Any words he speaks should be noted and pondered.

Path 22, the Path of Lamed

Letter of the Path: ל , Lamed (ox-goad).

Name of God: YHVH, the Tetragrammaton.

Astrological Correspondence:

    Libra, the Scales.

Tarot Correspondence:

    Trump XI, Justice.

Esoteric Title: Daughter of the Lords of Truth, the Holder of the Balances.

Path Text: *"The Twenty-second Path is the Faithful Intelligence, and is so called because by it spiritual virtues are increased, and all dwellers on Earth are nearly under its shadow."*

Mythological Principle:

    The Justice of Heaven.

Experiences of the Path:

    Narrow bridges and pathways; guarded gates and other barriers; images of duality and division; visions of past lives and their influence; trial before nonhuman judges.

Entities of the Path: Angels, people from past lives, gate guardians.

Magical Image: An arch of emerald green, bearing the letter Lamed in brilliant white upon its keystone. The door in the arch bears the image of Trump XI.

Colours: in Atziluth - Emerald green.

    in Briah - Blue.

    in Yetzirah - Deep blue-green.

    in Assiah - Pale green.

From Tiphareth, five Paths rise upward to link the sixth Sphere with the five above it. Three of those Paths cross the Abyss, the greatest of the barriers on the Tree, and pass into realms we can understand only in the most incomplete manner. The other two remain below the Abyss, and so enter into the world of ordinary experience in reflected form. These connect Tiphareth to Geburah and Chesed, the midpoints of the side Pillars and the great powers of polarity in the Tree's energetics; on a microcosmic level, they also form two of the three main connecting links in the Higher Self or Lower Genius, the hidden potentiality of the ruach.

The Path of Lamed, one of these, is also the first Path encountered on the upward journey which has no direct contact with anything below the Veil. This is an important factor in its symbolism, for this Path relates to an aspect of human experience which is often sought, rarely found, and never adequately defined. That factor is justice.

Much of the symbolism of the Path of Lamed relates directly to the idea of justice. This is appropriate enough, since the Path connects Geburah's power and harshness with Tiphareth's balance. At the same time, it stirs up a hornet's nest of questions, for there are few more contentious ideas in the Western world than this. Especially at present, when the most blatant greed and ambition are as often as not wrapped up in the language of "rights," to ask what justice is or might be is to plunge into a swamp of conflicting ideas where no trails and few signs lead through the murk.

In Cabalistic terms, this is as it must be. Until the Veil is opened for the whole world, justice can exist in Malkuth only in reflected, indirect forms. Until the Veil is opened for the individual, justice can be perceived by that individual only dimly, if at all. This is useful to keep in mind when thinking about one's own opinions. It is equally useful to consider when exploring the symbolism of this sometimes baffling Path.

✳　✳　✳

The Letter assigned to this Path is Lamed, which means "ox-goad". Nowadays this is an unfamiliar tool, but it was all but universal in the days when animal muscle rather than diesel fuel provided the motive force for agriculture. Oxen are very strong, very slow, and not particularly bright. To get them to move, and to keep them going in a straight line, takes considerably more than kind words. The ox-goad was designed to provide the needed persuasion. A long stick, curved and sharpened at the far end, it allowed the person behind the plow to jab the oxen pulling it when they strayed from a straight line or slowed down.

The image of the ox-goad serves as a symbol of balance in several different ways. The conflict of human cleverness and the stubbornness of oxen, forcing each one to conform to the needs and limits of the other, suggests one of these. Equally important, though, is the movement of the ox along a straight line, with the ox-goad ready to respond to any turning to one side or the other. A loss of balance, this image points out, is likely to result in pain. To the Cabalist, this principle is one of the basic rules of the game of existence.

The Name of God governing this Path is YHVH, the Tetragrammaton, the Name assigned to the element of Air. The symbolism of this Name is founded on the interplay of opposites, with Fire and Water, the energizing Yod and the receptive Heh, uniting in creative conflict to generate the universe. Using the same symbolism, the element of Air is itself the first child or product of the interaction between Fire and Water, the mean or balance between these opposing elements, and it is also the elemental correspondence of the Spheres of the Middle Pillar. Here again the imagery of balance is primary.

$$* \quad * \quad *$$

The next three correspondences of the Path deal directly with the symbolism of justice. The astrological correspondence for the Path of Lamed is Libra, the sign of the Scales. In the days before springs and digital readouts, weights were measured with a pair of scales, a simple pivoting bar with two pans for the substances to be weighed. The difference between the two sides showed instantly in the angle of the bar.

The scales are a symbol of equality, fairness, and precision; in the standard allegorical image of Justice, which appears on the Tarot correspondence of this Path, they represent all of these, and identify them as factors which go into the practical manifestations of justice. That image, however, also holds a sword. This can be seen as a representation of the Path as a whole, set between the balance of Tiphareth and the sword of Geburah, but it also refers back to the same point raised by the ox-goad. The sword in this image is traditionally identified as the symbol of punishment. It is the pain inflicted when balance is lost, and it cannot be excluded from an understanding of the nature of justice.

The Trump assigned to this Path, Justice, differs from the usual image of Justice in only one particular, but that one is of some importance. The ordinary image is blindfolded, to signify impartiality. The figure in Trump XI, on the other hand, is not. In esoteric symbolism, blindness is often used to represent the ordinary state of human awareness, while sight symbolizes the wider perceptions available to the magician or mystic. This points to the difference between "justice" as ordinarily perceived and justice itself as experienced beyond the Veil.

The Esoteric Title assigned to this Path refers again to the balances, but brings in another factor as well. The Path of Lamed is "the Holder of the Balances," but also the "Daughter of the Lords of Truth." Truth is not a simple concept; the symbolic nature of all human experience means that, in at least one sense, every human statement is and must be a lie, because it cannot capture the truth of any event. On a more pragmatic level, though, truth can be envisaged as an ideal, if not necessarily achieved; for justice to be the daughter of truth means simply that balance and punishment alike must rise out of an accurate sense of the situation involved. This is valid as a guide for human behavior; it is also true on a much broader scale.

✳   ✳   ✳

The Path Text, as usual, leads into issues of more complexity, although these again have to do with the idea of justice. The connection is not an obvious one, though, and a certain amount of deciphering is in order.

There are two different if related points covered in this Text. One is the connection between the Path and "spiritual virtues;" the other is the "shadow" which all Earth's inhabitants are "nearly under." The first sounds somewhat prissy to modern ears, the second ominous. Like so many first impressions, though, neither of these accurately reflects the meaning of this passage. The title given to the Path applies to both points, and suggests reliability.

The term "spiritual virtues" used in the first section does not refer to morality. Rather, the "virtues" referred to are like the virtues of medicinal herbs - that is, powers or effects - and "spiritual powers" has also been used as a translation for the same phrase. The point being made is that justice is a source of power. This may sound impossibly naive, but it is an important practical principle for the magician.

There's a tendency in modern culture to see ethical behavior as a weakness. Certainly it's true that if one wishes to play certain kinds of social games, such as politics, the habit of ethical behavior is a significant handicap. Such games do not make up the whole of life, though, and in terms of the deeper issues of human life - the attainment of happiness, wisdom, and that power of which political control is a cheap counterfeit - it is unethical behavior which is the weakness. All the various kinds of selfishness, ignorance and cruelty which make up human evil are impediments not merely to the magician but to any human achievement worth the effort.

Furthermore, human beings do not exist within a vacuum. All human action takes place within a larger context, affecting and being affected by larger forces. This is the point of the second part of the Text. The "shadow" referred to is a Biblical metaphor for protection and shelter, logical enough in the desert climate of the Middle East, and "all dwellers on Earth" - all beings presently at the Malkuth level - are "nearly" within the protection of a justice of more than human scope.

The operative word, of course, is "nearly." It's a matter of common experience that life isn't fair, and on its own terms this judgement is an accurate one. Once again, justice exists beyond the Veil, not below it. It is when the Veil opens that the force of justice begins to act directly.

In part, this is simply a matter of perception. Under ordinary circumstances, no one is a good judge of his or her own actions; the influence of the Negative Persona and of the weaknesses of the lower self act to skew judgement in the direction of self-interest with a monotonous regularity. The Opening of the Veil permits a clearer view, so that what once looked like the rankest injustice may be seen as the natural result of one's own follies. The traditional teachings about reincarnation suggest that this sort of insight often looks back to the effects of previous lifetimes, and experiences of this sort are not uncommon in certain kinds of work.

Still, there is another side to the sheltering shadow of justice, one suggested by the mythological principle of this Path, the Justice of Heaven. To pass the Veil is, in mythological terms, to enter the realms of the gods, and to do this is to invoke their judgement. One's own actions thus take on a much more immediate importance. Traditional lore has it that behavior on the part of a magician, ethical or not, has a much quicker and more extreme payback than the same behavior on the part of other people. This makes sense in theoretical terms; the magician has cleared away some of the impediments to the descent of powers down the Tree; the natural consequences of balanced, constructive action thus take shape more readily in the realms of experience. On the other hand, if the power he or she invokes turns into the sword of Geburah, the magician has no one else to blame.

Geburah, the Fifth Sphere

Title:	GBVRH, Geburah (Severity).
Name of God:	ALHIM GBVR, Elohim Gibor (Gods of Power).
Archangel:	KMAL, Kamael (He Who Sees God).
Angelic Host:	ShRPIM, Seraphim (Fiery Serpents).
Astrological Correspondence:	
	MDIM, Madim (Mars).
Tarot Correspondence:	
	the four Fives of the pack.
Elemental Correspondence:	
	Fire.
Path Text:	*"The Fifth Path is called the Radical Intelligence because it is itself the essence of Unity, uniting itself to Understanding, which emanates from the primordial depths of Wisdom."*
Magical Image:	A warrior queen in full armor, standing in a red chariot pulled by two roan horses, her head bare except for a crown, her dark hair loose, and a drawn sword in her hand.
Additional Symbol:	the pentagram.
Additional Title:	PChD, Pachad (Fear).
Colours:	in Atziluth - orange.
	in Briah - red.
	in Yetzirah - bright scarlet.
	in Assiah - red, flecked with black.
Correspondence in the Microcosm:	
	the will in Ruach.
Correspondence in the Body:	
	the left shoulder.
Grade of Initiation:	6=5, Adeptus Major.
Negative Power:	GVLHB, Golohab (the Burners).

The proper handling of the Pillar of Severity forms one of the more important tests that the Cabalistic magician must face. While its counterpart on the right side of the Tree of Life offers space for freedom and creativity, the left-hand Pillar teaches harder and, often, more painful lessons about the universe. Some part of these uncomfortable lessons have been discussed earlier in the sections dealing with Paths on the side of Severity, but their principal place on the Tree is in the fifth Sphere.

Geburah is the Sphere of conflict, discord and destruction; its symbolism is the symbolism of war; its function is that of cleansing and purification by fire. At the midpoint of the Pillar of Severity, it expresses that Pillar's nature in its most uncomfortable and uncompromising form. From Geburah, according to the traditional symbolism, come all those things which people fear and try to avoid: grief and pain and terror, violence and poverty, disease and death.

There's a natural human tendency to turn away from such things, to close one's eyes to the realities of chaos and suffering in our experience of the world. This tendency, in its proper place, has real value; in times of disaster, personal or collective, it enables people to shut their minds to horror and go on with life. Like all things, though, it becomes toxic when overdone. Taken to an extreme level, it leads to ways of thought which claim that the Geburah side of existence is illusory, that the various kinds of suffering that human beings undergo are in some sense less real than other aspects of the world we experience. Notions such as this have a long history, but they nonetheless add up to one more attempt by the human mind to substitute wishful thinking and self-interest for understanding.

It would not be necessary to make this point so strongly, except that in recent years these attitudes have become common in many spiritual and pseudo-spiritual movements. In some circles, anyone who even mentions the existence of suffering and evil is likely to be chided for being "negative" or "not spiritual enough". There are a certain number of people who have brought ideas from the Cabala into these contexts, and this has created some unfortunate possibilities for misunderstanding.

In view of this, it's as well to put matters plainly. Evil, suffering, death, pain and misery, all those things we try to avoid and hate to think about, have as much of a place in the Cabalistic magician's universe as any other human experience. They happen to everyone, including the most "spiritual" of people, and they play a significant role in the work of inner development. If life is to be understood, the place of suffering in it must be grasped, not ignored or waved aside. This, at least, is the traditional view of the magical Cabala; it could also be argued that it is the view of common sense.

Beyond this, there's a deeper philosophical issue involved, one that will lead closer to the core of the fifth Sphere's meaning. The attitudes just mentioned, considered closely, can be seen as products and symptoms of a deeper fallacy - the idea that the universe of human experience can be adequately judged by human ethical concepts like that of justice, that what seems "good" or "bad" to human beings is actually good or bad in some objective sense.

Take a moment to consider this notion. It runs very deep in the thought of the West, and mainstream religions as well as alternative spiritualities take it more or less for granted. There is an entire branch of Western theology, known as "theodicy," which exists for the purpose of explaining why God and the universe are good in human terms even though they usually don't look that way. And yet the entire notion rests on the claim that what the human mind perceives is an accurate copy of what it encounters, a claim we've already seen is untenable.

There are also the factors of self-interest and simple ignorance. To a three-year-old, the idea of eating ice cream and cookies all the time is good, while the idea of being made to eat vegetables is bad. To the child's parent, who has a somewhat deeper understanding of the way the world works, things are a little different. Given the significant limits on human perception and understanding, our ideas of goodness routinely have a definite ice-cream-and-cookies flavor to them.

It would be a mistake to take this, as some have taken it, to mean that all human ideas of right and wrong are meaningless. Those ideas, despite their limitations, have a definite use and value when applied by human beings to themselves; it's beyond this point that they fail. There's no point in accusing a cat of murder when it kills a mouse, or charging a tree with vandalism because it drops a branch on your windshield, and it's certainly no use to hurl reproaches at the universe when it fails to live up to human expectations. This is one of the essential lessons of Geburah, and leads to one of its most important gifts, which is serenity.

✳   ✳   ✳

The ideas just discussed may make the fifth Sphere sound as though, in human terms, it has no redeeming features whatever. This is far from the case. The unpleasant side of Geburah has been stressed in order to make certain points that need making, but this Sphere also shows a less forbidding face.

The title of the Sphere is, of course, Geburah, which in Hebrew means "severity" and gives a name also to the left-hand Pillar of the Tree. Much of what has been said about the Pillar of Severity elsewhere in this book can be applied equally well to the Sphere Geburah. In the dance of energy upon the Tree of Life, Geburah's role is primarily one of setting limits and countering imbalances, and this role is above all a healing and purifying one; in the universe as in the human body, uncontrolled growth quickly becomes cancerous.

The Name of God assigned to this Sphere is ALHIM GBVR, Elohim Gibor, and represents the fifth Sphere's relationship to the realm of absolute Reality. As mentioned earlier, the Name Elohim makes three appearances on the Tree of Life, all three in Spheres on the Pillar of Severity; here it is paired with the word Gibor, "power," which comes from the same root as the title Geburah and the archangelic name Gabriel, "Power of God." In this Name, the Reality beyond appearances is perceived in the form of sheer might, the power of the many-faceted Elohim. This power is a thing of Form, though, not of Force; it works to limit, to define and to control. In itself this power is not balance - that takes shape further down the Tree - but balance is impossible without it.

As other parts of the symbolism will show, this power is also a unity, and relates to the higher unity of the Supernals in unexpected ways. One example of this is the archangel assigned to Geburah, whose name is Kamael and means "He Who Sees God." The Briah correspondence stands for that aspect of a Sphere which exists in consciousness prior to perception; here it represents the power to focus consciousness, to turn awareness toward one object and exclude others. This, an essential part of the workings of awareness, is also the essential factor in all magical and mystical work, and this fact gives the archangel his name; only the perfectly focused consciousness can reach the highest levels of its own potential.

Every power, though, carries its risks with it, and this power of focus is the door to Hell just as much as to Heaven. To fill awareness with a single thing, shutting out everything else, is to approach that state of unbalanced energy which the Cabala sees as the realm of the Negative Powers. For this reason, older Cabalistic writings sometimes describe Geburah mythologically as the door - open to good and evil - by which the Negative Powers enter into the universe.

$$* \quad * \quad *$$

In Yetzirah, the realm of interactions between existence and consciousness in which the world we experience is born, the correspondence for Geburah is the Seraphim or Fiery Serpents. These dragonlike beings appear in the Bible as poisonous snakes, the ones whose bites the brass serpent Nehushtan was made to cure; echoing the Red Dragon of the Eden and Fall diagrams, they serve as a reminder of the destructive potential of this Sphere. They represent the experience of pain, the most powerful and effective of the limits placed on human beings. Pain, of course, is also the major motivation behind the work of inner development; we grow and change, most of the time, because it hurts too much not to do so. In light of the common dislike of this limiting force, it may be worth noting that traditional lore concerning angels identifies the Seraphim as spirits of love.

In the fourth World, the World of Assiah, the energies of Geburah take on a familiar form, and this is symbolized by the astrological correspondence of Geburah. Madim, Mars, is the planet which astrology identifies with conflict, opposition, and war. This is Geburah in its harshest and most uncompromising sense, made manifest in violence and destruction. Here the powers of ruin and chaos have their home. Again, though, these have a necessary part to play in the universe of our experience, whether we understand this or not.

✶   ✶   ✶

The Path Text returns to the issue of Geburah's connection with unity, and does so in bold terms. It describes Geburah as "itself the essence of unity," and links it directly to the Spheres Chokmah and Binah above the Abyss. It also names the fifth Sphere the Radical Intelligence; the word "radical" comes from a word for "root," and in politics a "radical" was originally someone who sought to make changes at the root levels of a problem. To call Geburah the Radical Intelligence is to imply that it approaches things in this way, which is entirely true. Taken along with the symbol of the Tree of Life, it also implies a specific direction for the energies of the fifth Sphere, since the root of the Tree of Life is in Kether, the Sphere of Unity.

Central to this idea is an important aspect of the fifth Sphere's meaning. Geburah is a power of limitation; as an aspect of consciousness, it represents the ability to limit awareness to a single object; as an aspect of human experience it stands for those things which most limit and constrict us. But to limit something, to restrict the number or nature of its acts or manifestations, is to move it in the direction of unity. It is thus part of the function of Geburah to enable created things to move in the direction of Kether; put another way, it is Geburah, and the Pillar of Severity in general, from which the way of Redemption is derived.

This point has practical applications, which will be covered shortly. It also has at least one more significance in terms of Cabalistic theory worth mentioning. As our discussion of Tiphareth's symbolism pointed out, those Spheres below the midpoint of the Tree deal primarily with the experience of separate individuality, those above the midpoint with the experience of unity. In Chesed and Geburah, that unity is a complex one, lacking the radical simplicity of the Spheres above the Abyss; nonetheless, both Spheres correspond to levels of consciousness at which the individual merges with the totality of experience. This is stressed by the Path Texts of both Spheres, which each include a reference to Kether. The two Spheres, though, express the link with unity in different ways; from the standpoint of Chesed, all things are one because they emerge from the same source; from the standpoint of Geburah all things are one because they strive toward the same end.

* * *

Of the remaining symbolism, the Magical Image requires a brief comment, if only because the version given here differs somewhat from the one which has been most commonly used in the magical Cabala over the last several centuries. This more common version has a warrior king, rather than a queen, as the central figure. Prejudices of an earlier time may have made a male figure here seem more appropriate, but in terms of its energetics Geburah is symbolically feminine, not masculine. A female figure in this image will therefore tend to work better in practical terms.

The pentagram or five-pointed star plays a critical role in the practice of ceremonial magic, and a ritual using it will be explored in detail later on in this book. It represents the powers of the four elements controlled and directed by the fifth, Spirit; it is also a traditional symbol of the human microcosm.

Of the will, an enormous amount could be written. As the expression of Geburah in human consciousness, the will is the principal source of strength in all magical working; in a real sense, the entire complex field of magical training can be reduced to a matter of the development of will. A quotation attributed to the 17th-century mystic Joseph Glanvill sums up the magical understanding of the will flawlessly:

> *"For the will therein lieth, which dieth not. Who knoweth the mysteries of the Will with its vigor? For God is but a great Will pervading all things by nature of its intentness. Man doth not yield himself to the angels nor to death utterly, save only through the weakness of his feeble will."*

There is, however, a certain risk of misunderstanding in this, for the ordinary idea of will in modern culture is badly flawed. The mention of "will-power" nowadays calls up images of white knuckles, gritted teeth, and muscular strain. All these are symptoms of internal conflict, and conflict - the result of division in the will - is the will's weakness, not its strength. Like Geburah, from which it derives, the will is founded on unity, and when it achieves unity it gains its ends without fuss or strain.

It is thus one of the chief concerns of the magician to learn unity of will, to will one thing at a time and to will it with the full force of the self. Reaching this state, for most people, requires coming to terms with various suppressed desires and needs; this is part of the interaction between Geburah and Netzach, mediated through Tiphareth. It is generally a slow process, but even the first small gains in strength and unity of will can have remarkable effects in terms of daily life.

One more point regarding the will may be worth making. Just as the levels of consciousness of the Spheres above Tiphareth have to do with unity rather than individuality, the aspects of the ruach linked to those Spheres are not "personal" in the narrow sense of that word. As the magician explores the nature of will, he or she will begin to discover that the will is not so much part of the self as something which works through the self, but which comes from beyond it. This recognition is an important step in the approach to the Abyss, and to the realms of unity beyond it.

$$* \quad * \quad *$$

The last part of Geburah's symbolism, the Negative Power assigned to Geburah, is named Golohab, a word that can be translated "burners" or "those who destroy with fire". (One modern Cabalistic writer has neatly translated it as "arsonists".) In traditional imagery, the Golochab are vast hideous heads with open mouths, belching smoke and flame like erupting volcanoes. Like the other Powers, though, this colorful image stands for a pervasive evil, not a monster out of fantasy but rather one of the monstrous cravings and actions that are all too real a part of our lives.

Geburah's position above the Veil has certain effects on its Negative Power. As we saw with the Tagiriron of Tiphareth, each of the Powers above the veil appears in two different forms: a lower form, which functions below the Veil in the realms of ordinary human awareness, and a higher form, which functions above the Veil and serves as a trap for the unwary on the spiritual quest.

The reflected form of the Golohab is found in hatred and cruelty. Common enough and obvious enough in our world, the power of hatred has an aspect which are not always recognized. The polarity between Geburah and Netzach often blends hatred with envy, so that too many times what we hate is also what we secretly desire. Here as elsewhere, our culture's blindness to the Netzach side of life involves huge if hidden costs.

The higher form, on the other hand, is somewhat rarer, and in some ways subtler. In discussing the Tagiriron, the Negative Power of Tiphareth, we saw that the way of the transformation of consciousness has its diseases. The first of these, represented by the Tagiriron themselves, is the tendency to dogmatism. The second often arises out of this first. If others do not accept the dogmatic "truth" offered to them, it can be easy for the dogmatist to conclude that these others are either incurably stupid or actually evil, either blinded or deliberately blinding themselves to self-evident truth. The result is another form of hatred, one which divides all people into those few who are capable of wisdom and the contemptible many who are not.

The temptation of Geburah, then, is spiritual elitism, the belief that only a fraction of human beings are worthy of the spiritual path. Along with this idea, most of the time, comes contempt for humanity, or that loud pity which is just contempt in a slightly veiled form. Another common expression is the belief in apocalypse, the idea of (and desire for) a catastrophe which will show the rest of the human race just how wrong it is. Phrased in this way, the idea sounds childish, and indeed it is - but the monumental folly and brutality which has sometimes resulted from this kind of thinking is anything but child's play.

In the face of the very real evils which exist in the world of our experience, and the equally real unwillingness of most people in the world to take responsibility for their own actions, the temptation of elitism can be a strong one. Still, it leads nowhere useful, and its chief function is to strengthen equally useless habits of thinking such as pride and self-righteous anger. More useful by far, although often more difficult, is the way of self-knowledge, which recognizes the flaws and follies as well as the capacity for growth that all human beings share, and sees the spiritual path in all its forms as a choice which is available to all.

Path 21, the Path of Kaph

Letter of the Path: ‬כ , Kaph (Hand).
Name of God: AL, El.
Astrological Correspondence:
Jupiter.
Tarot Correspondence:
Trump X, the Wheel of Fortune.
Esoteric Title: Lord of the Forces of Life.
Path Text: *"The Twenty-first Path is the Intelligence of Conciliation, and is so called because it receives the divine influence which flows into it from its benediction upon all and each existence."*
Mythological Principle:
Aspiration.
Experiences of the Path:
Flight, or views from a high place; journeys among or up mountains; brilliant light, often rainbow-colored; emotional exhilaration.
Entities of the Path: Pilgrims journeying; eagles and other winged beings.
Magical Image: An arch of clear violet, bearing the letter Kaph in brilliant white on its keystone. The door in the arch bears the image of Trump X.
Colours: in Atziluth - violet.
in Briah - blue.
in Yetzirah - rich purple.
in Assiah - bright blue, rayed with yellow.

Like the Path of Mem, on the far side of the Tree of Life, the Path of Kaph passes through the Veil without contacting Tiphareth, and forms part of one of the two side Pillars of the Tree. It has a similar role in the Tree's energy processes, and shares some important qualities: the oddly static balance brought about by the total dominance of one side of the polarity of Force and Form, noticeably, as well as an important place in the inner structure of Cabalistic practice. Just as the Path of

Mem and that of Nun mirror each other in certain ways, too, so do the Paths of Kaph and Ayin; both represent movement in the direction of Mercy, one from Netzach, one from Hod.

Still, these similarities do not add up to an identity by any means. Nor should these Paths be seen as nothing more than manifestations of the Pillars they help to form. Each Path of the Tree is a unique interaction between two Spheres, with its own distinct "personality". Just as the 23rd Path, with its watery symbolism and its focus on sacrifice, is more than a simple expression of the Pillar of Form, so the 21st Path also must be understood on its own terms.

Those terms are dominated by two elements which may look incompatible at first glance. The first is a quality of abundance, even extravagance, which draws on the imagery of the richness of the natural world. The second, seemingly in conflict with it, is a restlessness, a questing for change which no abundance can satisfy. These two both derive from the role and power of the Pillar of Mercy as the source of creative energy in the universe of our experience. In their higher aspects, these unite in a ceaseless fertility on all levels. Lower down, however, they can produce a sense of conflict between differing goals which is one of the hallmarks of this Path.

$$* \quad * \quad *$$

The letter of this Path, in some ways its most important symbol, is Kaph, which means "hand" and more particularly "open hand" or "palm". In physical terms, the human hand is among the most astonishing creations of nature, able to shape the physical level of experience in a remarkable variety of ways. The hands of a karate master can shatter concrete blocks; the hands of a skilled craftsperson can shape raw materials into any number of practical and beautiful things; the hands of a lover can awaken passion, and fulfill it. As a symbol, the hand has long been linked with ideas of mastery and creativity, power, structure, and rulership.

Additional meanings gather about the symbol of the open hand. Where the closed hand suggests ideas of withdrawal, containment, and reserve, the open hand symbolizes involvement and generosity. Even today, a generous person is often described as "open-handed".

The Name of God and the Astrological Correspondence assigned to the 21st Path both derive from the same symbolism, and both point to a significant fact about this Path. At several earlier points, the elusive and often misleading nature of the links between Path and Sphere symbolism has been mentioned. Generally, the Path assigned to a planet has no direct relationship with the Sphere of the same planet. There is one exception to this rule, however, and the exception is the Path of Kaph. To it are assigned the Divine Name AL, El, and the planet Jupiter - and the same Name and planet are among the correspondences of Chesed, the Sphere at the 21st Path's upper end.

These symbolic linkages are not accidental. Chesed is a Sphere of overwhelming creative and constructive power, the midpoint and primary focus of the energies of the Pillar of Mercy. In the diagram of the Lightning Flash, Chesed is the first manifestation of Reality below the Abyss. The Path of Kaph is entirely in its shadow, and carries its energies straight down the Tree to a receptive Sphere; under these circumstances, Chesed's power is a dominant influence on the Path.

This symbolic link expresses, as well, an issue in practical magic. Other Spheres may be elusive to the seeker, and must be reached by strange and even devious routes; not Chesed. The fourth Sphere, at least, may be found by going in the obvious direction. Like a lighthouse on the edge of an uncharted sea, it serves as a last point of certainty before the shadows of the Abyss close in.

The Name of God El has a great deal of importance in Cabalistic theory, but it will be best to consider it when the fourth Sphere has been reached. For now, you may find it useful to notice that the Path of Mem, this Path's opposite, shares its Divine Name: another example of the concealed unity within all of the Tree's oppositions. Jupiter, for its part, is the most important of the "benefics", or positively inclined planets, in astrology. Its influence tends toward optimism, generosity, and expansiveness, and it governs rulership, wealth, and increase.

✳   ✳   ✳

The Tarot Correspondence for this Path is Trump X, the Wheel of Fortune. The image on this card was originally another of the common visual symbols of the Middle Ages. In a time when most people could not read or write their own names, such images - carved in stone, shown in pageants, described in sermons - served a role in communication similar to that of the mass media of the present. The picture of the Wheel of Fortune brought home to its viewers the instability and impermanence of life in the world. In medieval art, it was usually shown with a whole crowd of figures on it, the one at the top crowned and robed as a king, the one at the bottom a starving beggar in rags. The circle of the wheel, connecting these two, suggested the then-revolutionary idea that king and beggar were ultimately the same under their garments, that the difference between them was not a matter of unchanging cosmic law but simply a result of different turns of fortune. As well, the image brought to mind the ups and downs of life on the individual level, reminding its viewers that no condition was permanent, that change was a constant part of life.

The point that this symbolism makes is that the good things in life may be enjoyed but cannot be relied on. The world of our experience contains many kinds of happiness, but it contains many kinds of suffering as well, and the factors which cause one or the other to put in an appearance are often largely outside of the ordinary channels of human control. Both, it should be remembered, are necessary for balance; attention to this point is one of the motivations for seeking balance on the individual level, so that it may be imposed less often from without.

The Esoteric Title suggests the same point. As Lord of the Forces of Life - not, you'll notice, the Forms - the Path of Kaph represents the descent of creative energy down the Pillar of Mercy into the realms of everyday human experience. Those forces take on forms which are sometimes agreeable to human beings, sometimes not; the same energies which cause a child to grow cause bacteria to multiply. Here again the richness of life and its harshness rise from the same root.

The Path Text, in turn, deals with the same creative power from a more exalted perspective. The Path is here called the Intelligence of Conciliation. Why? According to the Text, this is because the Path receives a "divine influence", which comes into it "from its own benediction (that is, blessing) upon all and each existence". What this implies is that the higher energies of the Tree (the "divine influence") descend into this Path because the Path's own energies have a creative role in the whole of the universe. This is a precise description of the working of the Pillar of Mercy, of which this Path forms a part. The term "blessing" or "benediction" has a specific technical meaning in traditional Cabalistic writings; it refers to those phases of the higher aspects of being which enter into contact with the lower, and contrasts with "holiness," which refers to aspects which remain forever separate.

The specific nature of the Path's effect gives the Path its title. It works to conciliate, to bring conflicting forces into harmony. This function comes partly from aspects of the fourth Sphere which are covered by its own Path Text, partly from the nature of the seventh Sphere, which links together individual things with the bonds of love.

✳   ✳   ✳

It is with the mythological principle assigned to the Path of Kaph that we return to its relationship with the Path of Mem. The two principles of Self-sacrifice and Aspiration unite in the symbolism of Tiphareth; divided, they form the polarity within which the opening of the Veil must take place.

The myths of aspiration tell of a person who seeks something great and achieves it; those of sacrifice tell of a person who has or is something great, and gives it up. In the whole process of the opening up of the Higher Self's potentials - a process which is not completed by the first journey up the Path of Samech - much is given up, and much gained. In every transformation, there is a tradeoff.

What is given up in the process is the self as it's ordinarily understood, a separate, isolated consciousness shut in its body like a chick in a shell. This experience of the self is not so much false as incomplete; it represents a fraction of the possibilities open to human awareness; it is, however, that fraction on which we base our sense of identity and of worth, and from which we measure and judge every part of the world around us. It is the most precious thing we have, and everything we value is related to it in some way.

What is gained is a broader selfhood which exists on the border between individuality and unity, which is capable of being separate but also of recognizing its connection to other centers of consciousness and of beginning to explore its oneness with those other centers. What is gained is the ability to shape experience consciously, rather than having it shaped unconsciously by unrecognized needs and energies and by powers from outside the self. What is gained, ultimately, is the freedom the chick gains when it breaks through the eggshell and wobbles out into a wider world.

The existence of esoteric traditions worldwide is evidence that, for many people, the trade has proved well worth making. Still, this decision is beyond all others one which each person must make for himself or herself alone.

Letter of the Path: ', Yod (Fist).

Name of God: ADNI, Adonai.

Astrological Correspondence:

      Virgo, the Virgin.

Tarot Correspondence:

      Trump IX, the Hermit

Esoteric Title: Magus of the Voice of Light, Prophet of the Gods.

Path Text: "The Twentieth Path is the Intelligence of Will, and is so called because it is the means of preparation of all and each created being, and by this intelligence the existence of the Primordial Wisdom becomes known."

Mythological Principle:

      the Wilderness Journey.

Experiences of the Path:

      Solitude; journeying through deserts and wild places; visions of the creation of the world; temptation by hostile or demonic entities.

Entities of the Path: Birds; tempting spirits.

Magical Image: An arch of yellowish green, bearing the letter Yod in brilliant white on its keystone. The door in the arch bears the image of Trump IX.

Colours: in Atziluth - yellowish green

      in Briah - slate grey.

      in Yetzirah - greenish grey..

      in Assiah - plum.

Although it exists below the Abyss, the Path of Yod possesses a quality which will become all too familiar when your work on the Tree rises to the levels above this highest barrier: the quality of paradox. The realm of the Supernals cannot be grasped from below. The closest approach to them which the human mind can make is the perfect union of perfect opposites. Though the 20th Path itself offers no way through the Abyss, its role as a link between Chesed and Tiphareth - between the first child of the Supernals and the reflection of Kether - gives it something of the same nature, a nature reflected in its symbolism.

This can be seen clearly in the Hebrew letter assigned to this Path. Yod literally means "closed hand" or "fist". In contrast to Kaph, the open and active hand of rulership and generosity, this hand is closed, its creative powers self- limited. As the closed hand can hide something within it, so the letter Yod has implications of concealment and hiddenness. In addition, Yod is linked symbolically with the idea of seed, specifically in the sense of sperm; this is meant to suggest ideas of hidden potential, of power and possibility held in reserve, of patterns which have not yet entered into manifestation. Just as a single sperm, so small it cannot be seen by the unaided eye, can set in motion the chain of events which results in the birth of a new human being, so the energies of the Path of Yod contain potentials which cannot be perceived easily but which can have startling effects over time.

In Cabalistic lore, this point is developed in two ways. First, as traditional writings point out, the entire Hebrew alphabet can be constructed out of the letter Yod turned, stretched or added to itself in different ways. Since the Cabala uses the Hebrew alphabet to stand for the whole range of basic interactions that structure the universe, this is more than a scholar's quibble. It implies that Yod, and the pattern of energies which it represents, is the source and template from which all others derive: in a sense, *the* letter, and so *the* Path.

It may seem odd, in this case, that Yod isn't the first letter of the alphabet, but this also expresses a point. Yod is the tenth letter, and this is held to symbolize the ten Spheres. The Tree of Life itself, then, is the source and template for the interactions between its Spheres; the descent of creative energy through each Path forms a small Lightning Flash, the ascent of awareness a Serpent in miniature. Also implicit in Yod's place in the alphabet is the idea that, though the letter symbolizes beginnings, these aren't beginnings out of nothing, nor do they take place in a vacuum. A seed must be produced and ripened by a plant, and must fall into fertile soil for a new plant to be born.

The second place where the letter Yod shows up in Cabalistic tradition is at once more familiar and more problematical. Yod is the first letter of the Tetragrammaton, the primary creative Name YHVH. In the context of this Name, Yod is the first spark of energy which gets the whole process of creation under way, and corresponds to the element of Fire, the Father, and similar concepts. As we'll see shortly, though, the letter Yod's own symbolism differs sharply; in a number of places, in fact, Yod's role on its own terms and its role in the Tetragrammaton are exact opposites.

This divergence is no accident, but rather a deliberate paradox. It can be resolved by considering the Tetragrammaton in the context of other Names of God used in the Cabala. The Tetragrammaton may be the most important of the Divine Names in practical terms, but it's neither the first in the creative process nor the highest on the Tree of Life. The Name AHIH, about which very little has been said so far, holds both of these honors.

The letter Yod, then, may be the beginning of the Tetragrammaton, but it is not the beginning of everything. This is the key to the paradox, and it is a key as well to the functions and energy relationships of all the Paths. To those things which come after the Yod of Tetragrammaton and are shaped by it, Yod is active and dominant; to those things which come before it and shape it, on the other hand, Yod is receptive, even passive. This is equally true, in Cabalistic thought, of everything that exists, and this point is one of the sources of balance in the universe.

$$* \quad * \quad *$$

The Name of God and the astrological correspondence assigned to Yod will help to clarify what was said earlier about the paradoxical nature of the 20th Path's symbolism. Where Yod in the Tetragrammaton represents Fire, and has masculine symbolism, these two entries are both linked to the element of Earth, and the second one is a feminine symbol. The Name of God ADNI, Adonai, is of course the Name attributed to Earth, and is used here for that reason; Earth here suggests the receptive side of the Path as discussed above. The zodiacal sign Virgo, one of the three Earth signs, is a more complex attribution and extends the Path symbolism in unexpected directions.

As a passive and receptive element, Earth needs the action of an outside force to bring about movement and change in it. Virgo, the Virgin, provides a concise image of the same idea. Biologically speaking, a virgin may be fully capable of reproduction, but as long as he or she remains virginal this capability is only potential. Without sexual contact with a person of the opposite sex, a virgin is for all practical purposes sterile.

Issues of virginity, like so many things having to do with sex, have been made far more garbled than they have to be by the Western world's intense ambivalence toward the realm of material experience. Social fashions in the West have tended to swing from prudishness (mislabeled "morality") to debauchery (mislabeled "liberation") and back again without passing through the more balanced middle ground between. Certain eras have glorified virginity, others have despised it, while still others have thought of it mostly as a kind of marketable commodity.

Beneath all this confusion, though, traces remain of an older understanding of virginity, one which dates from a time when the hidden side of things was more commonly a part of daily life than it is now. The details of this older understanding aren't necessary to the present subject, and involve (among other things) methods of magical control over the reproductive process that are not appropriate in the modern world, but two basic principles are worth discussing here. The first of these is the idea that the first use of anything, sexual energy included, has lasting effects on that thing. (It is for this reason that most of the old books of magic insist, and rightly, that magical tools should be "virgin" - that is, never before used - when they are prepared for ritual.) The second principle is that sexual energy is ultimately one form, an extremely pure and concentrated form, of the basic creative energy of the universe, and can be used for purposes other than reproduction, pair bonding, and pleasure. To redirect sexual energy in this way, though, normally requires that it not be expressed in the normal direction.

This is one of the significances of the Tarot correspondence of the Path of Yod, which is Trump IX, the Hermit. Another familiar image of the Middle Ages, this Trump shows an old man in a plain robe, with a staff to lean on and (often) a lamp to light his way. The way of the hermit was one of the common ways of spiritual life in medieval times; it involved renouncing not merely sexual life but ordinary human interaction as well. The same point appears, in turn, in the mythological principle of this Path, the Wilderness Journey, and the "temptation by devils" - the "devils" of natural human desires - which is sometimes a part of that journey was commonly a part of the lives of medieval hermits was well.

To modern eyes, the hermit's way may seem perverse, but it expresses a clear understanding of the nature of what we have called energy. In most cases, the creative forces which shape the universe of our experience have a natural way of expression. Broadly speaking, that way leads down the Tree, toward greater manifestation and complexity - but away from the goals of the mystic and the magician, who seek contact with the sources of energy itself. It is for this reason that the alchemists spoke of their transformative art as "the Work against Nature," and made that insight clearer in the motto "Nature unaided fails."

The critical word, of course, is "unaided." To oppose the normal flows of energy completely is to choke oneself off from the sources of life; to move unthinkingly with those flows is to be swept back into the same situation the way of Redemption seeks to solve. (Modern sentimentality about Nature to the side, it is precisely by "following Nature" - by, for instance, breeding to capacity, obeying the instinct of pack-loyalty, and responding to perceived threats with violence - that human beings have created much of their current predicament.) These are respectively the mistakes of Severity and Mercy, and as always the more useful way is to be found in the balance of the Middle Pillar.

✳   ✳   ✳

The Esoteric Title of the 20th Path is "Magus of the Voice of Light, Prophet of the Gods." There are three Paths which bear the title of Magus, and they occupy a special place on the Tree, expressing one pattern in three relationships to the Abyss. Their significance will be covered in a later section. As "Prophet of the Gods," though, this Path fills another role. A prophet communicates the will of the Unseen to the ordinary world and its inhabitants; the prophet's role is an active one, speaking to anyone who will listen, and contrasts with that of an oracle, whose function is the more passive one of answering questions. At the same time, it is central to their calling that prophets speak not for themselves but for a divine power, and the will which moves them is by no means always their own.

Other aspects of the Path of Yod are brought out in the Path Text, along with another example of the evasive nature of Path- Sphere relationships. The Path of Yod is here called the Intelligence of Will. Will, of course, is an attribute of Geburah, while the Path of Yod leads to Chesed. At the same time, the issues of virginity and the redirection of force mentioned above do relate to the fifth Sphere in obvious ways, and also to the exercise of will.

In exploring this paradox, it's important to remember that this Path is above Tiphareth, close to the Abyss. In fact, the same thing happens in a different way on the Path of Lamed, this Path's equivalent on the other side of the Tree, for justice - that Path's principal attribute - is also an important part of the symbolism of Chesed. The point is that at this level of the Tree, it becomes increasingly hard to draw firm boundaries. The Paths to Chesed rely on Geburah, and those to Geburah on Chesed, because all derive from the same unity - and return to it.

The rest of the Path Text deals with the 20th Path's function within the system of the Tree, and does so with a good deal of conciseness. The Path is called "the means of preparation of all and each created being;" this refers to its place between Chesed, where the macrocosm emerges from unity, and Tiphareth, where "each created being" takes shape as an individual entity. The energies which descend to Tiphareth by this Path bring the forces of the Pillar of Mercy into play in that process.

By the Path of Yod, in turn, "the existence of the Primordial Wisdom becomes known." The Primordial Wisdom is Chokmah, the second Sphere. From below, the Supernals are typically perceived (when they are perceived at all) in the synthesis we have called Aima Elohim; this synthesis takes most of its symbolism from Binah, and the darkness of the Abyss is thus in large part simply a reflection of Binah's own darkness and mystery. With the opening of the Path of Yod, on the other hand, something else begins to come into view, something of the side of Mercy rather than that of Severity, which lightens the Abyss and offers the first hope of a way across it. That way, as we'll see, is all but impossible to define, though it has often been the concern of prophets to do so. It can be experienced by the magician, but - as the symbolism of this Path would suggest - it must be experienced alone.

Path 19, the Path of Teth

Letter of the Path: ט , Teth (Serpent).

Name of God: ALHIM, Elohim.

Astrological Correspondence:
Leo, the Lion.

Tarot Correspondence:
Trump VIII, Strength.

Esoteric Title: Daughter of the Flaming Sword, Leader of the Lion.

Path Text: *"The Nineteenth Path is the Intelligence of the secret of all the activities of the spiritual beings, and is so called because of the influence that is diffused by it from the most high, exalted, and sublime glory."*

Mythological Principle:
Meeting with the Other Self.

Experiences of the Path:
Fire, sunlight, energy; solar symbols; rituals of initiation and purification; tests of strength and will; combat with animal or semi-animal opponents.

Entities of the Path: Initiating priests and priestesses; the animal twin or wild self.

Magical Image: An arch of lemon yellow, bearing the letter Teth in brilliant white on the keystone. The door in the arch bears the image of Trump VIII.

Colours: in Atziluth - lemon yellow.
in Briah - deep purple.
in Yetzirah - gray.
in Assiah - reddish yellow.

The Path of Teth is the second of the horizontal Paths on the Tree, and it links the two central Spheres of the side Pillars directly. There is no Path on the Tree which forms a more intense polarity or carries stronger energy flows. Other Paths participate in power, or are affected by it;

this Path embodies it in the purest sense. The symbols of the Path of Teth are symbols of power, and its tests are the tests of power; power, too, is the prize to be gained when the Path's lessons are learned.

All three of the horizontal Paths have a relationship with issues of power, but this relationship is shaped profoundly by the different positions of these Paths on the Tree. On the 14th Path, at the top of the Pillars, the opposition between Force and Form is resolved in the unity of the Supernals, and power manifests here as love. On the 27th Path, at the Pillars' feet, the solidification of the opposed powers brings them into explosive conflict. The 19th Path, located between these two, shares to some extent in the nature of both. Between Chesed and Geburah, the primary creative and destructive powers of the universe, the possibility of conflict always exists, and the spectacular levels of energy on the Path connecting them amplify the stresses of this interaction to the flashpoint.

The final step into conflict, though, is never taken. The perfect order of Chesed and the perfect discipline of Geburah combine into perfect control. Like a fighter pilot in flight, the 19th Path directs vast energies with small movements and subtle shifts, backed by constant vigilance and a thorough knowledge of the issues involved. Here, where powers blaze from Pillar to Pillar at the very edge of the Abyss, there can be neither room nor potential for error.

In practical terms, the Path of Teth has much to teach concerning the higher ranges of magic. Along with the Paths of Lamed and Yod, it forms a triangle of principles connecting the three Spheres of the Higher Self, and these principles are also the means by which these three Spheres are brought into balance. Many of the more advanced formulas of magical practice derive from this triad in one or another of its aspects.

*   *   *

The letter assigned to this Path is Teth, "serpent". The serpent is very nearly a universal symbol in the world's myths and spiritual teachings, and has shown up twice already in this book, as the Red Dragon of the two Eden diagrams and as the Serpent of the Tree of Life, whose windings trace out the way of Redemption. The serpent is often a symbol of energy in the purest sense, but it has another significance as well. In the Biblical phrase, the serpent is "more subtil than any beast of the field". This subtlety may be expressed in the highest forms of wisdom or the lowest kind of deceit, but in the context of great power it offers the one functional way of working. On the Path of Teth, in particular, the energy flows are strong enough that a direct attempt to shape them is like trying to turn aside the tides of the sea. Using subtle and indirect means, though, the energies of this Path can be tapped and used.

This point is also relevant to one of the other serpents just mentioned. The Serpent of the Tree of Life provides an image of spiritual progress which is based on precisely the subtlety just mentioned. A first glance at the Tree of Life might suggest that the Middle Pillar, by itself, is the only route needed for the upward journey. In practice, though, this direct approach generally fails. Without the balance provided by Hod and Netzach, the narrow way of the Path of Samech cannot be walked, just as the powers of Geburah and Chesed must be awakened and mastered before the door of the Abyss will open. Here again, a subtle and indirect approach works where a frontal attack does not.

✳   ✳   ✳

The next four symbols of the Path - the Name of God, astrological correspondence, Tarot correspondence and Esoteric Title - all come at the Path from another starting point. Each one, in a sense, builds on the one before it; although the starting point is far from the issues just discussed, by the time the sequence ends we'll have come around to a similar place, if from a very different direction.

The starting point is simple enough. The Divine Name ALHIM, Elohim, is assigned to this Path to represent the element of Fire, which well symbolizes the energetic nature of the Path. Similarly, the sign of the Zodiac assigned to this Path is Leo, the Lion, the strongest of the Fire signs. With Leo, though, a new aspect begins to emerge. This sign is associated with the Sun, and the Sun and the lion are both symbols which tradition links to the Sphere Tiphareth.

At first glance, the 19th Path may seem to have little to do with Tiphareth, since it has no direct contact with this Sphere. A look at the Tree of Life, though, will show the relationship. Tiphareth is the Sphere that brings Chesed and Geburah into harmony, establishing a polarity between these opposing forces. Before there can be polarity, however, there must be contact, and the Path of Teth is where this contact takes place. As the mean between the fourth and fifth Spheres, the 19th Path can be seen as a kind of first image of Tiphareth, mirroring the mighty force for harmony which will blossom a little further down the Tree.

At the same time, the Tiphareth symbolism doesn't override that of Fire. Even the lion, which dominates certain aspects of the sixth Sphere's imagery, is also the symbolic animal of Fire. As a wild animal, and, even today, a dangerous one to human beings, the lion also serves as a solid reminder that the energies of the Path of Teth are neither tame nor harmless.

The Tarot card assigned to this Path carries the sequence another step. Trump VIII, Strength, bears an image of a woman mastering a lion. In many decks, she is either opening or closing the lion's mouth. Despite the apparent conflict, the image contains no sign of struggle, or of resistance on the lion's part. This image combines the lion-symbolism just discussed with a reference to the 27th Path, for Peh, the letter of that Path, means "mouth" in Hebrew. Here the power of Teth is shown in the act of controlling the potential for conflict summed up in Peh.

All of these matters are summed up neatly in the Esoteric Title, "Daughter of the Flaming Sword, Leader of the Lion". The sword is a symbol of the element of Air; as the Vau of Tetragrammaton, Air is the product of the interaction between Fire and Water, just as the Path of Teth is created by contact between Geburah and Chesed, and Air is also the element assigned to Tiphareth. The sword is flaming, however, to show that Fire still governs this Path. The remainder of the Title restates the point made above, that the Path energies serve not only to carry enormous force, but also shape and direct that force to appropriate ends.

At the same time, of course, the Flaming Sword has another sense in Cabalistic tradition, and this opens up a further meaning of the Title. The Sword, as mentioned in an earlier chapter, is another symbol for the same descent of energies more often called the Lightning Flash, and represents the ten Spheres as modifications of a single creative energy. The "daughter" or product of the Spheres, the result of their interactions, would then be the twenty-two Paths in their established form - which could also be symbolized by the serpent, and thus the letter Teth. Here the sequence of images we have followed comes full circle.

*　*　*

The Path Text for the 19th Path takes the symbolism discussed above in another direction, one of the highest importance. The Path is here called the "Intelligence of the secret of all the activities of the spiritual beings," and this rather startling title is explained by a phrase which links it to an influence which descends from Kether. The Path of Teth, obviously enough, has no direct connection with Kether or with any of the Supernals, but the subtlety of the Serpent is not necessary here; to the extent that the Path of Teth is a first image of Tiphareth, it shares in the sixth Sphere's role as a reflection of Kether below the Abyss. Indeed, as the Path joins the primary polarities of the Tree together directly, it is in some ways a better image of the highest unity than Tiphareth itself.

It is in this image, then, that the "secret of the activities of all the spiritual beings" is expressed. One way of pointing toward that secret - for ultimately it can be known only by being experienced - is to remember that everything, seen from the realms above Malkuth, is a spiritual being, an aspect of unity, and participates in energies of universal scale. This is the point that the magicians of the Middle Ages tried to express with their lists of plants, animals, stones and metals which partook of the essence of a given planet or star. Nothing, however "material" it may seem to us, is merely dead matter. As we handle the things around us, we are shaping powers which reach back to the highest levels of existence. This, properly understood, is the key to the innermost secrets of magic.

Something of this same point is hidden within the mythological principle of this Path, which is Meeting with the Other Self. Myths of this type often involve struggle between a human hero and an animal or semi-animal opponent. This struggle, though, is a struggle which ends not so much in conquest but in a kind of union; Heracles defeated the Nemean Lion but thereafter wore its skin always; Gilgamesh and the beast-man Enkidu wrestled each other to a standstill and then became as brothers. The opponent in many of these myths, the animal twin or wild self, also appears in workings on this Path, and often in dreams as well. Feral, threatening, but also familiar, it represents the dawning awareness that the barrier between self and other, the comfortable inside and the unknown world outside, is itself an illusion - that what we experience and what we are ultimately are not two but one.

Chesed, the Fourth Sphere

Title:	ChSD, Chesed (Mercy).
Name of God:	AL, El (God).
Archangel:	TzDQIAL, Tzadkiel (Justice of God).
Angelic Host:	ChShMLIM,Chashmalim (Shining Ones).

Astrological Correspondence:
TzDQ, Tzedek (Jupiter).

Tarot Correspondence:
the four Fours of the pack.

Elemental Correspondence:
Water.

Path Text: *"The Fourth Path is called the Cohesive or Receptacular Intelligence, and is so called because it contains all the Holy Powers, and from it emanate all the spiritual virtues with the most exalted essences. These emanate, one from another, by the power of the Primordial Emanation, the Highest Crown."*

Magical Image: An old but mighty king sitting on a sapphire throne, robed in blue and violet, a golden crown on his head and a scepter and orb in his hands.

Additional Symbols: ———

Additional Titles: GDVLH, Gedulah (Majesty or Greatness).

Colours: in Atziluth - deep violet
in Briah - blue.
in Yetzirah - deep purple.
in Assiah - gdeep azure, flecked with yellow.

Correspondence in the Microcosm:
the memory in Ruach

Correspondence in the Body:
the left shoulder.

Grade of Initiation: 7=4, Adeptus Exemptus.

Negative Power: GAaShKLH, Ga'ashekelah, the Breakers in Pieces.

There is a sense in which the three Paths which lead up to Chesed sum up the entire pattern of the Tree below it. The 21st Path, beginning in Netzach, reaches into the realms below the Veil and summarizes the lessons of Force; the 19th Path, beginning in Geburah, crosses the edge of the Abyss to summarize the lessons of Form, while the 20th Path, beginning in Tiphareth, deals with the relationship between macrocosm and microcosm, and summarizes the lessons of the middle way between Force and Form.

All three of these Paths converge in Chesed. As the highest Sphere below the Abyss, Chesed is the level of awareness at which existence as we conceive it first comes into being. Here is the first extension of the creative Light in space and time, the birth of the macrocosm and of the dimensions of experience. In a sense, then, while the three Paths just discussed touch on the lower part of the Tree, the entire Tree from Kether to Malkuth is summed up in this one Sphere, as the full-grown tree is summed up and contained in the seed.

Above all, Chesed is the Sphere of creation, and the core elements of its meaning and symbolism derive from this fact. As the central Sphere and purest manifested aspect of the Pillar of Mercy, it also takes on the positive, expansive character of that side of the Tree. In addition, like all the Spheres outside of the Middle Pillar, it draws a certain amount of its meaning from the Sphere that balances it on the Tree's far side. Just as Hod and Netzach define each other by their conflict, Geburah and Chesed both derive a part of their identities from the fact of their opposition, and neither one can be clearly understood unless the other is taken into account. Where Geburah stands for limitation, Chesed stands for expansion; where Geburah represents violence, Chesed represents peace; where Geburah destroys, Chesed creates. In addition, though, there is a deeper link between these two powers. To the extent that Chesed contains all the Spheres below it within its own symbolism, Geburah is included therein. In a number of Chesed's symbols, the presence of the fifth Sphere shows clearly, and this reflects as well the unity of all opposites in the realms beyond the Abyss

✳   ✳   ✳

The Title assigned to the fourth Sphere is Chesed, which means "mercy", and refers directly to the Sphere's role as the clearest manifestation of the energies of the Pillar of Mercy. Like Geburah, which fulfills the same function on the other side of the Tree, Chesed is at a high enough level to express its Pillar's nature in pure form - without the muddying complexities of the Spheres below the Veil - while remaining below the paradoxical unity of the Supernals.

This statement may itself seem like a paradox, for as just mentioned the symbolism of the fourth Sphere includes elements of that of the fifth. Still, the confusion is apparent, not real. Geburah can be perceived in Chesed because Chesed's own nature, and that of the Pillar of Mercy as a whole, is to embrace and include all things. It is Severity, not Mercy, which excludes and limits.

As might be expected, though, Geburah's presence in Chesed's symbolism is most visible in those parts of the fourth Sphere's symbolism which face upwards, toward the Supernals. One example is the Divine Name assigned to Chesed, AL, which is pronounced El, and has no other translation but "God". This Name has been discussed in earlier sections as the first element in the Names ALHIM and ALVH, and as the central part of the composite Name ShDI AL ChI. In Chesed, it stands alone, representing the highest image of reality possible below the Abyss.

This image can be explored by way of the two letters which make up the Name. א, Aleph, corresponds to the element of Air and the Tarot Trump 0, the Fool; the first letter of the Hebrew alphabet, it represents the first outpouring of creative force into manifestation on the highest of levels, free of form or limitation; its name means "ox." ל, Lamed, corresponds to the zodiacal sign Libra and the Tarot Trump XI, Justice; it represents balance, equilibrium, and the idea of cause and effect. Its name, as you may recall, means "ox-goad". The ox and the ox-goad, motive power and directing limitation, represent in clear symbolic terms the potencies of Force and Form which, to the Cabalist, provide the universe we experience with its most visible and important polarity.

This Name has implications which go far beyond these concerns, and the polarity between its letters can be understood from a number of viewpoints. One of the more important of these may be found by considering these two letters as they relate to the rest of the Hebrew alphabet. If you take that alphabet in its usual order and divide it into equal halves, you'll find that Aleph begins the first half and Lamed the second. In one sense, this makes the two equivalent, but it also suggests an important difference between them. Aleph is at the very beginning of the alphabet while Lamed is effectively at its midpoint. Aleph's freedom, then, comes at least in part from the fact that it emerges first, before anything that might limit it has come into being; Lamed's balance, similarly, is the product both of its central position and of the fact that it exists in the midst of a universe of differing and sometimes contending powers.

The placement of these two letters on the Tree of Life also has a point to make. The Paths of Aleph and Lamed are respectively the beginning and end of the section of the Lightning Flash which runs from the first Sphere to the sixth. In terms of a division made earlier in this chapter, they frame the half of the Flash which has to do with unity rather than individuality. The Name El thus can be seen as a summation of the creative powers of unity.

The section of the Flash which runs from the sixth Sphere to the tenth, by contrast, can be summed up by the Hebrew word ThN, Tan, which is formed of the letters of the 32nd and 24th Paths. Tan is not a Name of God; rather, it means "dragon," and stands for the seven-headed Dragon of the Eden and Fall diagrams. The implication is clear enough. Creative power divided and individualized is of the nature of the Negative Powers; at the same time, it remains the descending light of the Infinite. As the myth of the Primal Worlds points out, even the demonic powers of unbalanced energy derive from the same unknowable reality, and share in the same unity, as everything else.

✳   ✳   ✳

The symbolism of the other three Worlds in Chesed is fairly straightforward. The Archangel Tzadkiel, "Justice of God," corresponds to the power of consciousness which enables us to perceive and compare many aspects of our experience at the same time; it is the basis of evaluation and judgement, and on a more basic level is the foundation of the experience of space. The Chashmalim, "Shining Ones," represent the process of outward radiation and expansion, while Tzedek, the planet Jupiter, is assigned by astrologers to rulership and greatness, to good fortune and to the simple physical expansion involved in feasting and similar enjoyments.

The Path Text, which comes next, will take up rather more time. It starts from the standpoint mentioned above, which sees Chesed as a summary of the Tree, and goes on in directions which have both theoretical and practical implications.

Chesed is called the Cohesive or Receptacular Intelligence. Both these terms, and the explanation given to them - that Chesed "contains all the Holy Powers" or Spheres - make it clear that Chesed can be seen as the context or framework within which the entire Tree of Life comes into manifestation. The expansive, inclusive nature of the fourth Sphere is itself a reflection of unity, the closest approximation to unity possible below the Abyss; it provides the background against which Geburah traces limits and Tiphareth brings harmony.

From Chesed, in turn, "emanate all the spiritual virtues with the most exalted essences." As we saw when the Path Text of the Path of Lamed was being considered, the word "virtue" should be understood in its older sense, as power. From Chesed, then, the highest of spiritual powers extend themselves into the realm of manifested reality. Also implied here is the point made in the Path of Lamed's Path Text, that what may as well be called goodness is a source of power. The blindness which makes severity, even destructiveness, seem stronger in human eyes than mercy is one of the more tragic consequences of the Fall.

Finally, the unity of Spheres as well as that of powers in Chesed is linked back in the Text to Kether. Each thing proceeds from the one before it because all things proceed ultimately from One. However, that One is itself an emanation; it proceeds, by way of the Three Veils, from the unknowable Reality beyond it. This last part of the Text thus reminds the student not to make the mistake of confusing the closest approach to that Reality with Reality itself.

✳   ✳   ✳

Like Geburah, Chesed has an additional title: Gedulah, which means "majesty" or "greatness." The additional titles of these two Spheres have an interesting relationship. The words Geburah and Gedulah are parallel, having similar sounds and the same number of letters; a similar link connects the word Chesed with Pachad, Geburah's additional title, "fear." This play on words helps to stress the relationship between the two Spheres.

Of the remaining symbolism, the correspondence in the microcosm and the Negative Power will require comment. The first of these is memory; this is part of the ruach, the great cluster of faculties which make up the conscious self in its full potential. It may not be clear why memory is assigned to Chesed, why memory deserves so exalted a place as the closest of the ruach's faculties to the neshamah and the Supernal Triad.

This may be less of a puzzle if it's remembered that, below the Veil, only the reflected form of this faculty is available to ordinary human consciousness. Of all of the parts of the ruach thus reflected, memory seems to suffer the most loss in the process. Experiments with electrical brain stimulation have shown that it's possible to call up memories of the past in perfect detail, and suggest that - barring physical brain damage - the memory may well retain an exact trace of everything which has been experienced. Yet it's an everyday fact of life that human memory is the most fallible of all data-storage methods. In particular, memory becomes utterly unreliable in the presence of strong emotions or belief systems. The inclusive nature of this aspect of Chesed leaves it entirely too open to distortion until the processes of memory themselves become fully conscious.

Even in its corrupted form, though, memory has astonishing powers. It is the medium in which each human being spends most of his or her life, the universe of consciousness into which all perceptions are fitted. Take a moment, now, to think about the places, people, and things that are important to you. How many of these are present to your senses right now? All the others exist, for you, only as traces in memory. Most of the things which have shaped your experience of the universe are present to you, now, only in memory - and this includes the half of the room which is behind your head as you are reading this.

To the Cabalistic magician, memory in its true sense goes beyond even this. Because it derives from a Sphere above Tiphareth, memory relates to unity as well as individuality; that is, it is not merely a personal faculty but a power of broader scope. Like will, memory has its roots beyond the self, and as the magician grows into contact with his or her Higher Self those roots provide a route to knowledge which transcends not only individuality but also space and time.

In the great flowering of the Western magical tradition during the Renaissance, magicians made use of these considerations to develop what was called the Art of Memory, a system of practices which opened up some part of memory's higher possibilities. This Art has been all but forgotten by later students of the esoteric tradition, but enough materials relating to it remain that it may someday be restored to the toolkit of the practicing magician.

$$* \quad * \quad *$$

The last symbol of Chesed which bears discussion is the Negative Power, the symbolic form of the Sphere in imbalance. Tradition gives to the fourth Sphere's Negative Power the name Ga'ashekelah, which means "those who break things apart", and the image of vast distorted giants with the heads of cats. As with the Negative Powers of Tiphareth and Geburah, the distorting effect of the Veil has to be taken into account here; the reflection of the Breakers in Pieces in the ordinary person will have one form, while for those who have glimpsed the realms beyond the Veil the corruptions of Chesed will take a different and more dangerous shape.

The cat as a symbol has a wide range of meanings, perhaps wider than any other animal's. In its negative senses, though, it typically stands for selfishness, for attitudes which place the ego and its cravings above all other things. The reflected form of the Ga'ashekelah derives from this; it is gluttony and greed, the expansion of Chesed distorted into a ballooning inflation of the self.

Above the Veil, in its turn, this vice becomes the foundation of the last and highest of the three temptations which lie between the first stirrings of the Veil and the door of the Abyss. The first of these, as we've seen, is the trap of spiritual dogmatism, the desire to petrify one's insights into a rigid parody of truth and defend it to the death. The second is the trap of spiritual elitism, the desire to despise the world for its blindness and withdraw into an shell of self-righteous contempt.

The third might be called the trap of spiritual tyranny. It comes into being when a mystic or magician decides that his or her insights confer the right (or, worse, the responsibility) to tell other people what they should do with their lives. It deepens when these attitudes are fed, as they usually are, by insecure people who seek some way to escape having to take responsibility for themselves. It ends, more often than not, with the mystic or magician becoming the center of a circle of devoted followers who have given up their own minds and wills and replaced them with those of their master.

As its correspondence with Chesed would suggest, this trap has to do with expansion, the expansion of the self. Its victim expands, though, not into the deeps of his or her own potential but across the boundary between one person and another. The followers of such a person become extensions of their leader's ego, absorbed to one degree or another into a surrogate unity of thought and feeling; they shrivel, while their master bloats. In turn, the inclusive nature of Chesed has its effect at this level as elsewhere; the mystic or magician who succumbs to this trap is likely to end up as the plaything of the whole range of Negative Powers, as the unthinking devotion of his or her followers offers opportunities for every kind of stupidity.

Examples of the Ga'ashekelah at work have provided the modern world with some of its more lurid news stories. The deeper impact of this sort of folly, though, goes beyond the scandals, the abuse and exploitation, or the body counts which not uncommonly result from it. The counterfeit unity of the spiritual tyrant and his or her followers - the "unity" of parasite and victim - is at once an obstacle to, and a flight from, the true unity which is to be found beyond the Abyss in the deepest places of the self. As a way to the completion of the self, this sort of folly is useless; for the Cabalistic magician, that is reason enough to avoid it.

Chapter Nine
The Tree Above the Abyss

With Chesed, the way of Redemption passes the last region of the Tree of Life which can be experienced, in any sense of that word, by the conscious self. The Paths and Spheres beyond relate not to the universe we perceive around us, nor to any of the higher levels we can learn to perceive, but to a realm beyond space and time in which the unchanging patterns of our experience exist in their pure state. From this realm, those patterns descend to shape the world we know; in this realm, in turn, dwell the immortal aspects of the human soul. For both these reasons, a grasp of the lore concerning the Supernals, and the Paths which link them to one another and to the rest of the Tree, is worth having, for their secrets touch on the deepest mysteries of the universe and of the self.

Path 13, the Path of Gimel

Letter of the Path: ג , Gimel (Camel).
Name of God: SHDI AL ChI, Shaddai El Chai.
Astrological Correspondence:
the Moon.
Tarot Correspondence:
Trump II, the High Priestess.
Esoteric Title: Priestess of the Silver Star.
Path Text: *"The Thirteenth Path is named the Uniting Intelligence, and is so called because it is itself the essence of glory; it is the consummation of truth of individual spiritual things."*
Mythological Principle:
Descent of the Divine.
Experiences of the Path:
Silence, empty space, imagery of the Abyss; deserts, oceans, uninhabited places; empty and silent temples; the vision of the Star in the East of Tiphareth.
Entities of the Path: Angels; silent priests and priestesses; masked figures.
Magical Image: An arch of blue, bearing the letter Gimel in brilliant white on its keystone. The door in the arch bears the image of Trump II.
Colours: in Atziluth - blue.
in Briah - silver.
in Yetzirah - cold pale blue.
in Assiah - silver, rayed with sky blue.

The crossing of the Abyss, like the opening of the Veil, is marked by a disruption in the usual ascending order of the Paths, a disruption which adds the risk of confusion to the other difficulties which must be faced here. Those difficulties are serious enough as it is. In turning toward the Supernals, the Cabalistic magician faces a realm in which opposites become identical and paradox is the closest approximation to the facts.

Beyond Chesed, conscious awareness cannot go even when it has been developed to its fullest possible extent. The Paths and Spheres above are not merely unknown, then, but in a real sense unknowable.

And yet, obviously, these Spheres and Paths have names, symbols, and traditional interpretations; a great deal of lore has gathered around them, and they play a significant role in practical work as well as theory. This is possible partly because so much of the magician's work with the Tree uses its reflection in Yesod, the Sphere of images, or in one of the other lower Spheres. Partly, though, it depends on a point of much deeper significance. The ruach ends with Chesed, true, but the ruach is not the highest aspect of the human soul. Above it is the neshamah, reflecting the Supernal Triad in the self, and what is unknown country to the ruach is home ground to the higher phase of the soul.

Thus the conscious mind, despite its limits, has a way to gain knowledge about the levels of Reality above the Abyss. In the experience of contact between the ruach and the powers of the self above it, images and understandings can be passed from higher to lower, communicating some glimpse of the nature of the Supernal realm. As with the parting of the Veil, too, these glimpses gradually broaden and deepen, until the two aspects of the self come to function as one.

Five Paths - the 18th, 17th, 16th, 15th, and 13th - lead up to the Supernal Triad from the levels below. Here, as with the Veil, the choice of a Path is more than a matter of convenience. The unity of the Supernals, though, makes the consequences of this choice rather different than those which face the magician before the Veil. All five Paths reach the goal. They do so, however, in different ways, and with very different results.

Of these five Paths, one - the 13th - is set apart in two ways. First, it is the only route across the Abyss which follows the line of the Middle Pillar, tracing out the way of balance up the higher half of the Tree. Second, it alone passes through Daath, the point of contact between higher and lower realms in the heart of the Abyss. Concerning Daath much can be said, and we will explore its symbols and meaning next; for now, it's enough to say that this quasi-Sphere offers a different means of interaction across the Abyss, one which goes far beyond what the Paths can offer.

It is by the Path of Gimel, then, that the magical Cabala directs the first journey toward the realms of unity. Just as the ascent from Malkuth began with the Path of Tau, and the first passage through the Veil with that of Samech, the first crossing of the Abyss follows the line of the Middle Pillar. Here as elsewhere in the work, balance is the first requirement.

✳   ✳   ✳

The letter assigned to this Path is ג , Gimel, which means "camel". This attribution comes from an old symbol for the Abyss, which likens it to a vast waterless desert which must be crossed by the Cabalist. Few creatures can cross any significant stretch of desert in safety, and a human being on foot is all but certain to perish. With the aid of a camel, though, the journey can be accomplished. On the one hand, this points to the need for care in choosing a Path across the Abyss. On the other, it points out that the strength needed to make the journey does not come from within the conscious self. It is the camel, not the rider, which takes step after step across the burning sand.

The next two symbols, the Name of God and astrological correspondence, illustrate this same point in another connection. At the same time, they provide another example - the most extreme on the Tree - of the complex nature of Path-Sphere linkages. The Name of God assigned to this Path is Shaddai El Chai, and the astrological symbol is the Moon. Both of these are symbols of the ninth Sphere, Yesod, which lies straight below Tiphareth, while the 13th Path lies straight above. Here, then, the way down becomes the way up in a dizzying inversion.

This attribution clarifies the point made above, and extends it into the realm of practice. The work of the magician in passing through the Veil is above all a matter of waking up, becoming conscious of the unconscious, acting from knowledge and deliberate choice rather than from reflex. Now, however, this must be reversed. At the edge of the Abyss, the magician must learn to rely on what he or she cannot know consciously, and to move in harmony with forces he or she cannot understand.

* * *

The Tarot correspondence of this Path develops the symbolism in another direction. At the same time, it provides a useful reminder of the fluid nature of the Cabalistic tradition over time. In its modern form, Trump II, the High Priestess, usually shows a veiled woman seated between two pillars, one black, one white. Lunar symbols appear on her clothes and headdress, and she often holds an open scroll or book on her lap. All of this is fairly straightforward: the pillars represent the Pillars of Force and Form between which the 13th Path runs; the moons symbolize the Moon/Yesod connection mentioned above; the book or scroll, as a symbol of knowledge, can be taken to represent Daath; the veil stands for the essential mystery of the Supernals. All in all, the card serves as a good summing-up of the symbols discussed so far, but very little more.

But this apparently straightforward Trump conceals a secret. The secret is not a matter of symbolism but of history, for the current version of Trump II is not the original. Earlier decks have an entirely different card in the same place: the Papess or Female Pope. Tradition connects this figure with the legendary Pope Joan, a figure of some notoriety in the later Middle Ages. According to the tale, a woman whose lover was a monk pretended to be male in order to live in his monastery. Her pretense of holiness was so convincing that she ended up being elected Pope - only to be found out when she went into labor in the middle of a Papal procession.

In some ways, the image of Pope Joan suits the meaning of the Path of Gimel at least as well as does the modern version of the Trump. Her message is simple, but critically important: things are not as they appear. Behind the stiff vestments and the regalia of power, something quite unexpected is going on. With the Path of Gimel, this is generally the case.

The Esoteric Title has to do with the same set of imagery as the modern version of the Trump, but it contains a reference to one of the most important traditional symbols of this Path. The "silver star" mentioned in the Title is also known as the Star in the East; some representation of this star is commonly placed on the eastern wall of lodge rooms in certain branches of the Western magical tradition, as well as in magically influenced organizations such as Freemasonry. It stands for an experience which is central to the Path's meaning. In magical work carried out on the Tiphareth level, it sometimes happens that unexpected power or insight will manifest itself, descending from the neshamah to the ruach. This experience, symbolized (and sometimes perceived) as light, marks the first step in the crossing of the Abyss, just as the "tremblings of the Veil" mark the beginning of the ascent to Tiphareth.

$$* \quad * \quad *$$

The Path Text places all these matters in their proper context. Of all the Texts, this is probably the least evasive; it has important things to say, and it says them as clearly as the nature of the Path will permit.

The Path of Gimel, then, is here called the Uniting Intelligence. Tiphareth, as discussed earlier, is the Sphere of individual existence in its most basic form, while Kether is the Sphere of absolute unity. The journey from the sixth Sphere to the first is thus a movement from separation to oneness, from the particular to the universal. The unifying process of that journey is "itself the essence of glory" - "glory" here, as elsewhere in the Texts, refers to Kether - because the essence of the first Sphere and the process of the 13th Path are alike the return of the many to one. That process, in turn, is "the consummation of the truth of individual spiritual beings" because the boundaries which divide each being from all others are imaginary - using this word in its exact sense - and exist only as a reflection of the unity and self-sufficiency of Kether.

It's worth noting that Tiphareth is the place from which this "consummation of truth" is experienced, rather than one of the higher Spheres. Tiphareth is the only Sphere below the Abyss which comes into direct contact with Kether; it reflects Kether, making each individual thing an image of the first Sphere's unity; at the same time, it is the highest point on the Tree at which individual beings exist as such rather than as aspects of a greater whole. To the sixth Sphere, then, each being ascends in search of truth; to the sixth Sphere, in turn, the energies of unity descend to bring that truth into being.

This latter point gives rise to the mythological principle of the Path of Gimel, the Descent of the Divine. Stories of gods and goddesses who visit the human world derive from this Path's principle; like Pope Joan, such deities are usually in disguise. Their function is not uncommonly to reveal some hidden truth to human beings, and that truth often involves the secrets of life and death.

Daath, the Gate of the Abyss

Title: DAaTh, Daath (Knowledge).

Name of God: AL, El (God).

Archangel: ————

Angelic Host: ————

Astrological Correspondence:
Sirius, the Dog Star.

Tarot Correspondence:
————

Elemental Correspondence:
Air.

Path Text: ————

Magical Image: A head with two faces, a female one looking upwards and to the left and a male one looking downwards and to the right, both framed in swirling silvery hair. Additional Symbols:

Additional Symbols: The empty room; the absence of all symbolism.

Colours: in Atziluth - lavender
in Briah - pale silver-gray.
in Yetzirah - pure violet.
in Assiah - gray, flecked with gold.

Correspondence in the Microcosm:
the conjunction of ruach and neshamah.

Correspondence in the Body:
the neck

Grade of Initiation: ————

Negative Power: SThRIAL, Satariel (the Concealers); AaGAL, Augiel (the Hinderers); ThAVMIAL, Thaumiel (the Twins).

Daath, the Gate of the Abyss, occupies the empty space in the center of the hexagon of Spheres that makes up the upper half of the Tree of Life. It has been the subject of a good deal of confusion in magical circles during the last century or so, for it fits into the scheme of the Tree awkwardly at best. It is neither a Sphere, an aspect of a Sphere, nor a combination of Spheres, although it functions as each of these in some contexts. Perhaps the best way to think of it is as an interface: the primary interface of the Tree, in fact, for it serves as a meeting point for nearly all the Tree's principal powers. As already mentioned, it links the Supernals with the Spheres below the Abyss, and this is central to its meaning.

It also, more directly, links Kether and Tiphareth. Daath serves as a representation of Kether below the Abyss, to such an extent that when we speak of Kether what we say usually has to do with its reflection in Daath. (This can become an obstacle at the higher levels of work; in the words of a Cabalistic saying, "when Daath is, Kether is not; when Kether is, Daath is not.") Daath also functions as a higher aspect of Tiphareth in some ways, a function mentioned in many of the older Cabalistic texts and suggested by the presence of Daath's title in the Name of God governing the sixth Sphere.

Daath also links Chokmah and Binah. This last role is the source of Daath's title, for the Hebrew language routinely uses "knowledge" as a term for sexual contact, and the union of Chokmah and Binah, Abba the Father and Aima the Mother, is often portrayed in frankly sexual terms. It is from this mating, in a mythic sense, that the universe is born. Daath thus defines the Middle Pillar, which might well be named the Pillar of Knowledge, and its role as interface is shared to one degree or another with all the Spheres of that Pillar.

But an interface is a boundary as well as a meeting ground; like a gate which may be opened or closed - an important symbol of Daath - it both permits and prevents passage. This is an important facet of Daath's nature. For the conscious self, questing up the Tree in search of the experience of truth, Daath is an impenetrable barrier. For the polarities which meet within it, Daath is the limit at which each gives way to its opposite. Daath thus relates to the Abyss as much as to the Middle Pillar; it is the intersection between these two, the point at which unity and separation merge - and divide.

The nature of Daath is made more complicated by its role in the mythology of Creation and Fall explored in an earlier chapter. Before the Fall, as Diagram 14 shows, Daath was the point at which the symbolic River Naher, the descending current of energy from the Supernals, was divided into the four rivers of Eden. After the Fall, as shown in Diagram 15, Daath became the highest reach of the Dragon, the point at which the waters of Life were corrupted by the dragon's venom into waters of death. At Daath, too, the four Kerubim and the Flaming Sword keep watch at the gate of the Higher Eden, at once a guard against the unbalanced powers below and a revelation of the way in which those powers can be overcome.

From this perspective, Daath's role as a barrier has been heightened by the Fall, while its role as a point of contact has been lessened - at least from a human perspective. Still, the Gate of the Abyss can be opened, and that opening is the supreme practical work of the Cabalistic magician.

$$* \quad * \quad *$$

The symbolism of Daath occupies an uneasy niche in the Tree's traditional imagery. Neither Sphere nor Path, it nonetheless has certain symbols corresponding to a Sphere, while at the same time it lacks some of the major symbolic expressions which define the other Spheres. It has no Name of God, no archangel, no host of angels, no Path Text assigned to it; such symbols as it does have do not always fit well in the structure of the Tree as a whole.

Its title, of course, is Daath, "knowledge." The sexual sense of this term is by no means the only one, or the only one of importance. Daath is knowledge in the sense of sexual union, the creative joining of polarities. It is also knowledge in the more usual English sense of consciously held awareness of a thing, for it is the basis of perception.

The ruach or conscious self, which tends to be regarded (and to regard itself) as the perceiving part of the self, is actually a structure or vessel for what we have been calling "awareness." A few moments of attention, though, will quickly show the difference between this structure and what it contains. If you observe yourself as you think and feel, you'll notice that the thought or feeling you perceive is different from the part of you that is perceiving it. The thoughts and feelings belong to the ruach; so do the reflections of imagination, will and memory in the lower self; so do the higher aspects of these faculties which awaken as the Veil opens. What, though, is the awareness itself?

It is in the answer to this fairly simple question that the complexities lie. In the traditional lore, the Chokmah and Binah of the microcosm - the chiah and neshamah - are said to reflect an aspect of themselves downward, into the Abyss, to form the part of the self which perceives the structures and sensations of the ruach, nephesh, and guph. This part of the self, which is Daath, is described as being like a flame set within the lantern of the lower bodies, and in this metaphor it emits rays of light which illuminate the things it perceives. This flame of awareness receives the power of perceiving from Binah, and the power of choosing what to perceive from Chokmah. It has something else from Binah, though: the first seed of individuality, a sense of distinction between subject and object, the perceiver and the thing perceived.

This seed is the kernel around which the other aspects of Daath form. It does not give rise to the full experience of individuality until Tiphareth is reached; in Chesed and Geburah it produces only a sense of differentiation within unity. Once the first distinction is made, though, the rest follows. This distinction is the beginning of the process of manifestation, and may be symbolized by the sexual act that is one meaning of the word "knowledge;" it also makes possible the perception that is the other meaning of the word "knowledge."

It is also the heart and essence of the Abyss. The distinction between the knower and the known is the first and last division of unity: the first made and the last released. Before it is made, the lower levels of the universe and the self cannot come into being, because there is no polarity upon which Creation can be based. Until it has been surpassed, until awareness fuses with the things perceived in the very act of perception, the way of Redemption cannot be completed and the unity of the Supernals cannot be regained. Once it has been surpassed, the awareness of Daath returns to its source in the union of chiah and neshamah and the cycle of cretaion is complete.

This may seem like the end of the individual self. It is not, although it may take some thought to see why. The return of awareness to its source does not nullify the creative act which brought the self into being. The ruach, nephesh and guph still exist; the neshamah, chiah and yechidah still exist. What has changed is the relationship between them. This new relationship can be represented, like the old one, as a center in the midst of the space between, a center which can again be called Daath. This center, however, is a point of direct contact between the neshamah in its pure form and the ruach in its completeness.

What is the effect of this change? To the neshamah, which exists in eternity, nothing. To the ruach, which does not, everything. The conscious self remains in existence, as we've seen, but the awareness which descends into it remains conscious of its unity with everything it experiences, conscious also of the presence and power of that unity in its own life and actions, and of its own transcendence of time and space through its origin in the eternal aspect of the self. The resulting being, aware of every level of experience from the unity of Kether to the material experience of Malkuth, is the microcosm as a complete reflection of the macrocosm - in the language of Cabalistic myth, the image of Adam Cadmon.

✳   ✳   ✳

The astrological correspondence assigned to Daath is the star Sirius, the brightest star in Earth's skies. The outer planets Uranus, Neptune, and Pluto might seem better candidates, but their symbolism (unlike that of the seven planets known to the ancient world) was not designed with magical principles in mind, and attempts to relate them to the Tree of Life have produced little more than confusion. The star Sirius, on the other hand, has been of high magical importance since ancient times, and the images and ideas built up around it are of great value. In modern magical writings it is often titled "the Sun behind the Sun;" it is equated with the Star in the East, and thus with the descent of forces to Tiphareth from the Supernals; in certain classes of practical work, its position in the sky is traditionally of some importance. As the brightest of stars, it holds a symbolic position between Binah's astrological correspondence, Saturn, and Chokmah's, the Zodiac, and thus also represents the contact between these powers.

Daath's correspondence in the Tarot is a vexing question. As it comes between the third and fourth Spheres on the Lightning Flash, it has been given the number 3 1/2 in some contexts; this is not simply Cabalistic humor, for as half of the important magical number seven, 3 1/2 appears in a range of Biblical and esoteric symbolism. At the same time, there is no 3 1/2 of any of the Tarot suits! Perhaps the best compromise assigns to Daath the 22 Trumps as a whole, for Daath's role as an interface is in some ways a summary of the principle behind all of the Paths.

Daath's elemental correspondence is less obscure. As a point on the Middle Pillar which, under some circumstances, functions as a Sphere, it shares the Middle Pillar's elemental attribution of Air. The ambivalent quality that appears in much of Air's symbolism fits well with the character of the gate of the Abyss.

The additional symbols assigned to Daath, in turn, are fairly straightforward, but they suggest an important practical principle. Human awareness has been compared to a room full of clutter, and much of the work faced by the magician is a matter of putting some sort of order into the confusion, so that things which are wanted can be readily found. This is only the first stage, though, and there comes a point at which the magician must turn his or her attention away from the mind-clutter in order to listen for the presence of something else. In doing this latter, awareness needs to be emptied, not merely organized, and among the things which need to go out with the trash are the symbols and principles of organization themselves.

This is the point made by the second of the additional symbols. The closest approach to the nature of Daath which can be made from symbolic terms is the absence of symbols altogether. This is a paradox, but it is also a practical guide. In Pathworking on the Tree, the most common sign that the level of Daath has been reached is that the images of the Pathworking fade out into blankness. Sometimes this will take place in Pathworking after Pathworking, until the colors of Daath appear in the inner sight to show that the way onward is open.

*   *   *

It is with Daath's correspondences in the microcosm and the physical body, though, that the most critical issues of magical practice emerge. As the link between the conscious self and the transcendent spirit, Daath is the medium through which all contact with the Higher Genius must take place, until the time comes when the Abyss is crossed once and for all. Like a gate, Daath may be open or closed, and it may also be opened to a greater or lesser degree. Completely closed, it is reflected in a complete blindness to anything outside the material aspects of life; as it opens, so open the higher levels of the self. Fully open, on the other hand, it permits the return of awareness to its transcendent source.

Traditional lore has it, as we've seen, that the full opening of Daath involves the highest levels of spiritual attainment. A partial opening of the gate, on the other hand, can take place on a much more modest level of development. Any glimpse of the Tiphareth level can waken the energies of the 13th Path and begin the process; as such glimpses are repeated, possibly over many lives, the process continues. The initial stages of the opening of the Daath center, in fact, are part and parcel of the work of opening the Veil, and the two become distinct only when the Veil opens and the Higher and Lower Selves merge in the full attainment of the Tiphareth level of consciousness.

The gradual opening of the Daath center is of the highest importance to the magician, for two reasons. First, the interface between ruach and neshamah is also said to be the interface between the parts of the self which perish with the death of the physical body and those parts which do not. As that interface becomes more active, more of the structure of the conscious self is preserved through the stages of death and rebirth, and lessons learnt in one life can be carried over to others with less difficulty.

Second, the interface between ruach and neshamah is a source of power as well as of knowledge. The River Naher of the Eden diagram represents the full creative energy of the Supernals in the macrocosm and microcosm alike. Poisoned, in the language of the myth, by the venom of the Dragon, it still flows, and the opening of Daath may also be symbolized as the loosening of the Dragon's hold on the lower Eden; the wider the gate opens, the more pure the descending stream. It's worth noting that the wholly material-minded tend to be remarkably passive, moved about only by biological drives or the acts and words of their leaders. The great magicians and mystics, on the other hand, have been men and women of astonishing personal power and vigor.

The physical reflection of the Daath center in the human body is in the neck and lower face, and contains the entire vocal apparatus. This is one reason why particular ways of speaking or chanting words have always been potent tools in the magician's kit.

✳   ✳   ✳

The remaining symbols given in the table belong to Daath only in a specialized sense. The three Negative Powers listed in the table correspond to the three Spheres of the Supernal Triad: the Satariel to Binah, the Augiel to Chokmah, and the Thaumiel to Kether. In the Fall, though, the Supernals remained untainted, and their equivalents among the Negative Powers cannot reach beyond the highest point of the Dragon's ascent. This "infernal triad" has its place in Daath, then, and provides the last and most dangerous traps faced by the magician on the way of Redemption.

These three Powers differ from the ones we've examined before in something of the same way those above the Veil differ from those below it. They correspond to three choices which may be made by those who awaken the full powers of the ruach, who successfully open the Veil and pass beyond it. These three choices have a certain resemblance to ideas and philosophies concerning the ultimate reality beyond our perceptions. In their reflected form below the Veil, in fact, they give rise to certain ways of thinking about the universe. In their pure form, on the other hand, they are not opinions but deliberate choices concerning the Supernal realm, made by human beings operating at the highest levels of power that conscious awareness can bear. Made with the full strength of the Higher Self, these decisions have potent consequences.

The Satariel or Concealers have the traditional image of a giant, horned demon's head hidden beneath a heavy veil. In reflected form, they represent the view that ultimate reality is nothingness, or that nothing actually exists: the standpoint of nihilism. In their pure form, they represent the decision to embrace the unity of the Supernals by rejecting all that lies below the Abyss.

The Augiel or Hinderers are given the form of distorted giants entangled in the coils of serpents. In reflected form, they stand for the idea that all that exists is precisely the flurry of experiences which the Cabala labels the World of Assiah, and that nothing beyond the realm of experience has any reality at all: the standpoint of relativism. In their pure form they stand for the decision to reject the unity of the Supernals in favor of the diversity of the realms below the Abyss.

The Thaumiel or Twins have the traditional image of twin heads borne on the wings of bats. They have no bodies, it is said, because they always seek to unite themselves with other beings and forces. In their reflected form, they symbolize the belief that the only thing that exists is oneself: the viewpoint of solipsism. In their pure form they symbolize the decision to see the conscious self as equal to, or containing, the Supernal Unity itself.

The pure forms of these Negative Powers can be put equally well into theological language. The Satariel, in these terms, represent the once-popular Gnostic attitude that sees Creation as evil, and rejects it in order to return to God. The Augiel stand for the corresponding attitude, quite popular nowadays, that sees the created world as the only reality and God as an illusion. The Thaumiel, finally, symbolize the always popular attitude that identifies the self as God. Alternatively, these can be seen from a philosophical standpoint, as three possible ways to relate the experience of change and impermanence to a transcendent, timeless realm of meaning: by denying that experience is real; by denying that the transcendent realm is real; or by taking the self which experiences as the transcendent realm itself.

These three horns of the Dragon, however, rise from a single head. The common factor uniting them looks back to Daath's relationship with Tiphareth, for all three of these Powers rise from the vice of

Tiphareth, which is pride. The Satariel reflect that pride which refuses to accept anything less than the highest as fit for the self; the Augiel, from that pride which refuses to accept that anything can exist outside its reach; the Thaumiel, for that supreme arrogance which makes the self equal to the unity of all things. Just as these mistakes are linked to Tiphareth, though, so is the knowledge which overcomes them, when the conscious self in Tiphareth recognizes itself and all other selves as reflections - nothing more, but nothing less - of the unity of Kether.

Path 17, the Path of Zayin

Letter of the Path: ז , Zayin (Sword).

Name of God: YHVH, the Tetragrammaton.

Astrological Correspondence:
Gemini, the Twins.

Tarot Correspondence:
Trump VI, the Lovers.

Esoteric Title: Children of the Voice Divine, Oracles of the Mighty Gods.

Path Text: *"The Seventeenth Path is the Disposing Intelligence, which provides faith to the righteous, and they are clothed with the holy spirit by it, and it is called the oundation of excellence in the state of higher things."*

Mythological Principle:
Love between Divine and Human.

Experiences of the Path:
Symbols of duality and unity, imagery relating to sexual love, contact with spirits, intuitive and oracular messages, images of the Abyss.

Entities of the Path: Androgynes and other dual beings; any of a wide range of spirits.

Magical Image: An arch of bright orange, bearing the letter Zayin in brilliant white on its keystone. The door in the arch bears the image of Trump VI.

Colours: in Atziluth - orange.
in Briah - pale mauve.
in Yetzirah - color of new yellow leather.
in Assiah - reddish grey, tinged with mauve.

In the work of opening the way across the Abyss, the four Paths to the Supernals which do not pass through Daath have a secondary place, but an important one. They do not, as the Path of Gimel does, help open the Daath center; their role has little to do with the bringing down of power from the Supernals or the transformation of the way of rebirth which the Gate of the Abyss has in its keeping. They do, however, permit communication between the ruach and neshamah, and such communication is a valuable gift in its own right. Each Path represents a different channel for this kind of contact with the Higher Genius, and each of these channels has a relationship with certain practical skills in the Cabalistic magician's toolkit.

Of these four Paths, the Path of Zayin is the first we will explore. Despite the comprehensive scrambling of Path numbers at this level of the Tree, this is the next Path in the order of ascent. It runs from Tiphareth up to Binah, the lowest Sphere of the Supernal Triad, linking the core Sphere of the conscious self with the realm of ultimate Form. To open it is to bring the imagination into harmony with the primordial forms which serve as "blueprints" for the manifested universe we experience. In practical terms, then, the Path of Zayin relates most closely to intuition.

The position of this Path above the Veil serves as a warning, though, that the relationships it represents do not appear in the realm of ordinary experience in anything like a pure or direct form. The "intuitions" experienced before the opening of the Veil are generally reflected through Yesod or Netzach, appearing as vague images or feelings which may or may not relate to anything at all. As the location of the Path shows, it is only once Tiphareth has been reached that these give way to the clear perceptions of intuition in its true form.

Still, the development of intuition can be a significant part of magical training even at the most basic levels. In many modern esoteric systems, the Golden Dawn system among them, this aspect of training is handled through the practice of one of the Western tradition's many systems of divination. To some extent, then, this Path has a special relationship to the work of the diviner, and in Golden Dawn practice it connects to the specific divinatory arts of geomancy, Tarot, and horary astrology. It should be understood, though, that the technical methods of divination are of value only as helps to the intuition, and as the Veil opens and the intuition grows clear specific techniques of divination may no longer be necessary.

* * *

Binah is the mother of Form; Tiphareth is the source of individual existence. On the Path linking them, issues of unity and individuality take on a heightened importance, and many of the symbols of the Path touch on these issues directly.

The letter assigned to this Path, Zayin, is one example of this. Zayin is the Hebrew word for "sword." The emergence of more powerful weapons has given the sword a golden tinge of nostalgia in modern minds, but it was the assault weapon of the ancient and medieval worlds, a precisely crafted device made for the purpose of killing human beings. The sword can symbolize the division of unity in the most radical of senses; a sword, after all, is simply an efficient means for converting human bodies from wholes to parts. Its form approximates a line, and as any student of geometry learns, a line is defined by two separate points and divides a plane into two equal halves.

As a symbol of the division of unity, the sword connotes the more destructive aspects of this process, and it links to beliefs of the Gnostic type which see the descent from unity to individuality as a fall or a mistake - a view which in its extreme forms has some relationship to the Satariel, the Negative Power linked to Binah.

The sword also symbolizes the element of Air, however, and that element plays a critical role in the Path's symbolism. The Name of God and astrological correspondence of the Path of Zayin both derive from it. The Divine Name attributed to this Path is the Tetragrammaton, the Name ruling Air, while the sign of the Zodiac assigned to the Path is Gemini, an Air sign ruled by the planet Mercury.

From Gemini, in addition, emerges another side of the Path's symbolism. This sign's traditional symbol is a pair of twins; in myth, these were Castor and Pollux, twin sons of the god Zeus and a mortal woman. Because of their mixed parentage, one of the twins was mortal, the other immortal. This can represent, in turn, the relationship between the mortal and immortal parts of the human soul, and this relationship is one to which the Path of Zayin has a particular connection. The ruach is centered in Tiphareth, the neshamah in Binah, and the Path connecting these suggests that the intuition is the most important of the routes of communication linking these two. In the higher levels of magical work, this becomes a point of some practical importance.

*   *   *

The next of the Path symbols develops the Path's meaning in a different direction. The Tarot correspondence for the 17th Path is Trump VI, the Lovers. The imagery on this card has changed substantially down through the years. The oldest image seems to have been nothing more mysterious than a young couple holding hands. Of the versions that followed, some showed a young man choosing between two women - bride and mother in some decks, bride and harlot in others - while others brought in imagery from the Eden legend or from stranger sources still. The Golden Dawn, taking the latter option, reworked the entire card on the lines of the Greek myth of the rescue of Andromeda from the sea-serpent by Perseus, and used this as a symbol of the relationship of the parts of the self, which is at least appropriate to the Path. Many of the most recent decks, finally, have turned back to the beginning of the circle and show a young couple holding hands.

This simplest form of the Trump is perhaps the most useful here, for it expresses the other side of the issue raised by the image of the sword. A cynic once pointed out that if all things are one, all sex is masturbation. Despite the sarcasm, there's a point to the jibe, for it's precisely the interaction between two different people that gives the act of love its special quality. In a broader (and highly metaphorical) sense, this same point holds for individual existence as a whole. Where the sword symbolizes the division of unity in its more negative senses, then, the image of the Lovers casts that division in a more positive light: not a fall from perfection but a reaching out to explore the possibilities of interaction and relationship. This set of ideas links into beliefs of the sort once found in Romanticism and now common to many so-called "New Age" ideologies. Such ideas see the breaking of unity as a positive step, a liberation from sameness - a view which in its extreme forms has some relationship to the Augiel, the Negative Power linked to Chokmah.

*   *   *

The Esoteric Title assigned to this Path returns to points raised earlier, while it also draws a valuable comparison. This Path is the only one which is given a plural title - again stressing its connection to issues of unity and division - and, as "Oracles of the Mighty Gods," it draws a connection between the Path and the intuitive powers discussed above.

The form of the Title, on the other hand, may strike a chord of familiarity. It closely parallels the Title of the 20th Path, "The Magus of the Voice of Light, the Prophet of the Gods." The parallel points up a contrast; this contrast is partly between the Force and Form sides of the Tree, partly between a Path below the Abyss and one which crosses it. Magus and prophet are both active titles, while child and oracle suggest receptivity. They represent two different ways of relating the self to the universe. By taking an active role, the magician comes into contact with the expansive energies of the macrocosm in Chesed; by turning to a receptive role, the magician interacts with the primordial forms underlying the macrocosm in Binah.

The Path Text approaches these same issues from a different direction. That direction is made more obscure than it needs to be by a terminology taken from theological sources. Terms such as "faith," "the righteous" and the "holy spirit" have been used and misused so often by the orthodox religions of the West that it can be hard to see past the thicket of connotations to the meaning intended.

Faith, to begin with, is not the same thing as blind belief. As discussed in an earlier chapter, it should be seen as an attitude of basic trust in the universe. As we'll see shortly, it has its roots in Binah, and at that level represents an awareness of the essential form which underlies the universe; we trust, ultimately, what we understand, and Binah is (in a special sense) the source of all understanding. Righteousness, similarly, has nothing to do with moralizing; it simply means being in a right relationship with the universe and the self. Finally, the term "holy spirit" (a better translation from the Hebrew would be "spirit of holiness") refers not to the third person of the Christian trinity but to the influence of the Supernals on the consciousness of the ruach.

The Path of Zayin, then, is the Disposing Intelligence - the word "disposing" meant "arranging" or "distributing" before it took on its modern meaning of "throwing away" - because through it the special gifts of Binah are given to the conscious self once this latter has brought itself into balance and harmony. These gifts include a basic trust in the universe, which comes through a grasp of the universe's underlying nature; they also include a range of subtle effects on the various levels of the aura, hinted at in the phrase "clothed with the holy spirit." These gifts, in turn, are the "foundation of excellence in the state of higher things," or in other terms the basis on which the higher levels of attainment on the magician's path can be reached.

The experience which underlies this Text, and which has deep connections to the receptive symbolism of the Esoteric Title, can be expressed in another way. As mentioned back in Chapter Four, the essential "otherness" of the part of the self above the Abyss has led some Cabalists to symbolize it as a separate being - as the Holy Guardian Angel, or as Adonai - and this symbolism appears as well in mythological contexts. There, it often takes the form of myths of love relationships between human beings and gods or goddesses. Such myths provide the mythological principle for this Path, and a study of this type of legend can provide useful insights into the dynamics of the 17th Path.

Path 18, the Path of Cheth

Letter of the Path: ח , Cheth (Fence).
Name of God: AL, El.
Astrological Correspondence:
                            Cancer, the Crab.
Tarot Correspondence:
                            Trump VII, the Chariot.
Esoteric Title: Child of the Power of the Waters, Lord of the
                            Triumph of Light.
Path Text: *"The Eighteenth Path is called the Intelligence of the
                            House of Influence, by the greatness of whose
                            abundance the influx of good things on created beings
                            is increased, and from its midst by investigation are
                            drawn forth the arcana and hidden senses, which dwell
                            in its shadow and which cling to it, from the cause of
                            all causes."*

Mythological Principle:
                            The Once and Future Monarch.
Experiences of the Path:
                            Boundaries, borders and shores; journeys
                            between worlds and times; images of contain-
                            ment or enclosure; relics of the distant past; an
                            often intense sense of waiting or brooding.
Entities of the Path: Phantoms of past ages; the Sleeping King or
                            Queen.
Magical Image: An arch of a rich amber color, bearing the
                            letter Cheth in brilliant white on its keystone.
                            The door in the arch bears the image of Trump VII.
Colours: in Atziluth - amber.
                            in Briah - maroon.
                            in Yetzirah - rich bright russet.
                            in Assiah - dark greenish brown.

The Path of Cheth runs from Geburah to Binah, forming the upper half of the Pillar of Severity. Like the Path of Mem below it, it has that peculiar balance which comes from the complete domination of one side of a polarity relationship. This quality of balance is heightened by the Spheres at either end of the Path, for the formative nature of Binah and the limiting power of Geburah both help to give this Path a characteristic mood of restriction, containment and control. It expresses the Pillar of Severity at its harshest, untouched by the balancing energies of the Middle Pillar or the harmonizing influence of Tiphareth.

This quality of the Path, however, produces not stasis and rigidity but immense power in motion. This may seem like a paradox, but it expresses the same law that comes into play whenever a gasoline engine is started or the trigger of a gun pulled. Gasoline or gunpowder, poured on the ground and lit, will produce a fire and little more. On the other hand, if either one is contained and restricted - enclosed within the rigid walls of a cylinder or a gun barrel - the energy they contain will be transformed into motion. The same is true of any source of energy, and above all of the human will.

To some extent, this ties into the issues of unity of will explored in our discussion of Geburah, but it goes beyond this as well. The principle of limitation, as it has been called, is one of the most important rules behind practical magic - and one of the least understood in modern times. Implicit in it is the entire art of talismans, and in another sense many of the technical methods of initiation derive from it. A detailed look into these matters would lead too far from our subject, but in a later chapter, some of the applications of this principle will be explored more fully.

In terms of the practical methods of the Cabalistic magician, though, the Path of Cheth has a different application. Like the Path of Zayin, it relates to the receptive side of the magician's work, and has its goal in Binah, the realm of ultimate Form. Where the Path of Zayin represents the art of divination, though, that of Cheth may be related to the various classes of magical work which we can call "visionary experience," and which in the Golden Dawn tradition are developed through practical methods such as scrying and Pathworking. As with the technical systems of divination, the specific methods of visionary work are useful mostly as helps to innate powers of the self - in this case, the subtle analogues of the ordinary senses which open on the less material realms of experience - and may be discarded as these powers become fully developed; in the training of the magician, though, the technical methods can have an important place. They represent forms - containers, in effect - for these often elusive abilities, providing structured channels through which hidden aspects of experience can be perceived.

✳　　✳　　✳

The letter assigned to the 18th Path is named Cheth, which means "fence" or "enclosure." In the largely rural and agricultural societies of the past, fences had an importance which modern city-dwellers rarely grasp. Pasture and farmland were the basis of survival, and wealth consisted largely of livestock - many old words for money literally mean "cattle." In such communities, fences served much the same function that bank accounts do now. These considerations gave the fence as a concept a role in the 18th Path's meaning which passes beyond the simple sense of containment into issues of value.

The next two symbols, the Name of God and the astrological correspondence, shift the major focus to the Path's place in the Tree rather than its own nature. The Name assigned to this Path is El, corresponding to the elements of Water, and the sign of the Zodiac is Cancer, the Crab, one of the three Water signs. The element of Water is the primary influence on the whole Pillar of Severity, governing both Paths and two of the three Spheres which form it. This reference to the most receptive of the elements stresses the essentially passive nature of the Pillar of Severity. Like the walls of the cylinder or the gun barrel in the metaphor used earlier, the energies of Form have the role of receiving Force, shaping it, and directing it toward an end.

The Zodiacal sign Cancer ties into this symbolism, but it has a lesson if its own to teach as well. Of all the animals known to the Middle

Ages, the crab best symbolizes the combination of containment and power which is central to the meaning of this Path. Enclosed in its hard shell, the crab is still capable of quick movement, and its pincers give it the option of attack. Like a man in armor, its very rigidity is a source of its strength.

The image of a man in armor plays a significant part in the next symbol of the 18th Path, although it is one element of a complex symbolism. The Tarot Trump assigned to this Path is Trump VII, the Chariot. Most versions of this card show a man in full armor standing in a chariot drawn by two horses; the horses may be replaced by sphinxes, or stranger beasts, but often one is black, one white.

The image of the chariot has a long and complicated role in the esoteric traditions of the Western world. It has been seen most commonly as a symbol of the self, with its horses the various drives and forces which must be harnessed and guided by the higher levels of the self. In nearly all versions of the Trump, however, the reins which would permit this kind of control are nowhere to be seen.

Implied here is the role of the neshamah, the spiritual self, in its relationship to the will in Geburah. In the image of the Chariot, it is the neshamah which is the true charioteer, and the conscious will is simply the vehicle through which the higher aspects of the self operate. (Technically, it is the chiah or spiritual will in Chokmah which works through the neshamah in Binah in this work of guidance; the references to Wisdom and Understanding in Geburah's Path Text apply to this.) The means by which this guidance takes place are not perceived by the conscious self. Hidden beyond the Abyss, they guide the chariot of the self without visible reins; the limiting and directing power of the will works within a context the ruach cannot see but cannot escape.

The Esoteric Title of this Path, in turn, refers back to much of the symbolism already covered. The Path of Cheth is "Child of the Power of the Waters" because of the dominant role of water symbolism on the whole Pillar of Severity, and because the Path descends from Binah, the Great Sea; it is "Lord of the Triumph of Light" because the midsummer solstice, the longest day of the year, takes place in the Northern Hemisphere when the sun enters the Zodiacal sign Cancer.

* * *

With the Path Text the focus of the symbolism deepens. Most of the concepts involved are among those dealt with by the other symbols, but the implications reach straight into issues at the core of the Cabalistic magician's work.

The term "house of influence" used in the Text was borrowed from the traditional language of astrology, and refers to the area or aspect of the universe which a given power is capable of affecting. As the Intelligence of the House of Influence, the Path of Cheth can be seen as the interaction which marks out these different areas or aspects, a role which has obvious connections with the Spheres this Path connects.

The Text goes on to point to two sides of this role, one as part of the way of Creation, one as part of that of Redemption. As a creative power, the "greatness of (the 18th Path's) abundance" increases "the influx of good things on created beings." This may seem like a strange thing to say about a Path on the Pillar of Severity, but the Text speaks of "good things" rather than some more formless concept such as "blessings." As a source of form, the Path helps shape the descent of creative power into concrete forms by distributing that power through the different "houses of influence," dividing unity into the abundance of the universe we experience.

As a redemptive power, on the other hand, the Path leads straight to the secrets of the visionary practices of magic. "From its midst," the Text continues, "by investigation are drawn forth the arcana and hidden senses" which are associated with it, but which ultimately come not from this Path but from "the cause of causes," Kether itself. The phrase "hidden senses" here could also be translated "hidden meanings" or "allusions." By probing the secrets of limitation, this part of the Text suggests, secrets and hidden meanings deriving from Kether - from the highest image of existence attainable by any level of the self - can be brought within reach of the conscious mind. Here again, as with the Path of Zayin, the workings of this Path allows a way of communication to be opened up across the Abyss.

The "arcana" or secrets hidden in this Path, in turn, have a strong effect on the way it tends to be perceived in the experiences of practical work. The feeling of waiting or brooding, and of the presence of something concealed just out of sight can be powerful when the Path energies are awakened in any way. This, in turn, has much to do with the mythological principle assigned to the Path of Cheth.

Most cultures have legends concerning a famous ruler or hero of the past who, although seemingly dead, will someday return. King Arthur is one of the most famous examples of the type, although he is neither the oldest nor the most widely known; much of Christian theology is founded on the attribution of exactly this myth to Jesus. In Pathworking, as in many myths, the Sleeping King or Queen is often found in an underground chamber or a silent hall, lying amid warriors and treasures. In many ways, this is a development of the image of the Drowned Giant of the Path of Mem, and represents the whole potential of the self, waiting for the time when all the prophecies of legend will be fulfilled.

Binah, the Third Sphere

Title:	BINH, Binah (Understanding).
Name of God:	YHVH ALHIM, Tetragrammaton Elohim.
Archangel:	TzPQIAL, Tzaphqiel (Contemplation of God).
Angelic Host:	ARALIM, Aralim (Valiant Ones).

Astrological Correspondence:
ShBThAI, Shabathai (Saturn).

Tarot Correspondence:
the four Threes and four Queens of the pack.

Elemental Correspondence:
Water.

Path Text:
"The Third Path is the Sanctifying Intelligence, and it is the foundation of Primordial Wisdom; it is called the creator of faith, and its roots are in Amen. It is the parent of faith, and from its virtues faith emanates."

Magical Image:
An old woman with long white hair, wearing a simple black robe, holding a rough wooden staff. She is facing toward the viewer's right.

Additional Symbols: All cteic (vaginal) symbols.

Additional Titles: AMA, Ama, the dark sterile mother; AIMA, Aima, the bright fertile mother; MRH, Marah, the Great Sea.

Colours:
in Atziluth - crimson.
in Briah - black.
in Yetzirah - dark brown.
in Assiah - gray, flecked with pink.

Correspondence in the Microcosm:
Neshamah, the spiritual understanding.

Correspondence in the Body:
The right side of the head.

Grade of Initiation: 8=3, Magister Templi.

Negative Power: None (see Daath).

A metaphor sometimes used in the magical tradition of the Cabala compares the crossing of the Abyss to a sea voyage into unknown waters. Like the captains of the age of European exploration, the Cabalistic magician at this point in the way of Redemption leaves the known world behind and sets out into uncharted regions. The Paths of Zayin and Cheth, to extend the metaphor, can be seen as the seas to be sailed, and Binah, the third Sphere of the Tree of Life, becomes the landfall on the far side of the ocean.

This metaphor has its greatest usefulness when working with reflections of these Paths in the Spheres of Netzach, Hod, and Yesod, where most of the work of the magician-in-training takes place. At these levels, the reflected Abyss can be crossed in meditation and Pathworking. As the ascent of the Tree continues and the Abyss comes closer, the metaphor weakens, and it must be discarded or reinterpreted when the magician comes to deal with the experience of the Abyss in its full reality. That ocean cannot be crossed by the ruach; it ends, like the ocean around the flat earth of ancient legend, in a sheer drop and a void. The world beyond it, in turn, is alien in a way which no new landfall on earth could ever be. Even the voyages of the Apollo astronauts, whose spacecraft turned the Path from Malkuth to Yesod into an orbital trajectory, reached a place more familiar than the one we're discussing.

The strangeness of the Supernal realm, its total difference from anything familiar, needs to be kept in mind constantly when the Spheres and Paths wholly above the Abyss are studied. The Supernals are the realm of unity: not a unity within which forms take shape, like Geburah; not a unity in which forces press outward, like Chesed; but utter unity, in which no division, no distinction, no separation can be imagined to exist. In Binah, that unity is the source of Form, while in Chokmah it is the beginning of Force; in Kether it cannot be defined even in so abstract a manner.

It may seem puzzling that the Cabala bothers to describe so thoroughly foreign a realm at all, especially since the ruach, the conscious self, can never do more than wrestle with reflections and paradoxes in the quest to deal with them. Still, as suggested before, the conscious self is not the upper limit of the human soul. To the neshamah, the chiah and the yechidah, the three highest aspects of the microcosm, this strange territory is home ground, and awareness of these levels may be gained as Daath opens. The ruach, ultimately, is merely a structure for awareness; to return to the metaphor, it is the ship in which the Cabalistic magician sails. That ship can complete only a part of the voyage before it founders. The remainder must be undergone by awareness alone, without any of the familiar structures that normally define the self. Like a castaway in some sailor's legend, it comes to the far shore of the ocean naked, bearing nothing but itself.

$$* \quad * \quad *$$

The need to construct symbols for Binah out of the realms of experience which can be comprehended by the ruach has produced a certain amount of dissonance in the symbolism of the third Sphere. Several different themes, not all of them easily compatible, move back and forth through its symbolism. One pattern, rising from Binah's role as source of the Pillar of Severity, includes symbols of darkness, limitation, and receptivity. Closely linked to this is a related set of images drawn from the symbolism of the Abyss. Another pattern, sharply different, stresses Binah's role as the source of form through imagery of fertility, birth, and motherhood. In addition, the place of Binah as the lowest Sphere not affected by the Fall has reshaped the third Sphere's relationship with the Spheres beneath it, giving rise to a pattern of images of warfare against the forces of evil.

The title of the third Sphere derives mostly from the first of these patterns. The word Binah, which can be translated "understanding," stands for the mode of knowing which receives what is known into a context; we understand something when we see its causes and its effects, its relationships and its meanings. While this form of perception is still a function of the ruach, it serves as the closest approximation we can reach to the mode of consciousness of Binah itself. It also stresses, usefully, that the relationship of Binah to Daath is in some sense like that of understanding to mere knowledge.

If this symbol makes allowances for the ruach's limits, though, the next does not. The Name of God assigned to Binah is YHVH ALHIM, Tetragrammaton Elohim, the conjunction of the great creative Name with the Powers. Both of these Names have appeared twice before in the course of our ascent of the Tree, and they make their third and final appearance here, above the Abyss. These two Names suggest differing, even opposed images for the Reality beyond appearances. The Tetragrammaton is an image of cyclic creative processes within unity; Elohim implies not unity but a diversity of powers bringing about creation through their interactions. The union of the two in one Name is deliberate paradox, a reminder of the limits of symbolism above the Abyss.

With the next two symbols, a new pattern enters the picture, and the imagery of struggle against negative forces takes on the principal role. The Archangel of Binah is Tzaphqiel, who is called the Prince of the Spiritual Strife against Evil, and the angels of Binah are the Aralim, "Valiant Ones." In the Worlds of Briah and Yetzirah, then, the third Sphere is to be seen as an active power opposing the forces of imbalance. This, as mentioned earlier, has largely to do with the myth of the Fall, but it also relates to Binah's position at the head of the Pillar of Form; it is not itself divided, but as the source of form it is the beginning of all division, and the limits of Geburah and the distinctions and definitions of Hod all descend from it.

The name of Tzaphqiel means "Contemplation of God;" he represents that potential in consciousness, unreachable by the ordinary mind, in which awareness comes to rest within the essential forms of all existence, knowing all things through union with their archetypes. This is the normal state of the neshamah. The Aralim, in turn, as the Yetzirah correspondence of Binah, stand for the processes of consciousness at this level.

In the world of Assiah, by contrast, the first pattern mentioned above comes back into play. Saturn, the astrological correspondence of Binah, stands for limitation and rest, age and inertia, and the effects of time. In practical working, Saturn is often used as though it were the correspondence of Daath, and this reflects an important point; in one of its senses, Daath is the image of the Supernal Triad as seen from below, and in that image the symbolism and power of Binah dominates. The role of the supernals as a limiting power plays a significant role in certain aspects of magical work.

*   *   *

The Path Text for Binah returns the focus to the work of Redemption. Binah here is called the creator, parent, and source of faith. Faith, as we've seen, can be understood as a basic quality of trust in the universe, a reliance on the existence of some sort of underlying pattern and purpose; it is the opposite of that common and destructive attitude which sees life as essentially meaningless and the universe as random or even malign. Faith derives from Binah because Binah, the source of Form, is equally the source of all stability and all predictable pattern.

The Text also calls Binah the "foundation of primordial Wisdom," a phrase which deserves some attention. Wisdom is Chokmah, the second Sphere, and the word translated "foundation" is Yesod, the title of the ninth Sphere. Yesod is the great center of solidification on the Tree, the point at which the energies of the higher Spheres take on the patterns of form and force that give rise to the experience of matter and energy in Malkuth. To call Binah the Yesod of Chokmah, then, is to assign it a similar role in solidifying and condensing the energies of the second Sphere, and this is one way of understanding Binah's function. Binah and Yesod are also connected numerically, since $9 = 3$ x 3, and share certain other symbols in some branches of the Cabalistic tradition.

Two other phrases in the Text deserve comment. One says of Binah that "its roots are in Amen;" the word Amen, now generally reduced to a sort of spoken punctuation at the end of a prayer, was originally one of the more important words of power, and in Cabalistic usage it is a title of Kether. The other phrase calls Binah the "Sanctifying Intelligence." To sanctify is to make holy, to bring something into relationship with the Eternal; the implication here is that it is through Binah that this process takes place, and Binah's place as the most accessible of the Supernals makes this sensible enough.

* * *

The receptive element of Binah's symbolism links with the imagery of fertility in the next several symbols of the third Sphere. It's a symptom of our culture's biases that the first of these is not a household term; cteic (that is, vaginal) symbols are just as common as phallic symbols in dreams, literature and life. The vagina is perhaps the most complete symbol of Binah. Receptive and dark, it encloses the act of reproduction, and from it issue the physical forms of new life. Its monthly bleeding (a link with Yesod, as tied to the cycles of the Moon) suggests also Saturn's role as Lord of Time; its salty secretions mirror the waters of the Great Sea, another Binah symbol.

Linked to this are two additional titles of Binah. Ama and Aima are Hebrew words for "mother." They differ only by the letter Yod, absent in one, present in the other. Yod can symbolize the sperm; because of this, and because of the numerical values of the letters which make up the two words, the first is called dark and sterile, the second bright and fertile. These are not, however, value judgements. Ama is Binah in its role as mystery and as source of limitation; Aima is Binah in its role as origin of all form. It is from Aima that the way of Creation is born, but the traveler on the way of Redemption will have more to do with Ama, for the secrets of the Abyss are in her keeping. She is the Lady of Silence, and of Sorrow.

The last of the additional titles of Binah has already been mentioned: Marah, the Great Sea. In earlier times, the ocean had the same sort of ideas associated with it that we now assign to outer space. Vast and largely unknown, it concealed dangers and treasures, lost civilizations and monstrous creatures; even those who traveled on it saw only what it chose to show them. All these things are compatible with the sense of mystery that is one of Binah's chief attributes.

The Great Sea also relates, in another sense, to the microcosmic correspondence of Binah, the neshamah. In one of the oldest metaphors in mysticism, the return of individual awareness to the source of all awareness is imaged as the return of a drop of water to the sea. This metaphor has its limits; from the perspective of the ruach, it is the sea that enters into the drop of water, linking it with all the oceans of the world without bursting it; from beyond the Abyss, on the other hand, it might be said that the drop never left the ocean at all! Still, it is a useful image, and it has an important role in some of the traditional symbolism of initiation.

The neshamah itself, as mentioned before, is the higher or spiritual understanding; it represents the root of the power of perception in the human soul, just as the chiah, the reflection of Chokmah, is the root of the power of action. As a power in the realm of the Supernals, the neshamah is beyond space and time, and the power of perception which comes from it is not necessarily limited by these factors. The Magister Templi, the magician who has crossed the Abyss to Binah, is said to be aware of past and future at once; the same power on a lower plane gives rise to some of the startling results of divination.

Path 15, the Path of Heh

Letter of the Path: ה , Heh (Window).

Name of God: ALHIM, Elohim.

Astrological Correspondence:
Aries, the Ram.

Tarot Correspondence:
Trump IV, the Emperor.

Esoteric Title: Son of the Morning, Chief Among the Mighty.

Path Text: *"The Fifteenth Path is the Constituting Inteligence, so called because it constitutes the substance of Creation in pure darkness, and it is said of these contemplations: it is that darkness spoken of in Scripture (Job 38:9), "and thick darkness a swaddling band for it."*

Mythological Principle:
the Monarch of the Golden Age.

Experiences of the Path:
Imagery of springtime and new life; the combination of solar and stellar symbols; the creation of the world, or of worlds; the vision of endless space.

Entities of the Path:
Royal figures with their retinue; angels; various classes of creative spirits.

Magical Image: An arch of bright red, bearing the letter Heh in brilliant white on its keystone. The door in the arch bears the image of Trump IV.

Colours: in Atziluth - scarlet.
in Briah - red.
in Yetzirah - brilliant flame red.
in Assiah - glowing red.

In climbing the Tree of Life, the one rule which holds good through all the confusions of Path numbering and placement is that the ascent to each Sphere begins from the lowest possible point. If Daath is counted as a Sphere - which, in some limited circumstances, it should be - this even holds good in the crossing of the Abyss; each phase of that crossing, to Daath, to Binah, to Chokmah and to Kether, begins from Tiphareth. Taken in a broad sense, this rule can be seen as a guide to the whole work of the Cabalistic magician, for it points out the value of basing each stage of that work on stages which have already been well mastered. In the crossing of the Abyss, though, it has a further sense. Each part of that crossing begins in Tiphareth; each extension of awareness into the highest possible levels of human consciousness, then, begins from the core of the conscious self, and rises from a foundation of self-knowledge.

This point is of special importance when the ascent to Chokmah, the second Sphere, is considered. From below the Abyss, the presence of the three Supernals is hidden within a darkness which derives from Binah, and it is Binah which provides much of the magical symbolism of these three highest Spheres, just as the term neshamah is used for all three of the highest phases of human awareness. This symbolism is based on experience, but it can lead into a trap.

That trap is the habit of thinking of the Supernals solely in Binah's terms, as dark, hidden, and void. It's true that these ideas may be applied to the Supernal realm. It's equally true, however, that their opposites may be applied just as accurately. In the unity of the Supernal Triad, all opposites are equally true, and just as equally false. The Supernals are dark, hidden, void; they are also bright, revealed, infinitely full; they are also none of these things, being beyond these and all other human labels.

The best way to avoid this trap, as the routes across the Abyss might suggest, can be found through the knowledge of the self which rises in Tiphareth. There, at the balance-point of the ruach, the unity of opposites is suggested by the harmony of polarized Spheres; there, where the unity of Kether is reflected in the consciousness of the self, some sense of the unity of the self can be gained through introspection. Each of the Paths rising upwards from Tiphareth, then, has something to teach about the relationship between the self and unity, a relationship central to the higher stages of Cabalistic magic.

The Path of Heh itself, the last of these five Paths, has a special relationship with the art of ritual magic. Like the Paths of Zayin and Cheth, it serves as a connection between the ruach and the higher centers of the self, but its endpoint is in Chokmah, not in Binah; it connects with the primal source of Force rather than of Form, and what descends it is thus power rather than perception. Where the Path of Zayin governs the work of the diviner and that of Cheth the path of the visionary, the Path of Heh can be seen as that of the ritual magician, who shapes power through symbolic action. Here, too, the Golden Dawn tradition offers a rich body of technical methods for the magician in training; here, too, these technical methods may be outgrown as the magician learns to use the natural powers of the self in a more direct manner.

*   *   *

In a broader sense, the Path of Heh deals with the whole relationship between power and the self. The letter assigned to this Path is central in this context. Heh is the Hebrew word for window, and in the days before effective indoor lighting windows were the most important way of providing light in houses and other buildings. Windows are not, however, light sources; they simply allow light from the sun to pass through walls to illuminate the rooms within.

The symbolism here is exact. Some magical theories have identified the source of the magician's power as the magician's own self; others have seen power as something present in various outside things - stars and planets, for example, or herbs and stones. In the magical Cabala, by contrast, these things are seen not as sources of power but as windows through which power passes, and the source of power itself is identified with the unity of the Supernals in its active form, which is Chokmah. In a broader sense, this is true not only of magical power but of every kind and manifestation of energy in the universe of experience.

The letter Heh, of course, has another role in Cabalistic thought as one of the letters making up the Tetragrammaton. Its symbolism in this context is a fairly precise opposite to the symbolism it has on the Tree. This is not an accident; the same thing is true of the letter Yod, and the apparent paradox is resolved in the way discussed in our study of the 20th Path. Like a window, the relationships of power symbolized by the letter Heh are receptive seen from one side and active seen from the other. Heh's receptive, symbolically female role in the Tetragrammaton is balanced by an active, symbolically male role on the Tree.

This active role dominates the next several symbols. The Name of God assigned to this Path, Elohim, and the astrological correspondence attributed to it, the Zodiacal sign Aries, both relate to the element of fire. Aries, a Fire sign ruled by the planet Mars, is the first sign of the traditional Zodiac, and its first degree marks the Spring Equinox. Chokmah is associated with the Zodiac as a whole, the belt of stars within which the Sun, Moon and planets carry on their immemorial dance; the descent of power from Chokmah through the Path of Heh to Tiphareth thus reflects, on a different level, the descent of energy from the Zodiac through the Sign Aries to the Sun in Spring.

✳ ✳ ✳

The Tarot correspondence of the 15th Path brings out this same active, energizing role in its strongest form. Trump IV, the Emperor, shows a crowned monarch on his throne, the orb and scepter of rulership in his hands. (Many modern decks give the throne a decoration of ram's heads, carrying on the Aries symbolism.) It's worth noting that this figure is an emperor, not merely a king. In the political thought of the Middle Ages, reflected here as elsewhere in the Tarot, the emperor was seen as the highest earthly ruler, superior to kings, subordinate only to God. Both the imperial houses of the Medieval world - the so- called "Holy Roman Emperors," who ruled most of central Europe, and the Emperors of Byzantium in what is now Greece and Turkey - claimed a special religious status as God's representative in political affairs. Most of the men who held these imperial titles couldn't have acted less like representatives of God if they had tried; still, the symbolism was potent enough to be copied, in the form of "Divine Right," by kings of a later age.

The political pretensions of these dynasties are of little importance here. Their symbolism, on the other hand, is central. The emperor as highest earthly power, and representative of a higher power still, relates well to the role already marked out for the Path of Heh. As ruler over kings, too, the emperor also puts a useful stress on the dependence of Tiphareth on the Spheres above it.

This pattern of symbolism reaches a culmination of sorts in the Esoteric Title of the Path, "Son of the Morning, Chief among the Mighty." The Mighty, as we've seen, is used in these titles to represent Chokmah and Binah, and the second half of this title is therefore properly a title of Chokmah itself. Its appearance here is nonetheless appropriate; this Path's imagery of rulership and power is a reflection of its role as a conduit for the forces of Chokmah; the Path, in one of its most important senses, is the clearest reflection of Chokmah below the Abyss.

The phrase "Son of the Morning" is more complex. This title is given in Biblical mythology to the Morning Star, and was then misapplied by Christian authors (along with the name Lucifer, "Lightbearer," also a term for Venus) to Satan. In the magical Cabala, which draws on both these traditions, it serves as a symbol of glory - and also of the arrogant pride which is the vice of Tiphareth and the pervasive fault of the powerful.

There is another side to these images of rulership, though. Many of the world's mythologies contain tales of a time in the past when peace and plenty on a grand scale were brought into being by the rule of a legendary monarch. These myths are sometimes mixed with those of the Paradise at the beginning of time, but the two are at root distinct. The monarch's role often links into old concepts of fertility magic, either in the most explicit sense or in more veiled terms. In the modern world, King Arthur is probably the most familiar of these figures, although a look through old mythologies - and recent political rhetoric - will provide many more examples.

The Monarch of the Golden Age, as we may term this mythological principle, often becomes the Once and Future Monarch of the Path of Cheth; this, and the similarity of the letters themselves, point to certain deep relationships between these Paths. Using the letters as images, we may say that the window closes, leaving the King sealed up in the enclosure of his tomb. It is central to the mythology of Golden Ages that they always end, and equally central that they may someday return.

∗   ∗   ∗

The Path Text moves from these matters to another aspect of the Path's meaning. As a flow of energy descending from Chokmah, the Path of Heh has a role in the process of Creation; this process and its interpretation is central to much of earlier Cabalistic thought, and though the magical Cabala tends toward other interests some traces of the older focus remain to baffle the unwary student. This Path Text, alone of the thirty-two, includes a reference to a Biblical quote; this is another older feature, deriving from the days when Cabalistic writings took the form of commentaries on Bible verses.

The subject of this Text, though, justifies the reversion to older forms. The Path of Heh, we are told, "constitutes the substance of creation in pure darkness." This darkness is described as a "swaddling band" (a cloth used to wrap newborns), and the imagery of darkness and containment identify this as a reference to Binah. It is also, in another sense, the Abyss, within which the first "substance of creation" is formed by the descent of light from Chokmah.

A detailed interpretation of this Text would require more space than the present subject will permit, for it refers back to accounts of Creation differing from the myth given in Part One of this book, accounts deriving from the Sepher Yetzirah and other ancient Cabalistic texts. The central point, for our purposes, is that the Path of Heh represents the most fundamental power at work in the process of Creation. It stands for a springtime not merely of the year but of all existence. The Text implies that the "substance of creation" - the underlying "stuff" of which all that we experience is made - is energy, the unbounded force of Chokmah.

Path 16, the Path of Vau

Letter of the Path: ו , Vau (Nail).

Name of God: Adonai.

Astrological Correspondence:
       Taurus, the Bull.

Tarot Correspondence:
       Trump V, the Hierophant.

Esoteric Title: Magus of the Eternal Gods.

Path Text: *"The Sixteenth Path is the Triumphal or Eternal Intelligence, so called because it is the pleasure of the Glory, beyond which is no other Glory like to it, and it is called also the paradise prepared for the righteous."*

Mythological Principle:
       The Keeper of Wisdom.

Experiences of the Path:
       Pilgrimage to temples, mountain hermitages, and similar places; imagery drawn from birth, sex, death, and other basic biological processes; communication of wisdom-teachings; visions of all of time.

Entities of the Path: Ancient wise beings, not always (or entirely) human; priestly figures engaged in ritual or teaching.

Magical Image: An arch of intense red-orange, bearing the letter Vau in brilliant white on its keystone. The door in the arch bears the image of Trump V.

Colors:
       in Atziluth - red-orange.
       in Briah - deep indigo.
       in Yetzirah - deep warm olive.
       in Assiah - rich brown.

The role of the Pillars in Cabalistic thinking has been stressed at a number of points in these pages. In some ways, these symbols of polarity and its resolution are more important practically, and more basic theoretically, than the Tree of Life itself. Partly, this is because the Pillars are more easily related to the realm of ordinary experience; it takes a certain amount of practice (as well as imagination) to learn to assign acts and perceptions to the Spheres of the Tree, but the play of opposites in everyday life is obvious enough that it can be grasped at once. Whenever a man and a woman unite to conceive a child, or sun and soil nourish a plant from seed to flower, the image of the three Pillars is manifest. On a grander scale, the whole process of Creation begins with the phase of Withdrawal, the creation of a space within God where God is not present, and the birth of the Tree of Life thereafter can be understood as the formation of a Middle Pillar of balance between God and the Void.

The seven Paths which trace the course of the Pillars within the structure of the Tree all possess something of this primal quality; all have, as well, the quality of balance, whether from the fusion of two powers or the dominance of one. Both these factors are at their strongest in the Path of Vau. As the higher half of the Pillar of Force, it represents the descent of creative power in its purest form, linking Chokmah, where all power comes into being, to Chesed, where the first energies of manifestation break forth below the Abyss. This same downrush of power holds the Path of Vau in a perfection of balance to which only the Path of Cheth, its equivalent and opposite across the Tree, can be compared.

The factors of primacy and balance shape much of the symbolism of the Path of Vau. Another factor, however, also has an important place. This Path deals with some of the highest levels of the Tree, but it does so by bringing the energies of these levels down into the reach of the conscious self. Its role here is, to a great extent, an anchoring one. In the work of the Cabalistic magician, it represents factors in experience and consciousness which can be relied on even in the Abyss, a background which provides context to the higher levels of the magician's journey. This role in the way of Redemption derives, in turn, from a similar role in the way of Creation; by bringing the creative force of Chokmah through the Abyss into the realms of manifestation, into the levels of the Tree where Force and Form unite in polar interaction, the Path of Vau can be seen as anchoring the primal powers of the universe itself.

This anchoring function is central to much of the symbolism of the 16th Path, and gives a sometimes startling "down-to-earth" flavor to some of that symbolism. The use of penis and vagina as images of the primary active and receptive powers of the Tree may serve as a reminder that the magical Cabala does not follow the rule of squeamishness which shapes so much of Western spiritual imagery.

A similarly down-to-earth quality can be found in the branch of practice which can be assigned to this Path. That branch is alchemy, the esoteric science and technology of physical matter. While modern attitudes too often dismiss alchemy as a futile attempt at making gold by inadequate means, or at best as a misguided approach to modern chemistry, this does a severe injustice to a subtle and complex field of knowledge. The alchemy of metals is only one of many branches of the art, and by no means the most important; there are alchemies of medicine and agriculture, of breath and etheric force, of mind and spirit, and many of these have much to offer even - or especially - to the present age. (Much of modern organic and biodynamic farming, for example, has its roots in older traditions of alchemical agriculture.)

Like the ritual magic which forms the practical application of the Path of Heh, alchemy is concerned with the descent of power from Chokmah, but where ritual work focuses this through the microcosm in Tiphareth, alchemy seeks it through the macrocosm in Chesed, where the Path of Vau has its lower end. To the alchemist, then, everything in the macrocosm is alive with power, and may be shaped and guided to a fuller expression of its innate energies through alchemical processes. As with the other practical arts we've reviewed in this chapter, these processes are defined by specific technical methods, but those methods may be - in fact, must be - set aside as the deeper potentials of the art and the self interact with each other.

The art of alchemy is the least developed of the major branches of esoteric practice in the Golden Dawn tradition; still, a method of alchemy was taught in the higher levels of training, and several alchemical manuscripts were studied intently by the Order's adepts. Of all the aspects of the tradition, this one may offer the widest scope for creative work at the present.

✳   ✳   ✳

The first symbol of this Path is the letter ו, Vau, which means "peg" or "nail." This image obviously ties into the idea of anchoring. As one of the simplest and, historically, one of the oldest methods of fastening things together, the peg or nail offers a prosaic image of a link bringing two separate things into a fixed relationship. Nails and pegs are normally distinct from the things they join, just as the Path of Vau has little symbolically in common with the Spheres it connects. Nor is the sexual symbolism implied here inappropriate; when two people make love, that act brings them into a specific (and, in etheric terms, semi-permanent) relationship; if circumstances allow, a child may be conceived who, while physically separate from both parents, creates another kind of fixed relationship between them. The letter Vau also has a role in the Tetragrammaton, of course, and as the Son within that Name it suggests many of the same concepts discussed here.

In the Tetragrammaton, the letter Vau corresponds to the element of Air, and if you've been paying attention you aren't likely to be surprised by the fact that Vau's own elemental symbolism points to the opposite element, Earth. The Name of God and astrological correspondence assigned to the 16th Path derive from this. As mentioned earlier, Earth has a special role as the sum or final unity of Fire, Water and Air, corresponding in a special sense to Spirit as the source or original unity of these three elements. Earth's qualities of stability and solidity also fit well with the character of the Path, suggesting the anchoring role already discussed.

Taurus also suggests several other points. The bull, its symbolic image, appears in another place on the Tree of Life - on the Path of Aleph, linking Kether to Chokmah. There is a sense in which the Paths of Aleph and Vau make up a single current of force, which reaches out from the unity of Kether to create and then establish the Pillar of Mercy. The planet which rules Taurus in astrological lore is Venus, suggesting the end of that Pillar below the Veil in Netzach.

One other facet of Taurus' meaning is of importance here. In astrology, the Moon is said to be "exalted" - that is, active in its most positive manner - in Taurus. What makes this interesting is that Cancer, the astrological symbol of the Path of Cheth, is ruled by the Moon, while the Moon itself is the astrological attribution of the Path of Gimel. All three of the vertical Paths across the Abyss, in other words, have a special relationship with the Moon. That relationship is not hard to fathom when it is remembered that the three Spheres directly below the Abyss are reflections of the three above, just as the light of the Moon is reflected from the Sun. A recognition of this fact is central to the opening of each of these Paths.

✳ ✳ ✳

Three other symbols of the Path draw on a different set of imagery. The Tarot correspondence of the 16th Path is Trump V, the Hierophant. This is another of those cards which has changed radically over the last few centuries. In the oldest decks it is simply the Pope, and shows the familiar image of the head of the Roman Church in his regalia. Like the Emperor, this image derived from medieval political life; the requirements of the Tarot's structure demand a spiritually oriented male figure at this point, to balance both the High Priestess (originally the Papess), the spiritual female of Trump II, and the Emperor, the worldly male of Trump IV. The power struggles between Pope and Emperor which convulsed the medieval world made the choice of this figure an obvious one, as did the Pope's then-unchallenged role as spiritual head of the Western world. Nowadays, though, both these factors are matters for history books, and with the change in circumstances a change in imagery was needed.

The word hierophant is Greek, and means "one who reveals the sacred." In ancient and modern initiatory systems, including that of the Golden Dawn's Outer Order, this word has been used for the central officer of the rite, the person who has the task of actually transmitting the essence of the initiation to the candidate. In a broader sense, the role of hierophant is that of linking the higher to the lower, the spiritual to the material, so that the powers of the higher levels shape the substance of everyday experience. This echoes the Pope's traditional role as Vicar (literally, "substitute") of Christ, the representative of God on Earth.

Implied here is the entire system of organized religion. While that system in the West is sinking into the last stages of rigor mortis under the pressure of bigotry, power politics, and greed, the essential concept is no more corrupt than that of any other human institution. In its proper place, an organized system of religious worship serves as an anchor linking the social order to the realm of the transcendent, not a nail driven through the human spirit.

Linked to this same concept are the Esoteric Title of this Path, "Magus of the Eternal Gods," and the mythological principle, the Keeper of Wisdom. The first is the second of three Magi on the Tree of Life; like the Path of Yod, "Magus of the Voice of Light, Prophet of the Gods," the Path of Vau helps trace a pattern on the Tree which will be discussed later in this chapter. The mythological principle, on the other hand, is another common figure in the world's legends and myths. The legendary rishis of India, associated with the seven stars of the Bear, form one example of this pattern; another is Mimir, the keeper of the Well of Wisdom in Norse myth. In Western esoteric lore, the most common figure to serve in this capacity is Melchizedek, the mysterious priest-king "without father, without mother, without descent, having neither beginning of days nor end of life." There has been a great deal written about this strange figure, much of it gibberish, but his name tends to appear wherever the esoteric traditions of the West emerge from hiding.

✳   ✳   ✳

The last symbol of this Path to be considered here is the Path Text. At first glance, this seems to lead off on a complete tangent from the rest of the symbolism we've discussed. The Path of Vau is described as the "Triumphal or Eternal Intelligence," as the "pleasure of the Glory" and as the "paradise prepared for the righteous." Once again, though, the language used by the Text misleads the modern eye; while the Text does point to a different aspect of the Path than we've examined so far, that aspect is founded on the symbolism already studied.

The "Glory," here as elsewhere in the Texts, is Kether. The word translated "triumphal" and "eternal" comes from the same root as the title Netzach, "Victory," and this and the reference to pleasure point toward the seventh Sphere. So, in turn, does the place of Venus as planetary ruler of Taurus.

The meaning of the Text is that the descent of power down this Path - or, more precisely, participation in that process - can best be described in human terms as joy. The heart of this factor, which also ties into the Venus reference of "Son of the Morning" in the Esoteric Title of the Path of Heh, will need to be covered in the next section of this chapter, when it appears in its most developed form.

What is to be made, though, of the reference to the "paradise prepared for the righteous"? This is subtle, but not beyond understanding. The point made here is that paradise, heaven, is not a place where souls sit on clouds strumming harps - or any place of any description at all. Rather, it is a state of consciousness, of a kind which we can best represent in the guise of an emotion. That state, in its more passive form, might be called joy; in its active phase, it has almost always been called love. The secrets of this state, as we will see, make up one of the most important issues in the work of the magician.

Path 14, the Path of Daleth

Letter of the Path: ד , Daleth (Door).
Name of God: YHVH TzBAVTH, Tetragrammaton Tzabaoth.
Astrological Correspondence:
    Venus.
Tarot Correspondence:
    Trump III, the Empress.
Esoteric Title: Daughter of the Mighty Ones.
Path Text: *"The Fourteenth Path is the Illuminating Intelligence, and is so called because it is that Brilliance which is the founder of the concealed and fundamental ideas of holiness and of their stages of preparation."*
Mythological Principle:
    The Marriage of Heaven and Earth.
Experiences of the Path:
    Images of the natural world and of the richness of Nature; images of polarity and sexuality; star and Zodiac symbolism.
Entities of the Path: The Goddess and the God.
Magical Image: An arch of emerald green, bearing the letter Daleth in brilliant white on its keystone. The door in the arch bears the image of Trump III.
Colours: in Atziluth - emerald green.
    in Briah - sky blue.
    in Yetzirah - pale spring green.
    in Assiah - bright rose or cerise, rayed with pale green.

The three highest Paths of the Tree of Life, like the three highest Spheres, have a special role in Cabalistic theory and practice. As patterns of relationship within the unity of the Supernals, they define the most basic elements of the Tree's structure, and form a template upon which every other kind of interaction - between Spheres, between Pillars, between Worlds - is ultimately based. The Paths of Aleph and Beth extend from Kether to Chokmah and Binah respectively, establishing the two sides of a polarity, while the Path of Daleth resolves that polarity in the act of creation. It's a pattern which has appeared again and again in these pages.

The first two Paths of this triad touch Kether, and this contact with absolute unity gives them an elusive quality which makes their symbolism a little like trying to catch hold of the wind. In comparison, the images and ideas assigned to the Path of Daleth may seem quite straightforward. To a great extent, this is an effect of familiarity, for this Path's keynote resonates down through the whole of the Tree. The other two horizontal Paths of the Tree, in particular, take their essential nature from the Path of Daleth; the fusion of energies on the 19th Path and the explosive collision of Force and Form on the 27th are both images, on different levels, of the primal union of the 14th.

At the same time, this familiarity conceals a radical difference, one which needs to be grasped if the symbols of this Path are to be read clearly. The Paths of Teth and Peh exist below the Abyss, and connect opposites to each other; the Path of Daleth exists above the Abyss, and connects unity to itself. The Paths of Teth and Peh, in turn, give rise to a unity on another level, that of Teth creating the unity of balance in Tiphareth, that of Peh the unity of powers in Yesod; the Path of Daleth, by contrast, gives rise not to unity but to the whole realm of multiplicity below the Abyss. Many becoming one, one becoming many: the two patterns mirror each other, but - below the Abyss, at least - reflection is not the same thing as identity.

✳   ✳   ✳

The symbolism of the 14th Path contains another form of union of opposites, as well. It joins images of creation and reproduction with concepts of spiritual transformation, bringing the ways of Creation and Redemption into a symbolic unity. This fusion relates to the unity of all things above the Abyss, of course, but it also has an important practical lesson to teach.

The letter assigned to the Path is ד, Daleth, which means "door." In the simplest sense, this refers to the union of opposites, in that a door connects two spaces separated by a wall. Note, though, that the connecting link implies the separation; a door standing by itself in the midst of an open field, for example, serves no purpose at all. The door as a symbol, then, implies union and division at once.

This symbolism may remind you of some of the ideas associated with Daath, the Gate of the Abyss - and it should. In one of its senses Daath is a downward projection of the Path of Daleth, a union of Chokmah and Binah projected into the Abyss, and Daath's function as a channel for creative forces is a development of the Path's creative power. Like a gate, as we saw, Daath can be open or closed, a passage or a barrier. Above the Abyss, in a realm where paradox is the closest approach to clarity, the door of Daleth is always both open and closed: unity and the division of unity in a single creative act, an act which cannot be distinguished from the Spheres which it unites.

This point is developed further by the name of God and astrological correspondence of the Path. The Name Tetragrammaton Tzabaoth and the planet Venus both refer to Netzach, the seventh Sphere, symbol of unifying force and, in human terms, of love. At the Netzach level of consciousness, love can be seen as a relationship between separate beings, but this way of perceiving functions only below the Abyss. Above it, separation and unity themselves fuse.

At the same time, the power of love in Netzach is itself a development of power in a broader sense. Netzach, at the foot of the Pillar of Mercy, takes the heart of its own nature from the head of the same Pillar in Chokmah; the two are different phases or manifestations of one force, and that force can also be described as love.

At the level of the Path of Daleth, love is the active form of unity, and unity is the source of creation, the channel by which Force enters Form to bring the world into being. This implies that, for the Cabalistic magician, love and power cannot be seen as two separate things. Like earlier comments about ethical action as a source of power, this is likely to sound like a pretty platitude in the cynical climate of the present. It is not. There is no power higher than love, no strength stronger, no protection more enduring - and this is true, in the most practical sense, in every aspect of magical training and work.

This can be difficult advice to follow, not least because the modern mind so often confuses love with addiction, with jealousy, with sex, with ownership. Still, if love is followed by way of compassion and acceptance, there is no better guide.

*　*　*

The Tarot correspondence of the 14th Path draws on another of the Path's reflections elsewhere on the Tree. Trump III, the Empress, once showed nothing more than the image of a woman in imperial robes and regalia, another borrowing from the ordinary world of the Middle Ages. As the cards changed and developed, though, new elements crept in; fields and forests appeared in the beckground; flowers and ripe grain rose up about the throne; in some decks the Empress became visibly pregnant. In many modern decks the image of this Trump has approximated another you may remember - the Magical Image of Malkuth, the tenth Sphere.

In one interpretation of the Tree of Life, Kether can be seen as the universe in a state of pure potentiality, Malkuth as the same universe in a state of complete manifestation, and the remainder of the Tree as the process which leads from one to the other. In this process the Path of Daleth forms the most crucial step, establishing the pattern of creation through polarity which governs everything that follows. Malkuth is thus the working out of the 14th Path's potential, as much as it is that of Kether.

In the Esoteric Title, the Path symbolism returns to points already raised; the "Mighty Ones," here as elsewhere, are Chokmah and Binah, and the Path of Daleth (and the universe created through it) their child. This same symbolism also governs the mythological principle of this Path, the Marriage of Heaven and Earth, and many of the ways this Path is experienced in practical work; the union of primal polarities from which all things are born, here as elsewhere, takes on the familiar imagery of human sexuality and draws on many of the most potent energies of human experience.

*　*　*

The Path Text, finally, leads off in a different direction. Here the symbolism of spiritual and magical development is central. The Path of Daleth is called the Illuminating Intelligence; the symbolism of light, as we've seen, is a commonplace in spiritual traditions worldwide, because some of the more accessible states of heightened awareness are often marked by the experience of brilliant light, giving rise to terms such as "enlightenment." Several of the esoteric traditions of the West draw distinctions between different kinds of this inner light. Such distinctions have a role here, for the Path is called "Brilliance;" in Hebrew, this is chashmal, the same word as the name of the angels of Chesed.

The point of this connection is clear when the rest of the Text is considered. The Path of Daleth, we read, is "the founder of the concealed and fundamental ideas of holiness," and of the "stages" by which these are prepared. To speak of ideas is to locate the discussion in the realm below the Abyss, where the conscious self shapes concepts, and the role of Chesed in organizing and recording such concepts is clear. What is implied here, however, is that there is a relationship between certain ideas held on this level and the creative forces of the 14th Path.

These ideas are the "fundamental ideas of holiness," but they are also "concealed." This concealment is not part of the concern with security which can be traced in certain parts of Western magical symbolism. Rather, these are concepts and ways of thinking about the universe which are central to the magical path, but which are not communicated because they cannot be. They rise from, and require, certain experiences and certain stages of inner transformation, and without these things the "concealed ideas" cannot be effectively communicated at all.

This sounds highly mysterious, but it is not so far outside of ordinary experience; a six-year-old child may learn the lyrics to a sexually explicit song while missing the point of the song completely; the clearest instructions for replacing a transmission will be gibberish to someone who has never looked under the hood of a car. With the coming of puberty, or an interest in auto repair, what was once nonsense becomes meaningful. The same is true of the inner secrets of the magical path.

There have also been, of course, secrets of other kinds associated with magical traditions, in the West as elsewhere. In part, these were reflections of the hard realities of an age in which public involvement with magic could amount to a death warrant; in part, they rose from an awareness of the potent inner effects of the experience of secrecy, effects we'll be discussing in a later chapter; in part, they came into being to guard certain powerful techniques from incautious or unethical use.

Most of these, which we might call the outer secrets of magic, have seen print many times in the last few centuries; the hidden teachings of the centuries can be had for a modest price in most well-stocked bookstores. The inner secrets of magic cannot. They can, on the other hand, be learned by anyone, with or without access to books, given effort, patience and the willingness to bear the burdens of self-knowledge: a modest price in its own way, given the scope of what it can buy.

Chokmah, the Second Sphere

Title: ChKMH,	Chokmah (Wisdom).
Name of God:	YH, Yah (God).
Archangel:	RZIAL, Raziel (Secret of God).
Angelic Host:	AVPNIM, Auphanim (Wheels).

Astrological Correspondence:
MZLVTh, Mazloth (the Zodiac).

Tarot Correspondence:
The four Twos and four Kings of the pack.

Elemental Correspondence:
Fire.

Path Text: *"The Second Path is called the Illuminating Inteligence; it is the Crown of Creation, the Splendor of the Unity, equalling it. It is exalted above every head, and named by Cabalists the Second Glory."*

Magical Image: An old man with a long white beard, wearing a plain gray robe and holding a rough wooden staff. He is facing the viewer's left, and looking slightly upwards.

Additional Symbols: All phallic symbols.

Additional Title: Abba, the Supernal Father.

Colours: in Atziluth - pure soft blue.
in Briah - gray.
in Yetzirah - iridescent pearl gray.
in Assiah - white, flecked with red, blue and yellow.

Correspondence in the Microcosm:
Chiah, the Spiritual Will.

Correspondence in the Body:
The left side of the head.

Grade of Initiation: 9=2, Magus.

Negative Power: None (see Daath).

The Spheres of the Supernal Triad always present a difficulty to students and teachers of the Cabala. Set above the Abyss, in a realm where the ordinary categories of thought and perception fall flat, they can be spoken of only in the most general and inadequate terms. It's possible that much of the sevenfold symbolism in Western magic grows out of a decision to solve this problem by not talking about the three highest Spheres at all! This is sensible enough from the point of view of the purely practical magician, since the Supernals have little to do with this level of magical work. For the true Cabalistic magician, on the other hand, the states of consciousness and experience represented by the Supernals are the supreme goal of the entire magical path, and something needs to be said of them, however inadequate that something must be.

At the level of Binah, this problem can still be avoided; since the third Sphere contacts the realms below the Abyss by way of Daath, the nature of this contact can be (and usually is) used to represent the nature of Binah in itself. With Chokmah, on the other hand, the difficulty becomes acute. Chokmah has no direct contact with the Spheres below the Abyss - the Paths linking it to Chesed and Tiphareth function, in a way impossible to show on a two-dimensional chart, through the mediation of Binah as expressed in Daath - and its powers come into reach of ordinary human consciousness only through other Spheres. To use a modern metaphor, it is like a light which shines through colored filters.

In another sense, of course, Chokmah is itself one of the filters rather than the light, for its energies derive from those of the first Sphere, Kether. Just as Binah conceals Chokmah, Chokmah conceals Kether, and each of these is less definable than the last. Binah can be grasped, in a highly limited way, through its reflection as human awareness; with Chokmah, that awareness dissolves into the more formless concept of power; with Kether, that power dissolves in turn into pure being - which itself dissolves into the Veils of the Unmanifest and the unknowable reality beyond.

✳   ✳   ✳

Chokmah's symbolism is predominantly a symbolism of power. As earlier sections of this chapter discussed, all the many manifestations of power on the Tree ultimately derive from the second Sphere. Chokmah represents the primal expression of force, the first and final movement of the principle of energy and change. In the context of esoteric tradition, the highest human expression of power is found in magic; Chokmah is thus the supreme Sphere of the magician, and it is no accident that the level of the initiation assigned to this Sphere is titled simply Magus, "magician."

The first of Chokmah's symbols, on the other hand, has a different focus. The title of the second Sphere is Chokmah, which means "wisdom." Knowledge, Understanding and Wisdom form an ascending scale of levels of perception; one may know something without understanding it, and one may understand it without having the wisdom to use it appropriately. It's important to note that while the words "knowledge" and "understanding" both imply an object - one knows something, or understands something - "wisdom" does not; it's impossible to "wise something;" one simply is, or is not, wise. On the other hand, to be wise is still to be something, while Kether, the next level of the scale, is not something but everything.

What's implied here is a subtle analysis of the Supernals, one which relates them back to the most basic analysis of the Tree discussed back in Chapter 1. There is only one thing which can be said about Kether, which is that it is. To speak of wisdom, though, implies two things, first that something is, second that it is something in particular - in this case, wise. To speak of understanding, in turn, implies three things: that something is, that it understands, and that there is something that it understands. To speak of knowledge, finally, implies four things: that something is, that it knows, that there is something that it knows, and that something - knowledge - comes out of its act of knowing. These four stages correspond to the letters of the Tetragrammaton, and also to the four Worlds.

In this sequence, the stage of wisdom is most critical, because it provides the context in which the whole process takes place; once "something is" gives way to "something is x," that x has a decisive effect on how the "something" is perceived. (Consider, for example, the power of statements of the "something is x" type in ordinary language: for instance, "that is a bomb" or "he is a loser.") This stage, which we may also call the stage of context or of definition, is equally critical in magical work; here as in the rest of life, how a goal is defined, and what context it is given, largely determines how and whether it will be reached.

Certain Cabalistic traditions, using theological language, describe Wisdom as a mighty goddess, the first creation and bride of God. The English language, on a different level, pays its own tribute to the idea of wisdom with the word "wizard," literally "wise person." For the practicing magician, a more useful tribute might be careful attention to the issues this idea raises, and to its applications both in magic and in everyday life.

* * *

The Name of God assigned to Chokmah is YH, Yah. This Name is made up of the first two letters of the Tetragrammaton, and like it is an ancient form of the verb "to be." Like the concept of wisdom, it suggests the first interaction between reality and its context in awareness. It represents as well the essential power behind polarity, combining active and receptive, male and female into a balanced unity.

The Archangel of Chokmah is Raziel, "Secret of God." Ancient legends relate that Raziel was the original source of Cabalistic teaching, which he taught to Adam in Paradise, and a book attributed to him - the Sepher Raziel - was one of the major texts of medieval Jewish magic. In less mythic language, he represents the state of awareness in which awareness itself merges into the single act of power which is the universe. His name also stresses the idea, mentioned before, that Chokmah is wholly hidden below the Abyss.

The angelic host attributed to Chokmah, in turn, is the Auphanim, "wheels." The idea that all action, on all levels of experience, moves in circles was a commonplace of the ancient wisdom traditions. Discarded by the founders of modern science, it has been rediscovered in the last century as part of the revolution in physics, with the odd result that some aspects of relativity theory would have made more sense to people who lived thousands of years ago than they make to most people today. This same idea, of course, is also a familiar concept in magical lore; the circular nature of magical action, as we'll see, structures both the methods of esoteric training and some of the common restrictions on the practical use of magic.

The astrological correspondence of Chokmah is Mazloth, the Zodiac. Here, too, circular patterns play an important part in the Sphere symbolism. The Zodiac is the circle of sky through which the Sun, Moon and planets appear to move when seen from Earth. In astrology, it provides the background of forces against which the planetary powers move and have their effects, just as the power of Chokmah provides the background for the whole energy structure of the Tree. Before the discovery of the outer planets Uranus, Neptune and Pluto, too, the fixed stars of the Zodiac were the next logical step outward beyond Saturn, the symbol of Binah and the furthest visible planet.

* * *

In the Path Text, the focus of the symbolism shifts from Chokmah's role in the magician's work to its relationship with the Sphere behind it, the highest goal of that work. In the Text, Chokmah is called the Illuminating Intelligence. The Path Text of the Path of Daleth uses the same title, but this is a result of translation; the Hebrew original uses two different words of similar meaning. Still, there is a definite relationship between the concepts. The illumination granted by the Path of Daleth, and the secrets revealed by it, both have their roots in the illuminating power of Chokmah, as the legends of Raziel mentioned earlier suggest. Here power, love, and illumination all appear, as they are, different names for the same transcendent force.

The Path Text goes on, though, to describe Chokmah in some startling terms. The second Sphere is called the "Crown of Creation;" "Crown," in Hebrew Kether, is the title of the first Sphere. Chokmah is also called "the Splendor of the Unity;" the Unity is Kether, and the title "splendor" suggests radiating light, an important part of Kether's symbolism. Finally, and most surprisingly, Chokmah is said to be equal to the Unity - that is, again, to Kether.

This can be read clearly only if it's remembered that both Chokmah and Kether are Spheres of the Supernal Triad, existing at a level of being where all things are one. Chokmah is indeed equal to Kether, in fact identical to it; it is the active side, as Binah is the receptive side, of a unity in Kether which is beyond even these categories. Kether itself, furthermore, is equally beyond all perception; everything which can be said about it, or thought about it, or known about it comes from Spheres below it, not from it as it is in itself.

The chief source for Kether's symbolism, in fact, is Chokmah. As the active side of unity, the source of power and of the process of creation, Chokmah is a workable approximation for the realm of pure unity symbolized by Kether. This is the source of the last part of the Path Text, which says that Chokmah is "named by Cabalists the Second Glory." Glory, here as elsewhere, is the Texts' term for Kether, and "the second Kether" is a more than workable description of Chokmah's role.

This last part of the Text has another point to make, though. To say that a certain title is given to Chokmah by Cabalists, specifically, is to suggest that the same title might be given to another Sphere (or the equivalent) by those who are not Cabalists. In fact, this is precisely the case, and much of the history of theology rests on the choice involved.

From the point of view of Christianity, for example, the Second Glory is not Chokmah but Tiphareth. The symbolism of Jesus and of Christian religious thought, from beginning to end, draws on images linked to the Tiphareth level of consciousness, and the issues of aspiration, sacrifice, and the relationship between the individual and God, which are central to Tiphareth, are also crucial in Christian theology. Equally, the vice of Tiphareth, the zealotry of spiritual pride, has been Christianity's besetting sin from the time of Jesus on.

From the point of view of Buddhism, by contrast, the Second Glory has generally been Binah. Despite the fact that Cabalism and Buddhist thought had only the most limited contact before the modern age, the issues and imagery central to Buddhism have a high degree of coherence with those assigned to Binah in Cabalistic thought, and the vice of Binah - the spiritual sloth which leads the mystic to turn his or her back on the experienced world in favor of passive absorption into the Void - has also been Buddhism's characteristic vice as well.

In many of the new Neopagan religions, finally, the Second Glory is Malkuth, and the central ideas and images of their theologies relate to the presence of the divine in every aspect of the material world, in the cycles of the year and of life. It remains to be seen how well these new faiths will deal with the already-emerging problem of material and sexual obsessiveness, symbolized in Cabalistic thought by Lilith.

The choice of an image for the highest reality, then, is of some importance. It should be said, though, that all these choices are valid; every Sphere of the Tree is an expression of the same reality, the same power, the same awareness which in the highest sense is represented by Kether. Different people will relate to the core issues of the mystical path in different ways, and for each of those ways there is a corresponding image of the Higher; this insight underlay many of the polytheistic faiths of the ancient world.

In the Cabalistic tradition, though, the primary image of Kether has generally been (as the Text suggests) Chokmah. The result is the abstract, rather impersonal idea of Ultimate Being which lies behind the complex symbolism and baroque mythology of the Cabala. From Chokmah, too, come the themes of power, of hidden truth, of illumination and love which have been central to so much of Cabalistic thought. In turn, the Cabala has the vices of its virtues; its besetting sin is the habit of turning away from the experience of unity into the construction of elaborate systems of theory and vision, cobwebs of the mind which obscure insight rather than furthering it: all a reflection, on the appropriate level, of the error of the Augiel.

Path 12, the Path of Beth

Letter of the Path: ב , Beth (House).
Name of God: ALHIM TzBAVTH, Elohim Tzabaoth.
Astrological Correspondence:
Mercury.
Tarot Correspondence:
Trump I, the Magician.
Esoteric Title: The Magus of Power.
Path Text: *"The Twelfth Path is the Intelligence of Transparency, because it is that species of Greatness called 'visionary', which is named the place whence issues the vision of those seeing in apparitions."*
Mythological Principle:
The Creation of the World.
Experiences of the Path:
Visions of creation, and of the emergence of form from formlessness; visions of past, present and future; the experience of Adam Cadmon.
Entities of the Path: Many-formed or shape-changing beings; Adam Cadmon.
Magical Image: An arch of bright yellow, bearing the letter Beth in brilliant white on its keystone. The door in the arch bears the image of Trump I.
Colours: in Atziluth - yellow.
in Briah - purple.
in Yetzirah - gray.
in Assiah - indigo, flecked with violet.

The three Paths which lead directly to Kether, the first Sphere, are far and away the most difficult of the Paths to master. As relationships between absolute undefinable unity, on the one hand, and each of the primary expressions of that unity, on the other, they function at a level so abstract and so inclusive that their symbolic expressions are more than usually unsatisfactory.

This is true, as we've seen, even of the Path of Gimel, which reaches halfway down the Tree to Tiphareth and relates Kether's unity to its reflection in the individual. It is true in a much greater degree of the Paths of Beth and Aleph. These two, the highest Paths on the Tree, relate unity to its two polar aspects of Force and Form, action and perception; processes within the Supernal Triad itself, they merge with the Triad's own symbolism and energies.

It may be worth noting that these parallel two other equally troublesome Paths further down the Tree. Kether and Tiphareth each stand at the apex of a pair of descending Paths, the only two places on the Tree in which a Sphere on the Middle Pillar is linked directly with lower Spheres to either side. This parallel is more than a matter of position; the Paths of Ayin and Beth have certain symbolic linkages, as do those of Nun and Aleph.

Still, there are important differences as well. Both pairs represent the extension of a balanced power into polarity; at the level of Tiphareth, this involves a risk of imbalance. Within the unity of the Supernals, by contrast, this risk is absent, and the symbolism of the higher Paths reflects this difference. In place of the grim figures of Death and the Devil, the symbolism of the Paths of Beth and Aleph places images of the highest stages of magical attainment.

✳   ✳   ✳

The first of the Path's symbols is the most general, and the most abstract. The letter assigned to the 12th Path is ב, Beth, which means "house." In esoteric usage, this word is applied very broadly indeed; the title "Intelligence of the House of Influence," given to the Path of Cheth, gives one example of this. "House" can mean container or context, surroundings or sphere of influence; as an idea linked to receptiveness, it relates to Binah and to the first Heh of Tetragrammaton. As a symbol of this Path, it suggests the coalescence of the receptive aspect of unity in Binah, forming a context within which the active aspect in Chokmah operates.

In older layers of the Cabalistic tradition, the letter Beth is a symbol of special importance. Cabalists working on the great project of interpreting the Bible noted early on that the first word of the Book of Genesis in Hebrew is BRAShITh, be-Rashith, "in the beginning." As this word begins with the letter Beth, that letter was held to contain the essence of the process of Creation, while Aleph, coming before it, was seen as a symbol for what came before Creation. While letter-analysis of this sort plays very little part in the magical Cabala, this particular analysis appears now and again in magical writings, and it has a definite application to the rest of the Path symbolism; as we'll see, the links between this Path and creative force are extensive ones.

✳   ✳   ✳

The next four symbols of the Path of Beth have a narrower focus; they deal with a particular aspect of the joining of Force and Form, rather than with that union as a whole. The Name of God and astrological correspondence assigned to the Path are both derived from the eighth Sphere, Hod. As the lowest Sphere of the Pillar of Form, Hod can be seen as the fullest manifestation of the patterns set in motion by the Path of Beth, and the only one of those manifestations which exists below the Veil in the realm of ordinary consciousness. Hod is also, and this is central here, the traditional Sphere of the art of magic.

It may seem strange that the Path of Beth should carry the symbolism of magic when Chokmah, so central to the magician's work, is on the other side of the Tree. In the realm of the Supernals, though, clear divisions are hard to come by, and opposites unite with an ease that frustrates the overly neat mind. As all three of the Supernals are one in essence, any relationship between two of the Supernals also involves the third, and in the relationship between Kether and Binah on the 12th Path the role of Chokmah comes to be played by the Path itself.

A significant part of the Path's symbolism, then, links with that of the second Sphere. The Tarot correspondence belongs, in part, to this pattern. Trump I, in the earliest decks, is called the Juggler, and shows a man in mountebank's costume behind a table covered with odd and usually undefinable objects. Later decks, renaming the card the Magician, turn the table into an altar, the assorted objects into the wand, cup, sword and pentacle of the mage, and the disreputable-looking juggler into a magician in his ceremonial robes. Both images suggest a link with Hod, since the god Mercury was the ruler of magicians and con-artists alike. At the same time, both images tie into old mythological concepts of creative power. Some of the most ancient creator deities are magician-tricksters, bringing forth the world by what sometimes amounts to sleight-of-hand. The Magician's mastery of the four implements of magic in modern decks also suggests the descent of power from Chokmah to the fourfold realm of Chesed.

The Esoteric Title of the Path builds on the same symbolism. The Path of Beth is called the Magus of Power, the third of the three Magi on the Tree. The interaction between the three Paths bearing this title is of the highest importance for the Cabalistic magician; it outlines the relationship between the self and the primal powers of creation at the highest levels of magical attainment. That relationship depends on the Spheres Chokmah and, as we'll see, Chesed as well, and it also has much to do with interactions among the ruach, the Daath center, and the neshamah.

From the point of view of the ruach, the summit of the magical path is reflected most clearly in the Path of Yod, the Magus of the Voice of Light, the Prophet of the Gods. From this standpoint, the magician is a voice and an interpreter for transcendent powers; he or she has entered into harmony with the creative forces of the universe, taking part in the dance of energies from which the world of experience comes into being, but in this work the magician's conscious self is little more than an instrument. From the point of view of the Daath center, between the ruach and the neshamah, the clearest vision of the magician's highest role is that of the Path of Vau, the Magus of the Eternal Gods; the forces of creation, in this image, work through the magician, who embodies the power of the eternal in the realms of manifestation. From the point of view of the eternal part of the self, finally, the best image of the magician is that of the Path of Beth, the Magus of Power. Here the magician shapes ultimate unity into ultimate form by means of ultimate force, and issues of "inside" and "outside" are meaningless within the oneness of the Supernals.

What is symbolized here is one of the more important effects of the crossing of the Abyss. Just as the awareness reflected in Daath is reabsorbed into the unlimited awareness of the neshamah, so the capacity for action reflected in Daath is reabsorbed into the unlimited power of Chokmah. Both these transfers involve a change in what might be called the center of gravity of the self, a shift from the ruach to the threefold neshamah. The ruach, which ordinarily sees itself as lord and ruler, passes on its authority to a higher aspect of the self; that higher aspect perceives, and acts, outside the limits of time and space, and under its direction the ruach often must move in harmony with powers it can neither see nor understand. On its own terms, then, the ruach at this level is like a prophet serving a power beyond itself; in its interaction with the neshamah in Daath, it is like a priest calling down an indwelling force; only the chiah itself, the Higher Will, is the true magician.

$$* \quad * \quad *$$

Just as the symbolism of the letter of this Path gave way to the narrower focus of the Hod and Chokmah imagery of the magician, the Path Text assigned to this Path takes a narrower focus still. The Path of Beth, it states, is called the "Intelligence of Transparency," is a "species of Magnificence called 'visionary,'" and is connected to the experience of seeing apparitions.

This Text, opaque though it may look at a first glance, is clear enough once the relevant parts of the Tree's symbolism are remembered. "Magnificence," here, is a translation of Gedulah, the alternative name of Chesed. (This is, in its own way, another link with Hod; you may recall that the Path Text of the eighth Sphere places the root of Hod in "the hidden places of Gedulah.") For "species of Magnificence" a modern reading might replace "aspect of Chesed" without much damage to the meaning. That aspect of Chesed which reaches out to relate to Tiphareth along the 20th Path already bears the title of

Prophet, so the idea that another is responsible for a particular kind of visionary experience does not seem out of place. As the Sphere of the macrocosm and the great expansive power of the Tree, Chesed tends to widen consciousness, to open up areas of perception normally closed to human beings. This makes it invaluable to the magician; Chokmah provides power, but Chesed provides the broadened awareness which enables power to be used rightly. It's worth noting that, just as the Path Text for this Path points toward Chesed, that of the Path of Yod mentions Chokmah. These two Paths trace out parallel courses on the Tree, and move in parallel in a wider context as well.

A little should be said, finally, about one more of the 12th Path's correspondences, an entity related to this Path and often seen upon it. The two Paths below which make up the Pillar of Severity both relate to variants of one mythic image; the Drowned Giant and the sleeping King both point toward a vaster and, possibly, an older figure. Adam Cadmon, the Primordial Human, is not only a Cabalistic concept; a primal being at the dawn of time, whose body becomes the raw material from which the universe is made, appears in many mythologies. The Hindu Prajapati, the Zoroastrian Gayomart, the Norse Ymir are all versions of this being; the Babylonian tale of Tiamat, nightmare goddess of the Great Deep, seems to be a distortion of it. The whole pattern, as we saw in Chapter 4, is a reflection of human consciousness upwards into the realm of unity, and grows into a recognition of the fact that we perceive the universe in the image of what we are or what we may be: in a crucial sense, the ultimate interaction between form and unity takes place in this act of recognition.

Path 11, the Path of Aleph

Letter of the Path: א , Aleph (Ox).
Name of God: YHVH, the Tetragrammaton.
Astrological Correspondence:
            Air.
Tarot Correspondence:
            Trump 0, the Fool.
Esoteric Title: The Spirit of Ether.
Path Text: *"The Eleventh Path is the Scintillating Intelligence because it is the essence of that curtain which is placed close to the order of the disposition, and this has a special dignity given to it that it may be able to stand before the face of the Cause of Causes."*

Mythological Principle:
            The Child of the Primal Void.
Experiences of the Path:
            -

Entities of the Path: -
Magical Image: An arch of pale yellow, bearing the letter Aleph in brilliant white on its keystone. The door in the arch bears the image of Trump 0.
Colours: in Atziluth - bright pale yellow.
            in Briah - sky blue.
            in Yetzirah - bluish emerald green.
            in Assiah - emerald green, flecked with gold.

The first of the Paths, the Path of Aleph links absolute unity with the power that is its most basic expression. In Cabalistic theory, which sees the Paths as the basic relationships which structure the universe we experience, it is the first of all relationships, and it relates to all the other Paths in something of the way that an original relates to its copies. It is the interaction between unity and power; between essence and the act which derives from that essence; between "is" and "does," noun and verb, being and becoming. From it, all else derives.

In every process of copying, some detail is lost; the 11th Path thus has a quality of completeness and universality which is not found elsewhere on the Tree. At the same time, as a relationship within the Supernal Triad, this Path can only be grasped in an abstract sense. Like the perfect circles and infinite lines of geometry, which can be imagined but never drawn, it evades more concrete forms of expression.

These two qualities, the universal and the abstract, have a dominant role in the symbolism and meaning of the Path of Aleph. Every relationship on the Tree, and thus (from a Cabalistic perspective) in the universe, can be seen as a specific form - a form defined and limited in some particular way - of this one primal interaction. Similarly, each of the symbols of the Path itself points toward some other Path or Sphere on the Tree, as though seeking examples of a process too general to describe in any other way; in Pathworking, the experiences and entities which arise on this Path follow no predictable patterns. Even when the Path's own role in the Tree is under discussion, it is the Spheres on either end which are referred to, rather than any particular quality of the Path itself. All things and none, it eludes definition just as the Sphere at its higher end, Kether, eludes any act of perception at all.

*   *   *

The letter assigned to this Path is א , Aleph, which means "ox." It's an odd fact of linguistic history that in many of the world's alphabets, the first letter has some relationship to cattle; this is true of our own letter A, which descends from a Phoenician copy of the Egyptian hieroglyph for "ox;" it is also the case even for such distant relatives as the Old Norse runic script. Some writers have suggested that this ties back to old astrological symbolism, from the days when Taurus rather than Aries was counted as the first sign of the Zodiac, or to related mythologies which place cosmic bulls or cows at the beginning of a great many creation myths.

An ox, however, is a bull that has been castrated, and this has a special importance in the symbolism of the Path. Oxen are huge and immensely strong, but that strength obviously does not express itself in a sexual form. The Cabala, as we've seen, uses sexuality as its most common metaphor for the process of creation through polarity, and the nonsexual power represented by the ox makes a useful symbol of a relationship in which polarity does not function. In one sense, of course, there is polarity on this Path, for the relationship between Kether and Chokmah itself forms a polarity; more broadly, though, polarity does not play a significant part in the Tree's structure until both Chokmah and Binah have been emanated. On the Path of Aleph, which traces the beginning of the Lightning Flash, the earliest phases of creation - phases in which the process of polarity does not yet dominate - still echo.

In older texts on the Cabala, as mentioned in an earlier section, the letter Aleph was used as a symbol for that which came before creation itself. While this derived from interpretations of Biblical texts which have little to say to the Cabala's magical tradition, it still fits well with the ideas discussed here. If, as Cabalistic thought holds, creation is essentially a matter of polarity, the Path of Aleph - a Path on which the first creative polarity has not yet formed - is indeed prior to it.

✳   ✳   ✳

The Name of God and astrological correspondence assigned to this Path both have to do with the Path's elemental symbol, the element of Air. This part of the Path symbolism leads in the opposite direction as the last, because Air relates to the Vau or Son of Tetragrammaton, the product of polarity in its most basic symbolic form. In the Divine name assigned to the Path, this opposition is at its strongest, for the Name linked with Air is the Tetragrammaton itself, the archetype of creation through polarity.

This apparent contradiction actually points toward the Path's character as origin and summation of all the Paths. The Path of Aleph itself is above the level at which polarity functions, but that does not mean that it has nothing to do with polarity, or with creation. Far from it; polarity may not be apparent on the Path of Aleph, but it is implicit in this first act of interrelation. Once primal power has emerged from primal unity, and then entered into a relation with it, the rest of the Tree in all its complexity follows.

The Tarot correspondence of this Path moves in yet another direction, one with deep implications. Trump 0, the Fool, has changed the details of its image over the years; older decks often show an old ragged man carrying a stick and chased or even bitten by a dog, while the newer decks generally clean up the image somewhat, showing a young man in princely garments whose dog trots beside him in a much more friendly fashion. The Golden Dawn itself, as it did with several other Trumps, went its own way with Trump 0, and its version of the card shows a naked child holding a wolf's leash while plucking a rose from a rose-tree.

The proper placement of the Fool in the Tarot deck has been the subject of an enormous amount of controversy and confusion in occult circles, and there are still several different opinions on the subject. This is not accidental; as mentioned above, the Path of Aleph can be seen as the source of all the Paths, and so in a precise sense the Fool can be validly placed anywhere on the Tree.

His relationship to the Path of Aleph, though, is paramount. The term "fool" was a professional title before it became a term of abuse; fools or jesters, the stand-up comics and commentators of the Middle Ages, had a valued place at the courts of kings. Behind their function, and linked to it in old records, it's possible to make out older, shamanistic traditions which saw madness as the close kin of trance, of wisdom and of death. The fool, the madman, the innocent came from outside the conventional order of things, at once threatening that order and offering it insights it could not reach on its own.

This social function is thus a mirror of the more general role of this Path. It also has certain things to say about the relationship of the magician to society, in earlier times as well as in the present. Few cultures have been entirely comfortable with their magicians; current opinion in magical and pagan circles to the contrary, the persecution of witches and sorcerers is not exclusive to Christianity, to monotheism, or to Western cultures. To be a magician is always, in some sense, to be outside the boundaries traced by society, and from this comes both freedom and vulnerability.

* * *

The Esoteric Title of the 11th Path changes the focus of the symbolism from the social world to the realm of philosophy and cosmology. This Path is named the Spirit of Ether; in the language of modern magic, "ether" is the subtle substance of the Yesod level of experience, so that once again we are left with an attribution of this Path that points somewhere else. From the perspective of Malkuth, ether is unseen, intangible, indefinite, and yet all the complexity of the material world derives from it. In this sense the Path of Aleph is the "ether" of the Tree, the abstract presence underlying the dance of form and force between the Spheres. The metaphor can be taken too far - the Path of Aleph can be considered as a "substance," but only in a vague and not especially useful sense - but it has its merits on its own terms.

The Path Text, as might be expected, deals with the Path in yet another of its aspects, and here the part of the Tree related to the Path is Kether itself. The Path of Aleph is called the "Scintillating Intelligence," and described as the "essence of that curtain which is placed close to the order of the disposition;" its "special dignity" enables it to "stand before the face of the Cause of Causes." Both the "Cause of Causes" and the "order of the disposition" are terms for Kether, within which the causes and dispositions of all things are contained. The role of the Path of Aleph, though, is an unexpected one; it serves as a "curtain" - the Hebrew word can also be translated "veil" - and the word given as "scintillating" has the sense of "glaring" or "blinding" as well. The Path of Aleph, then, is a concealment.

Implied here, subtly, is a link between the Path of Aleph and the Sphere Binah. Just as the relationship between Kether and Binah implies Chokmah, an implication reflected in the symbols of the Path of Beth, so the relationship between Kether and Chokmah implies Binah; if unity is to develop an aspect of force it must develop an aspect of form as well. Once again, the Path of Aleph proves to contain the whole structure of the Tree in latent form.

In many ancient mythologies, this sort of latent presence was represented by a mythic image, which is reflected in the mythological principle of this Path. The Child of the Primal Void is a figure which, like the primal bull or cow, tends to appear at the beginning of creation myths; without parents, without origin, it appears in dark water or mist, with all the powers of the universe present inside itself. In some myths it becomes the Macranthropos whose body is the raw material for the world; in others, it becomes the Keeper of Wisdom of the 16th Path, or the King of the Golden Age of the 15th; far down the Tree, it has an echo in some of the myths associated with the Path of Qoph. Like the Path of Aleph itself, it appears in many forms, and evades full understanding in all of them.

Kether, the First Sphere

Title:	KThR, Kether (Crown).
Name of God:	AHIH, Eheieh (I Am).
Archangel:	MIThThRVN, Metatron, the Prince of Countenances.
Angelic Host:	ChIVTh HQDSh, Chaioth ha-Qodesh (Holy Living Creatures).

Astrological Correspondence:
> RAShITh HGLGLIM, Rashith h a - G i l g a l i m (Beginnings of Turnings or Primum Mobile).

Tarot Correspondence:
> The four Aces of the pack.

Elemental Correspondence:
> Air.

Path Text:	*"The First Path is called the Admirable or Hidden Intelligence, for it is the Light giving the power of comprehension of that First Principle which has no beginning; and it is the Primal Glory, for no created being can attain to its essence."*
Magical Image:	The faint outline of a human face looking toward the viewer's right, seen through brilliant light. No details, not even gender, can be made out.
Additional Symbols:	The point, the crown.
Additional Titles:	Macroprosopus, the Greater Countenance; Amen; the Primordial Point; the Head Which Is Not.
Colors:	in Atziluth - pure brilliance.
	in Briah - brilliant white.
	in Yetzirah - brilliant white.
	in Assiah - white, flecked with gold.

Correspondence in the Microcosm:
> Yechidah, the spiritual essence of the self.

Correspondence in the Body:
> Above the crown of the head.

Grade of Initiation: 10=1, Ipsissimus.
Negative Power: None (see Daath).

In the Cabalistic magician's journey up the Tree of Life, the ten Spheres serve as the chief milestones along the way, marking stages of ascent and movements in the dance of energies. Each of thse milestones has its own character, its challenges to be faced and powers to be won; each can be attained in different ways and on different levels.

From one perspective, the first Sphere is simply the last and highest of these phases of the work. In another and deeper sense, Kether's role in the path of the magician cannot be equated with that of any other Sphere on the Tree of Life. The lower Spheres are stations on the journey; Kether is the journey's end. Similarly, when the Tree is considered from the standpoint of the Way of Creation rather than that of Redemption, Kether again has a place no other Sphere can claim, for the whole pattern of energies which are expressed and transmuted through the other Spheres have their origin in the first. All the powers and relationships of the Tree emerge from Kether, depend on Kether, return to Kether.

At the same time, it's a mistake to think of Kether as simply a sum total of the Spheres and Paths we've already examined. It's a mistake, in fact, to think of Kether as anything at all. All thought and all perception have their basis in difference; the idea of color would be meaningless, for instance, if everything in the universe was always and forever the same precise shade of green. In the first Sphere, there are no differences of any kind, and so thought and perception at that level are alike impossible.

Part of the nature of the Kether level of consciousness, then, is that it can be attained but not experienced; to attain it, precisely, is to pass from the experience of anything to pure experience itself. Dealing with Kether in any sense is like trying to solve a mathematical problem in which the most important term is equal to infinity. While it can be done, in certain ways, the result is unlikely to make sense in any ordinary terms.

*   *   *

These considerations may make Kether seem completely divorced from the ordinary world in which magicians, like everyone else, must spend the bulk of their time. This is an illusion, however, and understanding the way that the Kether level of experience and consciousness relates to everyday life is crucial if its potentials are to be opened up.

Kether and Malkuth, opposite ends of the Tree of Life, are by that very fact parts of a single continuum. Both are states of consciousness, ways in which human beings can experience the universe. Both are, as well, symbolic. There is a tendency, as common in modern times as it was in the ancient world, to think of less easily reached states of consciousness such as Kether as more "true" than the ordinary state of Malkuth. This is only accurate in a special sense. The experience of these other states gives a broader range of perspectives from which to approach a given experience, and phenomena which make little sense or have little importance from the standpoint of Malkuth take on very different roles at these different levels. Still, none of these perspectives, none of these roles, are "true." All remain symbolic expressions, reflections in consciousness, of a reality which none can grasp.

This is perhaps the central lesson to be learned about the first Sphere. The existence of one end of a spectrum implies the existence of the other; to suggest unity is already to imply the idea of diversity. In this way, Kether and Malkuth arise and depend on each other.

At the same time, one of the standard maxims of the Cabalistic tradition suggests that there is a subtle twist involved in this mutual dependence. "Kether is in Malkuth," it says, "and Malkuth is in Kether - but after another manner." Each Sphere contains the other, but in its own way. The unity of Kether contains the countless separate things of Malkuth as potentials within an undivided unity; the diversity of Malkuth contains the supreme unity of Kether as a "thing" in which all other things are contained. Thus in the theological language of the West, with its relentlessly material perspective, the term "God" may be used of that unity, and God and Creation set apart; from a Malkuth perspective, this is accurate and appropriate. In turn, the mystical traditions of the East, which tend to shun the Malkuth perspective, dismiss this separation as an illusion; from the perspectives central to these teachings, this too is accurate and appropriate.

To the Cabalistic magician, on the other hand, both perspectives - and others - are accurate and inaccurate, appropriate and inappropriate. Each has its uses, its strengths, and its failings. None is "true" in any absolute sense. Where mystics of many schools seek the transforming experience of "enlightenment," the magician recognizes this as simply one among many possible states of consciousness, valuable in some situations, less so in others. The magician also knows, as the mystic sometimes does not, that there are times and places in which the most earthbound sort of Malkuth-level consciousness is in fact the best way to face the situation at hand.

✻   ✻   ✻

Tradition assigns more symbols, titles and images to Kether than to any other part of the Tree of Life. This may seem strange, given that Kether's nature is said to escape human perception altogether, but the flurry of symbolism testifies to the weakness of the symbolic system rather than to its strength. Like the small boy in the snowball fight who threw as many snowballs in as many directions as he could in the hope of hitting something, the generations of scholars and loremasters who created the Cabala tried to "hit something" of the first Sphere by using every analogy which came to hand.

The first of these is the title of the Sphere, which is Kether, "Crown." This is partly a reference to the location of the Kether center in the physical body, partly a pun pointing to the connection between Kether and Tiphareth - a crown, after all, is what is above a king. It has a more specific role in magical lore, though, one which ties into some of the deeper symbolism of initiation.

In many cultures, religious art and mythology alike show holy people and supernatural beings with light about their heads, sometimes in the form of circular halos or flames, sometimes in the form of rays extending like horns from the forehead, more rarely in both forms. These two patterns can be linked to two different versions of the "Dying

God" type of myth, and thus to two different approaches to initiation - approaches which are often combined in modern magical traditions. The details of these systems aren't relevant to our subject, but the effect - a partly physical, partly nonphysical experience of brilliance around the head - is the source of the crown as a part of the regalia of kings. Once a way of augmenting the light of the halo, and later a replacement for it as the lore underlying the ancient kingships was lost, the crown still retains the round band and branching extensions of its original. For our purposes, it can serve as a symbol of spiritual power, as well as a reminder - critically useful in dealing with Kether - of the difference between image and reality.

The Name of God assigned to Kether goes a good deal deeper into the Sphere's meaning. The Name AHIH, Eheieh, is (like the Tetragrammaton) a form of the Hebrew verb "to be." The Tetragrammaton, though, is an ancient form, and its exact sense is not known. No such ambiguity surrounds the Name AHIH. It means, precisely, "I am."

"I am." You'll want to think about the implications of this statement. In Biblical mythology, it was the Name God used for himself in his revelation to Moses on Mount Sinai; not merely a human word for the Ultimate, then, it represents the Ultimate's own self-description. It is also the one accurate thing which can be said of Kether. "It is" cannot; so long as "I" and "it" are separate, the Kether state of consciousness has not been reached; in unity, there is only unity.

There is another sense to this highest of the Names as well. Through this book, the difference between symbol and reality, what can be experienced and what actually is, has been a central issue. From the standpoint we've explored, it may seem as though one's own consciousness is on one side of the wall between symbol and reality, while everything it tries to perceive is on the other. This is a useful habit of thinking, but it hides an important point.

All we can know is symbolic; at the same time, each symbol is a representation of something in the realm of reality. This is as true of human consciousness as it is of anything else. We cannot know ourselves directly, any more than we can know anything else, but by the same token what we perceive of our own awareness is a reflection of something, something which is part of the unknowable reality behind the universe we experience. The name AHIH, then, is also the one accurate thing each of us can say about ourselves.

The letters of the Name have their lessons as well; they represent the generation of the creative duality of YH out of the context of energies (H) rising from the Unmanifest (A). Thus AHIH, YH, and YHVH ALHIM, the Names of the Supernal Triad, are three stages of the emergence of the creative polarity symbolized by the Tetragrammaton, and are mirrored below the Abyss by AL, ALHIM GBVR, and YHVH ALVH VDAaTh as stages in the emergence of the diversity of existence implied by the Name ALHIM.

*   *   *

The Archangel assigned to Kether is Metatron, the Prince of Countenances, a figure we've met before. Ancient and somewhat heretical Jewish lore gives this archangel the title of "Lesser YHVH" and the role of God's second-in-command, both derived - like the name Metatron itself - from the figure of the savior god Mithras in the religion of the Israelites' Persian liberators. Other legends give Metatron the role of bringing others before the countenance of God, and these tales are the source of his usual title. As we've seen, Metatron is assigned to Malkuth along with Sandalphon, suggesting the link between the highest and lowest Spheres mentioned above. As the Briah correspondence of Kether, Metatron can stand for pure receptive consciousness without limit, free of both force and form.

The Angelic Host assigned to Kether is the Chaioth ha-Qodesh or Holy Living Creatures. There are four Creatures; each has six wings, suggesting Tiphareth; they each have four heads, human, eagle, lion and bull, corresponding to the Kerubim as angels of Yesod, and to the elements in Malkuth. As the Yetzirah correspondence of Kether, they represent the union of pure being and pure consciousness, which contains in it the seed of the Tetragrammaton and thus of the entire dance of force and form symbolized by the Tree.

The Assiah aspect of Kether, the astrological correspondence, is called Rashith ha-Gilgalim, "beginnings of turnings." In the Earth-centered astronomy of medieval times, the outermost sphere of the heavens was called the primum mobile or "prime mover," the source of motion for the whole system. This symbol stresses Kether's role as the beginning of all things, the source of all the energies of the Tree.

✳   ✳   ✳

Of the remaining symbols of the first Sphere, the Path Text is by far the most important, and as usual it leads straight into some fairly dense thickets of Cabalistic lore. It's worth noting that here, dealing with a Sphere best characterized by unity, the Path Text uses two different titles and discusses four different aspects. A paradox? Certainly, but one based on issues we've already covered.

In the Text, Kether is described as a light which makes it possible to comprehend the First Principle; it is also a Glory, with an essence no created being can reach. Light, First Principle, Glory and Essence are all terms describing Kether. As light, the most universal symbol of spiritual awakening, it governs the Way of Redemption; as First Principle, it is the source of the Way of Creation; its Glory is its effect on the rest of the Tree; its essence is itself alone. As a power shaping other levels of experience, it is named the Admirable Intelligence, while as a level beyond comprehension it is named the Hidden Intelligence. All in all, this profusion of symbols does a creditable job of summing up the aspects of the first Sphere's nature.

The additional symbols and titles given here are selected from a much larger collection, which can be found in most books on the subject. Many have applications to the Biblical mythology so central to the work of the early Cabalists; few have relevance to the magical Cabala as it's practiced today. Some that have are listed here. Of them, one in particular will repay study: the Head That Is Not. In the symbolism of the Tree of Life, Kether is the summit, the source, and the end; it is also a Sphere among other Spheres; it is also a symbol, an inadequate one, of a reality beyond its grasp. It is the head - and it is not. Above it, as mentioned back in Chapter 1, are the Three Veils of the Unmanifest,

Ain Soph Aur or Limitless Light, Ain Soph or Infinity, Ain or Nothing. Beyond these deliberately vague images, in turn, is a reality which can never be known, but which is the true summit, the true source, the true end.

Part Three

Practice of the Magical Cabala

Chapter Ten
Foundations of Practice

The material on theory and symbolism which has been covered in the first two parts of this book is only a part, and not a particularly large one, of the vast accumulation of Cabalistic lore which has been gathered together over the past thousand years or so, and which is involved in one way or another with the Golden Dawn tradition. It would be easy to expand on any of the points discussed so far in this book at much greater length, even without drawing on the immense resources of the Hebrew literature on the subject.

Too much theory, though, is not necessarily an advantage, nor is book-learning by itself enough to make a magician. In fact, the pursuit of hidden knowledge for its own sake has been an obstacle between many a would-be adept and the potentials of the magical path. The common notion that real mastery of magic depends on possessing some sort of exotic information is wholly misleading, as we've seen, and the most important "secrets" of magic to the novice are neither particularly exotic nor particularly secret.

What are these secrets, then? They are the same factors which bring success in any other human activity - a point which has led more than one magician to suggest that all human activities are ultimately kinds of magic. Because of the mystification that usually surrounds these factors in their magical setting, it may be more useful to look at them in another context.

Consider, for example, the situation of someone who wants to become a musician. That desire, alone, is powerless until it is expressed in action, and even then action alone is not necessarily enough. Our would-be musician requires three things in order to get from the desire to the reality. First, she needs to decide what kind of musician she wants to be - to choose, at least for the time being, an instrument and a broad style - and to settle on the steps she means to take toward that goal. Second, she needs to practice with her instrument as often and as regularly as she can. Third, she needs to learn from her practice, and to compare her present performance to her goals as a guide to improvement.

These same three factors - clarity of purpose, persistence of effort, and the ability to learn - are equally the keys to achievement in magic. They are also, precisely, the practical sides of the three Spheres of the ruach above the Veil. Clarity of purpose is a product of the imagination in Tiphareth, for the goals to be sought and the steps to be taken both must be imagined before they can be reached. Persistence of effort, in turn, is a product of the will in Geburah; and the capacity to learn comes from the memory in Chesed.

These three Spheres are at once the goals and the tools of the first great transformation facing the aspiring magician, the parting of the Veil of the Sanctuary. There is a sense, an important one, in which the whole work of that transformation is simply a matter of learning to use the half-developed potentials of these Spheres - of learning to imagine, to will, and to remember fully and clearly. More broadly, this same idea can be applied to the other Spheres of the Tree, so that the entire course of the magician's work can be seen as a quest to sense, to intuit, to think and feel, to imagine and will and remember, to rest and act and be, as these things can and should be done, not in the half-hearted and less than half-competent manner in which they most often are done.

Tools Of The Magician's Trade

The work facing the magician, then, is simple...but "simple" is not necessarily the same thing as "easy." To say that imagination, will, and memory are both the keys and the results of magical attainment is to point to paradox; a key locked inside the door it is supposed to open is little help to anyone. The metaphor isn't perfect, since each of us does have some trace of these three powers in reflected form, but the difficulty it suggests is still real.

Most of the techniques of magical training, from the most basic to the most baroque, are simply ways of getting past this difficulty: of strengthening or supplementing the ordinary supply of imagination, will and memory, so that the aspiring magician can become familiar with the possibilities of these parts of himself or herself, and so that he or she can make use of magical and mystical practices which demand more from them than most people are able to manage unaided.

There are a great many of these techniques in current use, and there are others which have been used in the past but have been discarded by most schools of thought in recent times. It was once common, for example, to subject novices to extremes of fear, humiliation or abuse in order to develop strength of will. It has also been common in certain magical traditions to use various drugs to loosen some of the inhibitions which block the free workings of the imagination. There are still books and teachers which encourage both these methods, but both tend to cause kinds and levels of damage which more than outweigh any good that might come of them. (Those magicians who encourage the use of drugs, and there are still some of them, may argue this latter point; still, neither frequent flashbacks nor a loss of short-term memory are helpful in magical work.)

In the main current of the Golden Dawn tradition, on the other hand, the methods used to supplement imagination, will and memory are far more prosaic, but rather more reliable. To supplement the imagination in its work of setting out goals and means, the tradition uses study; to strengthen the will in its work of building persistent effort, it makes use of routine; to strengthen the memory in its work of encouraging learning, it insists on the importance of keeping a record of work. These three things are the foundations of effective magical training, the most basic tools in the aspiring magician's toolkit.

Study In Magical Training

The role of study as one of these basic tools may seem to conflict with the somewhat harsh appraisal of esoteric knowledge which appeared at the beginning of this chapter. In its proper place, though, the study of magical traditions and theory can be a significant help to the aspiring magician. (Otherwise, much of this book would be a waste of paper!) The critical point here is that magical study is of value when it happens in the context of regular practice, just as magical practice gains depth and effectiveness when it takes place in the context of study.

The range of subjects which have a useful bearing on the subject of Cabalistic magic is vast, probably too vast for any one person to master completely. Dion Fortune, perhaps the most important theorist in the tradition in the first half of this century, suggested the modest goal of a solid general knowledge of all the natural sciences, plus history, mathematics, logic and philosophy, to say nothing of psychology and comparative religion, as a good starting place for the would-be initiate! The total amount of information to be had in each of these fields of study, of course, has increased many times since she wrote, and a number of other areas which did not exist at the time - for instance, systems theory and cybernetics - might usefully be added.

There is little point, though, in setting goals for the student which no one can reasonably be expected to reach. More realistically, the aspiring magician in today's world might focus on certain areas of study. The first of these, certainly, is magic itself; there is a great deal worth reading both in the classics of magical literature and in more recent works, in and out of the specific field of Cabalistic magic. Second, and closely related to it, is folklore and mythology, the soil in which all magical traditions have their roots and from which many of the formulae of practical magic derive. Any number of things might reasonably be third on the list - anthropology, comparative religion, philosophy, psychology - and any of these could be a valuable addition to a magician's body of knowledge.

Beyond these topics, the student of magic will find other areas of interest, and should follow up on as many of them as he or she wishes; there are few subjects which do not throw some light on the magical path.

Routine in Magical Training

Magic's role as one of the common interests of the counterculture in today's society may make the thought of routine seem out of place in a magical context; a good many people take up magic, or at least the pose of magic, precisely because it seems different from the routine, the ordinary and the predictable. At the same time, human beings are creatures of habit, and this fact - when understood and used - is one of the most useful tools of the magician in training. Anything done repeatedly tends to become a habit; if it is done in the same place, at the same time, or in the same situation, this tendency can become almost impossible to escape.

It can be a useful exercise, for the purpose of self- exploration, to give oneself a randomly chosen habit by making use of this principle. The use of habit and routine in modern magic, on the other hand, is more than a simple experiment of this kind. Properly used, habit becomes a support for the will, and difficulties which the will alone cannot overcome can quite routinely be passed through by the aid of automatic habit.

It is for this reason that the major schools of Cabalistic magic have always insisted that magical practice should be done every day without fail, if at all possible at the same time, in the same place, and following the same ritualized process. Once this has been done for a time, it becomes habitual, and when the habit becomes thoroughly established skipping a practice produces the same kind of internal upset as does skipping a meal. Much of the work described in the chapters ahead has to do with establishing a routine of practices and developing the elements of that routine, step by step, until simple rote practice gives way to progressively deeper levels of insight and attainment.

It's important not to go to the other extreme, though, by devoting too much time to magic too soon; that way lies burnout, and in some cases psychiatric problems. The routine of practice which will be suggested in the next several chapters can be done, in its simplest form, in half an hour to forty minutes each day. This is a good place to start for those with no previous experience at daily practice, and an amount of time which can be squeezed out of almost any schedule, however busy.

The Magical Journal

The last of the three basic tools we'll examine here, the magical journal, supplements memory in the same way that routine strengthens will and study helps imagination. Of all the higher functions of the ruach, the human memory is perhaps the least reliable; ten people seeing the same car crash recall and describe ten completely different sets of events, as the experience of countless law courts has shown. For the magician, this can become a critical problem, for there are no other witnesses to most of the truly important events of his or her path, and even the most deeply felt realization can fade from memory over time.

The solution for this problem is probably as old as the invention of writing. A record or journal of magical study and practice, kept up daily and reviewed at intervals, provides an anchor for the memory and a yardstick for progress. It's best to use a bound "empty book" or journal for this purpose - there are stages in the magical path where the idea of tearing pages out bodily and throwing them away is a tempting one - and keeping such a record with a computer is probably unwise for the same reason. Beyond this, the form and format of the record is a matter of personal choice. Dates, times, and details of practices are useful; so is an assessment, at intervals, of how your training is going. (Such assessments often make interesting reading after a few years have passed.)

The Watcher at the Threshold

The three tools of the magician just discussed have many applications, but their most important use comes into play after the work of training is begun and the first major obstacle on the path appears. The Watcher at the Threshold, to use the rather melodramatic name assigned to this obstacle in tradition, has been mentioned before in this book. It represents the central and most critical phase of a common pattern of events in the magician's development. Individuals differ, and so this pattern takes many forms; at the same times, there are certain factors at work in the modern world which tend to give the encounter with the Watcher a particular shape.

People take up the study of magic for many reasons, but there are very often two factors which would-be magicians nowadays have in common. One of these is an attraction to magic as a mask or pose, an image which can be used to replace one's own reflection in the harshly lit mirror of self-perception. The scandalous reputation of magic, and its persecution through most of the last several millennia, can make magic especially attractive to people who feel alienated from the power structures of Western culture. "Being a magician," in this sense, provides an identity and often - at least in cities of a certain size - a community, in which fantasies of persecution and omnipotence too often blend into a mix quite familiar to the students of social psychology.

But the comforting mask is only one side of the coin. The other side is a desire, often vague and unformed, for something which goes beyond the mere donning of a mask and a pose - something real in a sense neither the structures of the dominant culture nor those of the magical subculture can match. The force of this desire is not toward "being a magician" but, rather, toward becoming one. It's often the presence of this other desire which leads the would-be magician to magic, rather than any of the other possible countercultures in our society.

These two desires, mask and reality, move in harmony so long as the magical novice restricts his or her involvement to reading books and taking part in a few community rituals. When the novice moves on to regular practice, though, that harmony shatters; it's possible to be a magician or to become one - but not both. The disciplines of magical training are unfriendly to masks of any kind, even the magician-mask; fantasies of magical power and self-sufficiency run headfirst into the reality that the beginning magician can rarely control his or her own thoughts for two minutes together. On a deeper level, the goal of most of the basic magical disciplines is self-knowledge, and it is precisely the fear of self-knowledge which is the motive behind every kind of mask.

This fear, then, is the obstacle which must be overcome at or near the beginning of practical work. It can hide itself in any number of forms. Sometimes it disguises itself as boredom - and it's true that many basic magical exercises are dull. Sometimes it disguises itself as frustration - and it's equally true that many basic magical exercises are frustrating, even deliberately so. Sometimes it takes the form of some other interest, or a whole series of other interests, which lay claim to the time needed for magical practice - and it's true, of course, that magical training takes a certain amount of time out of each day. Sometimes, finally, it appears in its own form, as stark terror, rising up without warning and as often as not without explanation in the middle of some practice.

Whatever its form, there is no way around it, and only one way through: perseverance. To abandon practices at this point, or even to change them significantly, is to be defeated by the Watcher. To persist, despite boredom, frustration, the attraction of other activities, and the fear of change and growth, is to win. The Watcher may return - there are often more masks than one to cast aside - but each victory makes others easier to achieve.

It is here, ultimately, that the three basic tools of training mentioned earlier in this chapter come into play. All three are weapons against the Watcher. Study allows the novice magician to identify his or her experiences as part of a common pattern, and to face the Watcher from the standpoint of knowledge. Routine helps the novice to keep going with the practical work of training despite the pressures the Watcher may bring to bear. The magical journal permits each struggle with the Watcher to be compared with previous bouts and carried on with the help of past experience. It's possible to win through without these, but they make the process a great deal less difficult.

Elementary Practices

Beyond the three pillars of practice we've covered so far, there are a handful of basic practices belonging to the esoteric traditions of the

West which are best discussed here at the beginning. All of them are, or can be, learned and practiced from the first stages of magical training, and help lay foundations in various ways for the work to come. Two of them - daily recollection and the noon salutation - became part of the Golden Dawn tradition many years ago, and are covered in many other books on the subject; the other two - solar and lunar etheric charging - are borrowed from a related tradition, and are all but unknown in English-speaking countries. All four will prove of value to the magician in training.

Daily recollection is one of the oldest recorded practices of Western esotericism, dating back to the teachings of the mystical mathematician Pythagoras in the sixth century B.C.E. The essence of the practice has changed very little since that time, although there are variations in some of the details. The core of the original method is simplicity itself: one spends a few minutes each evening, before going to sleep, thinking back over the events of the day in the order in which they happened. Vast detail isn't necessary, but every significant event should be recalled to mind.

The point of this exercise is partly the same as that of the magical journal; recollection exercises the memory, and thus helps to strengthen this most fallible of the powers of the ruach. Partly, though, the habit of recollection is aimed at the broader goal of self-knowledge. This can work in obvious ways, as when an action or an attitude which seemed perfectly sensible at the time takes on a wholly different appearance in the cold light of memory. There are subtler possibilities involved, though. One of the ways in which human beings most often avoid self-knowledge is the habit of selective memory; we recall those things which bolster the self-image we wish to show ourselves, and do our best not to think about those which contradict it. The regular practice of recollection sets up a different rhythm of memory, one based on the simple sequence of events rather than on our personal preferences, and in this way helps to break down ordinary habits of remembering in favor of a less distorted approach.

The practice of the noon salutation also has ancient roots; mystics of the ancient Hermetic traditions of Hellenistic Egypt were performing salutations at various stations of the sun's path before the beginning of the Christian era. The sun's role in Cabalistic thought as an image of Tiphareth reflects in many ways its importance in more ancient traditions, and for many people the sun still forms one of the most effective symbols for the presence of the unity we've called God within the universe of our experience.

The noon salutation is intended to make use of this. Each day at solar noon, as the sun reaches its highest point in the sky, face due south. Visualize the image of the sun, and consider it as a symbol for what theologians might call the presence of God in the world of Nature. If you can do this in sunlight, good, but remember not to risk eye damage by looking at the sun directly. If you are in a place where you can do so unobserved, performing the Cabalistic Cross (as described in the next chapter) is a useful conclusion to the salutation; otherwise, simply hold image and contemplation for a moment, and then return to your ordinary activities.

There is one additional complication; the salutation should be done at solar noon, which is not necessarily the same as noon on the clock. You'll need to subtract an hour from clock time if Daylight Saving Time is in effect. Solar time also varies depending on how far you are east or west of the standard meridian of your time zone; the standard meridians are at 75 degrees west for Eastern time, 90 for Central, 105 for Mountain, and 120 for Pacific. Subtract four minutes from clock time for every degree of longitude west of the standard meridian; add four minutes for every degree east. (You can find the longitude of the place where you live in an atlas, or talk to a local astrologer.)

The noon salutation is useful for a number of reasons, some simple, some buried in the complexities of magical theory. At the simplest level, it's a valuable exercise in awareness to have some simple task to remember and perform at a fixed point in the middle of one's daily activities. On a deeper level, the act of calling a symbol and its meaning to mind again and again over a long period tends not only to energize that symbol but to open up a connection with the reality which the symbol represents - in this case, the presence of Tiphareth and the Tiphareth level of consciousness amid the seeming confusion of

Malkuth. Beyond this, there are a range of subtle relationships between the human microcosm and the sun on all the levels of experience, relationships which can be used to strengthen and balance the self in many ways.

The remaining elementary practices make use of this last level of interaction in a more focused way. The practice of solar and lunar etheric charging, while not specifically part of traditional Golden Dawn magic, is derived from traditions closely related to the Golden Dawn, and has links with a number of areas of the Order's work - notably, the largely neglected field of Golden Dawn alchemy.

* * *

Solar etheric charging, which we'll examine first, is done as follows:

First: On a clear morning before 10 am, in a place where you can stand in direct sunlight which does not pass through glass - a spot in the open air is best, but a room with an open window in the right place will work - stand facing the sun, eyes closed, with as much of your body as possible in sunlight. Raise your arms out to the sides, like the arms of a cross, palms forward. Breathe slowly, feeling the sunlight soaking into your body.

Second: After a minute or so, bend your arms at the elbow, bringing your hands inward and slightly up, so that they almost touch each other a few inches in front of your forehead. Your palms face inward. Visualize as clearly as possible light and heat flowing from your palms into your forehead.

Third: Move your hands together slowly downward from your forehead to your solar plexus, maintaining the visualization the whole way. When this has been completed, separate your hands with a broad sweeping movement, bowing as low as you can, and then return to the first position with arms spread wide. Repeat this whole process seven times.

Lunar etheric charging is done in exactly the same way, except that moonlight instead of sunlight provides the energy source for the work.

Lunar charging should only be done when the moon is waxing - that is, during the first half of the lunar cycle, from New Moon to Full Moon - and is best if done before 10 pm at night.

*　　*　　*

Both of these exercises are designed to influence the nephesh or etheric body. The sun is Earth's primary source of etheric energy as well as of physical energy, and charging the centers of the nephesh with solar force strengthens and energizes the whole structure of the etheric body. The etheric forces of the moon, by contrast, tend to produce increased sensitivity, especially toward subtle energies and the range of poorly understood perceptions we tend to lump together as "intuition." Done regularly, they help prepare the etheric body for the more intense energy flows of advanced magical work. Both practices also have positive effects on physical health. They can be done as frequently as circumstances allow, although more than one practice of each in twenty-four hours might risk a certain amount of temporary energy imbalance.

Chapter Eleven
Ritual Magic

Of the various kinds of magical practice, the one that generally comes first to anyone's mind is ritual. Even people who have only the dimmest notion of what magic is and what it does tend to think of magic in terms of weird rites complete with robes, wands, strange gestures and shouts of "Abracadabra!" Caricatured as this is, it nonetheless points in the right direction, for ritual - understood in its broadest sense - is the most important of the practical methods used by the magician.

We can define ritual, for practical purposes, as symbolic action. Every action done in a ritual context, whether it be the speaking of a word, the movement of a hand, the drawing of a breath or the building up of an image in the imagination, is a deliberate symbol. It means something, and something specific. In a well-designed ritual, these meanings resonate together like the notes of a musical chord, expressing a single pattern of meaning in a complete and balanced form.

From a Cabalistic viewpoint, this definition can be expanded a little, for the union of action and meaning in a well-made ritual works at every level of the Tree. Thus physical actions, etheric patterns, concepts, emotions, will and memory come together in a ritual under the direction of the imagination, which itself reaches upward toward the primal Form, Force and Unity of the Supernals. Seen in this light, then, ritual is a way of unifying the self on all its levels and directing it toward a single end. This combination of unity and direction makes ritual the magician's principal tool for action on any level of experience.

More exactly, this is what ritual is capable of being. Reaching the point at which that possibility becomes real takes a great many things, but most of them are a function of one: practice. Unavoidably, the first attempts at ritual will be a matter of fumbling with forms, memorizing words and gestures, and trying to perform these in the least awkward manner possible. Once these challenges are overcome, the inner aspects of the ritual have to be dealt with, over and over again, until the various levels of the rite come into harmony with one another and the first consistent effects start to show up. Even then, those effects must themselves mature and develop over time to reach their full potential.

All this may seem to make the practical use of magic a long and rather dreary process; if it takes years to completely master a given ritual - and this is in fact fairly common - how is the magician to respond to a new possibility or an unexpected emergency? Fortunately, the ritual forms used in the Golden Dawn system were designed with a great deal of built-in flexibility. Each ritual is built up out of smaller elements, which are to be practiced individually by the student, and most rituals can be directed toward any of a wide range of purposes by changing some part of the symbolism. Once the basic elements and their applications have been practiced, it's possible to assemble and work a ritual for almost any conceivable end in short order.

To master magical ritual, then, is less a matter of learning ceremonies by rote than it is one of understanding the formula of any given ritual - that is, its inner symbolic structure, the framework around which the details of the ritual are assembled. In turn, that understanding comes from experiencing the way in which that formula works out in practice. Here again, action and meaning must be brought together for the potentials of ritual to be awakened.

The Purposes of Ritual

To speak of the practical uses of magical ritual, though, is to touch on an issue which has caused a great deal of trouble in magical circles down through the years. Many writers draw a useful distinction between two kinds of applications of magic. The first, called "high magic" or "theurgy," consists of the use of magic to accelerate the spiritual development of the magician; the second, called variously "low magic," "practical magic" or "thaumaturgy," consists of the use of magic to bring about other kinds of change in any of the levels of experience. The first class is the more important, for the mastery of any kind of magic at all depends on inner development. What, though, of the second?

There are at least two questions tied up in this issue. First of all, what sort of practical uses does magic have? Second, and at least as important, what sort of practical uses should it have?

History has left the first question in a mire of confusion. At one time, it was considered sinful for Christians to believe that magic had any effect at all beyond that of illusion. Later, it was declared equally sinful for Christians not to believe that magic had effect! This latter period, the age of the great witch persecutions, saw the potential powers of magicians overstated to a preposterous degree by the propaganda machines of the Inquisition and its Protestant equivalents.

More recently still, of course, the pendulum has swung back the other way, and it is the closest thing to sin recognized by modern rationalism to believe that magic is anything but fraud or self-delusion. Some modern magicians have responded to this attitude by redefining magic as a kind of psychology, and accepting limits to its power in keeping with the opinions of modern psychological theory. Other magicians, rejecting this, have made claims for the potentials of magic which amount at best to wishful thinking.

In point of fact, we don't currently know what limits exist on the power of magic. It's clear that magical processes can affect the whole range of experiences which are usually called "subjective" or "psychological" in our culture, and those "objective" or "physical" things most closely linked to this side of experience - for example, the functioning of the immune system and the physical body in general - seem also to be open to magical influence. On the other hand, claims of the more extreme kinds of power over the "objective" or "physical" side of experience - for example, the levitation of heavy objects - seem to fall flat in practice. Between these two extremes is a wide gray area of possibility, in which the actual limits seem to lie. A great deal of experiment and, above all, honest assessment will have to come before any more definite line can be drawn.

The question of what purposes are appropriate for magic - that is, of magical ethics - is equally confused; a great deal of nonsense has been written on the subject of the use and misuse of magic. The spectrum of opinion runs all the way from those who threaten dire consequences for the least use of magical techniques for anything but mystic attainment, to those who hold that the whole purpose of magical training is godlike power over the world and the attainment of all one's material desires.

These extremes can, as usual, be discarded, but the way of balance between them needs to be traced out carefully. Perhaps the best guide to this is the principle of the circular nature of magical action, mentioned in the discussion of Chokmah's symbolism in Part Two of this book. This principle has been the subject of a great deal of mythologizing in ancient and modern times alike - the "threefold return" of current Wiccan lore is an example - but it expresses a useful truth. Every magical act affects its source as well as its target. If you set out to destroy another person by magic, you will be attuning your consciousness to energies of hatred and destruction, and those energies will take shape in your life just as effectively as they will do so in the life of your intended victim. If you set out to control another person - which is what most so-called love spells amount to - you will weaken your own will to the same degree that you override the will of your target. The same processes which allow magical acts to shape the experience of another person will just as easily allow those acts to shape the experience of the magician. In this there is no one acting as a judge, no "occult police" of the sort beloved of certain magical writers; it is simply a matter of cause and effect.

The much-despised Golden Rule - treat other people as you would want them to treat you - might well be used as a yardstick in considering the practical uses of magic. So, on a higher level, might the ideal of love found in the symbolism of the Path of Daleth. Still, a common proverb offers perhaps the clearest advice in these matters. In magic, as in the rest of life, what goes around comes around. In the case of destructive magic, too, there's another proverb worth considering: lie down with dogs, get up with fleas.

In considering any use of magic for practical ends, it's necessary to have a goal - not simply a vague idea, but a precise goal thought out in detail, which you can express clearly in a single sentence. Here again, the issues of magical ethics are important. Are you sure that you actually want what you think you want, and are you sure you want to live with the consequences of getting it?

It's also important to make your goal exactly the thing you want. There's a story, well-known in magical circles, of a man who tried to use a visualization technique to get money. He visualized himself handling huge stacks of bills. Shortly thereafter, he was hired by a bank - where he spent eight hours a day, at a modest wage, counting huge stacks of other people's money. The story is funny enough, but there have been any number of other people who have made the same mistake in less harmless ways: who have wanted security but made money the goal of their actions, or wanted love but made power over someone their goal, or wanted peace but made isolation their goal, and who got the thing they sought and not the thing they actually wanted.

From the standpoint of the magical Cabala, there is a sense in which every goal other than the Great Work of spiritual transformation is an example of exactly this kind of mistake; it's a central teaching of the whole Western magical tradition that we must find our happiness through the restoration of inner wholeness before we can find it anywhere else. At the same time, there are times when it's appropriate to change our surroundings as well as ourselves, and practical magic is one of the tools available to the magician for this part of the work.

Beginning Ritual Practice

There is much more which could be said on the subject of ritual, and fortunately much of it has been said elsewhere, in the classic books on the subject. For the purposes of this book, though, the points mentioned above will be enough. What remains, centrally, is the actual practice of magical ritual. While the full subject of ritual work demands a book to itself, we can explore this branch of Cabalistic magic through two of the most important basic ritual practices in the tradition.

In the Golden Dawn, the first ritual which was introduced to the Neophyte was a short ceremony called the Lesser Ritual of the Pentagram. This rite has been borrowed by a wide range of groups, and most people involved in the magical community nowadays are at least slightly familiar with it. Despite its simplicity, it has a great deal of depth, and contains potentials which can be discovered only through a great deal of practice.

Like the more complex rituals which follow it, the Lesser Ritual of the Pentagram has the quality of flexibility mentioned above, and the symbolism of the ritual can be changed to produce one of two different effects: invoking (the gathering of energy) or banishing (the dispersal of energy). To perform the ritual, you will need privacy, and a space large enough to permit you to move in a circle a few feet across. The ritual is performed as follows:

First: Stand in the center of the space, feet together, arms at sides, facing east. Pause, clear your mind, and then visualize yourself expanding upward and outward, through the air and through space, until your feet rest on the Earth as though on a ball a foot across. Raise your right hand above your forehead; draw it down, palm toward your face, visualizing a beam of light descending from far above your head. Touch your fingers to your forehead, and visualize the descending light forming a sphere of light, the same size as the Earth beneath your feet, just above the crown of your head. Vibrate the word ATEH (pronounced "ah- teh").

Comment: Vibration, as the word is used in magical contexts, refers to a special way of speaking or chanting words of power or Names of God. It can best be described as a kind of humming or droning chant. To begin learning it, make the sound "aaah," extending it as far as breath will allow, while changing the tone and the shape of your mouth until you feel a buzzing or tingling feeling at some point in your body. With practice, this feeling can be directed to any point inside or outside of the physical body.

Second: Draw your hand down to touch your solar plexus, just below the lower point of the breastbone, and visualize a shaft of light descending from the sphere above your head to the visualized earth beneath your feet. Vibrate MALKUTH (pronounced "mahl-kooth"). Bring your hand back to the center of your chest, and then over to the right shoulder; visualize a beam of light extending from the vertical shaft to a point just past your shoulder, where it forms a sphere of brilliant red light, the size of the others. Vibrate VE-GEBURAH (pronounced "veh geh-boo-rah"). Then bring your hand straight across to your left shoulder; visualize a beam of light extending from the center of your chest to a point just past your shoulder, where it forms a sphere of brilliant blue light the size of the others. Vibrate VE-GEDULAH (pronounced "veh geh-dyoo-lah").

Third: Join the hands in front of the center of the chest, fingers together and pointed upwards, palms touching. Visualize the Earth and the three spheres of energy joined by the cross of light. Vibrate LE-OLAM, AMEN (pronounced "leh o-lahm, ah-men").

Comment: These first three steps form what is called the Cabalistic Cross. The words, which are in Hebrew, are an ancient ritual prayer borrowed by Christian churches many centuries ago; in translation, it reads, "Unto Thee be the Kingdom and the Power and the Glory forever, amen." The words Malkuth, Geburah and Gedulah point to its obvious Cabalistic meaning; it maps the Tree of Life onto the physical body; together with the imagery of expansion in the beginning, it identifies the magician with Adam Cadmon. On a less symbolic level, it also energizes and balances certain centers in the nephesh of the magician. This latter effect can (and should) be strengthened by focusing the vibration of each of the first four words into the sphere of light being formulated, and that of the last words into the image of the cross of light.

Fourth: Step to the eastern edge of the space in which you are working. With the first two fingers of your right hand (the others and the thumb folded back), and the arm itself held straight, trace a pentagram some three feet across in the air before you. To invoke, trace the Invoking Pentagram in Diagram 17; to banish, trace the Banishing Pentagram. These should be made as even and exact as possible. As you trace them, visualize the line drawn by your fingers shining with blue-white light.

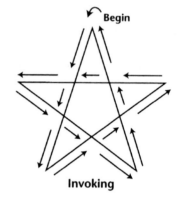

When you have finished tracing, point to the center of the pentagram with your fingers and vibrate the Name YHVH (pronounced "yeh-ho-wah").

Fifth: Holding your arm extended, trace a line around a quarter circle to the southern edge of the space in which you are working, visualizing that line in the same blue-white light. Trace the same type of pentagram in the south, with the same visualization; point to the center, and vibrate the Name ADNI (pronounced "ah-dough-nye").

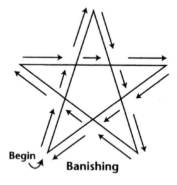

Sixth: Trace the line around a quarter circle to the western edge of the space and repeat the process, this time vibrating the Name AHIH (pronounced "eh-heh-yeh"). Then trace the line around a quarter circle to the north and repeat, this time vibrating the Name AGLA (pronounced "ah-geh-lah").

Comment: The pronunciation of these names is a matter of tradition, and thus unavoidably of disagreement. The Tetragrammaton, in particular, has been the subject of a whole series of disputes down through the years. Jewish tradition forbade it to be spoken aloud at all, and the Golden Dawn accordingly taught members simply to pronounce the letters aloud - "Yod Heh Vau Heh" - when vibrating. While this is functional to some extent, it was a significant break with the traditions of Western magic.

The Tetragrammaton is one of a whole family of names of power used in the ancient world; here as elsewhere, the differences between monotheist orthodoxy and paganism are far smaller than either side likes to admit. Classical Latin pronounces J as Y and V as W, and so the name "Jove" used for the Roman god Jupiter was actually pronounced "Yo-weh;" the Greek mysteries made use of words of power such as "Io" and "Evoe," and the Gnostics used names such as "Iao" and "Ieou" frequently in their writings. All of these words of power are variations on a specific pattern of vowel sounds used in many spiritual traditions. The early Christian scholars who first translated the Bible into Latin, who were by no means ignorant of the deeper side of pagan spirituality, accordingly wrote the Tetragrammaton as "Jehovah," pronounced "Yehowah," and it was this pronunciation which was standard in Western magical circles from the early Middle Ages up into the nineteenth century. In practice, this pronunciation of the Name tends to have a more potent but also more balanced effect than others.

The pronunciations of other Names given here, and elsewhere in this book, follow standard Golden Dawn practice.

Seventh: Trace the line back around to the east, completing the circle. You are now standing inside a ring of visualized light, with a pentagram shining in each of the four quarters. Return to the center and face east, as you were at the opening, but raise your arms to the sides like the arms of a cross, palms forward. Say aloud:

"Before me, Raphael (pronounced "ra-fa-ell"); behind me, Gabriel ("gah-bree-ell"); to my right hand, Michael ("mee-ka- ell"); to my left hand, Auriel

("oh-ree-ell"). For about me flame the pentagrams, and upon me shines the six-rayed star!"

Comment: While naming the archangels, visualize them as conventional angelic figures, larger than human height and blazing with light. Raphael wears yellow and violet, and carries a sword; Gabriel wears blue and orange, and carries a goblet; Michael wears red and green and carries a staff; Auriel wears every shade of earth and green growth, and carries a disk bearing a pentagram. When the pentagrams are mentioned, visualize them as clearly as possible. When the six-rayed star is named, visualize a Star of David on the front of your body, about two feet across, the upward-pointing triangle red, the downward- pointing triangle blue.

Eighth: Repeat the Cabalistic Cross, steps 1-3. This completes the ritual.

∗ ∗ ∗

This ritual is the most basic of a series of ceremonies using the same formula. In it, the magician aligns himself or herself with the source of power through the Cabalistic Cross; a space is then defined for that power, first with symbols and Names at the edges of the space, then with an invocation of balanced forces at the center; finally, the magician repeats the first step to link the structure thus created with the power at its heart. The whole formula has certain links with that of the Golden Dawn's Equinox Ceremony, one of the most fascinating (and least often understood) of the Order's rites. In this particular application of the formula, this pattern is combined with a symbolism based on the numbers 4, 5 and 6, representing the Spheres of the higher aspects of the ruach as well as the macrocosm, the microcosm, and their interaction; it can thus be seen as a simple invocation of the Higher Self.

In its banishing mode, by far the most common in practical use, the Lesser Ritual of the Pentagram is often treated as a purely protective or defensive technique, and the pentagrams and circle traced around the area are seen as a barrier against hostile forces. While there is some truth to this conception - the pentagrams and circle, with practice, form a tangible presence on the etheric level - it's more useful to think of the Pentagram Ritual as a way of establishing balance at either a raised or lowered level of energy, with effects which extend beyond the limits of the traced circle. The banishing form of the ritual, then, decreases the amount of energy present, and at the same time imposes balance on it: a process which is highly disruptive to a hostile entity or a magical attack, but which also has a range of other possible uses, many of which have nothing to do with this sort of protective work.

Other rituals using the same formula can be found in books on Golden Dawn ceremonial magic. For now, though, the most useful thing to do is to concentrate on this one. It should be performed every day for at least two months before going on to the other ritual given in this chapter. Do it in its invoking mode on one day, its banishing mode the next, and continue to alternate; pay attention to the differences in any effect you may notice. As with every practice, write up an account of each performance of the ritual in your magical journal.

Opening the Centers of Power

The Lesser Ritual of the Pentagram is the most basic of the building blocks of Cabalistic magic; every major ritual, and many of the minor ones, begins and ends with it. In its banishing mode, which is the one used in such contexts, it clears away conflicting energies in advance of ritual work, and closes down the energies of the ritual itself once the ceremony is complete.

The next piece of ritual work to be learned is based on a different formula altogether, and has different uses. The Middle Pillar exercise, as it is called, is rarely if ever done as part of any other ritual. It is just as important for the ritualist in training, though, for its purpose is the opening up of energy centers within the body. These centers, which were mentioned back in Chapter Four, correspond exactly to the four Spheres of the Middle Pillar, plus Daath. Their awakening is probably the most important task faced by the beginning student of ritual, for it is through these centers that the forces used in ritual are gathered, directed and put to work.

Like the Lesser Ritual of the Pentagram, the Middle Pillar exercise has been borrowed and adapted by many groups within the magical community, and many people will have had some exposure to it. Unfortunately, the version which was the starting point for most of this borrowing and adaptation had been the subject of a certain amount of tinkering, involving the placement of one of the centers and the pattern of the circulation of energy. The original form, which is given here, is designed to bring about certain very specific changes in the structure of the etheric body, and these are not accomplished by the more common version of the exercise. If you are familiar with the Middle Pillar exercise, therefore, you'll want to note any differences between the version you have learned and the one given here, and pay attention to any differences in the results.

✳   ✳   ✳

The requirements for the Middle Pillar exercise are the same as those for the Lesser Ritual of the Pentagram. The exercise is performed as follows:

First: Perform the complete Lesser Ritual of the Pentagram in its banishing mode, as described above.

Second: Standing in the center of the space, facing east, with legs together and arms at sides, turn your attention to a point infinitely far above your head. Visualize the point shining with light, like a star. Next, drawing in a breath, visualize a stream of light descending from that point to the area just above your head, where it forms a sphere of intense white light about eight inches across. The bottom of the sphere is just above the crown of your head. Concentrate on the sphere, thinking of it as Kether, while you breathe slowly and deeply four times; on the fourth outbreath, vibrate the Name AHIH (pronounced "eh-heh-yeh"). Try to make the vibration resonate within the sphere of light itself.

Third: With the next inbreath, bring the stream of light down to the middle of your throat, and there form another sphere of light of the same size, this one a soft gray color. Concentrate on it, thinking of it as Daath, while you breathe slowly and deeply four times; on the fourth outbreath, vibrate the Name YHVH ALHIM (pronounced "yeh-ho-wah ell-o-heem). Again, try to make the vibration resonate in the sphere..

Fourth: In the same way, establish the golden sphere of Tiphareth at the level of the heart, and vibrate the Name YHVH ALVH VDAaTh (pronounced "yeh-ho-wah ell-o-ah vah da-ath"); the violet sphere of Yesod at the genitals, and vibrate the Name ShDI AL ChI (pronounced "shah-die ell chye," with the "ch" as in Scottish "loch"); and the sphere of Malkuth at the soles of the feet, which may be black, dark green, or the four Briah colors of the Sphere, and vibrate the Name ADNI HARTz (pronounced "ah-dough-nye ha ah-rets").

Fifth: Pause, and then direct your attention upwards again toward the Kether center above your head. Draw in a breath, and visualize a shaft of brilliant light descending with the inbreath to the Tiphareth center at your heart; visualize the Tiphareth center shining more brightly as you breathe out. Repeat this process four times; on the last outbreath, the Tiphareth center should blaze like the sun.

Sixth: Draw in a breath slowly, feeling the air pass through your nostrils and down your windpipe. Visualize it as passing into the Tiphareth center at your heart, and from there out to your left side, down the left flank and leg, to the Malkuth center at the feet. Hold the breath there for the same amount of time you took to breathe in, then breathe out at the same pace, visualizing the breath passing up the right leg and flank, in to the Tiphareth center, and then up and out the windpipe and nostrils; then, hold the outbreath for the same amount of time. (It's helpful to count mentally from one to four during each of these four phases - inbreath, hold, outbreath, hold - to get the rhythm; this is an application of the Fourfold Breath, which will be introduced in the next chapter.) Make the visualization of the moving breath as concrete as possible, so that you feel the path of the breath down and up again as though it were a physical movement. Repeat this whole process four times.

Seventh: Pause, and then perform the Cabalistic Cross as given above to close the exercise.

*   *   *

The formula of the Middle Pillar is fairly straightforward to anyone with a background in the Cabala. Like the Cabalistic Cross, it identifies the magician with Adam Cadmon, symbolically fusing the individual and the universe. Within this fusion, though, it sets in motion some specific changes: first, it energizes the centers in the physical, etheric and astral bodies associated with the Spheres of the Middle Pillar; next, it brings the Kether and Tiphareth centers into closer contact; finally, it connects the Tiphareth and Malkuth centers using etheric substance drawn from the breath, cleansing and balancing both centers and indirectly passing on the energies of Kether to the center governing the physical body.

It's worth noting that there are a whole series of further developments of the Middle Pillar formula, which are based on the various formulae of initiation used in the Golden Dawn and which take these transformations of the etheric body to a much greater degree. These are well beyond the scope of the present book, but can be worked out fairly easily by anyone familiar with the Order's papers on the inner side of ritual.

The effects of this exercise vary depending on the etheric condition of the person practicing it. Improvement in physical and emotional health is perhaps the most common effect, the opening up of what are sometimes called "psychic" abilities another result that often appears. To avoid overload of the centers, it should be done no more than once each day, at least for the first year of training. Once each day, on the other hand, is also a fair minimum. Once the two months' work on the Lesser Ritual of the Pentagram has been finished, the Middle Pillar exercise should become the daily practice of any student of Cabalistic magic. It takes only about fifteen minutes to do, and those fifteen minutes are the most important investment of time it's possible to make in the early stages of magical training.

Chapter Twelve
Meditation

As a part of magical training in the Golden Dawn tradition, the technique of meditation is less well known than ritual, but it is very nearly as important. Where ritual forms the central active technique, meditation is the most useful receptive technique. Where ritual shapes energies, meditation shapes the forms of awareness; where ritual builds on symbolism, it's through meditation that the symbols to be used are made a part of the self.

In some ways, it's unfortunate that the word "meditation" is the only common term in English for the range of inner techniques that are based on specific modifications of receptive awareness. Originally, the term (meditatio in Latin) simply meant thinking, especially deep or drawn-out thought. Applied to the Catholic practice of directed thought about religious ideas, it was used for want of anything better to describe the not particularly similar methods used by Oriental monks and mystics. Once broadened this far, the meaning of the word proceeded to stretch completely out of shape, with the result that nowadays, "meditation" is used by many people to refer to practically any kind of spiritual or pseudo-spiritual exercise.

For our purposes, on the other hand, this word "meditation" will be used to refer to a specific (and in some ways rather difficult) skill: the ability to use a symbol held in the mind to come into contact with the deeper reality which that symbol represents. If you have had experience in the past with Oriental methods of meditation, this sort of work may seem rather strange to you, and the methods used to learn and perfect it may seem stranger still. At the same time, the system of Cabalistic meditation presented here is founded on some of the core elements common to spiritual practices everywhere.

It should be said at the outset that the system of meditation presented here, while based on the method used in the Golden Dawn, is only one out of many kinds of Cabalistic meditative work. Some of the others differ in almost every imaginable way from the method taught in this book. None of them, and certainly not this one, should be thought of as the "real" or "correct" system. Like any living thing, the magical Cabala has grown and branched out in many different ways; the scale and diversity of such methods are a sign of vitality, not of confusion or error. The particular choice of methods made by the Golden Dawn is followed here largely because it works well for most students within the context of the Order's system as a whole, given the essential qualities of effort and perseverance.

Preliminaries to Meditation

The method of meditation given here, then, is based on the symbolic material discussed earlier in this book. Those symbols, one at a time, are to be taken into the mind, explored, studied, turned over and over again in thought, as though they were parts of some complicated machine which you are trying to understand. Each symbol, then, is to be fitted back in its place, so that the machine - to continue the metaphor - can be turned on and set in motion.

In some ways, then, this form of meditation is not that far removed from ordinary thinking. The critical difference is that, in meditation, you will be thinking about one thing and one thing only, for the entire time of your meditation. This is not that unfamiliar a state - most people experience it now and then, when deeply absorbed in a problem or the like. However, trying to do it at will, every day, can be another matter entirely!

Some fairly simple factors will help you achieve this skill. It's best not to try to meditate within about two hours after eating a meal, or when you are tired; both of these tend toward drowsiness, and this can be a major source of interference. Loud music or television close by is another hindrance, and should be avoided if you have the option.

It's best, as Chapter 10 pointed out, to set a specific time for your practice session each day, and to stick to it. In the case of meditation, perhaps the best time of all for many people is early in the morning, preferably first thing on waking up. At this hour there is often little background noise, and the stresses and confusions of the day will not yet have established much of a foothold in your mind.

Meditation - First Stage

You have chosen a time and are ready to start, then. The next task at hand is developing the basic skills you will need for the meditative work. At once the most basic and the most important skill you will need to learn for this work is a state of relaxed concentration. Note the word "relaxed"; the last thing wanted here is the kind of tense teeth-gritting inner war that the word "concentration" usually suggests. The following exercise will help you begin to learn how to reach this state, as an initial step toward the practice of Cabalistic meditation. Do it each day during the period you've set aside for practice.

For this exercise, you'll need a quiet and not too brightly lit space to work in, and a chair with a straight back and a seat of a height which, when you sit on it, will permit your feet to rest flat on the floor and your thighs to be level. You will also need a clock or watch placed where you can see it without turning your head. Sit down with your feet and knees together, your back straight but not stiff, your hands resting on your thighs. Your eyes should be open, looking ahead but not focusing on anything in particular.

Take a few moments to be aware of your physical body. Start at the top of your head and work your way downward to the soles of your feet. Pay special attention to the tensions you feel. Don't try to relax them, or to change them in any way; simply be aware of them. Over time, this simple act of awareness will weaken and eliminate your body's tension patterns, by bringing to consciousness the rigidities of thought and emotion that underlie them. Like so much in meditation, however, this process must be allowed to move at its own pace.

Throughout all of this, and all of the exercise to follow, keep as still as possible, without fidgeting or shifting, but without a forced stiffness. The goal here is to put your body in a state of balanced and relaxed poise, in which it will not interfere with the work you're trying to do. Be aware that this goal may take a great deal of practice to reach! Most students will find that itches, cramps, and the like will get in the way, and these obstacles will often become more rather than less frequent as time goes on - for a while. Eventually, given persistence, the body learns to relax into the meditative position, and these difficulties come to an end.

When you have finished with the brief assessment of your physical body, then, turn your attention to your breathing. Draw in a deep, slow, even breath, while counting mentally from one to four; hold the breath, counting from one to four; let the breath out, slowly, counting from one to four; finally, hold the breath out, counting from one to four. Begin again with the inbreath and the count. When holding your breath, don't close your throat. The breath should be held in or out with the muscles of the chest, so that a sharp tap on the chest will drive out air. All this breathing should be done through the nose, and the mouth should be gently closed, with the tongue resting against the roof of the mouth.

While you are breathing, your mind will want to run off along various trains of thought. Don't let it. Keep aware of the rhythm of the breathing, the feeling of the air moving into and out of your lungs. When your mind slips away into inner chatter, as it will, bring it gently back to your breathing. It will slip away again, and again, and again. Bring your attention back to your breathing. With practice, you will find yourself able to keep it in place for a moment here and there, and in those moments you will find an odd kind of calm but watchful clarity arising. This is the state you are trying to achieve. Don't be upset if it disappears as soon as you become aware of it. Return to the exercise, and in time the clarity will reappear.

In the first week or so of practice, you should do this exercise - the fourfold breath, as it's called - for at least five minutes by the clock. Thereafter, ten minutes should be the daily minimum. Any more than twenty minutes would probably be too much at this point.

Obviously, this is not the kind of symbolic meditation we have discussed. The skills it teaches, however, are of crucial importance for the more advanced practices you will be working with further on. Furthermore, this particular exercise is used to clear the mind before real meditation, and to return to ordinary consciousness afterwards. Time spent mastering it will not be wasted.

Meditation - Second Stage

The first stage of meditative practice serves as an introduction to the kind of focused awareness you will be using throughout these exercises. It should be practiced, as given above, for perhaps one month before going on. Here as elsewhere in Cabalistic work, you will find that the best advice is found in the old Rosicrucian motto, Festina Lente - make haste slowly. An attempt to rush through the stages of training will only result in longer delays to make up skipped work later on.

Before you begin the second stage work, then, review your practice journal, and compare your work in the first stage with the instructions given above. You may find that little lazinesses have crept in, or that entire parts of the exercise have been forgotten. This is common enough, and is by no means a disaster, provided only that you correct the mistakes and go on. This, of course, is often the hardest part!

At length, when you are ready to begin work on the second stage, turn back to Chapter 1, read the paragraphs discussing the first Sphere, and then set the book aside. Sit in the same meditative posture, spend a minute reviewing your body's tensions, and then begin the fourfold breath as described in the first stage. During this breathing period, you should not think about the Sphere, or about anything else. Simply be aware of the rhythm of your breathing, and allow clarity to establish itself.

After about five minutes of this, change from the fourfold breath to ordinary, slow breathing, and begin thinking about the Sphere. Recall as completely as possible the description from the text. Go on to think about the idea of the Sphere in a general way, without allowing your mind to wander off the subject. Finally, out of the various ideas or images that have arisen, choose one train of thought and follow it carefully out to its end. Again, keep your mind on the subject. If it wanders away, bring it gently back to the track and start again.

You'll want to spend fifteen minutes at this, then return to the fourfold breath for a minute or two. When your mind is again clear, end the practice session. Be sure to note down the images and ideas that came up in the meditation. Please note that you'll want to do the Spheres in their numerical order - Kether first, then Chokmah, then Binah, and so forth. Meditate on a different Sphere each day, and when you finish the sequence start at the beginning again with Kether. You should plan on going through the complete sequence at least four times before going on to the next phase of the meditative work.

This is the first and most basic kind of Cabalistic meditation, and the key to much of the work you'll be doing in the course. It may seem simple or even boring, but this method contains depths that will not become apparent without time and patient practice. Your goal should be to keep the mind gently but firmly focused on the chosen subject, with the same kind of relaxed concentration you've learned to give to the rhythmic breath exercise. When this is attained, the path to the deeper forms of Cabalistic meditation will be well begun.

Meditation - Third Stage

The third stage of your meditative practice follows closely on the second stage, as given above. The framework will be the same in this and all subsequent meditative work: the awareness of the body and its tensions, followed by five minutes of the fourfold breath, followed by the meditation proper, and then a few cycles of the fourfold breath to close.

The new portion of this stage begins with the end of the first period of fourfold breath. At this point, return to an even, slow rhythm of normal breathing, clear your mind as much as possible, and in that clarity visualize the Magical Image of Malkuth, as given in the table in Part II of this book. Build up the image one portion at a time, in as much detail as you can, and then try to see the entire image clearly all at once. Your goal should be to see the young woman on the black throne as clearly and distinctly as if you were looking at her with your physical eyes. At the same time, visualize the entire space around you becoming a featureless sphere colored according to the part of the Tree on which you are working, using the Briah color of the Sphere or the Atziluth color of the Path - in this case, citrine, russet, olive and black. This assemblage of imagery will take time and practice to achieve, of course, but with practice you will find that it helps focus the mind on the subject of meditation to a remarkable extent.

Once you have constructed the image, hold it in your mind as clearly as possible, excluding all other thoughts to the extent that you can. In that period of clarity, repeat the Divine Name assigned to Malkuth silently four times. Finally, allow the Name and the image to fade from awareness.

For the first two or three sessions of meditation you spend on any given Sphere or Path, it will be best to do nothing more than this, although you should continue this building up of the image for the whole of the fifteen minutes you've allotted for the meditative work. Thereafter, this sequence should be used as a preliminary step in your meditations, lasting a few minutes at most.

Another, less tangible element may begin to enter at this stage. Each Path and Sphere of the Tree has a mood or emotional tone corresponding to it, arising from its energies the way the mood of a piece of music arises from the interplay of sound. As English lacks a vocabulary for expressing the finer shades of emotion, these moods have not been included in the tables of correspondences, but they form an important part of the complete pattern of meaning on the Tree. As you work with the images and ideas corresponding to the different Spheres and Paths, you are likely to find that these have definite effects on your emotional state; pay attention to these, particularly while visualizing the Magical Images, and over time these effects will coalesce into a clear and stable perception of emotional correspondences. The importance of this perception can hardly be overstated; among other things, it provides one of the most accurate ways of testing material received in visionary states.

At this point, then, you have completed and released the visualization of the Magical Image and the colored sphere of the part of the Tree with which you are working. Next, as in the second stage meditations, call to mind the subject of the meditation, think about it in a general way for a time, and then choose some aspect of it and follow this out as far as you can. The one variation here is that the specific aspects are to follow a particular order.

As a result of the Fall, each of the Spheres enters into human consciousness first in the unbalanced form of its Negative Power, and this must be met and overcome before the balanced form under the presidency of the Divine Name can be experienced. Your first topic for meditation in the third stage, then, will be the image and meaning of Lilith. Review the discussion of Lilith and her symbolism in Chapter 7 before you start the meditation, and then seek to understand the role of obsessive fear and desire in yourself, in the world, and in the tenth Sphere.

Three to five sessions of meditation should be a minimum for this work. Afterward, spend at least the same number of sessions meditation on the symbolism and meaning of the Divine Name Adonai ha-Aretz, again using the material in Chapter 7 as a starting point. Go on to the Archangels, Angelic Host, and Planetary Sphere assigned to Malkuth, taking each one as a subject of meditation in turn, and exploring it as thoroughly as you can. When this has been completed, go on to the remaining symbols of the tenth Sphere, taking them as topics for meditation in whatever order you choose.

When you have worked through the full set of symbols of Malkuth, then, go on to the 32nd Path. Here the symbols may be taken in the order given in the table in Chapter 7, or in any other convenient order. Explore them as you did those of Malkuth. You will want to have a thorough grasp of them, and of their meaning, before you go on to the process of Pathworking and begin the visionary ascent of the Tree.

When you have finished your work on the 32nd Path, continue with the rest of the Tree, taking the Spheres and Paths in the order set out in Part II of this book. Each Sphere and Path, explored in this way, will take perhaps a month to work through, perhaps longer. The entire process of ascent thus involves something like three years' work. This is a significant commitment, of course, and you are the only person who can decide if it is one you are willing to make.

Over the course of this stage, you should gradually increase the time you spend in the central, meditative phase of each practice session. By the time you have worked your way up the Tree to Kether, you'll want to be spending thirty minutes in the meditations if at all possible. Here, perhaps more than anywhere else, you will probably tend to mislead yourself; the clock in the room you use for your meditations will become your best ally - if your most hated one!

Meditation - Fourth Stage

When the ascent of the Tree through meditation and Pathworking has been completed, and the symbolism of the Spheres and Paths is familiar to you on more than a surface level, the last stage of this sequence of meditations begins. Here the techniques are the same as those of the third stage; what changes is the goal and direction of the work. Your task at this stage is to synthesize the various elements of the Tree into a unity, and the tools you will be using are the elements of the Tree's inner structure discussed in Chapter 2.

Start, then, by linking with the energies of Kether through its Magical Image and Divine Name, just as though you were about to meditate on its symbolism. The topic for your meditation, though, is the highest of the three major triads on the Tree, as seen from the perspective of Kether. Explore the ways in which the three Spheres and three Paths making up that triad interact with one another. Trace the connections between Kether's symbolism and that of the other parts of the triad.

In these meditations, strive to remain in Kether's perspective the whole time, to the extent that this is possible. Measure all things against the yardstick of absolute unity. Your work in the third stage meditations will have given you some grasp of the way that Kether relates to itself, the special quality that makes the first Sphere what it is, and this should be used as a guide for this fourth stage work.

Next, in other sessions, shift your viewpoint to that of Chokmah by linking with the second Sphere's energies through Image and Name, and exploring the first major triad from the perspective of pure dynamic force; later still, do the same from the perspective of Binah.

Further meditations in the same sequence will explore the rest of the major triads, the three pillars, and the minor triads. When you have worked through these thoroughly, so that each relationship within them makes clear sense to you, go on to the Sword and the Serpent: that is, first, seek to understand every one of the Spheres from the perspective of each of the Spheres, and then explore each of the Paths from the perspective of every one of the Paths. Finally, unite the entire Tree of Life in your meditations, so that you grasp the relationship of each of the thirty-two Paths of Wisdom to all of the others.

All this will involve a certain amount of repetition, both of third stage and of fourth stage material. This is deliberate, and to some extent necessary, as insights will build on insights through meditative practice; the relationship between Kether and Chokmah looks different on its own than, say, when the interactions of both to Binah have been understood. By the time the entire sequence has been completed - a matter of several more years, if the work is done with the thoroughness it deserves - your conceptions of some of these relationships will have changed dramatically as new levels of understanding become familiar to you.

This completes the sequence of meditations given here. It does not complete the range of uses of this powerful method of magical work. The same skills which you'll have developed in working your way up and down the Tree of Life can also be used for a wide range of other explorations in, or outside of, the Golden Dawn's tradition of the magical Cabala - to study the art and science of sacred geometry, for example, or to wrestle with the meaning of the enigmas of the alchemists, to explore the deeps of magical philosophy or the inner structure and working of the traditional rituals of initiation. Like a skeleton key, the technique of meditation unlocks many doors.

Chapter Thirteen
Pathworking

The disciplines of ritual and meditation form the foundation of practice in the Golden Dawn's magical Cabala. The skills developed through these techniques provide the basis for the whole process of inner development. They are not, however, the only branches of practice in the tradition; there are a wide range of other methods used in training and practical work.

One of these other techniques is the art of Pathworking - the ascent of the Tree of Life by way of the powers of the imagination. In Pathworking, the Cabalist moves from Sphere to Sphere through intensely visualized journeys along the symbolic landscapes of the Paths. In turn, these journeys open up the Paths on other levels, linking and energizing the structure of the Tree within the consciousness of the magician.

The methods of travel used in these inner journeys are based on the same principles of symbolic thought we've presented already - with a critical difference. Unlike the Spheres, which are perceived in the same manner and through the same or similar symbols by every human being, the Paths are personal experiences which must be understood by way of a personal symbolism.

A number of writers in the tradition have said that "the Spheres are objective but the Paths are subjective." This is a somewhat clumsy way of expressing the issue; Spheres and Paths alike have aspects which could be called objective and subjective, and only the teaching of the Four Worlds adequately explains the way these interact; still, the point this saying makes is an important one. The Spheres can be given an extended system of images and symbols which can awaken the full range of Sphere energies and potentials in anyone who works with the Cabala; to a significant extent, the Paths cannot.

Why should this be so? The answer can be found in a distinction we pointed out earlier, between two aspects of the Paths. On the one hand, each Path is a point of contact between two Spheres, a channel for the play of energies between one level of Reality and another. On the other hand, each Path is a route of travel upon the Tree, a shift in awareness by which Cabalists move from Sphere to Sphere. We can think of these two as the theoretical and practical meanings, respectively.

In the theoretical sense, the Paths are primary elements of the universe as the Cabala understands it, as "objective" as anything can be. In the practical sense, by contrast, things are less clear-cut. Since every human being has a unique mental structure, and responds to experiences in unique ways, the means of moving from one level of awareness to another will be somewhat different for each individual who attempts it. Symbols and transformative tools that will work flawlessly for one person may completely fail to work for another. Thus, while it's entirely possible to seek an understanding of the Path's theoretical nature through meditation on the traditional Path symbols, trying to use these to travel the Path directly is much more problematic.

To speak of Pathworking in this context is to risk a certain amount of confusion, because the term "Pathworking" actually has come to mean two very different kinds of magical practice, and the meaning most common in current occult circles is not the one that will be used here. In this common meaning, a "Pathworking" is a guided visualization, read aloud from a prepared text, which may or may not use Cabalistic symbolism at all. The events of the meditation are preplanned in detail, and the people experiencing this sort of Pathworking visualize themselves going through the events and encountering the beings described to them.

Such guided meditation work has a place in magical practice, especially in the early phases of training in group work. As a method of personal exploration of the Paths of the Tree of Life, on the other hand, it leaves much to be desired. Since the Spheres are common to all beings, while the Paths are much more personal, the Spheres can be given elaborate, interlocking systems of symbols that can be used to communicate something of their essence to the student, but the Paths require a much more open approach; all that tradition can provide is a handful of images to serve as signposts, pointing in the direction of the real experience of the Path. Once these signposts have been learned and understood through meditation, any actual progress along the Paths has to be made by individual understanding of unique personal experiences. To replace this with a set of predesigned guided visualizations is a mistake, because no one set of images will work properly for all people; more than this, presenting any fixed set of experiences for a Path may cause students whose personal experiences are very different to miss the Path entirely.

The Technique Of Pathworking

There are several points which need to be raised before we go on to the details of the method. The first of these has been mentioned before, but deserves repeating: meditation and ritual, not Pathworking, make up the foundation of practice in the magical Cabala. Some groups both inside and outside the Golden Dawn tradition, losing track of this, have become little more than clubs for a kind of "astral tourism," doing Pathworkings and similar kinds of work to the exclusion of anything else. Most of the time, this is harmless if unproductive; in some extreme cases, certain of the people involved have become so deeply caught up in their own imaginations that psychiatric problems resulted.

For this reason, it's considered best for beginners to take up this branch of work slowly, and in the context of regular practice of more stabilizing kinds. For the first year or so of your training, then, twice a week might be a sensible maximum. For this and other reasons, too, it's a good idea to attempt a Pathworking on any given Path only after the Path has been explored in third-stage meditation.

With this out of the way, we can now turn to the actual mechanics of Pathworking. The basic framework of the practice will be the same as the one you're using for meditation; thus, you'll begin by taking the meditation posture, being aware of your physical body, and then clearing your mind with several minutes of the fourfold breath. Next, you'll need to visualize the magical image of the Path you intend to travel, just as you did for the meditations on that Path, and hold this as clearly as possible in your mind. Then, slowly, visualize the door swinging open, until you can see what lies beyond it. You may find that some image appears there at once; if not, visualize a tunnel through the substance of the element of the Path - rock for a Path of Earth, for instance, or billowing cloud for a Path of Air - running off into the distance.

Now, slowly and clearly imagine yourself rising from your chair, and walking up to the doorway - and through it. The door remains open behind you.

Keeping your mental image of what lies beyond the doorway as clear as possible, go forward along the Path. Allow your mind to add details to the tunnel: changes in direction and color, objects in the way, doors, rooms, entities. At first, you may see very little in the way of spontaneous images; you may even see nothing at all besides bare tunnel walls. This shouldn't be a cause for worry, however. With a little practice, you'll find that the imagery will begin to take on a life of its own. The Path may widen out into a cavern, pass beneath an underground waterfall, descend a narrow stairway, or come to a place where some object or being is waiting.

When you decide to bring the Pathworking to an end, imagine yourself stopping and turning around, then walking back along the way you came. Visualize each of the landmarks you passed on the way in, and pass them by, just as if you were retracing your route along a physical path. When you come to the door again, walk out through it and feel yourself sitting back down in your chair. Watch the door swing slowly but firmly closed. Concentrate on this image for a few moments, then clear your mind with several cycles of the fourfold breath before ending the practice.

You may find yourself a little disoriented afterwards; if so, try eating something. Very few things close down the visionary senses more thoroughly than food in the stomach. It can also be useful to move around and to do routine activities - washing dishes and the like; this helps reorient the awareness back to the Sphere of Malkuth and the realm of everyday life.

Linking With The Spheres

A somewhat more complex method, which can be added once you've gained some experience with the simpler version, involves putting the Path in its proper place on the Tree of Life. This is done by adding a new element to the preparation. After clearing your mind with the fourfold breath, but before doing anything else, call up in your mind's eye the colored light and magical image of the Sphere at the lower end of the Path, as if you were beginning a meditation on that Sphere. Enter as fully as possible into the Sphere's mode of consciousness. As you do so, allow the imagery to change; let the magical image become the center of an imagined circular space colored the Briah color of the Sphere, and let this become a circular temple, with doors in the wall corresponding to the magical images of the Paths which connect to that Sphere. At this point, imagine yourself rising from your chair, and go to the portal-image of the Path you intend to travel; from here, travel along the Path until you feel that your journey has reached a conclusion, then visualize the end of the Path before you. This is a double door set in an archway like that of the Path's magical image. The door, however, is the Briah color of the Sphere at the upper end of the Path, and it bears the symbol of that Sphere's astrological correspondence. (Thus, for instance, the door at the upper end of the 32nd Path will be the violet of Yesod, and will bear the crescent symbol of the Moon.)

Spend some time building up this image before going on. At this point one of two choices is available to you. If the Sphere at the Path's upper end is not one you have explored in meditation, turn around and go back the way you came. Visualize yourself journeying all the way back, returning to the temple of the Sphere. Visualize the door of the Path's image closing, then release the imagery and close the session of practice in the usual way.

If you have already gained a solid grasp of the Sphere at the upper end of the Path through your meditative work, on the other hand, the pattern changes. When you have reached the end of the Path, stand before the door of the Sphere, and see it slowly open in front of you. Beyond it is brilliant light of the same hue as the door. Step forward into the light; it becomes a temple of the Sphere around you, with the magical image of the Sphere at its center. Enter into the mode of consciousness of the Sphere as intensely as you can. In front of the magical image, you'll find a chair. Feel yourself sitting down in it, and once you are settled, allow the chair in which you are sitting to become the chair in which your physical body rests; clear the images from your mind and close with several cycles of the fourfold breath. It's not necessary for you to return along the Path or reestablish yourself in the Sphere where you began; you simply return to ordinary consciousness directly from the higher Sphere.

This may seem surprising, but it follows from basic Cabalistic understandings concerning the higher levels of human awareness. Whether we are conscious of it or not, all these levels are in operation at every moment; it is precisely because we are not usually conscious of this point that the summits of human possibility can seem so far out of reach. The act of rising from Sphere to Sphere thus is not a journey into an alien environment; rather, it is a reaffirmation of potentials which are always present to human consciousness. So long as the practice itself is ended with a definite act of closure - the purpose of the final period of fourfold breath, in this as in other contexts - there is no value in shutting down one of those potentials even in symbolic form. Quite the contrary; the act of opening up a Path in this manner will help foster the opening up of the same Path on other levels and in other ways. This can be used, in fact, as a deliberate practice for personal transformation.

For similar reasons, Pathworkings should always go from a lower Sphere toward, or into, a higher Sphere, never vice versa. (In the symbolic language of Cabalistic theory, it might be best put this way: the Path of the Sword is already established; it's the Path of the Serpent that demands our efforts.) You retrace your steps back down to your starting point in your initial workings of any given Path simply because each Pathworking should end in a definite level of consciousness, rather than somewhere in the indeterminate space between. Both varieties of Pathworking - the exploration Pathworking, which starts and ends at the same Sphere, and the completion Pathworking, which traverses the Path from Sphere to Sphere - have their place in the toolkit of the magical Cabalist; the first is more useful in discovering one's own personal approach to a Path, the second for tracing the ways in which that approach connects to the Spheres; the one is primarily a help to meditation, while the other has broader effects.

The transformative power of completion Pathworkings, in turn, requires a certain amount of care in handling; like any transformative technique, this one can go awry if used clumsily. In this case, the most important restriction is a simple one: your first set of completion Pathworkings on the Tree of Life should follow a balanced order of ascent, from Malkuth to Kether. The standard order is the traditional Path of the Serpent, the order in which the Paths appear in Part II of this book. Taken in this order, the effects of these Pathworkings will balance one another, so that the long-term changes in awareness and energy this practice tends to bring about will unfold with a minimum of disruption.

It's also best to do several exploration Pathworkings on any given Path before attempting a completion working, to lay the ground for a smooth transition from Sphere to Sphere - and, of course, it's vital to support the whole process of Pathworking with practical work in meditation.

Pathworking And Meditation

At this point, the linkage between Pathworkings and meditation requires a certain amount of discussion. Meditation - it bears repeating - is the core receptive practice of this system, Pathworking a development growing out of it; the depth and value of your experiences in Pathworking will be powerfully affected by (in a real sense, in fact, dependent on) the extent to which you prepare yourself through meditation.

This preparation has two aspects. On the one hand, the mental training of meditation is the most important single skill that can be brought to the Pathworking process; the more effectively you can clear and focus your attention, and keep stray bits of interior chatter from interfering with the rising of imagery, the more vivid and powerful your pathworking experiences will become.

On the other hand, a solid grasp of the traditional symbols of the Path you are traveling will help you make sense of the experience, and to navigate amid what can often be confusing and uncertain imagery. If that grasp of the symbolism has at the same time been communicated to the deep levels of consciousness through meditation, the symbols can become a shared language linking conscious and nonconscious aspects of the self; images from your meditations which surface in Pathworkings can be read and understood with a high degree of clarity, and used as keys to less easily grasped symbols.

For this reason, as mentioned before, it's a good idea to complete the third-stage meditation on any given Path before exploring that Path in a Pathworking. Depending on your time resources, you may wish to complete the entire third-stage meditation sequence before going on to Pathworking, but it's often most useful to ascend the Tree in meditation and Pathworkings at the same time: finishing the meditations on the traditional symbolism of each Path, then doing a series of Pathworkings on that Path and meditating on the images and events you experience.

This last use of meditation is one of the most valuable, and most often neglected, parts of the Pathworking process. After your first Pathworkings, in particular, you'll probably find yourself wanting to go right back out through the door the next day. Not so fast! Please remember that Pathworking is meant to assist meditation, not to serve as an astral vacation. You noted down everything you saw during your Pathworking in your magical journal (didn't you?) and now is the time to put this to use. Spend two or three sessions of meditation, at least, going over the images and events of the Pathworking, treating them as symbols in the same sense as the traditional symbols of the Tree, and exploring their links to the ideas and images you already know. If you need more time to be sure that you understand the symbols, take it. One Pathworking which has been fully explored through meditation will be more valuable to you than a dozen that you barely comprehend. Only when you feel that you've gotten everything you possibly can out of one Pathworking should you go on to do another.

Helps To Pathworking

When done by an experienced Cabalist, a Pathworking can become an intensely vivid adventure, a kind of waking dream in which symbols come to life and the bare framework that tradition provides for each Path is fleshed out by personal knowledge and vision. Although it's likely to be some time before you achieve this level of skill, there are some steps you can take to help you get the most out of your Pathworkings.

The most important of these can be summed up in two words: go slow! Never take a Pathworking further than you're comfortable going. Particularly on your first few experiences, go only a short distance beyond the door, and in all cases pay close attention to every image you encounter, no matter how unimportant it seems. If an image appears vague or blurred, as is likely at first, pause before it and try to perceive it with as much clarity as possible. It's important, too, to treat whatever you meet on the Path as real, for the duration of the Pathworking. If you come across the image of a living being, pay attention to what it says; if you encounter a physical object, deal with it as you would a similar object in the material world. The more you behave as though the experiences of the Path are real, the more real they will become for you.

One caution does need to be made regarding your dealings with the apparently living beings you may encounter during a Pathworking. Some of these are honest and will teach you things of value, but others are not and will try to deceive you. You may find it difficult to think of "imaginary" beings in these terms, but experience will quickly teach you that such beings can have a life of their own and behave in the most unexpected ways. If you have trouble believing this, think about the people in your dreams, and the way their behavior is independent of your will.

There are a number of effective ways which Cabalists have found to tell the one type from the other. The first of these you should learn, and a habit you should make universal in your Pathworkings, is the practice of challenging any being you meet with the Divine Name governing the Path you're on. For the 32nd Path, therefore, you'll want to ask the beings that you encounter, "Do you come in the Name of Tetragrammaton Elohim?" If an entity says "yes" or repeats the Name, it is probably honest. If it says "no" or does not answer, command it to leave by the same Name, and wait until it's completely gone before proceeding with the Pathworking. If it resists leaving, use the Pentagram in the manner covered in the chapter on ritual. All this may seem bizarre or silly, but you'll soon learn the value of such tests.

It's possible to make use of this method of testing with the Divine Name in a more active mode as well. At the beginning of a potentially difficult Path - one on which you have had trouble before, or one which crosses one of the major barriers of the Tree - it can be a good idea to call out, "In the Name (whatever Name of God governs the Path), I seek guidance upon this Path. May a guide be sent to me!" Remain at the beginning of the Path, then, until a being comes; test it by the Name, and if it passes the test accept its guidance on your journey. Similarly, a guide of this sort can be summoned elsewhere on the Path, if no progress seems to be being made or if hostile or dishonest beings are active. Here again, such approaches require a certain suspension of disbelief for most people, but the technique has been found to work well by generations of Cabalists.

Testing With The Path Colours

The art of Pathworking, as we've mentioned before, is a fairly recent addition to the toolkit of Cabalistic methods. It has proved itself as a useful and valuable technique, and many if not most of the groups working in the Cabalistic tradition today make use of it. It needs careful handling, however. Some groups, and some individuals within groups, have approached Pathworking in the wrong way, and many of these have found themselves in a great deal of confusion and some real trouble.

There is, in fact, a trap built into Pathworking. It can be avoided, but doing so takes careful handling and a certain amount of hard common sense. What is this trap? Quite simply, the risk of picking up images in a Pathworking that have nothing to do with the Path being worked.

The principle behind Pathworking (and a number of similar

techniques) is the useful fact that a mind focused on a particular symbolic pattern tends to pick up images from the Sphere of Sensation which are in harmony with that pattern. In general, this works quite well, but several factors can introduce errors. The most important of these, in the early stages of training, is instability of mental focus. How often, as you try to build up a symbolic image or concentrate on a topic in meditation, does your mind go wandering off in another direction? These other thoughts take shape in the ether around you, and bring in their own trains of related images, in the same way as the image or topic you intend.

This is normal, in the early stages of the work, and will become less of a problem with time. For now, though, it means that your Pathworkings are likely to be a mixture of useful images and worthless ones, like a radio signal in which the message is mixed with static. As long as this continues, you'll need some means of sorting out the two. Fortunately, there are a number of such methods.

One of the most useful means of examining the images from your Pathworkings involves the colors of the Paths as given in the various tables. So far these have been of little importance, but now they come into their own.

The method is conveniently simple. Both while actually doing a Pathworking, and while considering the results afterwards, keep the colors of the Path you're traveling in mind. Objects and entities which appear in these colors are likely to belong in the working, while those with different colors more than likely do not. Thus, for example, if the image of a warrior in red armor appears in a working of the 31st Path, he probably belongs there; if the same warrior shows up on the 29th Path, his color gives him away as an intrusion.

This method can be refined in certain ways, using the Four Worlds system which underlies the color correspondences of the Tree. Each Path has four colors given, one for each of the Worlds. As you'll remember, the Worlds can be used to represent the four stages of the process of perception: Atziluth for the thing perceived, Briah for the structure of the perceiving mind, Yetzirah for the series of events that bring these two together, and Assiah for the final result, the perception in the mind. Every perception you have, of course, is in the World of Assiah by definition, but your perception can be affected by one of the Worlds more than the others. This is what the colors can be used to reveal.

For example, in a Pathworking on the Path of Resh, you might encounter a king dressed in robes of golden yellow, who tells you certain things. The table for the 30th Path lists golden yellow as the Briah color of the Path of Resh. Because of this, you may wish to think of the king's message as having to do chiefly with the inner structure of your own consciousness. In your meditation on this element of your Pathworking you'll wish to explore the king's words with this in mind. You may determine, for instance, that the message is of particular value to your Pathworkings because it expresses some part of your personal response to the Path, but you might be slow to offer it as advice to anyone else for the same reason.

An image which is in the Atziluth color of the Path will tend to refer to the Path as it exists in itself, and may deal with the meaning of the Path on an abstract, impersonal level. An image in the Yetzirah color should be carefully studied for clues concerning the magical applications of the Path, while an image in the Assiah color will tend to refer to the way the Path's energies manifest in the world of everyday experience.

Testing With The Planetary Letters

Another method of testing imagery seen in Pathworkings makes use of a different part of the Cabala's symbolism. A somewhat more advanced technique, it requires a certain amount of experience with the Pathworking process, and a certain amount of self-knowledge as well. This new technique is meant to supplement the method of testing by colors, not to replace it; it allows you to test the images which you encounter during the Pathworking process in a more subtle way, and it permits a better understanding of the sources of the "static" that so often gets in the way of that process.

Before you begin using this method, you'll want to read through a number of Pathworkings you've already completed, and try to get a sense of the possible sources of the "static" that may have contaminated them. The most common sources of interference fall into seven categories, which are assigned to the seven "double" or planetary letters of the Hebrew alphabet:

Memory is assigned to the letter ת , Tau;

Deliberate construction is assigned to the letter כ , Kaph;

Anger and impatience are assigned to the letter פ , Peh;

Pride and vanity are assigned to the letter ר, Resh;

Sexual fantasies are assigned to the letter ד , Daleth;

Simple imagination is assigned to the letter ב , Beth;

Wandering thoughts are assigned to the letter ג, Gimel.

These attributions, which differ somewhat from the usual meanings of the planets, should be memorized for use in Pathworkings. (They derive from traditional systems of esoteric medicine and psychology, among the most thoroughly forgotten of the old magical arts of the West; they have other uses as well, but those do not concern us here.)

Both the letters and the categories they represent should be kept in mind during the Pathworking process. When you encounter something which makes you suspect you are picking up interference, simply trace the appropriate letter before you with your visualized hand, and see the letter take shape in white light. Hold the image of the letter for a short time. If the suspect part of the Pathworking blurs, changes, or vanishes, imagine yourself speaking the Divine Name assigned to the Path four times, and if this does not cause the intruding image to vanish, use the Pentagram as mentioned above.

A mastery of both these methods of testing, by colors and by letters, will do much to keep your Pathworking experiences balanced and constructive. Common sense and a sense of humor, though, will do more. Pathworking can become a powerful tool for the deepening of understanding and the opening up of the hidden possibilities of the mind. At the same time, there are risks in this sort of work; the magician who ventures out on the Paths in this manner will encounter lies, distortions, deliberate obscurity, and flattery, and if he or she takes the experiences of the Paths at face value the result will be confusion or - in the most extreme case - madness. Here as elsewhere in magical work, where the rewards are significant, the dangers are real.

Chapter Fourteen
Prayer

Of all the various technical methods of mysticism and magic which are part of the Golden Dawn tradition, the art of prayer has received perhaps the least attention in modern magical writings: this, despite the detailed discussion of the methods and purposes of prayer in many older esoteric texts. There is a tendency in some magical circles, in fact, to think of prayer as something incompatible with the theory and practice of magic, or - worse - as a kind of half-hearted attempt at magic on the part of those whose theology won't let them go further.

There is a certain validity to this claim; it is based on a drastic misunderstanding of the nature of prayer - but that misunderstanding is itself very common nowadays, even (one might even say especially) in those religions which stress prayer most. For the sake of clarity, we'll need to look at this mistake in some detail before the way of prayer in the magical Cabala can be described and explored.

What is prayer, then? To most people in our society, in or out of the orthodox religions of the West, it's generally thought to be the practice of talking to God in order either to please God by praising him or to ask for the things one desires. (Those with Protestant backgrounds may recall the lines from the hymn "Sweet Hour Of Prayer" - "...that bids me, at my Father's throne, make all my wants and wishes known.") Both these notions, common as they may be, are odd ones, to say the least - in terms of common sense as well as the theology of those same religions.

In the first case, the objection is simple: what possible use could the creator and master of the universe have for human flattery? The second case involves subtler contradictions. If God is omniscient, to begin with, he already knows what you want; in fact, he has known it since before the beginning of time. What is the point of reminding him? Similarly, if God always wills what is best for everyone, and that will is infallibly carried out, then to ask him for something he hasn't given you is to ask him to give you something which (whatever your own opinion in the matter) is less good than what you have already! This sort of paradox can be piled up almost indefinitely.

Both these notions of prayer are founded on a single assumption, which is the root of the problems they present. That assumption is the idea that the point of prayer is the effect it has on God - whether by pleasing him, or by inducing him to grant favors, or in some other way. To think of prayer in this way is indeed to turn it into a kind of magic, and often enough a lukewarm one at that. It is also to miss the point of the exercise. The purpose of prayer is found, quite simply, in its effect on the person who prays.

To give the orthodox religions their due, this same point is central to the higher understanding of prayer in most major traditions; this has been recognized within the current religious mainstream by more than a few people, and revivals of older and more honest conceptions of prayer have a noticeable following at present.

Certain of these same conceptions underlie the approach to prayer used in the magical Cabala. We can begin to explore that approach by way of a point raised in Chapter 7, in the discussion of the Name of God attributed to the tenth Sphere. Human beings tend, at the Malkuth level of consciousness, to perceive the universe of their experience in human form; these habits of thought lead us to envision the ultimate reality - that unknowable cause of our perceptions, which we have called God - as a person rather than, say, a stone. This is purely a matter of symbolic experience, of course; like any of our perceptions, it says a good deal more about ourselves than it does about what it seems to describe; it also plays a significant part in bringing about exactly the garbled understanding of prayer discussed above. As a matter of symbolic experience, though, this habit of thought opens up some unexpected possibilities, because the way we relate to people has depths not often realized.

Kether, as the traditional saying has it, is in Malkuth; and Malkuth is is Kether, but after another manner. Most of the time, in the Malkuth level of consciousness, we relate to our surroundings as a collection of objects, hard surfaces beyond which our awareness does not penetrate. We encounter these objects, perceive them, act on them or are acted on by them, and go away. Under certain circumstances, though, this experience transforms itself unexpectedly into an experience of unity. This can happen in certain kinds of interaction with the world of nature, and this has given rise to various traditions of nature mysticism.

More often, though, it happens in the more intense kinds of human interaction, especially in that interaction we term love. This has given rise, in turn, to various traditions of erotic and romantic mysticism, as well as a great deal of the language we use to speak of love.

This same quality of interaction, finally, can also exist on the Malkuth level between a human being and existence itself, using the experience symbolized by the Divine Name in Malkuth as the symbolic form of the Reality beyond perception. In this personal interaction with the Infinite, Kether becomes present in Malkuth; unity and individuality fuse, and the awareness of the person who enters into this relationship participates in both these states at once. That fusion is symbolically at Tiphareth, although the experience of it is not always or even usually linked to an opening of the Veil, and it is to Tiphareth that the personified image of Reality - in Cabalistic terms, Microprosopus, the Lesser Countenance; in theological language, God in the usual sense of the word - is assigned.

This is the effect of prayer at its highest. For the ordinarily religious person, the follower of the Open Path, this effect offers one of the few ways to transcendent experience. For the mystic, in the usual Western sense of that word, the way of prayer offers a primary tool for transformation, one which has been developed in some remarkable and powerful directions in some branches of the orthodox religions of the West. For the magician, finally, the way of prayer offers a second means of transformation, which can be used along with the methods of the Secret Path to provide another way to that Path's highest goal.

From the point of view of the magical Cabala, then, prayer is a direct means to the experience of the highest level of human awareness, the closest approach we can make to that reality we have called God. It is not principally a way of bringing about change in the universe of our experience, although it can cause such change; any transformation in consciousness has effects on our experience of the world. Its primary effect is neither on God nor on the world, but on the magician himself or herself. It is a mystical practice, in the strict sense of the word; it leads to unity rather than to power, and thus serves as a balancing force and a source of guidance in the magician's journey.

Three Grades of Prayer

Unlike some other kinds of practice, prayer is not easily classified along the lines of developing technique or specific attainments; a single method may be used from the beginning of the work to its fulfillment, and beyond, while the various experiences and phases between these two points tend to blur into one another in a way that frustrates the orderly mind. Still, in order to talk about the subject at all, some sort of framework needs to be used, and a modification of one framework used in certain branches of the Golden Dawn tradition will serve our present needs.

In this classification, prayer may be divided into three grades, corresponding to the three levels of initiation used in a Golden Dawn offshoot known as the Cromlech Temple. Their names in the sources refer to these grades, and aren't necessary for the present purpose; we may as well call them simply the first, second and third grades of prayer.

Prayer of the first grade corresponds, roughly, to the ordinary idea of prayer; that is, it approaches the hidden reality in the same way we normally approach a person, through the act of communication. In this grade, the magician prays in words, addressing some conception of divinity. It's wisest not to visualize an image, or to make the idea of the power you are addressing too concrete. In some contexts, especially in certain classes of ritual, this is useful, but here it may interfere with the further stages of the work.

Set aside a few minutes each day, then, and talk to the most abstract idea of God with which you're comfortable; say to it whatever you would say if you could speak to the cosmos as a whole and be heard; if those words express anger, frustration, resentment, or what have you, that's fine. The goal here is not to parrot some ideal of reverence, or to praise or flatter the Infinite - again, what possible use could God have for your flattery? - but to become used to relating to the universe in a different and very specific way.

Depending on past experience - those with previous ties to orthodox religion may have more trouble with this practice, or less - this first grade of prayer may take days, weeks, or months to begin showing signs of deepening into something more than a kind of talking to oneself. Those signs may include anything from a simple sense of something listening to the words, on the one hand, to visionary experiences and upsurges of unexpected and wildly intense emotion on the other. In either case, it's best to simply persevere with the practice, and with your other practices.

The transition from the first grade to the second grade of prayer should be allowed to happen by itself. It takes place when the topic of speech in prayer changes from whatever it may be - and, as mentioned above, it may be anything - to one's own spiritual state. This is the point at which mysticism enters the way of prayer. Religions of the kind which tend to foster guilt often stress confession of sins at this stage; those religions which prefer to foster feelings of impurity put more stress on purification. In the magical Cabala, which sees little value in either of these notions, the focus of this grade might well be the quest for transformation and wholeness. Still, the straight road here must be found by each person, alone; there are few things so intensely personal as this.

Prayer for transformation has been at the center of many systems of Western magic; the book of Abramelin, which is little more than a collection of prayers in its practical sections, and the original Enochian system of John Dee may stand as examples. There is, however, another grade of prayer, which is the prayer of silence, the third grade of prayer in the classification we are exploring. The transition to this grade, like that to the second, should be allowed to happen of itself. It occurs when the verbal mind stops coming up with words to say, and all that remains is focused attention turned toward something the lower self cannot perceive at all. In Cabalistic terms, Daath at this point returns to its source in the Supernals. This state, too, must deepen; its first stages may resemble nothing so much as blankness of mind; its further stages pass step by step into the hidden places of unity. Beyond this, there is little which can or should be said concerning it.

Helps To Prayer

Like any other practice, prayer benefits from the triple support of study, routine, and the keeping of the magical journal. Books of that odd emotional quality which seems to direct the mind toward the things above it are useful in study; so are the writings of the great mystics of East and West. As for routine and the magical journal, prayer should be handled in these respects like any other practice.

It's often useful, especially for those who have left a religion in which prayer was common, to use a physical posture for prayer as unlike the traditional one as possible. One approach which has proved useful is that of borrowing the posture, opening and closing of magical meditation. Sitting upright on a chair, with the body in a state of balance and the mind centered through the fourfold breath, is worlds apart from the usual habit of kneeling on the floor with bowed head and folded hands. The seated position, and the emotional quality it tends to evoke, are entirely appropriate to the magical art of prayer; to put matters perhaps too harshly, it is the position of a free human being freely seeking the source and ground of existence, not that of a slave pleading for favor.

For similar reasons, it can be useful to avoid the orthodox Western phraseology of prayer, with its use of parental terms for the Infinite. The ultimate reality is no more a father, or for that matter a mother, than it is a grandchild, and - especially in the present time, when relationships between parents and children seem to be more than usually complicated - this sort of terminology tends to bring a load of emotional baggage with it. Here again, though, this will need to be decided on the basis of personal needs and experiences.

This last comment applies, in the broadest sense, to all the details of prayer. Partly this is an effect of the underlying principle of prayer itself; a personal interaction will be shaped by personal factors, whether that interaction is with another human being or (to fall into theological language one last time) with God. On a deeper level, though, it has to do with the presence of Kether in this kind of magical work, a presence which dissolves all hard and fast rules in unity. Your contact with this unity - a unity in which you yourself take part, knowingly or not - must be sought by way of a path which, in the end, is nothing other than yourself.

Chapter Fifteen

Magical Cabala in Daily Life

One difficulty faced by many magicians nowadays, in and out of the Golden Dawn tradition, is the apparent gap between magic and the world of everyday life. In the fantasy fiction loved by so many people in the magical community, magicians save vast realms and cast down the forces of evil; in what we tend to call real life, on the other hand, students of magic are more likely to save coupons than kingdoms, and the opportunities to fight against evil - while they certainly exist - tend to be on a distressingly small and personal scale. This kind of dislocation between grand ideals and petty realities plays a certain role in giving magic its current reputation in society at large, just as it has a good deal to do with the posturing and grandiose claims rather too common in the magical community.

This gap, though, is more apparent than real; it has less to do with the nature of magic - or of the world we perceive around us - than with the common modern habit of seeing other times and places through incurably rose-colored glasses. Behind the glossy images of Merlin's myriad clones lie older figures which, stranger and far more compelling, are nonetheless a good deal more prosaic: Myrddin Wyllt, half-mad prophet of the Caledonian woods, soaked to the skin and shivering in the rains of winter; John Dee, who sold books from his library to pay for groceries while he and his scryers searched after the secrets of the universe; the odd assortment of men and women from England's middle class who created and shaped the Hermetic Order of the Golden Dawn. It needs to be remembered that these, not the constructs of fantasy fiction, are the real magicians, and their work took place in worlds which were not, ultimately, all that different from our own.

From the standpoint of the Cabala, this same idea can be expressed in a slightly different way. The ten Spheres of the Tree of Life are the ten levels of experience and awareness in which the magician operates, and one of them, Malkuth, is the realm of everyday life. The everyday world, in other words, is itself a realm of magic. Different levels, different realms, are best suited to different kinds of magic; the question then becomes, what sort of magic best fits the nature of Malkuth?

Training the Awareness

Like most simple questions, this one has a complicated answer. To some extent, all magic takes place at least partly in Malkuth, since the physical body and the circumstances of ordinary life play at least some part in shaping every kind of magical work. On the other hand, certain kinds of work - Pathworking is one example - involve moving the focus of awareness away from the material level.

These are balanced by other practices which direct the magician's attention straight toward the details of everyday life and of sensory experience. Harder to systematize than the core practices of ritual and meditation or auxiliary arts such as Pathworking, these practices can be classed together under the general label of "awareness exercises." They form a useful and sometimes neglected field of Cabalistic practice.

Perhaps the simplest awareness exercise, but among the most useful, is the practice of mentally linking material things with their equivalents in Cabalistic symbolism. This is especially valuable when first learning the symbols, or when working with them in a sequence of meditations. During the month or so spent doing third-stage meditations on any of the Spheres, for example, it can be illuminating to note anything you encounter which seems connected to the Sphere you're exploring;

between meditations on Netzach, for example, you might make a point of noticing those things which remind you of the seventh Sphere, from green plants to displays of emotion; between meditations on Kether, you might try to notice anything which seems connected in some way to the idea of unity. Related to this, and a test of your grasp of the symbolism, is the practice of choosing an object or event at random and thinking through its connections to the symbols of the Tree. These are not simply mind-fillers of the crossword puzzle variety, although they can be used (or disguised) as such; they teach the novice magician to begin to think in terms of the Cabala in the context of daily living.

It's also useful to expand these practices in ways which exercise the imagination, the will, and the memory. For instance, you might try to notice and keep a running count of every red thing you pass along a ten-block walk. In itself, this sort of practice is pointless; it does not matter in the least, of course, whether there are 334 red objects along a section of a given street, or ten times that many. Such exercises are calisthenics of the mind, though, and they develop skills of awareness and perception in the same way that the apparently pointless movements of physical calisthenics build strength.

Living Deliberately

The same principles can be applied to a wider range of activities in daily life, and here they can easily become more than simple exercises. One of the things magicians and mystics of many different schools have pointed out, again and again, is that most people tend to go through life as though by reflex. The force of habit, which we explored earlier as a help to the magician's work, has a less pleasant side; it is a tyrant which rules many lives. Patterns of behavior set in motion at one point in time often continue long after they have stopped being useful or even harmless. The same is true of the fixed habits of thinking that we label "opinions" or "beliefs." Caught in such patterns of habit, we too often stumble from one crisis to another, blaming the universe around us for disasters which we have created ourselves.

The magician, by contrast, learns to live deliberately - to choose his or her actions and reactions, rather than to have them chosen by the force of habit. This doesn't mean that all habits of thought and action are to be abolished. On the contrary, it means that the habit-making powers of the mind are to be explored, made subject to the control of the ruach, and used when - and only when - they are the appropriate tool for the work at hand. The magician is the master of habit, not its slave.

How is this done? The critical factor, here as elsewhere in the work, is awareness. The same kind of focus and clarity which meditation turns on the symbols of the Tree can be turned on the events and actions of daily life. When this is done regularly, it gives the magician a broader perspective on his or her own behavior, and once this perspective begins to emerge changes can be made as choice and circumstances suggest.

Some students of magic have tended to neglect this first step, and respond to the idea of living deliberately by trying to make wholesale changes in their lives all at once. Almost always, these attempts fail. This is partly because trying to act without awareness in these matters is a little like trying to drive a car while blindfolded, and can produce an equal amount of wreckage. Partly, though, these failures come about because strong habits are often responses to emotional turmoil, and changing the habit generally involves facing the emotions involved. It's wisest, therefore, to learn to observe the self before trying out any changes; it's also generally wise to start with minor habits, and - at least at first - to make one change at a time.

Perhaps the most useful exercise in learning to live deliberately is the practice of recollection, which was discussed in Chapter Ten. By training the magician to remember and assess the events of daily life, the practice of recollection has effects which reach beyond its basic role of memory training; it leads, in time, to the ability to leave the context of habit and expectation and to see one's own actions in a clearer light.

The Purposes of Secrecy

One of the more frustrating aspects of the gap between magical ideals and contemporary realities comes out of the reputation, or rather the multiple reputations, which the magical arts and traditions have in the Western world at present. Several thousand years of history come between the words "I am a magician" and any hope that this statement will be understood by the majority of those who might hear it. Between the Christian view that magic is by definition the worship of malign powers, on the one hand, and the rationalist view that magic is by definition fraud or delusion, on the other, there's often not much space left for magicians to define themselves to the world.

The traditional response to this difficulty has given rise to a good deal of confusion on its own. Secrecy was a hard necessity in the days when even the rumor of involvement with magic was enough to bring a visit from the Inquisition; it remained useful in later times, when fear of magic gave way to ridicule and such rumors could ruin careers and bring the threat of commitment for insanity. Nowadays threats of this kind are rarely a problem for most magicians, and this point has led many in the magical community to denounce secrecy as cowardice and to challenge people to stand up in public for their beliefs. It has also helped create a highly visible magical subculture with its own fashions of speech, dress and ornament, a subculture willing and even eager to announce its interests to the world. In this context old habits of secrecy may seem outdated, to say the least.

At the same time, secrecy is more than simply a means of protection. It is also, crucially, a method of magical training. The discipline of secrecy teaches the novice magician to think before speaking, and to judge words and actions alike against the yardstick of a broader purpose. It is thus a powerful awareness exercise, and it also fosters the skill of living deliberately.

More subtly, it brings about a change in the way the magician-in-training relates to the social environment. That environment is above all else a web of communication, made up of a whole range of verbal and nonverbal actions. Most of it goes on unnoticed; we don't often think about the purposes of "small talk", or the messages which may be communicated by a particular piece of clothing. Still, those purposes and messages exist, and they have powerful effects both on our interactions with other people and on the way we relate to ourselves. It can be an instructive experience to explore these effects consciously

- for example, to go into a public place three times on three different days wearing sharply different styles of clothing, and to pay attention to the ways these influence not only other people's behavior but one's own feelings and thoughts. More instructive and more magically important, though, is the experience of breaking the web: moving outside the ordinary patterns of social communication into the undefined space beyond.

The web can be broken in many ways. Most of these, however, produce only negative results in those who experience them; much of the almost instinctive fear so many people have of the mentally ill rises from the fact that madness cuts its victims out of this web of communication; similarly, a good deal of the psychological damage suffered by children in abusive families comes from such families' absolute demands that certain subjects and certain incidents, however traumatic, must never be made part of the web. A good percentage of humanity's more irrational acts come from processes of this kind.

The voluntary discipline of magical secrecy, by contrast, breaks that web in a specific, limited, and controlled way. The secret - and it can be any secret, about anything - is by its very secrecy outside the social environment, but since the fact that there is a secret is itself part of magical secrecy, only the person keeping the secret knows that a break in the web exists. The magician who maintains secrecy thus stands on the border of the social environment, half in, half out. He or she can take part in the web freely, but must do so consciously, for a lapse into unthinking behavior risks disclosure of the secret. At the same time, the secrecy of the magician is voluntary, not forced, and covers only a small part of the magician's total life. In traditional magical lodges it may involve nothing more than a few passwords and symbolic gestures and the details of a certain number of rituals - and yet this can be enough to reshape one's approach to the entire social environment.

The practice of magical secrecy thus turns the very fabric of the social environment into a realm of awareness and, with practice, of conscious action. This builds on the principle of living deliberately, but it goes far beyond that. It is the basis of much of the traditional image of the magician, and many of the powers credited to the great mages of Western history have their source here rather than in any more obviously "magical" type of work. Once the countless small messages passing through the social web are brought into consciousness, they can be read, shaped and directed by the magician deliberately, with remarkable effects on the social environment.

None of this, of course, means that the modern Cabalistic magician should maintain secrecy on the traditional scale; there are times and places for speech as well as for silence. Here as elsewhere, unthinking habits are likely to be a burden rather than a help, and a rigid custom of secrecy is as unproductive - and as annoying! - as the kind of occult fashion statement which bellows, "Hey, I'm a magician!" from a block away. Rather, the magician should be able to be open about his or her work when this is appropriate, and equally should be able to remain silent about it, nonverbally as well as verbally, when this is more useful. Once again, awareness and conscious choice are the critical factors, and balance the most useful path.

The Cabala as a Way of Life

Beyond these specific issues - of awareness training, of living deliberately, of secrecy - the whole practice of the magical Cabala has effects in the realm of Malkuth. Any activity which makes more than a small demand on time and energy tends to shape the rest of life around it; the lives of the athlete, the artist, the musician show the impact of these fields of effort in ways which go far beyond the limited time spent in practice and performance.

So, too, the magical Cabala is a way of life, for those who study and practice it, and whose lives are changed by it. The magician does not stop being a magician when he or she gets up after a meditation or clears away the tools of ritual. All of life, in one way or another, is drawn into the work of magic.

In many systems of spiritual development, this process is systematized by rules of life, simple or complex. Some of these go into enormous detail, ranging from food taboos, through rules for associating with other people, down to instructions on which side to lay on while sleeping! Such rules can be useful, in the same way as the rule of secrecy; they teach self-discipline and conscious action, and they can be used to give symbolic overtones to the whle structure of daily life. At the same time, they can easily be turned into habits as rigid as the ones they replace, and in this way they often become burdens rather than tools.

The magical Cabala jettisoned all this - and it once had an enormous amount of it, borrowed from the vast body of Jewish religious law - well before the formulation of the Golden Dawn tradition. As a result, the Cabalistic magician-in-training is left to settle the details of his or her way of life without this kind of guidance. This avoids some problems, but it raises others, especially for the unwise and overly self-centered. It can take a certain amount of time and suffering to realize that a lack of fixed rules is not the same thing as a lack of responsibility. Such, ultimately, are the risks of freedom.

As a student of the magical Cabala, then, you face the task of deciding for yourself what the work means to you, and what place it will have in your life. There may be changes required to make that place fit for habitation, but it's rarely a good idea to try to force these. More useful, and more in keeping with the principles we've explored, is the slow but steady process of growth that will come naturally with time and magical practice. Instead of trying to reach an ideal at once, it can be wisest to seek a response to each situation, based on your sense of what's happening and your understanding of the principles involved. You're likely to make more mistakes this way, but you're certain to learn more about yourself and magic alike.

Here the practice of recollection, as discussed earlier, and your magical journal are among your best allies. It's been suggested that forgetfulness is the source of most human folly, and certainly a clear memory of unpleasant results is one of the best cures for the desire to do something stupid. Learning to remember, and remembering to learn, are thus crucial in the day- to-day process of the Cabalistic path.

As you proceed along this path, deepening your understanding of yourself and of the forces which surround and shape you, you may find that some of the ways of life that fit best with the practice of Cabalistic magic correspond quite closely to certain notions which might be called "goodness." The idea that ethical behavior is a source of strength to the magician has been raised before, and it deserves mention here, because it can play an increasingly important part in the life of the Cabalistic magician as the work of the Way of Redemption goes on. Still, personal experience is among the best of teachers, and this book is not about morality; you'll want to find your own way, step by step, through that particular tangle.

Bibliography

A tradition as diverse as the magical Cabala cannot be contained within the covers of any one book. The principles, symbolism and practices covered in the pages you've read are one way to approach the riches of that tradition; as mentioned elsewhere in this book, though, there are many others.

The books listed here offer one way to begin exploring some of those other approaches. They represent a small portion of what's available concerning the magical Cabala, and an even smaller portion of the total range of available books on magic. They have been listed here because each of them, in one way or another, shares certain themes or practical methods with the material covered in this book, and so may be particularly useful to its readers.

One source, though, deserves being listed out of place. Israel Regardie's *The Golden Dawn* (Llewellyn, 6th ed. 1989) is a collection of most of the theoretical papers, rituals and other materials of the Hermetic Order of the Golden Dawn, the most important of the magical orders active at the end of the last century. Regardie presented the Order's papers largely as he rfound them, and as a result the material in the collection is poorly organized and often obscure; still, as a source for information on the magical Cabala, no other book is even in the same league.

Some other books which may be useful are:

Cicero, Chic and Sandra Tabatha. *Secrets Of A Golden Dawn Temple* (Thoth Publications, 2005). Covers the construction and use of magical implements in the Golden Dawn tradition.

Crowley, Aleister. *Book Four* (Weiser, 1980). An introduction to the basic concepts of mysticism and magic; like much of Crowley's work, quirky but useful.

- . *The Book Of Thoth* (Weiser, 1969). Crowley's last major work, a study of the Tarot which goes deep into Cabalistic theory.

- . *Magick In Theory And Practice* (Dover, 1976). A study of the principles of magic, from Crowley's somewhat odd viewpoint. The appendices at the back, which give a wide range of practical techniques, are worth the price of the book by themselves.

- . *777* (Weiser, 1973). Crowley's edition of the extensive Golden Dawn tables of correspondences.

Davidson, Gustav. *A Dictionary Of Angels* (Macmillan, 1969). The one thorough book in English on the names, legends and powers of angels.

Fortune, Dion. *The Mystical Qabalah* (Weiser, 1978). A superb although somewhat dated book on the Tree of Life.

Godwin, David. *Godwin's Cabalistic Encyclopedia* (Llewellyn, 3rd ed. 1994). An essential reference work on Hebrew words used in Cabala.

Mathers, Samuel L. *Astral Projection, Ritual Magic And Alchemy* (Destiny, 1987). A collection of Golden Dawn papers not included in Regardie's collection, including some important technical papers.

Regardie, Israel. *Ceremonial Magic* (Aquarian, 1980). A study of ritual methods in magic, with extensive practical instructions.

- . *The Middle Pillar* (Llewellyn, 1970). An interpretation of the Middle Pillar exercise.

- . *The Tree Of Life* (Weiser, 1969). A study of the purposes and meaning of magic, still among the best modern works on the subject.

Index

Other titles from Thoth Publications

MAGICAL KABBALAH
By Alan Richardson

The Magical Kabbalah is a revised and expanded re-release of an Introduction to the Mystical Qabalah which was written when the author was a teenager, has never been out of print in 30 years, and is regarded by some as the clearest, simplest, and most effective book on the topic ever written.

This excellent introduction presents a spiritual system that anyone can use to enhance his or her life. The reader learns how the Kabbalah can and should be self-taught, without joining expensive groups and paying for dodgy teachers with dubious motives. Whatever your spiritual path these tried and tested methods will expand your consciousness and broaden your grasp of the Western Esoteric Traditions as they exist today. They will also show how each person can help expand these traditions and become self-initiated in safe and potent ways.

Explore both the theories and principles behind ritual practice. Explore the ways in which the Kabbalah - the Tree of Life - can apply to (and make sense of) every aspect of everyday life. Perform astral magic, use the Tarot for self-exploration, energise ancient myths to make them come alive, revisit past lives, build patterns in your aura, work with the imagery of Egyptian and Arthurian magic, banish unpleasant atmospheres and create gates into other dimensions.

ISBN 978-1-870450-53-9

PRINCIPLES OF ESOTERIC HEALING

By Dion Fortune. Edited and arranged by Gareth Knight

One of the early ambitions of Dion Fortune along with her husband Dr Thomas Penry Evans was to found a clinic devoted to esoteric medicine, along the lines that she had fictionally described in her series of short stories *The Secrets of Dr. Taverner.* The original Dr. Taverner was her first occult teacher Dr. Theodore Moriarty, about whom she later wrote: "if there had been no Dr. Taverner there would have been no Dion Fortune!"

Shortly after their marriage in 1927 she and Dr. Evans began to receive a series of inner communications from a contact whom they referred to as the Master of Medicine. Owing to the pressure of all their other work in founding an occult school the clinic never came to fruition as first intended, but a mass of material was gathered in the course of their little publicised healing work, which combined esoteric knowledge and practice with professional medical expertise.

Most of this material has since been recovered from scattered files and reveals a fascinating approach to esoteric healing, taking into account the whole human being. Health problems are examined in terms of their physical, etheric, astral, mental or spiritual origination, along with principles of esoteric diagnosis based upon the structure of the Qabalistic Tree of Life. The function and malfunction of the psychic centres are described along with principles for their treatment by conventional or alternative therapeutic methods, with particular attention paid to the aura and the etheric double. Apart from its application to the healing arts much of the material is of wider interest for it demonstrates techniques for general development of the psychic and intuitive faculties apart from their more specialised use in assisting diagnosis.

ISBN 978-1-870450-85-0